GARY

JACK TINKER

JACK

TINKER

A LIFE IN REVIEW

James Inverne

OBERON BOOKS

LONDON

First published in 1997 by Oberon Books Ltd
(incorporating Absolute Classics)
521 Caledonian Road, London N7 9RH
Tel: 0171 607 3637/Fax: 0171 607 3629

British Library Cataloguing in Publication Data:
A catalogue record for this book is available from the British Library.

ISBN 1 84002 018 0

Cover design: Andrzej Klimowksi
Back cover and endpaper cartoons: Gary Smith
Typography: Richard Doust
Printed in Great Britain by Arrowhead Books Ltd, Reading

For Jack, hope you like it

ACKNOWLEDGEMENTS

I could not have even attempted to explore the vast treasure trove of Jack's work without the aid and assistance of certain people. Therefore, my most sincere thanks to:

James Hogan, my publisher, for his advice and trust; everyone who helped me at the *Daily Mail*, particularly the librarians who somehow managed to work around my blundering search for needles in haystacks; the Brighton *Evening Argus* for kindly allowing me access to their archives; also, to everyone who contributed, giving up their time to speak to me and often pointing me in fruitful, hitherto unsuspected directions; to Sir Cameron Mackintosh for the title of the book; to a lady who helped me stay pointed in the right direction, the mercurial Jill Samuels. Above all, to Sir David English for his active support throughout. Finally to my mother and father who, as ever, have had a lot to put up with.

CONTENTS

List of Contributors   *viii*

List of Illustrations   *ix*

Foreword   xi

Introduction   xiii

1   King of the Musicals   1

2   Jack on Will...   53

3   More First Nights   70

4   The Battle of Edinburgh   122

5   Broadway vs the West End   133

6   Taking the Temperature   152

7   There's No Business...   192

8   Star Quality   202

9   The Critic: Friend or Foe?   247

Epilogue   265

Index   271

CONTRIBUTORS

Sir Alan Ayckbourn
Michael Barrymore
Cheryl Barrymore
Lionel Bart
Steven Berkoff
Melvyn Bragg
Kenneth Branagh
Michael Coveney
Michael Crawford
Stephen Daldry
Paul Daniels
Nicholas de Jongh
Dame Judi Dench
Sir David English
Sir Richard Eyre
Bruce Forsyth
Maria Friedman
Julie Goodyear
Sir Peter Hall
Herbert Kretzmer
Linda Lee-Potter
Lord Andrew Lloyd-Webber
Sir Cameron Mackintosh
David Nathan
Benedict Nightingale
Elaine Paige
Denis Quilley
Dame Diana Rigg
Willy Russell
Antony Sher
Ned Sherrin
Wayne Sleep
Charles Spencer

ILLUSTRATIONS

The publishers are grateful to the following for permission to include their material in this book. Despite our best efforts, it has not been possible in every instance to contact the copyright owners of certain photographs.

Dustjacket – *Daily Mail*
Cartoons – Gary Smith
1 – Michael Brennan
2 – *Daily Mail*
3 – Mike Forster
4 – Reg Wilson
5 – *Daily Mail*
6 – Alastair Muir
7 – Ken Towner
8 – Neville Marriner
9 – *Daily Mail*
10 – M. Courtney-Clarke
11 – Alan Davidson
12 – Ivan Kyncl
13 – Ken Towner
14 – John Swannell/The Really Useful Group
15 – John Haynes/Royal Court Theatre
16 – Paul Smith
17 – M. Debuskey Associates
18 – Phillip Jackson
19 – James Gray
20 – ATV Photo
21 – Dave Bennett
22 – Alastair Muir
23 – SOLO
24 – David Rice-Evans
25 – Dave Cromd
26 – Neville Marriner
27 – Alan Davidson

FOREWORD

I was Jack's editor and we had a lot of things in common so we became close personal friends. That does not often happen between editor and journalist – the relationship is usually somewhat double-edged. We managed to ride the switching modes, where one minute I would be giving him an instruction or changing his copy, then later we would be laughing and gossiping. It never became a problem.

Jack first came to my notice when he was on the Brighton *Evening Argus*. He wrote to me and asked for a job, enclosing some of his work. I had just become editor on the *Daily Sketch* and was looking for new, young staff. We met, the chemistry was right, so I hired him as a diary and general feature writer. Later I launched him as Richard Woolfe, the fearless *Sketch* diarist.

However, I knew that he wanted to write reviews and there was never any question that he would ever end up doing anything else. Four or five years after we both moved to the *Daily Mail*, an opening for a critic occurred. By that time a kind of lethargy had overtaken critics, partly to do with changes in Fleet Street. People were either reviewing shows from the final preview, or else the reviews did not appear until thirty-six hours after the first night.

This was completely wrong, as far as I was concerned. I spoke to Jack, and told him that we must re-establish the great theatrical tradition where the reviews are written at lightning speed with white-hot emotion. Jack was absolutely suited to doing just this. So we persuaded the theatre owners to put the opening nights start times back to 7.00pm.

The *Daily Mail's* audience is very interested in theatre. Jack and I built on this and resolved to make the newspaper foremost in Britain for theatrical criticism. I told Jack he would always have the same spot in the paper, on page three.

Both of us had similar tastes when we were growing up – we were seeing exactly the same films at opposite ends of the country. We were swept away by the classic scene from the MGM musicals, where the cast of a show would all go to a hotel and wait for the papers to appear. It was that excitement which we sought to re-establish in London, and we succeeded.

In the end all the papers restarted printing reviews in their last editions. It was Jack's skill and talent in leading the way that brought about this revolution. It was perhaps his greatest contribution to the two professions he so loved.

Sir David English
Chairman & Editor-in-Chief
Associated Newspapers Ltd

INTRODUCTION

For most of the 20th century British theatregoers have been treated to a rich outpouring of expert critical opinion. Several national dailies, a handful of specialist theatre magazines and a thriving local press have ensured that hardly any new play or show reaches the stage without public comment. From James Agate to Kenneth Tynan or Harold Hobson, to name a few, theatre critics have sometimes become 'stars' in their own right. And in the theatre community, at least, the names of most of today's critics are household words. Jack Tinker, however, writing for the *Daily Mail* for over a quarter of a century achieved a unique distinction. He became the people's critic. This book is as much about Jack Tinker himself, as seen through his writings, as it is about his long-running commentary on theatre and show business.

It was obvious that Jack adored theatre in all its forms. As the impresario, Sir Cameron Mackintosh says: 'He was a curious amalgam of a critic and a fan.' Almost singlehandedly he put paid to the lie that popular newspapers' readers are not interested in theatre, and all credit to the *Daily Mail* for providing Jack with the vehicle through which he could speak to millions in punchy, arresting language.

When he died suddenly in 1996 at the age of 58 his death was felt throughout the world of show business. The West End, in particular, knew that a friend and ally had been lost for ever. Many theatres dimmed their lights as a mark of respect, an honour previously accorded only to the likes of Sir Henry Irving and Lord Olivier. Performances of *Cats, Miss Saigon*, and *Les Miserables* were dedicated to his memory, and soon afterwards a memorial service in his beloved Theatre Royal, Brighton, was packed fit to burst with celebrities, friends, relations and members of Jack's wider family of *Daily Mail* readers from across the country. A recording of *Send in the Clowns* was played and, as one, the buzzing audience fell quiet. That silence, as Sondheim's heart-wrenching melody sang into the auditorium, was the most eloquent silence some of us had ever encountered. The beautiful old theatre where Jack began practising his trade had never seen anything like it.

A few months later, thousands of admirers flocked to the London Palladium for a gala show in his honour. So prestigious was the line-up that columnist, Linda Lee-Potter commented: 'No impresario could ever afford to put it on.'

The familiar image of Jack, diminutive, dressed in style, impish and witty remains with us for now. But for how long? This book is intended to preserve his memory and a flavour of his life's work.

That Jack loved his work was obvious to everyone. He was a veteran first-nighter whose verdict was eagerly awaited, or feared, next morning.

But he was also a serious debater of theatrical issues. Though he never published a collection of his reviews and articles. Asked whether he had ever considered the prospect, he noted that he would want it set in some sort of context, but was not sure quite how it should be done. Sadly, his untimely death provides the impetus. The context chosen here is simply the progress of theatre during his long career, a platform from which we can once again hear Jack's 'voice'.

Given his enormous output, capturing Jack's inborn enthusiasm for theatre has not been difficult. His articles are shot through with wit and vigour, and never less than entertaining. But doing justice to his life's work is another matter. Over a career in the popular press lasting nearly thirty years he was bound to write articles and reviews on a wide range of theatre and showbiz topics, leaving a legacy which amounts to one of the longest continuing critical discussions in a single newspaper in existence. In the space of 300 or so pages, we can only hope for a snapshot of his total output.

The problems of selection are on a large scale, particularly as in a tribute of this kind we wish to sense the character of the man himself. Any compilation of his work must, therefore, strike a balance between the reviews that typically reflect Jack's outlook and personality and those covering productions and performers which people would naturally expect to be included. What did Jack think of Pinter and Stoppard? What did he say about *Aspects of Love, Les Miserables* and *42nd Street*?

Invidious choices have to be made, hence the decision to place due emphasis on Jack's extensive coverage of musicals, the genre he so loved, and other showbiz events, perhaps at the expense of 'serious' drama. And readers of any critical survey need familiar reference points, Shakespeare being the obvious example. But with so much else to cover, a panoramic view of Shakespeare productions over the last quarter of a century is impossible. But Jack loved great performers and there is room here to at least focus on a few key interpretations of the great Shakespearean roles.

With all these demands in mind, this collection, mainly of Jack's best-known pieces, has been assembled under appropriate headings; and, since he made himself so much a part of 'the business,' rather than just a critical onlooker, the selection is interspersed with comments drawn from interviews with some of his contemporaries in the world of theatre.

Jack's critical output actually spanned thirty years from his first job as a young critic on the Brighton *Evening Argus* to his page 3 slot on the *Daily Mail,* the job he held until his death. As Associated Newspapers Chairman and Editor-in-Chief, Sir David English, says in his foreword, the reviews were written in a white-hot state of emotion at the end of the performance, in time for the early editions. This restored the first night review's news status, and perhaps in spite of his vast knowledge and understanding, Jack never lost his gift for making news out of theatre.

A journalist to his fingertips, he served a typical apprenticeship on local newspapers. He joined the Brighton *Evening Argus,* after three years training on the *Surrey Advertiser.* He quickly became the theatre critic, a job he no doubt relished. There was plenty to write about, Brighton being a major tour date for shows en route to the West End. As well as establishing a reputation for incisive, witty criticism ('A poet!', according to Sir Ralph Richardson), he soon made a name for himself as a glittering raconteur. Tales of Tinker holding court, performing to an enthralled audience on The Brighton Belle railway service, are legion. There was to be more than a little of the performer in him as later stage appearances attest.

After a few years in Brighton greener pastures beckoned. In 1971, he received the call to Fleet Street. His departure from the *Evening Argus* was marked by the presentation of a wooden spoon – 'to stir things up in the West End as you have stirred them up down here', explained Alan Melville, President of the Society of Brighton and Hove Entertainment Managers. That is precisely what Jack did. After a year as a diarist on the *Daily Sketch*, the newspaper merged with the *Daily Mail* and Jack finally assumed his position as theatre critic.

A man of many parts

There was Jack Tinker the critic, and there was the lesser-known Jack Tinker, the author of two books: *The Television Barons* (1980) and *Coronation Street – 25 Years* (1985). He also devised stage shows including *Merman – The Lady and Her Songs* (1985) and *In Praise of Rattigan* (1984). Lastly, there was Jack Tinker the stage creature – star of his own one-man show, *An Audience and a Critic* (1994), not to mention the scene-stealer of sundry charity galas, and other showbiz events.

His work was officially recognised several times: dubbed critic of the year in 1982, 1989, 1991 and, posthumously, in 1997, he was also awarded the *De Courcy Critics Circle Award* of 1991. After his death the newly-refurbished Lyceum Theatre named a section of the Champagne Bar 'Jack's Corner,' and The Critics Circle Drama Section dedicated *The Jack Tinker Award For Most Promising Newcomer* to his memory.

On a personal level, Jack was a popular figure in the business and with his readers, but respect for him goes deeper than that. Whatever his views on any specific production, he remained a loyal friend of the theatre itself. Of course, there were shifts in taste and contradictions as the years went by – witness the modification of his views on *Les Miserables* which falls only just short of back-tracking. Was he wrong first time round? – or as Lyricist Herbert Kretzmer suggests, did he warm to the show in the end? Or was it a case of a critic gently acknowledging that in the end the punters rule? Some might ruefully add: 'if there's time for word of mouth to spread before the show closes.'

Sometimes the sparring between critic and performer becomes a knockabout display of mutually incompatible attitudes. As Jack himself wrote: 'In the full glare of Edinburgh's annual media circus, Mr Stephen Berkoff, actor, author and director extraordinaire, publicly moderated his offer to murder the *Guardian*'s Nicholas de Jongh only slightly. Critics, he conceded, were after all necessary to our daily functions, like toilet rolls.' Berkoff explains the context in which he made this remark, not in earnest, but as part of the fun of the occasion. Nevertheless, it pinpoints the residual antipathy between critic and performer; and some would argue, even on the receiving end of a bad review, that critics perform rather more than just a necessary function. Indeed, could theatre survive in the long run without the critic's gift for spreading highly infectious *good* news when it is warranted? That said, a review still has to be news, not advertising. News cuts both ways, and ultimately we depend on our critics overall to introduce a note of balance into a business which would otherwise be awash with hype.

Balance was one of Jack's trade-marks, and his trade-marks were indelible. The reviews from the Brighton *Evening Argus* in the early Sixties are as punchy as anything he wrote in the *Daily Mail* towards the end of his life. In particular, Jack always made the effort to understand what each production or work was trying to achieve; and if it did not work, to highlight the reasons why. One conspicuous example of his insight at work is his coverage of Sondheim's *Sweeney Todd*. When it first opened at the Theatre Royal, Drury Lane, in 1980 Jack recognised its merits and was at pains to praise the composer's worthy efforts to break the mould of musicals. But he observed that the staging did not serve the piece well and prophesied that the show would find its time. He was proved right when the show was revived at the Royal National Theatre in 1993. It played to packed houses and its run was extended.

The grammar school boy

Jack Samuel Tinker was born on 15th February 1938 and raised in Royton. His natural instinct was to seek out the limelight: 'I felt compelled to live smack in the centre of places with distinct and vivid personalities of their own,' he wrote. So he packed his bags and moved south.

Flamboyant as he often was, he was by no means all for himself. He had great reserves of kindness and humility. Once over lunch in his beloved West End haunt, The Ivy restaurant, Jack told me of the greatest compliment he had ever been paid. He was passing the Phoenix Theatre, where *Blood Brothers* was playing. I remember the story more or less as follows:

'This enormous muscle-bound yobbo deposits his bulk in my way, glowers down at me and says, "You're Jack Tinker aren't you?" I nervously confess that I am, looking for my escape. Suddenly he breaks out into a smile and shakes my hand. Then he points to my rave notice plastered outside the theatre, says, "I've just seen that show, and you got it dead right – dead right!" '

The fact that Jack had touched this man, who inhabited such a different lifestyle had thrilled him deeply. 'If I can reach people like that, make them go to the theatre' he enthused, 'then I feel it has all been worth it.'

He could, of course, be controversial. During a performance of his one-man show, an audience member accused Jack of being responsible for his daughter failing her eleven-plus. Apparently, she always read Jack's work, and had got into the habit of beginning all her sentences with And's and But's. In vain did the critic try to explain that this is standard practice in journalism. The man threw a bundle of Jack's own cuttings at him, with all the offending words circled in red ink. Finally, he was thrown out. Such demonstrations were rare, and even added to Jack's appeal.

The great debate

Much of Jack's writing is concerned with preserving a state of balance in the theatre, so that the entire spectrum has room to flourish. In Chapters 4, 5, and 6, covering the Edinburgh Festival, Broadway and other broad issues, he tries to encourage this equilibrium – balance between the Edinburgh Fringe and the official Festival, a more even range and quality of work on Broadway. Particularly fascinating are his comments on the already difficult balancing act of the critic. If he was amused and sometimes concerned at some performers' extreme reactions to bad reviews, he was outraged when he thought individual critics were accorded too much power – hence his annoyance with the *New York Times*'s Frank Rich. He unleashed a dazzling barrage of offensive and defensive manoeuvres to keep his beloved theatre on an even path of progress. Passionately protective of the critic's right to express his honestly held opinions, he was sensitive to the proper limitations of that privilege. Balance, balance, in all things, balance.

Jack may have been sometimes amused by the changes in the theatre world, often encouraged, occasionally angered. One thing was certain – if anything threatened to affect the sanctity of British theatre, his piercing gaze would be turned upon it. Hence the new depths plumbed by Sarah Kane at the Royal Court with *Blasted* provoked his wrath (and how!). Equity – the guardian of actors' rights – found itself the victim of a fierce attack from Jack when its intention to announce a strike posed a serious problem to the industry in general. And those who are entrusted with the standards of the great flagships of the nation's theatre – the Royal National Theatre and the Royal Shakespeare Company were closely watched. If they triumphed, Jack led the applause. If not...

Some new developments were regarded with cautious optimism – the age of huge sets, the arrival of radio mikes and new technology. And the foundation of any healthy theatre environment, new writing, was closely examined. Jack looked for the strengths, but was quick to point out the failings, to avoid any hint of long-term damage.

Aspects of 'the outside world' which he brought into his column became grand scenes in life's long-running show. Yet it also worked the other way round – the world of entertainment itself was, in Jack's philosophy, an essential commentary on life. When he writes about *Coronation Street,* for example, he is not simply talking about a popular television show. Jack loved these characters. To him, and to millions, they bring comfort, joy, and an awareness of human nature – essential ingredients for life and for theatre.

Star quality was a gem that also entranced Jack throughout his career, though it did not blind him to a performer's failings. Many times he tried to analyse it, to define the ingredients which make a star, and – one feels – was never quite satisfied. Yet he was keenly aware of the peculiar pressures of stardom as well as its rewards, always appreciating the human side to the star, the frailties and the personal victories. He seemed to share in the pride of those personalities who have attained their dreams against the odds, such as Sir Robert Stephens, or Lord (Lew) Grade. Nothing delighted him more than seeing a falling star manage to rise again. It was with such a flush of pleasure that in 1994 he hailed Michael Barrymore's conquest of his inner demons.

All in all, I hope this compilation does justice to Jack's valued and informed enthusiasm for a financially precarious business, often under political and commercial pressure, and always vying for the punters' attention in competition with cinema, TV and clubs; a noble business perhaps, which needs its friends, and for which an insecure future can always be taken for granted.

One final thought. The Brighton *Evening Argus* once asked Jack what he would like for an epitaph. Without skipping a beat, he answered: 'Loved the show, loathed the finale.' He was, as so often, speaking for all of us.

James Inverne
London, 1997

1

KING OF THE MUSICALS

Joseph and the Amazing Technicolour Dreamcoat
Music by Andrew Lloyd Webber, lyrics by Tim Rice
Albery Theatre
***Daily Mail*, 19th February 1973**

The golden wheat after the corn

If I were rich beyond the dreams of Paul Getty (or even Elizabeth Taylor whose imagination might conceivably be less limited), I would hire myself a theatre. In it I would stage the last act of this smashing show. And I would be my own most fervent customer.

There can surely be few more pleasant ways to pass 55 minutes of one's day than in front of Frank Dunlop's brilliant presentation of the original brainchild from Messrs Lloyd Webber and Rice.

Lamentably a querulous commercialism deems this not to be enough. A whole new first act has been brought forth in order that West End audiences may relish the resounding hit musical already raved over on its appearances in Edinburgh and at the Roundhouse. Ray Galton and Alan Simpson have been drafted to produce the dialogue for this addendum to the Scriptures. They have yielded a great deal more corn than Joseph later stores in Pharaoh's granaries against the years of famine.

The filial warfare between Jacob and Esau is unaccountably transferred to the highlands of Scotland, and there it could stay. With only Tim Rice's simple recitative to link the bouncy numbers, the story of Joseph romps along. Surely the original good Jewish boy to strike it rich in an alien land. Quite right that Gary Bond makes him so acceptably self-satisfied.

Once we are in Egypt there is also Gordon Waller going through his Elvis Presley routine and almost through his tight white satin jump suit. A Pharaoh fit to make the Sphinx split her sides laughing.

***Daily Mail*, 13th July 1973**

New colour for the dreamcoat

This was always a tiny, burnished gem of a musical. From Edinburgh via the Roundhouse it twinkled brightly. But an ugly commercial and crass setting threatened to eclipse its gleam when it first opened in the West End earlier this year. An incongruous first act tacked on the beginning cross-grained the talents of Galton and Simpson with

Rice and Webber. Now, however, courage and taste are belatedly triumphant.

The whole of that first act has been pruned. And a trio or so of bouncy new send-up songs are added to the remaining original hour of pure delight. And what have we got? We've got a show as tuneful, sharp and wholesome as anything you are likely to see this side of the Testaments.

Peter Blake oomphs his way through the role of Pharaoh, now that Gordon Waller has relinquished Elvis Presley's second-skin clothing.

It is not often a management comes clean mid-run and says: 'We were wrong.' Perhaps others will learn that more is not always better, and trust the public to realise that a brief burst of enchantment is better by far than a large wedge of boredom. Theatre, unlike other commodities, is still not subject to weights and measures inspection for the price of a ticket.

Evita
Lyrics by Tim Rice, music by Andrew Lloyd Webber
Prince Edward Theatre
Daily Mail, **22nd June, 1978**

Viva Evita!

Forget the ballyhoo... the show really is a total triumph

In the unlikely event of my verdict having any effect whatsoever on its box office success, I must first report that *Evita* is a technical knockout, a magnificent earful, a visual triumph and a wow. But better still, it is the first intelligently adult, political musical to be staged here since *Cabaret*.

Ignore all the ballyhoo. The wildness of the first night audience proclaims that *Evita* is not history being regurgitated, it is history being made. London has seen nothing like it, and it was actually born here.

Now, if this sounds like overkill it is fully justified. Andrew Lloyd Webber and Tim Rice have taken one giant step forward since the innocent days of *Jesus Christ Superstar*. They have created, not a musical, but a full-scale modern opera, full of soaring choruses, decked out with delicate arias and linked with witty recitatives.

Of course, the story of Eva Peron, the sinning patron saint of Argentina's post-war poor, is in itself a gift. It combines all the elements of Cinderella, Lady Macbeth and Lorelei Lee.

The miracle is that under the direction of that most subtle and tasteful of showmen, Hal Prince (he, indeed, staged *Cabaret*), all the potential of her story is realised with stunning visual effects that have nothing at all to do with lavish trimmings.

Prince's theatrical economy can only make one marvel. He sets the song *Goodnight and Thank You* to one revolving bedroom door. With each rotation Evita emerges bidding goodbye to another, richer and grander peignoir. Thus is established the indelible image of her horizontal rise to fame and fortune. Who needs words with bold pictures like this?

What one does need, of course, is an Evita who can live up to the legend. And though Mr Prince hands Elaine Paige no star entrance (she wanders on in grey following her own coffin) and no applause-winning exit (she succumbs to cancer in a plain hospital bed) everything that happens in between establishes Miss Paige as the perfect Evita. A private hell-cat and a public princess.

She approaches the microphones to sing the show's best known song, *Don't Cry for Me Argentina* in a shimmering Dior mountain of tulle like a royal bride. And even when she is competing with the fascinating blow-up newsreel shots of the real Evita, it is Miss Paige's Evita who holds the stage – a diminutive look-alike star who grabs her rainbow's end only to find stardust has as little substance as sawdust.

The standing ovation from the audience at the end and Miss Paige's own streaming tears heralded the birth not only of a new star but the success of a considerable actress. In case we come to admire Miss Paige's Evita along with her doting peasants, there is David Essex's cynical (and extremely impressive) Che Guevara on hand to prick every one of her hot-air balloons the moment it takes off into the clouds.

This is not a eulogy to the lady, but a highly moral warts-and-all portrait. Indeed they have ducked nothing. In fact, the evening only hiccups once, and that is because the most haunting tune *Another Suitcase, Another Hall* has to be hung on a character who contributes little to the fast-flowing story. It is, nevertheless, beautifully sung by Siobhan McCarthy.

But what is this nit-pick in an evening that never looks anything less than a total artistic triumph?

The King and I

Music by Richard Rodgers, book and lyrics by Oscar Hammerstein II
London Palladium
Daily Mail, **13th June 1979**

The King has me really puzzled

It is curiously disconcerting to discover that money does not talk. At least not in this lavish no-expense-spared-memory-lane revival of the old Rodgers and Hammerstein goldie, it doesn't.

Oh, it shouts loud enough. Cash registers jangle louder than the temple bells from the moment Mrs Anna sets a Victorian button-shoe on the soil

3

of old Siam. But what I missed amid all the rapturously-received opulence was that still small voice of the story-line.

This production treats the whole thing like a too-familiar opera. Played straight out front, with the dialogue treated rather as tiresome time-wasting between those luscious Rodgers numbers (surely one of his most lovely and lyrical scores), the folksy appeal of the well-meaning school-marm and the stubborn autocratic monarch runs dangerously close to sounding offendingly patronising.

Mrs Anna herself needs a great deal of help to stop the part becoming something of a pill. And 28 years after he first created the title role on Broadway, Yul Brynner seems strangely reluctant to give such aid. Indeed, he appears disinclined to give very much, saving his presence. This, with eyebrows etched like forked snake tongues across his bald dome, is still admittedly considerable.

But he goes through key numbers such as *Puzzlement* lightly, as if rendering a favourite party piece. Is this really a man torn between opposing mysteries of the universe, or someone playing a part one time too many?

From where I was sitting it was the latter. And incidentally, since I was sitting in the fifth row, why could I only, at times, catch every fourth word of his delivery?

However, Virginia McKenna gamely battled on to win our hearts despite a grumbling microphone and having her own heart melted through the back of Lady Thiang's (Hye-Younce Choi) head in the glorious *Something Wonderful* song.

Director Yuriko has been singularly unsuccessful in marrying oriental formality with Western musical conventions – and surely this is the message of the entire show.

Sweeney Todd

Music and lyrics by Stephen Sondheim, book by Hugh Wheeler
Theatre Royal, Drury Lane
Daily Mail, 4th July 1980

I can't see the demon barber making a killing with this

It cannot be read as an encouraging omen that the acclaimed (eight *Tony Awards*) Broadway version of this blood-thirsty musical thriller closed at the weekend with a £200,000 loss.

Of its high artistic merits, there can be no doubt. Sondheim's insistent and strident score turns the legend of Fleet Street's demon barber into another landmark in his mission to lead the popular American musical into the realms of literate opera. And with Hal Prince staging it like something between a Brecht satire and a gothic *grand guignol*, its aspirations are impeccable.

Beneath a huge, rotting warehouse roof, the saga of Sweeney Todd's revenge on a corrupt cesspit society is played out with scarcely any dialogue but lashings of spurting blood to accompany his 20 victims down the trap door to Mrs Lovett's pie-shop. Yet, though I smelt lots of realistic cooking I did not scent a smash hit. The theme itself is hardly one to bring coaches rolling in, and Sondheim's deliberate operatic treatment does not make it instantly accessible. When I first saw the play by Christopher Bond down at Joan Littlewood's Theatre Workshop in Stratford East, it seemed ideal material for its setting.

Delivered with direct guts (if you'll pardon the expression) it had an honest integrity. Sweeney himself became almost a hero; a man who had been the victim of a villainous judge who had sentenced him to life banishment for a crime he had not committed, and then raped the barber's young wife and abducted his daughter.

Sondheim has stayed true to this concept but somehow its appeal becomes swamped by the show's own cleverness. There is a curious lack of incisiveness in some of the playing, too.

Though Denis Quilley, a fine actor and singer, is strong and broodingly vengeful, his sense of outraged injustice did not connect itself to my sympathies. I can only assume that Sheila Hancock's gallery of grotesque mannerisms as Mrs Lovett were intended as an ingratiating cover-up for the fact that she, like me, did not consider the terrible price of meat sufficient reason to go into wholesale slaughter.

All this said, I wish the venture nothing but well. It is brave, daring and attempts something new which is a cut above most things in the West End at the moment, if I may use the term in this context.

They're Playing Our Song

Book by Neil Simon, music by Marvin Hamlisch, lyrics by Carol Bayer Sager
Shaftesbury Theatre
Daily Mail, 2nd October 1980

Beware! This show is a real stunner

If, like me, you're a sucker for old-fashioned sentiment heavily chromium-plated with a tough Broadway gleam then it is about time you rediscovered the Shaftesbury Theatre.

The building has been so long off the map of West End hits it had acquired the welcoming chill of a mausoleum. But now revamped and looking as good to eat as a wedding cake it has the show to bring a smile to its facelift.

Perhaps *They're Playing Our Song* is not the greatest musical ever written. For a story which boasts a hit composer and a top lyricist as its hero and its heroine, and uses their chequered collaboration as its sole plot, we might have been forgiven for expecting something a little more ambitious in the way of knock-out music.

Still, Marvin (*A Chorus Line*) Hamlisch and Carol (*Nobody Does It Better* etc.) Bayer Sager have produced one genuine showstopper in the title song and at least one memorable torch number in *I Still Believe in Love*, which has the distinction of being reprised by Johnnie Mathis on tape – and that is a good deal more than most musicals offer anyway.

However, what sells the show to me is not only Neil Simon's sinewy dialogue but the entire packaging of this Broadway hit. It comes gift-wrapped for success.

The technical effects are often stunning – at one point almost literally. The car carrying Tom Conti to his climactic romantic rendezvous with Gemma Craven overshot its mark, revolving into a massive scenic flat. 'Stop!' yelled the hapless Conti, just in time to prevent the scenery swiping the West End's most bankable male star into oblivion.

A mere technical hitch that unfortunately wasn't all right on the night. But it brings me to two of the most engaging performances currently in London. Mr Conti as the laconic composer who lives in luxury on Central Park, and Miss Craven as the volatile lyricist who lives in chaos in cast-offs from old shows, give Neil Simon's lines an appealing warmth without ever losing their bite.

They're backed by three alto egos apiece, which not only makes for funny visual effects but also comes in handy for backing groups to their singing. Apart from the couple's rampant egos constantly undergoing work-outs on assorted couches and in bed, the other fly in their creative ointment is Leon, the unseen boyfriend of Miss Craven who phones every time the plot needs an upper.

One day I shall write a thesis on modern fiction which relies entirely on someone you never see, starting with *Rebecca*. Meantime let us be grateful to Leon for providing Mr Conti with such lines as, 'I could have taken Valium but I couldn't unclench my teeth!'

It is a skilled, professional and glossy evening.

Cats

Music by Andrew Lloyd Webber; based on verse by T S Eliot
New London Theatre
Daily Mail, 12th May 1981

A marvellous heap of rubbish

This non-stop hymn of praise to our feline friends (and enemies) must deserve to succeed if only because so many diverse talents have been invested in it. T S Eliot and Andrew Lloyd Webber to name but six.

6

In case anyone gave up reading papers and watching TV for Lent and then decided to kick the habit altogether, it had better be explained that the young Lloyd Webber took the old Eliot's collection of fey rum-te-tum verses dedicated to the mysteries of the cat – *Old Possum's Book of Practical Cats* – and set them to music. Very fine, if deliberately derivative, music it is too.

The result is possibly the most spectacular heap of rubbish ever spread around any West End theatre. I say this with no disrespect, I hasten to add. For the entire New London Theatre has been brilliantly converted into one huge refuse dump. Surely no auditorium can ever have been more effectively or dramatically used. Cats eyes peer out from the darkness from every conceivable angle and about a quarter of the audience revolves along with the central acting area when the show begins.

It becomes clear from the outset that this is an experience rather than a musical. Performers in cat suits writhe on to the stage from dustbins, outsize car bonnets and seemingly nowhere to introduce the mysteries of the Eliot cats.

Personally I have long lived without voluntary contact with cats of any kind, due to a chronic allergy brought on by their fur and dangerous apoplexy provoked by their antics on my patio. So I was not exactly a walk-over for this reunion with Growltiger, Rum Tum Tugger, Mungojerrie and Rumpelteazer, Macavity or even Gus the theatre cat. They have all felt the blunt end of my garden broom since Eliot tried to make us see them with sentimental eyes.

Yet despite a certain amount of innate preciousness and total lack of any plot, the evening conspires against all but the meanest minds. Through their sheer energy and endurance in Gillian Lynne's continuously sinewy choreography, the cast works a collective and individual magic.

They are as motley a bag as you could find along any catwalk. Brian Blessed as Old Deuteronomy, looking like an Ancient Greek god on his way back from Hades; Elaine Paige as Grizabella, the cat too hot to include in Eliot's book, looking like a lady who has been kicked out of a cat house; Wayne Sleep as Mr Mistoffelees, looking like a cat who would like to walk alone if allowed to; Paul Nicholas as Rum Tum Tugger, looking as if someone from Adam and the Ants as a cat who has just pinched the cream; Bonnie Langford as Rumpelteazer, proving that this little kitten has grown into a real trouper.

The show stands or falls by their individual bravura – it is very episodic, and some are more bravura than others. I never cease to marvel at the British public's ability to applaud indifference at the expense of artistry. Little Miss Langford's acrobatic artistry I have already extolled. Wayne Sleep redeems an indifferent tap routine with grim balletic magic in the second half. And Elaine Paige's finale as Grizabella, ascending like a redeemed feline Mary Magdalene on a jet-propelled car tyre and magic staircase into the sky, was the stuff showbiz is made of.

CAMERON MACKINTOSH

Half the time I had to remind myself that Jack was a critic. He was like a very good friend and even if I had not seen him for months it would feel as though I had just left him. I first met him thirty years ago, when he was at the *Argus* and I was taking my tatty old tours around the country and poor old Jack had to review them. He had already made quite a splash at that paper, at a time when Brighton was a very important date. An awful lot of theatre people lived there and Binkie Beaumont used to bring his shows there just prior to the West End. He was a great friend of the manager of Brighton's Theatre Royal, Melville Gillam. When the Binkie era ended, Melville was forced to take in a wider variety of productions – my little Agatha Christies were plainly there under sufferance. Therefore, Jack was exposed to an unusually diverse range of shows.

Jack was particularly amused during a performance of my production of Alan Ayckbourn's *Relatively Speaking*. The star was Dora Bryan, who was very close to Jack. To Gillam, though, she was not glamorous enough. At the end of the show, Dora told jokes, a routine that the audience loved. Just before the Brighton opening, Gillam went up to her and condescendingly said: 'I do hope, Miss Bryan, that you are not planning to make any of those terrible speeches. This is a first-class playhouse. I expect you to do the show and nothing more.' When the moment for her routine arrived, Dora told the audience what had occurred – 'This is a very posh playhouse,' she told the packed house. At that point, right on cue, her dog Dougall marched up to her and was greeted with 'What are you doing on stage, Dougall? You're scratching, love. Have you caught fleas in Mr Gillam's dirty old dressing-room?' Gilly was positively steaming, while Jack and the audience roared with laughter.

You always knew that you were on better ground with him, though, if the show had a bit of glitz and glamour. Jack was a curious amalgam of a critic and a fan. He would fall over himself for a *42nd Street* or a *Crazy for You*. He found it more difficult to take on board a musical drama, for example *Les Miserables* or *Cats*. In the former he did recognise the power of the score, but could not reconcile that kind of story being a popular musical – hence his famous phrase, 'The Glums'. Even with *Cats*, if you read the original review, Jack did not really get it initially. The rave headline, which we used in the publicity, was not written by him. That kind of show jarred for him. Whereas he loved something that was imbued with the tradition of the great musicals, on which he was brought up. To be fair, the majority of critics are like that. The difference is that Jack was never scared to nail his colours firmly to the mast.

It meant that, although he was brilliant at finding new talent and finding new playwrights, he was not as adept at spotting new trends in writing for musical theatre. That is something that very few people in this country are good at.

I love a *42nd Street* as much as anybody. There will always be room for that kind of show. What it cannot do is drive the theatre forward. Those shows are essentially reviews, taking the best elements of the past and presenting them in the new way. That is one kind of musical. Another is the re-interpretation of the great shows, *Guys and Dolls*, *Carousel* and so on. Then you have musicals which come out of the ether, from the side. Shows like *Hair*, *Rent* and *Cats*. They follow no known pattern, and have a premise so off-the-wall that they cannot possibly be repeated. You need a balance of all three to keep musical theatre alive.

Barnum

Music by Cy Coleman, lyrics by Michael Stewart, book by Mark Bramble
London Palladium
Daily Mail, 12th June 1981

Beat the drum – it's brilliant!

'Barnum's the name and hokum's the game,' cries Michael Crawford ecstatically very early on. And by the end of a remarkable evening during which Mr Crawford and this extravagantly talented company have performed every miracle short of flying without wings while hatching eggs, I would gladly have marched through Piccadilly beating a big drum on behalf of Barnum's brand of hokum.

For this is not merely a razzmatazz musical biography of the man who lent his name to America's three ring circus. In truth, it tells us very little about Phineas Taylor Barnum, apart from facts such as his marriage to a strong-minded woman, his scruple that nothing was too large or too small to promote for profit, and his brief love affair with the Swedish nightingale Jenny Lind.

What it is most definitely, however, is a mammoth celebration in the idiom of the Big Top of the human spirit over life's mundane impossibilities.

Barnum was a man who, in his own words, paints his world in 'fire engine reds, Kerry greens and buttercup yellows.' It is a message we are in sore need of, in these impossibly mundane times.

To him, general Tom Thumb, the smallest man on earth, or Joice Heth, the oldest woman, were not freaks. They were creatures made exceptional by some divine Providence, and raised on high above their fellow men.

To bring this exhilarating, if salutary, thought home to his audience, Michael Crawford sings while walking a tightrope, slung across the Palladium's yawning proscenium, leaps into a box from a trampoline, performs all manner of conjuring illusions, and finally sky-dives from the roof of that theatre to the stage down a loose-slung rope. And you ain't seen nothin' yet!

However these are just (just!) tricks of his trade: superb bonuses. Crawford's central performance has about it a crusading zeal which touches the entire audience with its message and was for me the real heart of a show which is all heart or nothing.

When they rose to give him a standing ovation, it was much more than just a tribute to a great performer pulling off one more success; more than just an appreciation of an entertainment which begins the moment you enter the foyer, with jugglers and clowns besieging the aisles.

I saw strong men weep – Kenny Lynch to name but one. And for that there must be some higher explanation than the fact that once again the British have proved they can stage a Broadway hit and bring something fresh and native to its polished professionalism.

Let it be said here that on-stage there is not a man or woman who does not earn his or her place and keep thrice over. They juggle, they dangle from trapezes, they play instruments, they walk the high wire, they conjure and play a host of roles.

Conspicuous among this roll-call of honour is William C Witter, a tireless ringmaster and spectacular performer. Also we must, in this context, acknowledge the sterling support of Deborah Grant as his sparring-partner wife, and Sarah Payne, who makes Jenny Lind an appealing version of Britt Ekland with voice and talent.

But over and above all this, there is Crawford's own personal gospel: if it can't be done, try it.

This, of course, is the urge that is the hope of the human race. It is why the Wright Brothers wanted to fly, why Michelangelo painted the ceiling of the Sistine Chapel, and why anyone does anything that is not strictly necessary.

Art, said George Jean Nathan, the great American critic, is a reaching out into the ugliness of the world for vagrant beauty and the imprisoning of it in a tangible dream.

This show is that tangible dream. If it is a musical with only one decent tune and a book with only one slim theme, then this is the triumph of hokum over mediocrity. And it is art of the highest order.

MICHAEL CRAWFORD

When we did *Barnum*, Jack's review was the first I read. It was excellent. Then, when we revived it with a different cast, it was the *Mail* verdict that I was anxious to see. Did Jack think it was a mistake to come back? Would he like this company less? On the opening night, we were all celebrating in an Italian restaurant around the corner from the theatre. I had a fixed smile on my face, but the grin was false. Not until someone brought in his review, if anything even better than his original reaction, did I feel that we had genuinely done it. Jack was one of the key figures when my career began to flourish, certain phrases stay with one as a performer throughout one's life, whether positive or negative. His comments, for me, were positive and a great encouragement.

Jack describes *Barnum* as a triumph of theatricality rather than plot. That is how the work first impressed me when I saw it in New York. Then Glenn Close and Jim Dale were in it, and the chemistry between them was not all that it could have been. I saw possibilities of going even further with the piece, in terms of the energy needed to sell it (something that Barnum himself might have agreed with). That had to come from everyone, not just me.

That company was the most cohesive that I have ever worked with – particularly when we took it to the Victoria Palace. We had to be an intensely close team, because everyone was doing dangerous things, relying on everyone else. We used to go in without fail at 4.00 every afternoon for a circus warm-up. It was not compulsory, but everyone was there – including the musical director, Mike Reed.

People moved their day around that, despite all the inconvenience. We did that for about eighteen months – a big chunk of our lives. All of us became extremely close, sharing our happiness, our sorrows, our well-being, our illnesses. When you saw somebody smile at someone, you knew it was genuine. There was the extra energy I envisaged.

Guys and Dolls

Music and lyrics by Frank Loesser, book by Abe Burrows and Jo Swerling
RNT Olivier
***Daily Mail*, 1st November 1982**

A guy called Paul makes the dolls sizzle...

On those rare and miraculous occasions when they perfect perfection itself, it is a privilege and a boast to be there. And so it was the night the National Theatre unveiled the replacement cast for their Empire State-sized hit, *Guys and Dolls*.

Back in March I was grabbing at superlatives to describe Richard Eyre's sizzling production of this street-wise classic where every number falls over itself to steal the show. But a second visit to view the replacement cast sends me reeling out of the theatre to report that until you have seen this line-up you ain't seen nothing yet. Those who have stayed on have become better than anyone has a right to expect.

And the newcomers – Paul Jones to name but a zillion reasons for indulging in a second sitting – lend an added brio that sets the entire production apart from anything else to be seen in town at the moment.

Nothing I have ever seen on Broadway has surpassed the excitement now generated non-stop from the stage of the Olivier Theatre. This is not a cast of British actors letting down their hair for a piece of enjoyable slumming. It is a high-octane ensemble company showing the American theatre that given the goods, they can deliver them as well as the best.

Of course the continued presence of Miss Julia McKenzie is sufficient in itself to ensure my vote for the *Best Musical Performance of the Year,* even before the nominations are listed. Miss McKenzie as the eternal fiancée, Adelaide (she of the perpetual psychosomatic cold) appears to be visibly liberated by the vibrant new hot blood around her.

From the moment she burlesques her way wickedly through her floor show routine, *A Bushel and a Peck,* to her heart-rending reprise of Adelaide's lugubrious lament, she is clearly the mistress of the hour.

Now, however, she has a wizened, beaten Nathan Detroit in the crushed shape of Trevor Peacock to stir her maternal yearnings. And she can confidently take her performance up a decibel or so knowing that there are two young lovers on hand to take handsome care of Damon Runyon's parallel romance between the cocksure Sky Masterson (Paul Jones) and his mettlesome Salvation Army conquest, Sister Sarah (Belinda Sinclair).

Mr Jones oozes the sort of sexual self-confidence that cries out for a good woman like Sarah to tame; vocally and visually he is matinée idol material (another *Best Performance Award,* surely).

Frankly, I can't think of anywhere I'd rather be than this fastest floating crap game from New York.

RICHARD EYRE

There was a lot of opposition when I did *Guys and Dolls.* Many people questioned whether this was the sort of thing that the National Theatre should be doing. Most of that dropped away when the critics saw what the show was. The piece thoroughly vindicated its place at the National Theatre, partly because it is a classic piece of romantic comedy, and partly because it is done in a way that would never have been attempted in the West End. The values that I applied to it were the values of the National Theatre – a responsiveness to text, to truthfulness and to a kind of veracity. Although it is a fairy tale about New York, I brought to it the same values that I would bring to, say, a production of *Much Ado About Nothing.* It was individually characterised, the quality of the acting had to be as high as in any other National Theatre production. In a West End musical you would usually get two or three powerful performances at the centre and then there is a falling away. Whereas, at the National Theatre you expect casting in-depth across the board, and a fastidiousness in all areas of presentation. The critics, including Jack, appreciated this.

Camelot

Book and lyrics by Alan Jay Lerner, music by Frederick Loewe
Apollo, Victoria
Daily Mail, **24th November 1982**

Santa Claus to the rescue

God bless Prince Andrew for switching on the lights of Regent Street in the nick of time. Three cheers for Santa Claus for getting early to the grotto.

For how else would the hapless Richard Harris have survived the ignominy of his unorthodox first act exit except in the spirit of the panto season? Mr Harris was forced through circumstances beyond his control to retreat behind the theatre's thick drapes crawling on all fours, having had his retreat cut off when the curtain came down behind him.

True, the sight of his velvet-clad rump rather spoiled the splendour of his heroic posture, legs akimbo, the sword Excalibur held aloft. But what can you do with this broken-backed hobbledehoy charade except serve it as a seasonable pantomime? It was never a half-decent musical and it never will be. The tunes do not improve with the years.

Even the best of Frederick Loewe's pedestrian score is merely a muddied reflection of his previous lilting successes from *My Fair Lady*. Listen hard to Mr Harris's tortured King Arthur intoning *How to Handle a Woman* and you cannot fail to hear eerie echoes of *I've Grown Accustomed to Her Face*.

You also recognise *On the Street Where You Live* in *If Ever I Should Leave You*. And the limp social coyness of *How Do the Simple Folk Live?* is simply *Wouldn't it Be Luvverly?* draped in cobwebs.

The truth is that as a major stage show for the Eighties it is barely watchable. Lerner tailored the book and lyrics – based on T H White's Arthurian eulogy *The Once and Future King* – as the flagship for the Kennedy vision of a New Camelot. And some of the script could have come straight from a campaign speech writer. 'This is the time when violence is not strength and compassion is not weakness,' cried King Harris rousingly just before that wretched curtain cut him off in his prime.

Even in its days dressed up to the wimple, the show was never a critical hit. And no one will accuse this mordant revival of hiding its faults under largesse. The sets look as if they have been dredged from the bottom of Arthur's lake and the costumes from one of the less spectacular Palladium yuletide offerings.

Accidents apart, Richard Harris does what he can with what he has. He sets his face in a convincing medieval mask of suffering after dispensing with a little light frolicking in the cause of a youthful flashback.

His Guinevere is the breathtakingly beautiful Fiona Fullerton, who captures the spirit of the season and plays the evening as if about to sprout the wings of the Good Fairy. To complete the eternal triangle that wrecks the Round Table there is a full square and very un-French Lancelot from Robert Meadmore.

But the yeast which leavens the loaf is Robin Bailey's bluff King Pellinore. No Wenceslas was ever more welcome than he.

Starlight Express

Music by Andrew Lloyd Webber, lyrics by Richard Stilgoe
Apollo, Victoria
***Daily Mail*, 28th March 1984**

First class to success!

I waited a few moments just in case Mr Lloyd Webber had one of his scene-stealing announcements for after the show. A public separation; a secret marriage. But no. This time all an anxious PR caught me by the sleeve to whisper were a few explanations as to why the microphones had played up.

So the only news Mr Lloyd Webber will make this morning is the sort that is written in international currency. I prophesy this show will keep bankruptcy from the door for another decade or so.

It may not be much of an innovative musical – there are synthesised echoes of many an old score to be picked up along these tracks. But it is one hell of a roller coaster spectacle.

The theatre, brilliantly done over by John Napier, is ringed by a three-tier racetrack with clear perspex crash barriers and a massive suspension bridge floats as its centrepiece. Around this the cast race and rumble, pretending to be trains (have you ever read what Mr Freud used to say about people who fantasise on the subject of trains, by the way?).

'A total media concept,' I hear my good friend Dame Edna Everage dubbing it, ever the one to be aboard the latest band wagon-lit.

Appropriately for the subject, the show started late and there was the odd technical hitch. But there is no denying that once aboard, this streamlined Inter-City evening only occasionally runs out of steam.

If you wanted to be picky with the railway officials en route you might complain that it is almost vulgarly sentimental to wax nostalgic about steam-engines – Mrs Thatcher wouldn't thank you for that one little bit, with the coal industry in the state it's in. But as Lloyd Webber's new collaborator Richard Stilgoe makes it clear in his book, they have very strong views about the rivals to steam.

Diesel is a no-good leather boy in rock 'n' roll gear; Electric shows up as an androgynous black funky guy who talks a lot about AC/DC and wears clothes you couldn't take home to your mother.

In between a bit of in-fighting for the favours of the best looking tenders (or the tenderest best lookers) a race is run and run with Stephanie Lawrence bathed in a pink spot and frantically trying to cling on to the right guy in the end. Now I won't spoil all by telling you who wins but it wasn't either of the big bad boys and it would have made the perfect ending to a children's bedtime story. No matter. When did cold logic figure in a spectacle?

When Richard Stilgoe's lyrics need to be funny they are. And when they seek to be romantic there is mercifully enough to look at so that you do not hear lines like: 'I believe in you completely, though I may be dreaming sweetly.'

As far as concepts go, it must be said that Trevor Nunn's impeccable sense of direction makes up for any disappointment in Arlene Phillips' choreography. Though heavens, what can anyone ask of a cast like Lon Satton, Miss Lawrence, Jeff Shankley (Diesel), Jeffrey Daniels (Electric) and Ray Shell (Steam – though his friends call him Rusty and much more besides, I shouldn't wonder).

So, in lieu of anything else to report at this opening night, I can only say that this show could well set another track record for Mr Lloyd Webber.

West Side Story
Book by Arthur Laurents, music by Leonard Bernstein, lyrics by Stephen Sondheim
Her Majesty's Theatre
Daily Mail, 17th May 1984

A classic sadly dated by events

Surely it can't be 25 years since I queued around the block for the privilege of standing at the back of the stalls in this very theatre to see this very show? Well, it is and I did.

Then, of course, we had seen nothing like it. Heard nothing like it. And we could scarcely believe it when we had. It was a show for its time which dragged the musical kicking, screaming and ultimately bleeding into the second half of the 20th century. The hair-trigger tensions generated by Jerome Robbins' dance routines fairly set the theatre alight. And I remember a shocked headline in the *Daily Telegraph* demanding: 'Does Stage Violence Really Have a Serious Effect on Children?'

Today it is revived as a revered classic and as a classic it passes muster. But it seems curiously distanced now. Almost romantically quaint with its *Romeo and Juliet* love story force fed into the framework of a New York gangland backstreet setting.

With the awful reality of our own social conflicts, and teenage urban violence, erupting around us in every major city suburb the sheer theatricality of the piece now makes it feel rather stale and artificially structured rather than rough, dark and dangerous as it appeared then.

Even the imposing brownstone New York tenements on the stage look practically cosy compared with Britain's decaying high-rise council wastelands, which themselves were brand new when this show was born.

This said, it is a luxury to sit back and recall a time where numbers crowded each other out for a place in the memory. Compare Bernstein's score and Sondheim's lyrics with the puny one-song (if that) hits that litter the West End these days.

Without *West Side Story* it is doubtful if we would have had the likes of *Cabaret*, *Chicago*, *A Chorus Line*, and our own *Blood Brothers*.

This young cast of eager unknowns do their best to give it full justice. But Tom Abbott's faithful period reconstruction of the original lacks the precision and the nerve-stretching tension of that long ago blockbuster. There is no George Chakiris to give the Sharks their dangerous bite; no Chita Rivera to lend the Jets their exotic glamour.

So it is the lovers who stand out as this revival's greatest strength. As Maria, Jan Hartley has a dark fragile beauty and a voice that soars magnificently through those great love songs, *Tonight*, and *I Feel Pretty*. Steven Pacey as her ill-fated Tony may strain a little in his serenading of her name, but there is never any doubt as to his feelings.

42nd Street

Music by Harry Warren, lyrics by Al Dubin, book by Michael Stewart and Mark Bramble
Theatre Royal, Drury Lane
Daily Mail, 9th August 1984

Dazzling – it's fresher and faster than Broadway!

Finally it's here. The father and mother of all showbiz musicals. The one that has everything it is possible for a musical to have and still plenty more besides. Fresher and faster, if that were possible, than I remember it on Broadway, too. Never in a lifetime's theatre-going have I seen a chorus with more youth, zest and dazzle than this home-picked exuberant troupe of hoofers.

From the moment the curtain hangs a fire on 40 pairs of furiously-tapping feet, there is the crackle of energy, excitement and success in the air. Oh dear, I'm already talking in incoherent hyperbole. Yet if I started to list all the good and sensible reasons why you simply must see this show to believe it, we'd be here all day and you'd still be none the wiser.

For *42nd Street* has always been touched by a shimmer of indefinable magic. It sprang out of Hollywood's urge to banish the stark realities of the Thirties Depression with all the things it could do best – songs that have become standards, dance routines by the great Busby Berkeley that have become legends; innocent backstage fun dispensed by Ruby Keeler and Dick Powell which has endured across the decades.

What producer David Merrick has done, with his usual shrewd flair for capitalising on success, is to put the story back where it belonged – in the theatre. Where else could the tale of a young chorus girl from Allentown who became a star overnight pack a greater punch? Like all the best ideas, it is blindingly simple. But from here on Mr Merrick has left nothing to chance. The best songs are rifled from other movies of the same era (*Dames* from *Dames*, for example).

The choreography of the late Gower Champion – who died on the day the show opened on Broadway, thus beginning the almost mystic quality that has grown up around the piece – is the finest epitaph any artist could wish. And there was not a boy or girl on that stage last night who did not do his memory proud.

As for the other stars, well at last London has entertainment big enough to encompass the magnificent techniques of Miss Margaret Courtenay. Miss Courtenay plays the big-hearted Broadway broad who writes shows and dolls out wisdom. And no one delivers a wisecrack to such effect as she.

Ruby Keeler's original brand of innocent mischief is, of course, a hard act to follow. So the triumph of Clare Leach is all the more remarkable, and to see Miss Keeler herself standing in a box leading ovation after ovation at the end of this blissful evening was no more than her efforts deserved.

It is to Miss Leach that the suave James Laurenson delivers that monumental showbiz cliché: 'You're going out there a youngster but you're gonna come back a star.' And Miss Leach makes you believe every word of it.

It was a rather muted London return for Miss Georgia Brown as the star who blows it. But this is to quibble. It will be a long time before we see the like of *42nd Street* at Drury Lane again.

If you had to analyse objectively the show's gut appeal, it would be simply its optimism. The theme of the unspoiled innocent triumphing against all the odds is perennial. And if it is as superlatively well done and well intentioned as here, it can lift the heart and raise the spirits as nothing else.

17

Les Miserables

Music by Claude-Michel Schonberg, original text by Alain Boublil and Jean-Marc Natel, lyrics by Herbert Kretzmer
RSC Barbican
Daily Mail, **9th October 1985**

The life and hard times of Les Glums

The Royal Shakespeare Company have elected to join forces with the commercial theatre and man the barricades to bring the musical version of Victor Hugo's marathon sweep through French social history to the Barbican. They have, needless to say, more than half an eye on making a killing in the West End later. There are, however, two major and maybe insurmountable obstacles to this happy outcome and neither of them is the title.

First, there is the sheer scale of the material to be condensed and sustained in manageable musical form. The paperback translation of the original novel runs to 1,232 pages. To pack all this, or even a portion, into three and a quarter hours of non-stop operatic treatment, encompassing such grandiose themes as revolution, human degradation, spiritual retribution, obsessive guilt and the triumph of true love might seem like attempting to pour the Channel through a China teapot.

In Paris, however, the enterprise has already proved a runaway triumph. The French take their great literature to heart; one small reference to such events in the narrative is enough to sound a clamour of collected national conscience through to such an audience. To us, more familiar with Dickens than Hugo, these shorthand effects turn this anguished vision of intertwining destinies into a series of mere coincidences, and his tidal wave of emotions into ripples of cheap sentiment. The hero Jean Valjean (Colin Wilkinson), for example, has no sooner escaped from the chain gang than – in no more time than it takes to sing a song and nip into the wings for a change of costume – he is a successful factory owner and mayor of the town.

The second and equally serious difficulty this bold Gallic import will have winning popular Anglo-Saxon approval, is in the staging. True, there is some thrilling music to stir the action along and no-one is more deft at pinning a French tune to an English ear with appropriate lyrics than my esteemed colleague Mr Herbert Kretzmer. But the directorial team of Trevor Nunn and John Caird who imaginatively turned *Nicholas Nickleby* into the biggest transatlantic triumph in the history of the Royal Shakespeare Company, have found little verbal excitement or novelty here, despite the resources amassed to little effect on their stage.

When Hugo wrote his novel he claimed that the vision of Hell that Dante brought through poetry, he hoped to achieve in prose. There is nothing so potent in this musical staging. It leaves one curiously uninvolved. Despite the grandeur of the music, *Les Miserables* has, sadly been reduced to *The Glums*.

The Phantom of the Opera
Music by Andrew Lloyd Webber, lyrics by Charles Hart, book by Richard Stilgoe and Andrew Lloyd Webber
Her Majesty's Theatre
***Daily Mail*, 10th October 1986**

He's Phantastic!

Four words sum up the unstoppable success of Andrew Lloyd Webber's triumphant re-working of this vintage spine-tingling melodrama. Stars, spectacle, score and story. Together, they add up to that old magic ingredient: theatricality. There is simply nothing on Earth to transport you so quickly or so far into phantasy than a feast of illusion. And Hal Prince's production stints nothing in providing an unending banquet of the stuff. When I get my breath back from gulping down as much as is decent at one sitting, let me deal with each item in turn.

First, the star and the evening's greatest surprise. Were it not that I personally know Michael Crawford's singing teacher to be the kindest and mildest of men, I would swear that Mr Crawford had sold his soul to the devil to acquire the rich and powerful voice with which he floods the theatre and holds us hypnotised in his presence.

The mask that for most of the evening obliterates half his face only hints at the physical horrors beneath it. But by the time his golden-voiced protégée has torn it aside to reveal a peeling skull and rotting flesh, he has utterly established the phantom as one of the enduring tragic figures of the modern musical; a man with a tender, gifted and loving soul whose only crime was to have been born a freak. It is surely one of the great performances, not only in a musical but on any stage and in any year.

In this Mr Crawford is indeed fortunate to be partnered by someone as illustrious and exotically voiced as Sarah Brightman. I can think of no other actress whose glorious operatic range can match a stage presence so delicately vulnerable or exquisitely beautiful.

On now to the full throttle spectacle that Maria Bjornson has conjured up to encompass all the diverse elements of the evening. Giant chandeliers plummet from on high; great gilded angels bear Mr Crawford skyward as he sings out his heart to heaven; a lavish fancy dress masquerade underlines the sinister nature of disguise; high-camp pastiches of less than grand opera strike just the right note of comic relief while a lake of lights floats us down to the Phantom's lair beneath the great Opera House of Paris.

As for the score, it soars and instils itself into the mind like some half-forgotten refrain from Verdi, taking the story line on in great sweeps of musical sound. In its unabashed romanticism it reminds us that the *Phantom* is at heart a simple tale of unrequited love, as inspiring and moving in its way as *Romeo and Juliet* or more appropriately *Beauty and the Beast*. Yet to underline the sheer theatricality of the piece the Phantom does nothing so mundane as die for love. He vanishes in a blink before our eyes.

True there are faults, but to pick now would be churlish and irrelevant. Mr Lloyd Webber has another long-term tenancy and his wife has established herself as a star of status. As for Michael Crawford, there is just no other artist in this country today who can touch his command of a stage or match his daring in meeting a new challenge.

Evita
Music by Andrew Lloyd Webber, lyrics by Tim Rice
Prince Edward Theatre
Daily Mail, 3rd February 1988

Adios Evita, we won't forget you

If any critic took his seat in the newly named Prince Edward Theatre on that tumultuous first night in June 1978 imagining that one word he published next morning would alter the short-term destiny of *Evita*, then he must have been half-blind and totally daft. This was the show, the first of its kind, which came fully-packaged, critic-proofed and stamped all over with success. It was, I wrote at the time, not history being regurgitated but history being made.

Now, nearly eight years later, *Evita* is finally ending its record-breaking London run. It closes on Saturday after nearly 3,000 performances. Every major West End musical since has hoped and strived to repeat *Evita*'s enviable formula. Few if any have ever got it quite so right.

First there was that unstoppable album. Released two years before the show even previewed, it had already made the words and music of its creators, Tim Rice and Andrew Lloyd Webber as well-known to world-wide audiences as their own national anthems.

The life and death of Eva Peron had all the ingredients of Cinderella, Lady Macbeth and Lorelei Lee. But how to put all that across in two and a half hours? Yet who except the writers and producers, at that time even cared! Julie Covington, chart-topping star of the hit record, was by now making the show headline news all over again.

'Earning money is a drag,' declared Miss Covington, as she spectacularly bowed out of the decade's most coveted role with no explanation other than: 'I just didn't want to do it.' From that moment the search to find her replacement took on *Gone with the Wind* glamour.

I've often wondered since if she ever had cause to regret those words. But certainly Elaine Paige, who emerged to grab her pot of gold at this particular rainbow's end must have gone down on her knees to thank Miss Covington for them.

Thus, before the first rehearsal had been called, the real-life drama of an unknown girl stepping into a star role had already bound the myth of *Evita* to the public's imagination with hoops of steel. True, Miss Paige was hailed as an overnight star. But looking back, away from all the euphoria, it has to be admitted that any actress-singer of her professional pedigree (belty little roles in less memorable musicals) could have pulled off a personal triumph that night.

Marti Webb, Stephanie Lawrence and Siobhan McCarthy all went on, justifiably, to star in their own West End musicals. Jacquey Chappell became the fifth *Evita*, to be succeeded last May by Kathryn Evans. She was bored with life as a housewife so her husband, former Blue Peter presenter Peter Purves, suggested she go back on the stage. She sensationally pulled off the big part. She takes *Evita* to Manchester after Saturday's closure in London. Miss Lawrence, if I have to be ungallant enough to choose, was for my money the most complete *Evita* of them all – though she confessed to me that she didn't even get past the first audition in that fevered search for the first *Evita*.

What gave them all the perfect *Evita* showcase, however, was undoubtedly Hal Prince's masterly staging. A veteran of an enviable string of Broadway hits, he brought a sharp intellect and high tone class to a story many had predicted would be squalid, or at best sanitised. Using only the images of beds and doors for the settings he chronicled Eva Peron's horizontal rise to fame, fortune and immortality with an indelible visual impact.

The now familiar music and lyrics worked their magic all over again. And when Elaine Paige moved out, puppet-like and dressed in a mountain of white tulle, to belt out the show's great stopper, *Don't Cry for Me, Argentina*, there could be no-one in the audience who doubted that the British musical had at last grown-up.

This was indeed the first adult political pop opera to be originated in London since John Gay staged *The Beggar's Opera*. And after it no subject could be considered taboo or too unlively for a musical setting.

It had broken many moulds. For starters, Hal Prince had given his star an entrance which must have gone almost unnoticed by everyone except her nearest and dearest behind their opera glasses. Just one of a crowd of peasants following Evita's coffin. Her exit was no less downbeat. Frightened, and for once alone in a bed, the skeletal figure simply succumbed to her cancer. But in terms of theatre it was shattering.

Since that night of so many thousand nights which followed, I have been back to see the magic worked again no fewer than five times. The spell has never failed. There is, sad to say, no sure-fire formula to hand down to posterity as a lesson to any who come after – except for all-round excellence. It just so happened that at the right time in their careers Messrs Rice and Lloyd Webber found themselves joined together in an enterprise in which they both passionately believed. They were fortunate enough to have the right manager in David Land, shrewd enough to market their music to the right producer, who in turn came up with the right cast and the right director. All this – and the right publicity in all the right papers. It takes this and much more to make the sort of history *Evita* has made. The West End will seem somehow incomplete without it.

ANDREW LLOYD WEBBER

I think Jack meant that the British musical had 'grown up' with *Evita* in various ways. The subject matter that we had chosen – which is hardly the most overtly commercial – was the first time that the musical had tackled something like that. Before *Evita*, one thought of the British musical as *The Boyfriend* and *Salad Days*. This was new.

Secondly, it was the first British musical that was really able to take its original production around the world. *Jesus Christ Superstar* travelled internationally, but with different stagings. *Evita* had one, and it was Robert Stigwood who taught me how to duplicate shows. Then, when I met Cameron Mackintosh later on, I was able to tell him how Robert used to do it. This interested Jack because he also knew Robert.

Carrie

**Music by Michael Gore, lyrics by Dean Pitchford, book by
Lawrence D Cohen
RSC Stratford-upon-Avon
Daily Mail, 19th February 1988**

Oh dear girls, what a dreadful Carrie on

Here is neither the time nor the place to debate how the publicly-owned Royal Shakespeare Company came to be privatised as an out-of-town try-out venue for Broadway. This troubled musical is in enough trouble without political controversy.

First, we are forced to ask ourselves why anyone with a glimmer of instinct should want to set Stephen King's vengeful novel of an adolescent's supernatural powers to music? Then why like this, with a score you usually hear escaping unbidden from someone else's Sony Walkman on the Tube?

These are questions which quickly clamour for an answer before the plot is even half set (or, in this case, congealed) when the lustrous Miss

Barbara Cooke, woefully miscast, is forced to lend her wonderful voice to a lament on the religious significance of women's monthly curse. I must warn the faint of heart, and those with pretensions to good taste, that this misguided aria is graphically signalled by a schoolgirl shower scene.

In the film version, of course, the rather tawdry Hammer-horror elements of the plot were redeemed by a Hitchcockian sense of *grand guignol*. Director Terry Hands, alas, has found no cohesive idiom to join together the jangle of the music, the tensions of the unsavoury story, the go-go choreography, a pantomime Cinderella transformation and sundry hi-tech stage designs. It looks and sounds a mess.

An expensive mess. And nearly a nasty mess, too, when Ralph Koltai's clinical mechanical set all but decapitated poor Miss Cooke as she gathered breath to heap more fire and brimstone on her persecuted daughter, Carrie.

Broadway's reclaimed heroine, Miss Cooke, is one of nature's serene saints struggling to transform herself into a monster of religious repression. For any failure to do so convincingly, she is blameless. Blameless, too, is the show's shining reason for our pilgrimage to Stratford to catch its brief stay: Linzi Hateley.

Miss Hateley is a 17-year old drama school graduate with a voice like an angel who can turn treacle lyrics into purest honey. I hope sincerely that Broadway takes Miss Hateley to its heart. It can take the rest wherever it pleases.

Metropolis

Music by Joe Brooks, book and lyrics by Dusty Hughes and Joe Brooks
Piccadilly Theatre
***Daily Mail*, 9th March 1989**

Scene-stealing scenery – but an out-of-date time machine

The first glaring irony of this flagrantly expensive spectacular is to take a parable about a world where machines take over from men and rob them of their dignity... and deliberately turn it into a musical where the scenery takes over from actors and steals all the notices.

It is perhaps worth remembering that Fritz Lang's epoch-making Expressionist movie of the same name and theme flopped at the box office. But at least it had the singular virtue of being silent. No such luck here.

With ne'er a tune to trouble the toes nor a lyric worth repeating, and dialogue spoken in the sort of Sunday voices usually reserved for infant school nativity plays, the effect is to make *Les Miserables* seem frivolous. 'Tree, sun, flower, bird,' intones Judy Kuhn, who has forsaken the pallor of Broadway to walk this deadly treadmill of industrial woe and who even now must be putting in long distance calls to her agent.

She is speaking to a class of bewildered infants who have spent their entire life underground amid Ralph Koltai's truly amazing setting. 'Things we might never see again,' she warns them. Two and a half hours later I felt very much the same. Miss Kuhn had, in the meantime, been metamorphosed from a caring rebel-rouser into a disruptive robot and back again into Goody Twoclogs by a mad scientist (Jonathan Adams). And Brian Blessed had made several impressive entrances and exits in all manner of floating command capsules.

The second great difficulty is, of course, that as a glimpse into the future it is all so sadly out of date. Far from the machines which run our lives needing armies of human toilers to keep them operating, quite the reverse has happened.

By a neat coincidence, a very unfunny thing happened on my way to the theatre. I passed through one of London's increasingly common underground cardboard cities full of today's destitute humanity. Of course, their redundant plight has no doubt been, directly or indirectly, brought about by the very computerised efficiency of today's machines. So the show's prophecy proves as empty as its songs.

There are some truly thrilling voices frittered during the course of this £3 million extravaganza. But their effect is merely to interrupt what narrative there is and give us more time to gaze at Mr Koltai's massive array of giant cog wheels, laser light effects and the transparent lifts which signal an entrance, or better still, an exit. The audience received it ecstatically. They must have been backers or mad or both.

Aspects of Love
Music by Andrew Lloyd Webber, book and lyrics by Don Black and Charles Hart
Prince of Wales Theatre
Daily Mail, 18th April 1989

Lloyd Webber dares and comes up with yet another winner

Never expect the expected from Andrew Lloyd Webber. Those who go to the Prince of Wales in search of the flamboyant theatricality of the *Phantom*, the pyrotechnics of a *Starlight Express* or the pulsating action of *Cats* will look in vain.

This is the work with which he takes the musical full circle back to its original roots. If *Phantom* was grand operetta, *Aspects* is pure opera, a theme in five keys with several variations. Yet who among us would presume to guess what creative sprite prompted him to turn David Garnett's delicate novella into a full scale opera?

But one thing is certain. Only Mr Lloyd Webber would dare the risks entailed. Indeed probably only Mr Lloyd Webber *could* dare such risks. For this is uncharted territory on so many fronts. Not least the theme which floats through fast-shifting passions and long-term affections which effectively bind together five people across three generations; a sort of *la ronde en famille*.

But let us not worry our pretty heads with the complexities of the plot just yet. What you all want to know is: has the maestro of the great Western musical pulled off another multi-million dollar smash hit... this being the sort of headline jargon Mr Lloyd Webber's work invariably attracts.

The fact is that he has achieved something far more subtle, possibly even more rewarding. Though not all the aspects of *Aspects* are as happy as the music, notably the insistent love theme that runs through the tangle of its complex story, *Love Is Everything*, the song with which Michael Ball's exquisite voice – accompanied only by a piano – begins the evening.

Mr Ball, when we meet him, is the cherubic 17-year-old precocious schoolboy about to throw himself at the feet of a stranded actress and embark on a series of romantic adventures which will last well into manhood. The actress, a vibrantly intelligent and commanding performance by American, Ann Crumb, who couldn't be more typically French if she had been called *Croissant*, marries Mr Ball's rich uncle instead and the interchange of partners begins.

I'm sure it probably helps to have invested an evening reading the book prior to investing in tickets. Who goes to an opera without knowing the story?

Although Maria Bjornson's settings appear strikingly plain and simple, they are nonetheless on a substantial scale. Thus the action never quite manages to flit from mood to mood as the music and the deliberately simple lyrics by Don Black and Charles Hart demand. And too often what should seem light and ambiguous comes across as faintly mundane or even slightly sleazy.

What redeems all their actions should be the sensation of people who have the style and daring to – as the uncle's mistress puts it – 'roll the dice and drink the wine.' Mr Lloyd Webber has certainly rolled the dice and drunk the wine. Whether the public are prepared for such a show of courage or not time will hardly tell. The show is booked out enough already for it to be counted a box office success.

It is, however, no mean achievement to have taken such a huge artistic gamble and come within an ace of the jackpot. For by the second act, when director Trevor Nunn has more established the bitter-sweet content of the piece, we really do begin to enter into the fascination the five main characters hold for each other.

Echoes of Miss Crumb's first caprice with the virginal Mr Ball haunt the stage when he, in turn finds himself falling for the teenage daughter she has had by his elderly uncle (I told you this wasn't going to be your average musical plot).

A perfectly delightful performance from Diana Morrison absolves these exchanges from either nymphet prurience or worse. She had the disarming charm of an assured, yet innocent, adult child. Exactly what one imagined in the pages of Garnett's original concept.

No writer, composer or artist has ever fulfilled him or herself without testing new territory. It takes courage and a sure nerve, not to mention the sort of bankable reputation of Andrew Lloyd Webber.

But in art as in less high-minded spheres, who dares wins. And the daring shown here tonight deserves to win our admiration, even if it leaves some hearts cold and does not please everyone. That, anyway, is not what I guess to be the name of this particular game.

Miss Saigon

**Lyrics by Alain Boublil and Richard Maltby Jr, music by
Claude-Michel Schonberg
Theatre Royal, Drury Lane
Daily Mail, 21st September 1989**

Miss Saigon: a triumph and a shattering experience

The story of *Madam Butterfly* is rapidly overtaking that of *Romeo and Juliet* as a sure-fire crowd-pleaser however and wherever you tell it. Shifted to the shameful carnage of America's military adventures in Vietnam, and given the unashamed gut force that marks the work of Messrs Boublil and Schonberg – the team that launched *Les Miserables* on its world conquest – it maintains all its tried and true theatrical potency. Yet also something more.

It has both the courage and the compassion to confront the brutal facts of its situation with a commendably small attempt to decorate the tale with the trappings with which musicals usually sugar unpleasant pills. No *South Pacific* this. Yet it has the power to move one to tears at the mess Mankind can inflict upon itself and also to fill the heart fit to burst with the simple nobility of its heroine's capacity to rise above it. I can think of few modern musicals which can make this claim, and I speak as one of the few who found *Les Mis* most mizzable.

Part of the evening's exultant triumph must, of course, go to its Young Turk director, Nicholas Hytner. He sustains an emotional hold on the audience with a staging that is deceptively uncluttered and lean. It is, in fact, highly complex and knows when to go for the jugular or bring on the razmatazz.

A giant golden statue of Ho Chi Minh is hauled upright like some threatening totem to add dramatic chill to the separation of the young Vietnamese girl and her GI lover. While, in a song that remorselessly mocks the all-American dream while seeming to parade it, a dreamlike phantom chorus high-kick and sashay as a block-long Cadillac glides into view baring a brazen beauty queen. Brecht and Weil could not have capped such conceits.

This latter *coup de théâtre* happily brings us to the hitherto unexplored talents of Mr Jonathan Pryce. An actor of demonic daring always, here he proves himself to be a master of musical insinuation possessed of a voice most singers would envy. As the girl's opportunistic pimp, he creates a fascinating character, snakelike arrogance matched to the survivor's slimy charms, and fair bowls us over.

As for the protagonists of the story, I can only report that the world-wide search for a Miss Saigon has yielded a talent of shattering emotional depths in Miss Lea Salonga. Her suicide to give her small (scene-stealing) son a better life with his father in America is built up to with hypnotic grace, integrity and a wonderful singing voice. And in Simon Bowman she has a worthy foil.

Her tragedy involves all our guilt. The point is forcibly made in the opening song of the second act by Peter Polycarpou, singing his lungs out on behalf of the *bui-doi* – half-caste – children left behind in Vietnam after America's ignominious withdrawal. An evening of shattering dimensions.

The Hunting of the Snark
Book, lyrics and music by Mike Batt
Prince Edward Theatre
Daily Mail, 25th October 1991

Dancing towards disaster with the Snark

It took the best part of my day to beat the strike which paralysed Paris yesterday and return to London in time for this monumental piece of unremitting folly. For just as Cameron Mackintosh was giving the French a taste of deeply motivated musical enterprise with *Les Mis*, the West End was being subjected to the sort of meaningless spectacle which has left French audiences brain dead for decades.

Mike Batt gives a whole new meaning to that phrase 'All off my own Batt' by being responsible, not only for the music, lyrics and book but also for the direction and design.

In truth, he shows flair and enterprise in each department. Backed by the mightiest orchestra seen on any stage outside the Royal Albert Hall, the middle of the road music swirls around amplified to studio perfection by microphones glued on the artists' cheeks, chins and foreheads like so many monstrous carbuncles on the faces of well-loved friends.

What are we to make of a show whose only real daring, apart from conspicuous cost, is to write its own epitaph as an Act One finale. A number staged like the showstopper from *42nd Street* and sounding like Barry Manilow's club song, it is prophetically titled *Dancing towards Disaster*. I would discuss the performances of such diverse talents as Mark McGann, David McCallum and the maverick Kenny Everett if I could fathom out exactly what they were doing there.

However the show's catastrophic misjudgment, on a scale worthy of *Springtime for Hitler*, is to take Lewis Carroll's tantalising nonsense poem about the mythical Snark and trample its ephemeral magic into the ground with the hobnailed boots of Mr Batt's fatuous musical analysis.

McCallum, lightly disguised as Carroll, assures us that the master had no thought other than to amuse with his tale of the Snark and its ill-assorted hunters. But Mr Batt, out of hell, perversity or spite, thinks otherwise. In a parade of portentous or pretentious lyrics, Mr Batt imposes all manner of motives and messages on those mellifluous lines of poetry.

It will be a long time before we see such a display of one man's private obsessions turned into such pulverising public capers.

Blood Brothers

Willy Russell
Phoenix Theatre
Daily Mail, 16th December 1991

Blood sheds a sad story of family fate

The more often I have the good fortune to revisit this extraordinary musical, the more convinced I become that Willy Russell has written the seminal musical of our times. My excuse to indulge – for the eighth time – in Russell's brilliant mix of modern morality tale and ancient folklore is its rehousing in London's Phoenix Theatre.

And my astonishment at the richness of his achievement as writer of book, music and lyrics only increases. As a story of twins separated at birth and doomed by fate to die together, it marries all the passions of a sharp social perception to a gritty suspense narrative that keeps one on the edge of one's seat throughout.

The whole of it is unified and orchestrated by a thrillingly lyrical score. It is powerfully sung here, notably by Stephanie Lawrence as the hapless working-class mother forced to give away one of her babies to her middle-class employer, and Carl Wayne as the ever-present avenging Angel of Death. It is a huge, complex canvas of inner-city life, class distinction and earthy Liverpudlian humour. What Willy Russell achieves, however, is to imply the whole with bold, brash strokes.

There is a simply wonderful performance from Russell Boulter, taking us from the rough and tumble carefree, tough-love childhood of the twin left at home to grow up through an agonising adolescence, to a premature and increasingly bitter maturity. The inevitability of his fate builds up to overwhelm them all with the awesome tread of Greek mythology. The man who gave us *Educating Rita* and *Shirley Valentine* can also claim to have created the British musical's most matchless heroine in the stoic, large-hearted Mrs Johnstone.

Stephanie Lawrence's performance brings an extra resonance to the role, not least in the evening's constant hymn to that icon of tragic destiny, Marilyn Monroe. Ms Lawrence, you may remember, had the great misfortune to play Marilyn incandescently and matchlessly in a show which died the death. What crueller fate than that?

Moby Dick
Book and lyrics by Robert Longden, music and additional lyrics by Hereward Kaye
Piccadilly Theatre
Daily Mail, **18th March 1992**

Lunacy on the high seas with the ship's Belles of St Trinian's

It is at times undoubtedly mad. It is at times flagrantly bad. But there is such a lunacy and anarchic energy about this bizarre show that it could win a devoted cult following among those in the know.

The West End would be a poor place indeed if it did not have room for such a piece of blatant and outrageous impertinence. I am not saying I swallowed it whole, like Moby devoured Captain Ahab's right leg. Oh no. There were times when I felt the cast were attending a far funnier party when we were. And that does tend to freeze the smile.

But consider the premise. A sort of St Trinian's school of the most wayward pupils, ruled over by a transvestite head teacher, decides to put on a ghastly sixth form musical version of *Moby Dick*. With me so far? You won't be much longer. Any acquaintance with Herman Melville's worthy classic is as helpful as a road map of Hong Kong in the middle of the Sahara Desert. It would be confusing enough to have all the men aboard the Pequod played by girls in the first place. But as some of the original 'girls' are, in fact, played by boys (or at least my programme tells me so), the cross-dressing becomes nothing if not baroque.

Some of it is wildly funny – not least the pregnant 'girl' (Earl Tobias) whose high-camp impersonations of every drag queen's favourite galaxy from Garland to Davis keeps our minds tactfully off the Adventures of Captain Ahab. It also keeps author Robert Longden's off them, too. His is clearly an off-the-wall talent which can resist no gag, good or bad, if it sparks off a song or saves a little serious plot-setting. Like the bright but naughty boy at school, he'd much rather throw paper darts than turn in an essay.

The songs are certainly worth the tricks he employs to introduce them and they are marvellously sung. Room to mention only Hope Augustus' lusty renderings as Ahab's wife, Theresa Kartell's sexy cannibal Queequeg, Joanne Redman's pert and precocious storyteller and Mark White's endearingly inappropriate Irish Jig, smilingly prophesying the entire crew's doom.

Of Ahab's legendary obsession with hunting down the whale which lunched on his leg we have to trust to Tony Monopoly's rather precarious sense of double identity and entendre. As the headmistress he adopts a swooping, Nellie Wallace stance, and as the headmistress-acting-the-mad-captain, he does more of the same, only wearing black panda eyes and a white cricket pad. What he lacks, however, is a true sense of bravura camp. And this is what the part cries out for. But heaven knows, there's plenty of it about elsewhere.

CAMERON MACKINTOSH

Jack saw *Moby Dick* for what it was. Most of the critics anyway did not understand that I did not produce this show in the way that I normally would. At the time I was in America supervising *Miss Saigon*. I gave the author £25,000 to put it on at The Fire Station. It was a wild idea, which went extremely well there. The mistake which I made was to move the show, which needs a small house, to the thousand-seater Piccadilly Theatre in the West End.

It came off playing to 4,500 people a week, which is hardly a flop. The trouble is that it had been allowed to balloon. The show that I had given the go-ahead to, which had twelve people and three musicians, had expanded to a cast of thirty and five or six musicians. That did not suit the piece. Also, people came to see a Big Show. Alain Boublil said to me, 'It is not the kind of show we expect from you.' My job is in fact to find anything with promise. Interestingly, the show continues to be done in Europe. One day someone will find the correct mad way of doing it here.

There was a degree of glee when it was panned. Most of the critics in this country get extremely protective of the classics. Michael Billington, whom I respect greatly, gave me the worst review I have ever had from him. He got into such a stew about the fact that this could be done to *Moby Dick*, a great novel being turned into a musical. The same was true of *Les Miserables*. The Americans loved both shows and *Moby Dick* did well out there. They enjoy irreverence, but our critics get very stuffy. I suppose it shows the difference in our cultural upbringing – America's first experience of theatre was through burlesque.

Starlight's Super Stars
Daily Mail, 28th November 1992

Not that Sir Andrew Lloyd Webber needs his income boosting or his fame enhancing, and certainly me putting in my halfpennyworth will not affect his fortunes one jot.

But I came away from his revamped version of *Starlight Express* this week rejoicing that success and wealth have not dulled the cutting edge of his drive to improve and perfect even the most unpromising of his output.

It is eight and a half years since I and my ilk (a good collective noun for critics, ilk) gave his hectic roller-skate extravaganza a coolish welcome. And while I have championed *Aspects of Love* as possibly his most interesting score to date and have returned to *Phantom of the Opera* on at least eight occasions, and *Evita*, *Cats* and *Jesus Christ Superstar* almost as many, nothing has ever tempted me back to *Starlight Express* on an off-duty night.

When my granddaughter was born (and don't start me off on that obsession) I made a list of shows I prayed would still be running when she was old enough to kidnap for an introduction to the theatre. For I do believe that children's taste is far more eclectic and adventurous than most parents realise.

My eldest daughter was taken to see Marlene Dietrich's one-woman concert at four and a half and sat there enraptured in wonderment at the magic and mystery of it all. She remembers it to this day. All three daughters were practically weaned on the comic genius of the likes of Max Wall or Ken Dodd.

But back to *Starlight Express*. I had never thought to include it on my Grandparental Must-See list. To me it was consigned to those landmarks which Japanese tourists gawk at because it is there.

So it was a double surprise and pleasure to discover a reborn theatrical delight. The show, with five different numbers and a good (or rather all indifferent) half-hour cut from the replanned plot, is an escapist joy. Almost a decade on, its young cast has an energy that makes you weak to behold. The choreography has grown daring and dangerous with the performers' confidence on the roller skates. And there is not a hint of the cloying air of tentative worthiness which hung over the original.

Sir Andrew cheerfully acknowledges the limitations of the earlier version. 'We got it slightly wrong at the beginning. I wanted it just to be two hours of great fun for the kids,' he told me with an engaging simplicity rare in creative people. 'It was coming to the end of its natural life and I wanted to see if I could refine it and give it new life.'

Well, you can't say fairer than that, can you? And fun it most certainly is. So, I have revised the sainted grandchild's curriculum accordingly. I can't wait for her to toddle into that theatre and marvel at the pyrotechnics of those racing roller-ball engines. And after the ovation it received on its grand-reopening night, I have absolutely no fears that it will not still be there. My only worry is: will I last until then?

Carousel

Music by Richard Rodgers, book and lyrics by Oscar Hammerstein II
RNT Lyttelton
Daily Mail, 11th December 1992

Sheer genius bustin' out all over

Carousel is, of course, one of the all-time great musicals. Emotionally challenging, musically enthralling, sociologically adult and, in its day, astonishingly sexually precocious, it pointed the way forward to everything that followed.

More than a decade ahead of *West Side Story*, its plot embraces wife-beating, attempted murder, ill-starred love, suicide and redemption. Thirty years before Andrew Lloyd Webber, or Sondheim, it has sung-through dialogue which can still teach today's practitioners, who insist on setting such banalities as 'pass the pickles' to music, how to cut the mustard.

This said, Nicholas Hytner's triumphant Royal National Theatre production stands as a beacon in its own right. It takes all the show's finest qualities and defines them and refines them afresh.

A classic production of a classic musical and one which frankly I do not expect to see bettered in my lifetime.

From the very moment of the overture, with its strong, familiar tunes exquisitely orchestrated and brought to breathtaking dramatic life by Bob Crowley's economically ingenious settings and the late Sir Kenneth MacMillan's thrillingly expressive choreography, you know you are in the presence of a master-work in the hands of masters.

By the time the principal players have made their first impact you also know the evening is of a rare calibre indeed.

In Joanna Riding's grave and determined Julie and Michael Hayden's hunky, self-regarding Billy we have a leading pair of players who, one feels, could be totally at home as Romeo and Juliet and still sing the socks off any score you offered them.

Their long *If I Loved You* duet spells out the very anatomy of unassuageable physical attraction. Equally, the splendid Janie Dee and

Clive Rowe illuminate the other side of love's coin with such memorable standards as *When the Children Are Asleep*. As a bonus, we are treated to Patricia Routledge setting the precise emotional tone on such diverse mood-poems as *June Is Bustin' Out All Over* and *You'll Never Walk Alone*.

The entire evening swims along on this high tide of enchantment, moving you to laughter and tears by turns. It confirms Mr Hytner as one of the finest directors of modem times.

Sweeney Todd
Music and lyrics by Stephen Sondheim, book by Hugh Wheeler
RNT Cottesloe
***Daily Mail*, 3rd June 1993**

Razor-sharp, a rare and wondrous treat

Here at last it is. The production of Sondheim's most (if I may use the word) meaty musical that I have waited to see these past 13 years. Not exactly holding my breath, you understand. But certain, somewhere in the recesses of my instinct, that there must be the perfect way of staging this most difficult, defiant, yet musically devastating of musicals.

In 1980 at Drury Lane, its gory *grand guignol* wit and subterranean social issues were all but submerged in the coat of showbiz gloss which had been applied like bad varnish.

Now director Declan Donnellan at the Royal National Theatre has stripped it down to its bare bones (there I go again. Sorry, it's difficult not to catch its note of salacious *sangfroid*). And we can see what a very rare and wondrous thing Mr Sondheim had created.

Based as it was on Christopher Bond's play, it has a taut, deliberately melodramatic storyline of a barber robbed of his wife and a daughter by a lecherous old judge who deported him.

Understandably, he returns in some considerable state of fevered vengeance against the human race in general and the judge (Denis Quilley, advanced now from his original role as Sweeney) in particular. Less easy to comprehend, is the motivation of his blood lusting accomplice Mrs Lovett, pie-maker extraordinaire. Surely not just the high price of meat?

Yet Miss Julia McKenzie, that most versatile mistress of all the Master's music, gives us not a second to dwell upon this. I had thought she reached a career pinnacle in his sublime *Into the Woods*. But no. Miss McKenzie discovers another even higher summit here to scale.

Musically, as I hinted, the score is one of his most demanding. Its sudden, unexpected key changes and mood swings jangle the nerves, keeping one never far from the edge of one's seat. Yet Miss McKenzie makes it seem as easy as falling off a barber's chair and augments it with as bravura a performance of black comic acting as you could wish.

As Sweeney himself, Alun Armstrong's pale, pudgy face is frozen in torment, and his diabolical passion is never at issue. His singing voice, perhaps. Nevertheless, thanks to him the blood-soaked barbarity of the second act treads that precarious path between genuine Gothic horror and the deepest black comedy in a way one would never have thought possible.

All director Donnellan uses to suggest the stinking social cesspit of Victorian London is a door here, a staircase there and a chorus of prowling citizenry eavesdropping on all the nightmares and singing like a dream.

The audience, like children satiated on the thrill of fear rose and yelled their rapture. Quite right too. A thrilling evening by any standard.

DENIS QUILLEY

Jack got it absolutely right with *Sweeney Todd*. I agree that Hal Prince's original staging was clever, but it lacked concentration. All the great things that were happening all over the place were completely peripheral. All the main action took place in the middle of the stage in a little truck, about ten feet high and twelve feet square, which became Mrs Lovett's pie shop and my barber shop above. And all these bridges going up and down and heavens knows what was completely extraneous. When I played the role again, succeeding Alun Armstrong at the National Theatre, by contrast the set was simply a little black box and everything was concentrated on the central action, which made a huge difference. Jack's review was very perceptive, he always saw things in a clear perspective.

Sunset Boulevard
Music by Andrew Lloyd Webber, book and lyrics by Don Black and Christopher Hampton
Adelphi Theatre
***Daily Mail*, 13th July 1993**

Triumph for the Phantom in reverse

And just when we least expect, it, Sir Andrew Lloyd Webber sneaks another little opus into the West End. What a pickle! For those of you who haven't been listening with the ears of a bat or looking with the eyes of a hawk these past few months, it may come as a shock to learn he has been taking a nostalgic stroll down *Sunset Boulevard*.

A trip, I must report, which has yielded him some of the mega-possibilities offered by his earlier brush with *Phantom of the Opera*. For *Sunset* is *Phantom* in reverse. A female monster stalking her prey in her own twilight world, enticing the fly of her desire into it with spider-like cunning.

Billy Wilder's Fifties black-and-white classic of the silver screen – which introduced us to the indelible legend of the ageing movie star,

Desmond – was heaven-sent for the particular hyper-theatrical spin Sir Andrew has proved he can bring to the most unexpected themes.

With all its undoubted splendours – a towering baroque fantasy set of Norma's Hollywood mansion, the movie screen which turns into the bottom of the fateful pool from which we gaze up to see her dead young lover floating above, Norma's final descent down the vast ornate staircase with that eternal entreaty: 'I'm ready for my close-up, Mr De Mille' – *Sunset* lends itself as readily to the theatre as it does to the screen.

However, that the result seems something less than the sum of so many glowing parts is, I feel, due mainly to a loss of strong focus on the part of director Trevor Nunn.

When I saw this piece in embryo at a private showing last year, it gripped me until the tears sprang unbidden.

For Don Black and Christopher Hampton's book and lyrics touch on all the themes guaranteed to touch me most close to the heart. The need for magic in every life – Norma in her heyday has supplied myths to millions and is now in an oblivion of her own dreams; the unequal nature of love itself – both she and Joe, the out-of-work writer she lures fatefully into her lair, have the most lethally mismatched gifts to offer: his youth, her wealth...

Trevor Nunn, sadly, muffles its impact with untypical Barbara Cartland gush. I could not believe it.

Perhaps there is also a touch of *Evita* vamping in the sung dialogue between some splendid songs – a habit I would gladly pistol-whip to the bottom of the nearest pool myself. I would die happy never again to hear anyone sing: 'Have some pink champagne.'

All this said, the show resurrects itself to heights of genuine triumph, not least when Miss Patti Lupone is flinging out Norma's deepest delusions.

With the profile of an eagle and a predatory prowl, she may not have the true hauteur of a great silent movie queen. But give her a song to belt out – such as *With One Look* or *As if We Never Said Goodbye* – and she shows us exactly the quality it takes for a star to be born.

One of my sneaking reservations about the film was always William Holden, who won the role only as a last-minute replacement for Montgomery Clift.

Kevin Anderson offers no such doubts here. This is a sex symbol beyond Norma's ken and era. A moody, amoral character whose fatal flaw is that he does have a heart.

If I seem slightly less than totally overwhelmed in spite of this, it is nothing for the box office to worry about. And certainly nothing wrong which can't be fixed.

And that's another difference between the theatre and the movies.

Grease

Book, music and lyrics by Jim Jacobs and Warren Casey
Dominion Theatre
Daily Mail, 21st July 1993

Slick revival is a certain hit

Nothing and no one will stop this whim-wham show roller-coastering to a smash hit. The West End is obviously sitting up and begging for its juvenile brand of broad and brassy mindless escapism. If a musical as original, witty and sophisticated as *City of Angels* cannot find an audience, then obviously anyone with an eye for success will go to the opposite end of the spectrum. And here it is. An amiable 20-year-old satire on a 40-year-old youth culture.

I say this in no spirit of sorrow or anger. For only a curmudgeon could ignore the undoubted zest and commercial appeal of this blatant piece of Fifties kitsch pastiche of high school hops, pouring scorn on Sandra Dee look-alikes and aping James Dean wannabees.

To one who has lived through all this twice, if not three times (for heaven's sake it was my youth they were parodying back in 1972 and it was the unknown Richard Gere – making his West End debut and farewell who helped to put the winklepicker in), it would seem we have come full circle. Safe sex is, after all, now back in fashion.

Yet cynicism aside, the show does have a vibrant life all its own. And though it has incorporated many of the hit songs from the movie, there is nothing in it as dated as John Travolta...

The first big question about this latest revival must be: can Craig McLachlan cut the mustard away from the TV soap? Answered in one: this guy is potentially one of the hottest properties to hit the West End in any era.

The second, slightly smaller query must be: does he out-class his compatriot, the sainted Jason? Put it this way: what Elvis Presley was to Tommy Steele, Craig is to Jason. He's a raunchy, sexy presence with a wry, sly sense of humour and some slick comic timing. Debbie Gibson as the despised Sandra Dee-goody-goody also has her charm.

There are, too, a couple of stunning numbers belted across by Drew Jaymson (the ambiguously titled *Mooning*) and the unlikely named Sally Ann Triplett (*Look at Me, I'm Sandra Dee*) which are the benchmark of the show's musical aspirations.

Yet what makes it a copper-bottomed coach party plunderer is the driving exhilaration which erupts in Arlene Phillips' high-octane choreography, and the terrific sounds which drown out any fuddy-duddy demand for rhyme or reason.

It's simply a feel-good evening. Those of you who ask for more should have gone to see *City of Angels*.

Aspects of Love

Music by Andrew Lloyd Webber, lyrics by Don Black & Charles Hart
Prince of Wales Theatre
Daily Mail, **22nd December 1993**

Exquisite reprise of love songs in the key of life

One of the silliest statements in the welter of Sunday supplements last weekend was the assertion that 'There is no sex without guilt.' Andrew Lloyd Webber's *Aspects of Love* is, in fact, a celebration of, among much else, the total denial of this. It also examines the complexities of love on many levels, warning against the destructive power of jealousy for that which you can no longer possess.

Which is why, despite the flaws in its first, overblown West End production, I have always felt it is possibly his most daring and original project. Now, for a brief Christmas season before it goes out to tour the country, this exquisitely concise and precise new revival reveals its emotional intensities in all their subtleties.

Stripped of the previous directorial baggage, it comes alive as a piquant Mediterranean *La Ronde*, a love-go-round within a family, utterly true to the spirit of David Garnett's original novella.

Across and between the generations, a torch of passion is passed back and forth. The 17-year-old boy elopes with the struggling young actress who, in turn, goes off with his rich and elderly uncle. The tale is taken up again when their teenage daughter falls in love with her now grown-up cousin, reconciled at last to the loss of his first love.

To bring all this off and rescue it from the mundane and the shabby demands simplicity and cunning from both director and cast.

Which is exactly what it gets. Kathryn Evans as Rose, the girl who incites excitement wherever she goes, not only has the voice of an angel, but also that special quality to elevate the woman's caprices into recognisable high style and generosity of spirit. Her final lament for her indulgent dead husband – *Anything But Lonely* – is a spine-tingling affair, which has the audience roaring its appreciation.

Of course, the musical's great recurring anthem *Love Changes Everything* – sung powerfully and hauntingly by Alexander Hanson as the boy who links the generations in loops of love – is still the evening's eternal showstopper. But for those who still claim this is a one-song show, may I recommend a special hearing of *The First Man You Remember*.

As sung by Gary Bond, the ageing roué, to his young daughter, the lyrics of Don Black and Charles Hart deserve to become a lasting standard. A song which speaks as eloquently of a father's devotion to his child as a young man's passion for his first love. Like Gale Edwards' production, it is sweet, simple, yet full of echoing depths and dark shadows.

Sunset Boulevard

Music by Andrew Lloyd Webber, book and lyrics by Don Black and Christopher Hampton
Adelphi Theatre
Daily Mail, 20th April 1994

Now she's ready for the close-up, Mr De Mille

After the most expensive intermission in the history of British musicals, the first question to be asked is: was the wait worth it? Well, from where I was sitting, I would say that Sir Andrew Lloyd Webber's great gamble has already paid off with the richest dividends, artistically speaking. Visually far more tasteful, far more taut in its narrative and far, far more intense emotionally. These are just some of the rich bonuses reaped in this highly-publicised revamp of a show which, it is now admitted, opened too big, too loud and too soon. The expensive lessons learned in its Los Angeles transfer have brought it back far closer to the tightly-told Gothic Hollywood love tangle so perfectly preserved in Billy Wilder's classic movie.

The considerably toned down settings mercifully now no longer overwhelm the central characters or their situation. Certainly not Miss Betty Buckley's statuesque Norma Desmond. Mind you, it would take a great deal more than a floating baroque palace to eclipse her grandly imperious hauteur.

From her first big number – the resounding *With One Look* – Miss Buckley serves notice that we are in a very special presence and very privileged to be there. The audience immediately rewards her with an ecstatic ovation most actresses would be gratified to receive as a final curtain. But we ain't seen nothin' yet. Nor heard it. For her voice has both the power and the subtlety to seduce an audience into slavery. By the time she descends that sweeping, gilded staircase to deliver Norma Desmond's fabled lunatic command – 'I'm ready for my close-up, Mr De Mille' – she has conquered a crowd even glitzier and ritzier than those present at the official opening night, so many months, lawsuits and backstage histrionics ago...

It takes a courageous – and very rich – man to admit: 'I was wrong; let's try again.' I only hope Sir Andrew's courage pays off as readily at the box office as it has done on stage. For this is now a show which deserves to be seen and set alongside his past mega-hits.

ANDREW LLOYD WEBBER

I got to know Jack by about 1981, when *Cats* was on. He could be relied upon to be impartial no matter what the situation was. There was a period, though, when he was pretty disgruntled about everybody and everything. I produced a play called *Lend Me a Tenner*, a farce that was actually rather funny. Jack did not like it, and wrote that the only good thing about it was the set. So I wrote to the *Daily Mail* and promised to send him the set as a present as soon as the show closed, but I warned that it would be a long wait. It became a running joke between us. I kept ringing him up to say:

'Jack – very worried about the figures this week for *Lend Me a Tenner*, you'd better get ready, the set will be coming soon.' That went on for the two years that the show ran, and we had a huge laugh over it.

After that, we had lunch every four months or so, just to keep up.

He loved *Sunset Boulevard* when it was done at my festival at Sydmonton Court, but thought that it had gone wrong in London. Then, when we revised it, he liked it again. I know that what he was saying was true. When we premiered that show, it had probably the best reception of anything that I have ever done. Yet something was lost in the translation.

I have a theory about musicals, that they are best not seen until they are about four months into their runs. They take a while to settle down. The only show that I have not altered once it has opened is *Phantom of the Opera*. *Cats* had ten minutes taken out of it and was reworked quite considerably after it opened, although nobody realises it. We experimented quite a bit. There was even one number that we completely re-staged three months down the line. *Evita* was also cut by about five minutes. You need to get a show as right as possible by the opening night, but after that they remain very much works in progress.

Fiddler on the Roof
Book by Joseph Stein, music by Jerry Bock, lyrics by Sheldon Harnick
London Palladium
***Daily Mail*, 29th June 1994**

Treacle that sticks in the throat

What a difference 30 years can make to our perception of a much-loved musical. *Fiddler on the Roof* has a great heart. It was written with moral hindsight and high hopes when the world had not long recovered from a life and death struggle against the evils of Nazism.

The barriers of racial prejudice were falling apart and new freedoms seemed endlessly possible. Today, however, the world is a darker and infinitely more deadly place. There is ethnic cleansing on a scale we though impossible ever again when we thrilled to this folksy story of Jewish survival amid the dreadful pogroms of Tsarist Russia.

Joseph Stein's book could afford to lay on the treacle of sentimentality with a trowel. The sufferings and fortitude of Tevye the Milkman and his family belonged to another age.

Now, sadly, such a social soft-centred whimsy is almost obscene in the face of the atrocities being daily committed on minority tribes and religions on our own European doorstep. It would have been fascinating to see the show given a radical new and hard-edged production...

But no. The revival is in aspic. It is Topol, that most lachrymose and sentimental of actors, who is once more wearing the show's throbbing heart on his own sleeve...

But there is no real rage at the cruel injustices his intimate friend, God, heaps upon his kith and kin, his village and even his horse. At the moment his young daughter decides to marry out of the Jewish faith, the final affront to all his unswerving trust in tradition, the anger is comic. It brings forth laughter not pain.

Still, there are songs which refuse to lie down and live insistently in the memory, springing to life most marvellously, even in this rather sub-Jerome Robbins tribute. Moreover, anything which reminds us , however tactfully, what it means to be turned overnight into refugees for no better reason than one's race or religion is as welcome as a candle in a naughty world.

As Topol himself says when urged to take an eye for an eye and a tooth for a tooth: 'That way the world would be full of blind and toothless people.' A moral we could do worse than hugging to ourselves today.

Oliver!
Music and lyrics by Lionel Bart
London Palladium
Daily Mail, **16th December 1994**

Oliver! Back to the West End for more

The show is back – thirty-four years after it first proved that the British really could teach the world how to write musicals after all. Moreover this lavishly mounted, lovingly re-worked, lustily sung revival demonstrates that Lionel Bart's great achievement in *Oliver!* is that it can still show a clean pair of heels to many of those which have followed.

It is a production which as well as giving sparklingly fresh and alive versions of all the old show-stopping familiar tunes – an all but forgotten art form these days – it also serves up a bright and shining new musical star in Sally Dexter as Nancy, plus the most original new child wonder with Adam Searle's beguilingly brazen Artful Dodger.

To my knowledge, Miss Dexter has never before sung a note on any West End stage. Her acting ability has even been a joy, yet she gives us a Nancy full of life, fun and frolic who literally lights up Fagin's dark cellar with her merriment. Her full-belt rendering of the show's great heart-stopping love song, *As Long as He Needs Me,* is one of the most stunning moments of musical theatre currently to be seen in London.

Of course, producer Cameron Mackintosh has judged the times exactly ripe for a revival of this landmark musical. In 1960 when it began its first record-breaking run, going on to storm the citadels of Broadway and Hollywood with its adroit retelling of Dickens' horrifying story of poverty, juvenile delinquency and urban degradation, such things were of distant history. Today the Fagins and Dodgers are visibly back among us, and the Workhouse seems only another social reform away.

The cryptic lyrics of Bart's ironically jaunty *Gotta Pick a Pocket or Two – In this life / One thing counts / In the bank / Large amounts –* could be the anthem of the past decade. Thus director Sam Mendes has cleverly pointed up the cruelties and privations suffered by young Oliver without losing the beat of the great heart which carries the story along.

Jonathan Pryce's laconic Fagin is a wearily benign, self-mocking con-artist. While it is almost impossible to believe that before his murderously psychotic Bill Sykes, Miles Anderson once essayed the title role in the RSC's first *Peter Pan.*

True, the evening takes a dangerously long time to hit its stride. But there is no doubt as to its success or its longevity.

As the facade of St Paul's sweeps into magnificent close-up on the wings of the Bart's infectious hymn of welcome, *Consider Yourself,* we know that *Oliver!* is back home where it belongs. In the heart of London, and in the hearts of its ecstatic audience.

LIONEL BART

Before meeting Jack, I generally avoided critics. I thought it might make it difficult for them to do their job. I went down to Brighton soon after we began to get friendly. We walked along the pier and I discussed this problem with him. 'Don't worry about it Lionel,' he replied, 'because I will never actually slag you off in any way unless it's constructive. It will be spontaneous and it will be constructive. And because I love you and what you do, it can't be anything but that.' He decided to give me first-hand experience and invited me to be his date for a bunch of shows and to sit with him while he wrote his reviews immediately afterwards. I did this – we went to a dozen or more together. People were going around calling me a 'critic's moll!' Nevertheless we became great friends.

Because Jack was such a theatre enthusiast and loved the game which we are in, it shone through his writing – it was not about what a smartypants he was or how well he could write the Queen's English. He was trying to help people rather than destroy them. Jack was perhaps the last of the old-time critics that wrote immediately after the show – it is terrific to be spontaneous like that. You turned to read the *Daily Mail* first because it was hot off the opening night. I love that old showbiz circus parade feel of next-day reviews.

I once went to supper with Jack and Nicholas de Jongh. They told me that their nicknames were 'Smear' and 'Gush'. Sitting there, they looked like a couple of Hogarthian drawings. It all added spice to the world of theatre.

Jack narrated a concert of mine once, at the Dome in Brighton for an AIDS charity. About two or three thousand people turned up – it was on a Saturday and a Sunday. It featured a cast of thousands, gleaned from all the amateur theatres and opera societies in Sussex. They performed songs from six of my shows, against this huge set of scaffolding that was meant to emulate that for *Oliver!* They perched Jack on the top of this very high edifice, despite the fact that he had terrible vertigo. But the little peacock could not resist the chance of narrating from such a prominent position. He even sang a song – *In the Land of Promises*.

It's difficult to say yet what mark Jack made in the long term. But then, it is difficult to pin down any of the finest commentators in that way. They all had pros and cons. Ken Tynan was brilliant, but acerbic. When I saw Ken speak in his first public debate at the Oxford University Union, he followed a youth who had a dreadful stutter that was quite difficult to listen to. The ruthless Tynan's opening line was, "Now that we all once again have a roof over our mouths...", which about sums him up. Milton Shulman was often bitter. Jack was at the opposite pole. Noël Coward also could be very biting, but never to the detriment of people's spirit. He was not the cynic that people thought. Neither was Jack. He liked a little dish, as we all do, but it was not a dirty dish.

Les Miserables

Music by Claude-Michel Schonberg, original text by Alain Boublil and Jean-Marc Natel, lyrics by Herbert Kretzmer
Royal Albert Hall special concert performance
***Daily Mail*, 30th September 1995**

Flop that left us far from miserable

The overnight prognosis on *Les Miserables* was not a healthy one. Astonishing as it may seem, when it opened at the Royal Shakespeare Company's Barbican headquarters on October 8, 1985, many critics, myself included, judged it to be overlong, muddled and a tad pretentious. Of the thrilling quality of its music, however, there was scarcely a dissenter.

Well, yah, boo and sucks to such carpers. Next Sunday at the Royal Albert Hall, Cameron Mackintosh, the impresario whose passionate belief in *Les Mis* has nurtured it across the decade until it has been seen in more than 30 world-wide productions, has prepared something of a triumphalist treat.

Two hundred and fifty artists, all of whom have appeared in this critic-proof piece, will assemble for a grand concert version. Backed by 100 musicians, singers such as Colin Wilkinson, the original leading man, Michael Ball and Ruthie Henshall, for whom *Les Mis* was a stepping stone to stardom, will relive their past glories in a show which now has a life all its own.

It has made millionaires of its original creative team and has more than justified Cameron's dogged faith.

This could be taken as a lesson on the worthlessness of critics in general and a sackcloth and ashes confession from me. It is neither. For by the time Cameron had moved the show into the West End, many faults had been rectified. And with each new production there has been a fresh reappraisal so that slicker, cleaner improvements have continually been incorporated into the original.

My daughter took me to witness this at the opulent Paris Gala Cameron had arranged for the show's return to its native city. It was a triumphant night. Almost 25 minutes shorter than when I first saw it, it was extended by as long again when the Parisians gave it an ovation that lasted almost exactly the same time. The reviews which followed were ecstatic.

Indeed, if this ebullient, full-throated, exhilarating and tightly drilled version had been the one we had seen at the Barbican, the notices, certainly mine, would have been very different.

Yet the bitter irony is that the Paris production of the show is the only one which has ever flopped. I could almost have predicted this simply from observing the chic first night audience. They arrived horrifically late and appeared utterly resistant to any entreaty to sit down and see their beloved Hugo in musical form. They had clearly come to see each other. And although they were overwhelmed by what they eventually gazed upon that night, nothing was going to break the national habits of many lifetimes.

The fact is that no self-respecting Frenchman will ever commit himself to booking theatre seats in advance – as the rest of the civilised world must do. They prefer to keep their diaries optional in case an appealing dinner date presents itself. Food, and the company kept while eating it, is their premier theatre experience.

By contrast, the London production at the Palace Theatre is booking as far ahead as March 1996 and has more than £2 million of the punters' money invested in that advance.

Cameron is one of the most generous souls I know, as well as being one of the great benefactors of our arts. Why he has no honour, at the very least a knighthood, for his charitable works alone is a mystery.

HERBERT KRETZMER (Lyricist of *Les Miserables*)

A well-known quotation in Boswell's life of Dr Johnson illustrates what makes Jack special. Oliver Edwards says to Johnson: 'I have tried too in my time to become a philosopher, but I don't know how. Cheerfulness was always breaking in.' That is what Jack had. I can think of a few critics who are by nature morose. Even when they explode into enthusiasm about a play, they drag their own particular anxieties in with it. They may have appreciated it, but you never have a sense that they had a good time. The element of personal joyousness is something that distinguished Jack from every other critic I have known. He did not have to invent that quality, it was in his genes. That is why he was so adored.

On *Les Miserables*, though, Jack got it totally wrong at first*. It is no abuse of my friendship and love for him to say so. He must have had a very bad dinner that night. It was a particularly dyspeptic review. I entirely respect the fact that he did not have a very good evening, nothing can change that. However, the phrases and language he employed, and the line he adopted in reviewing *Les Miserables* seemed unnecessarily sour. I told him many times afterwards that he was a very good critic but a lousy prophet. His piece predicted that the production of *Les Miserables* at the Barbican would not make it to the West End, for reasons which he specified. I was far from happy with that, because it is not part of the critic's job to seek to influence the judgement of those who might bring a show into the West End. He can review the play, and impresarios can draw conclusions from his writing as to the quality of the show. But to go out of his way to discourage any such move was an unfriendly act. It added a certain tension to our friendship without affecting it too much. The show took off at such a rate of knots within a matter of weeks that it is tempting to quote Winston Churchill, 'There is only one thing to be in victory and that is magnanimous.'

Besides, I think that Jack himself felt a little chastened by the tremendous success of *Les Miserables*. He sought in various ways, if not to recant, then to soften the blow. When he saw it in Paris, he suddenly discovered all sorts of brilliances and wonderful aspects in the play. Jack always insisted that it had been tightened up and revised after the original opening. That is not true, we lost half of the song *Little People*, because we felt that it was a little too cockney-sparrowish for the dramatic situation. What actually happened, I feel, is that Jack heard the show more and more as it succeeded around the world and gradually persuaded himself that it had been made tauter. He simply increasingly came to like it.

Interestingly, an enduring myth has grown up around *Les Miserables* that it survived a uniformly bad press to become a hit. In fact, one only has to look at the papers of the week when it opened, to see that for every bad review there was another that was ecstatic. We had an

* For Jack Tinker's first review of *Les Miserables* see page 18.

44

unfavourable review in the *Observer*, yet on the same day the *Sunday Times* hailed the show's 'blazing theatricality'. We had a cool review from Irving Wardle in the *Times*, and yet an abundantly generous reception from Michael Coveney in the *Financial Times*. Benedict Nightingale and Michael Billington loved it. By the end of the week, delighted articles in *Time* magazine and *Newsweek* put *Les Miserables* on the shopping list of every American touching down at Heathrow. The reason for this myth is largely due to Jack's review, which shows his influence. The show was aimed at Middle England, and Jack was the laureate of that middle-of-the-road, middle-brow sensibility.

I have also sometimes wondered whether Jack wrote what he did to show that he was his own man. He and I worked on the same newspaper, and that perhaps worked against me. Sometimes a critic can be subliminally anxious to show that he can criticise even those whom he knows well. So the harshness of his line could have been a declaration of independence, no bad thing in itself.

Company
Music and lyrics by Stephen Sondheim
Albery Theatre
Daily Mail, **22nd March 1996**

Taking pleasure in this Company

Do yourself (and Mr William Kenwright) a great and lasting favour. Get a ticket for the Albery Theatre and see Stephen Sondheim's seminal musical performed with more power, more wit and more raw emotion than ever before.

It was the late Kenneth Tynan who declared that a truly great production – either through its comedy, tragedy or originality – should make you more aware of why you are alive.

Sondheim's splendid mould-cracking musical does in plenty. Indeed, its final liberating anthem, *Being Alive*, could clearly have been written expressly for Tynan's demanding requirements. It deals, in one exultant, climactic hymn, with the overwhelming human need which lies at the heart of our capacity for love. And only when that dependency is realised and admitted can any relationship hope to thrive.

I have always had a special affection for this particular musical. It was the first Broadway show I saw on my first New York trip, and it changed my entire vision of the capability of this hybrid art form. Ever since then I have availed myself of every possible opportunity to see it wherever it is performed.

Yet never have I seen it revealed in all its emotional complexities so vibrantly as it is here. Director Sam Mendes has found the key to the show's heartbeat. His imaginative restaging unlocks the show's dramatic drive by streamlining the complex interaction so that it appears to take place almost entirely in the sitting room or the imagination of his central character, Bobby. And his terrific award-winning cast do the rest.

Adrian Lester's performance as Bobby, everyone's easy-going best friend or possible lover, has deepened and grown since the show first surfaced at the intimate Donmar. He fills the Albery's space with the amused, bemused bewilderment and subtle pain of a man unable to explain the hollowness of his own apparently fun-filled existence.

Sondheim fills this background with a resounding score and some of his most lethal lyrics – liberally scattered among the couples and girlfriends who compete for time and space in his life. Collectively they paint a sharp, wry portrait of New York life in all its urban confusions.

There is the mocking, sophisticated taunts flung at full throttle on the *Ladies Who Lunch* – a number which Miss Sheila Gish has now made entirely her own. For a brief second in her gutsy anger she lets her guard slip. And in that instant she reveals, as few have ever dared before, the empty void and ensuing panic at the centre of her own being. For this moment alone she is more than worthy of her *Olivier Award*.

Yet the evening abounds with felicities like this. A quirky, haunting West End debut from Hannah James gives a complete new level of comic poignancy to the lilting one-night-stand duet, *Barcelona*.

And there is a genuine mad pre-nuptial terror in Sophie Thompson's complex counterpoint duet together with Michael Simkins' patient groom in *Getting Married Today*.

I could go on ticking off the multitude of joys to be found at the Albery. But it is best to discover them for yourselves and make Mr Kenwright a happy man. He is the brave producer who has transferred this living gem to the West End.

Passion

Music and lyrics by Stephen Sondheim, book by James Lapine
Queen's Theatre, Shaftesbury Avenue
Daily Mail, 27th March 1996

Never mind the music, this is a night that belongs to Maria

There is no doubt about it. The Olivier Award-winning Maria Friedman is not only among the finest singers on London's musical stage at the present time. She is its greatest actress.

Without her mesmerising performance – cast courageously against type as the plain, neurotic and clinging Fosca in Stephen Sondheim's latest journey into the labyrinth of the human heart – the evening could well have been retitled *Songs to Cut Your Throat By*.

There is a strange and perverse quality in Sondheim's work. In the glorious revival of *Company*, where he is writing of a hero whose capacity for love has been frozen, he produces songs and musical themes of pulsating excitement.

Here, however, where he and his librettist James Lapine are exploring the very nature of our most irrational emotion – passionate love amounting to obsession – his music remains remorselessly academic.

Not a single song rises to meet the demands the story makes upon it. Based on a rather over-heated romantic movie, his score on this occasion remains irritatingly cool and dispassionate.

This is unforgivable. Even if he had confined himself to the lush waltz-time of the period, he should have produced at least one musical moment to lift us from our seats.

As it is, only Miss Friedman, her singing voice severely under-tested, contrives to do this by the sheer force of her physical presence.

A chronic invalid, filled with self-loathing and emotionally crippled by an early reckless marriage, she nevertheless gradually wears down the resistance of a dazzlingly handsome army officer based in her colonel cousin's battalion.

It seems an improbable premise. He is already in love with a beautiful married lady. Moreover, he is played by Michael Ball, the glimpse of whose bare buttocks in the opening scene might be considered by some to be worth the price of the ticket alone. Yet Miss Friedman transcends all this. She allows you to know the rapacious power of the weak. And when she comes blinkingly down for her curtain call, the immediate standing ovation which greets her tells its own story.

Thanks to her, this is as moving, thought-provoking and as memorable as we have come to expect from Sondheim. But I would be most reluctant to see it again without her.

MARIA FRIEDMAN

Jack seemed to know so much about lots of people. He was very discreet, so you always felt that you were talking to somebody who was going to respect what needed to be kept private. He was a human being, a caring man first, and a journalist second. He was a man that I trusted. My mum loved him – he always remembered her, which made her day.

I met him initially in a restaurant, after a show. He got up and thanked me for my performance, and I thanked him for his review. After that, I got to know him because he quite often did the compèring of the galas, the shows that I was in, at which point it stopped being a critic/performer relationship, it just became one performer to another.

47

He was a brilliant compère. One of the first times I ever saw Jack in a gala he was dressed as a boy scout with a hockey stick. I noticed him frantically practising in the wings, way beyond the time everybody else had finished preparing. From time to time he rushed upstairs to avoid someone to whom he'd just given a terrible, crushing review. Finally, there was the very witty sight of him in a boy scout's costume, diving into my dressing room, saying 'Do you mind if I just hide here for a moment because so and so has just walked past.'

Jack's own performances were very good. He was nervous, but very erudite. He really took it seriously, like everything he did. He wanted to be good, he so wanted to please. An entire audience would be captivated by him, he would get them laughing as one. Often, the scripts would be quite ploddish and he'd just leave them, freefall, and the evening would take off.

I think he really did care about performers. Because he was also a performer himself he knew what the process was and that you can damage that irreparably, if you're too loutish about it. But he was always witty as well, if he was going to lay into somebody you couldn't help but smile.

He had a huge influence on me. During a period when I had been unemployed for a very long while, I was sitting up in bed, opening my mail, and a friend came in and said 'Have you seen this article?' It was a double-page spread with Antony Sher, Maggie Smith and me on it. There I was, without a job, yet on that page. I was so completely bowled over – then the phone rang. I picked it up, absolutely blasé, convinced that it must be somebody phoning to tell me they'd seen this article. It was the Post Office tower, telling me that they were just about to disconnect my phone.

The contrast was fantastic. If they had phoned five minutes beforehand I would have been utterly distressed, because I just felt like I had no future. Then out of the blue I read this article and when I got this phone call I smiled. I knew that somebody somewhere thought that I was all right. I wrote Jack a card, telling him how that morning went, in the form of a play. And I was told that he kept it.

There was another time when I was unemployed, a very bad emotional time in my life. I had decided not to do any work for a while. And Jack, who I very rarely saw socially, phoned me up at home – I don't know how he got my number – and said 'I think it's about time you went out young lady.'

I didn't want to go out, but he insisted that I accompany him to the *Evening Standard Awards*. I protested, but he said 'I think it's about time that you got back to work.' He took me on his arm, as a guest to the awards, and sat me in the most glamorous company. I was escorted around the room as though I were the Queen.

I was an unemployed girl who was having a really tough time, and those are the sort of things that you never forget. He didn't need to do it, and from there I got work. People saw me with Jack and people suddenly remembered me. He never pried, never asked me a personal question, but I always knew that he cared.

When he went I really felt on my own.

Martin Guerre
Book by Alain Boublil and Claude-Michel Schonberg, music by Claude-Michel Schonberg, lyrics by Edward Hardy
Prince Edward Theatre
Daily Mail, 11th July 1996

C'est magnifique, mais ce n'est pas la Guerre of subtle passions

What with the upsurge of blood-thirsty religious certainties, from Bosnia to Northern Ireland, the boys who brought us *Les Mis* and *Miss Saigon* must have thought they were onto an instant crowd-pleaser here. By returning to the tumult of French history they were, after all, going back to the familiar roots which made their original fortune. After all this classic story of duplicity, of stolen identity, of illicit love, has already produced two hugely successful movies and endless retellings.

Moreover, the backdrop of 16th century religious bigotry in rural France no doubt persuaded Boublil and Schonberg that here were very fruitful modern parallels.

Alas, it also seems to have blinded them to the subtle human passions which are what makes the story of Martin Guerre the endlessly fascinating drama it has become. They have stripped it to the bare essentials and stayed mainly with its social and religious obsessions.

However, instead of simplifying matters this only confuses the absorbing human conundrums that lie at the heart of the piece.

Why does the real Martin Guerre quit his wife and land to disappear for seven long years? Why does the village so willingly mistake the impostor and take him, in the case of his wife, so literally to their bosom? And most important of all, why does that wife who has waited so chastely for the return of her ne'er-do-well husband suddenly surrender her virtue to a man she knows to be a stranger?

All these issues the book and Edward Hardy's work-a-day lyrics carefully duck. The narrative comes in arbitrary bursts and the great epic moments from *Les Mis* and *Saigon* are totally missing.

Indeed, there is the deadly air of worthy endeavour hovering over the piece, so unusual in the work of director and co-adaptor Declan Donnellan. True, there are some visually and musically affecting moments to lift the spirits. The stomping pagan dance rituals of the virile peasant villagers speak volumes of hidden cruelty and dark passions.

There are, too, occasional moments of genuine tenderness between Iain Glen's personable impostor and Juliette Caton's radiant wife-who-waited. Unfortunately Miss Caton's character has been reduced to a cipher of feminine docility instead of the defiant and liberated woman I had always understood her to be.

Mr Glen tosses a mane of hair most manfully. But any complexities in his character have, like the rest, been ironed out as crisp as newly-laundered bed linen.

The same goes for Matt Rawle, the rightful Martin Guerre. What makes him suddenly M. Bon Homme remains largely a mystery.

There is the familiar swelling of the Schonberg score to carry the evening along. But too much of this echoes hits we have known before. However, who am I to pour *eau froide* over the proceedings? An ecstatic audience roared its appreciation. And, anyway, I am the one who said *Les Mis* * was too long.

* See reviews of *Les Miserables*, pages 18 & 42, and Herbert Kretzmer, page 44.

Musical of the year 1996

Aarhus, Denmark
Daily Mail, **27th September 1996**

First stage on road to stardom

The making of a hit musical is as mysterious and elusive as it is ultimately lucrative. Even now, Sir Cameron Mackintosh, that maestro of the mega-musical blockbuster, is struggling to turn around the fortunes of his latest, *Martin Guerre,* by relaunching it next month with a drastic revamp.

According to Don Black, one of Britain's greatest lyricists and no stranger to triumph on the musical stage (*Billy, Tell Me on a Sunday, Aspects of Love* and *Sunset Boulevard*), it must begin 'with a hunger'.

'Andrew Lloyd Webber has proved there is nothing you cannot write a musical about, but all the ingredients have to be exactly balanced. There has to be a clear, central vision. And all that comes very rarely,' he says. Just how rarely this is, Mr Black has of late spent a great deal of time finding out. He has been president of the Grand Jury for an international competition to find the best unproduced musical in the world. There were 300 entrants from 28 countries and the only consolation – or not, as the case may be – to the likes of Mr Black was that all had to be submitted in English.

'I was longing to hear a lyric which had something new to say and in a different way – something a bit more profound than "please don't leave me," ' he confessed just before Sir Peter Ustinov and Julia McKenzie revealed the winners in the unlikely setting of the hi-tech concert hall in Aarhus.

'We had half a dozen *Rasputins*, several *Jekyll and Hydes* and the odd *Crippin*. The oddest one was about Kayote fishing – but it was disqualified,' said Black. 'Shall we just say that it was easy to spot that, for some, English was not their native tongue.

In the event it was three English-speaking nations – the US, the UK and Ireland – which dominated the lavish prize-giving gala directed by Miss McKenzie and boasting an all-star cast, including Denis Quilley, John Barrowman, Bonnie Langford, Joanna Riding, Claire Moore and Al Jarreau – which must have rather disappointed our hosts who, in the shape of the Danish Broadcasting Corporation, the Danish Radio Concert Orchestra and Bang and Olufsen, had forked out £80,000 in prize-money, as well as some generous hospitality to their international gathering of judges, performers, musicians and journalists.

For my money – and 40 grand of theirs, too – there was one clear winner. Curiously, however, like all the other English-speaking finalists, it had looked outside its native soil for inspiration. The California-based *Enter the Guardsman* was, in fact, based on Molnar's famous Hungarian comedy. Yet its book (by *Tony Award* nominee, actor Scott Wentworth) fairly fizzed with the kind of sophisticated wit all too seldom heard on the musical stage in these sung-through days. And its music and lyrics (Craig Bohmler and Marion Adler) skipped effortlessly from the dialogue.

As a small-scale chamber piece, it had style, charm and humour – and if I were Sam Mendes, I would be high-tailing it to LA to snap it up for the Donmar Warehouse.

The British, who have long been teaching our American cousins how to cut the musical mustard, were by no means eclipsed. The talented George Stiles proved a triple winner. Already a protégé of Sir Cameron with his charming *Just So* musical, his collaboration with Paul Leigh, *The Three Musketeers*, netted them the £20,000 second prize. While his other entry, a musical rework of *Peter Pan* with *Just So* partner Anthony Drewe and veteran word-magician Willis Hall, won a special commendation which carried with it Bang and Olufsen's state-of-the-art hi-fi equipment plus a further £5,000 for the Best Song (*When I Killed Peter Pan*, vigorously sold to the black-tie audience by Denis Quilley).

Musketeers was, in fact, the favourite choice of Bjorn Ulvaes, one quarter of the late Abba and, with partner Benny Andersson, part-composer of *Chess* and one of the Grand Jury, too. 'I think it has great commercial potential,' he said.

However, the Brit contingent stuck out doggedly (and open-handedly) for the US's more elegant *Guardsman*. And if the other runner-up was any indication of the quality of the rest of the 300 hopefuls Mr Black and his Grand Jury had to sit through, my heart indeed goes out to them. Ill-advisedly written as an all-American tribute to the Scots lover-poet Robbie Burns, *Red, Red Rose* dredged up every cliche in the musicalbiog lexicon. Not least of which was using *Auld Lang Syne* as a finale and rendering the immortal *My Love is Like a Red Red Rose* into the kind of Muzak you would walk up ten flights of stairs to avoid hearing in a lift. Not even the highly personable John Barrowman, in a swirling kilt, could redeem it.

However, Ireland got its nose past the post, too, and collected £5,000 for a sweetly sentimental piece called *The Sea of Emotion*, by Paddy Meegan, as the Most Promising Newcomer. But the ride had obviously been a bumpy one for the multi-national Grand Jury. 'We had a great deal of head-shaking and mutterings of 'it won't mean anything in Malmo,' president Black said rather wearily when it was all over.

2

JACK ON WILL...

The Merchant of Venice
William Shakespeare
Theatre Royal, Brighton
Brighton *Evening Argus,* 12th February 1964

Shakespeare all dressed up for export

The British Council have decided to dress up Shakespeare in the finest silks and satins, endow him with lavish sets, and send him on a grand tour of Latin America and the Continent to celebrate his 400th birthday. Personally, I can't help regretting the British Council's choice in honouring the Bard's birth, especially since they are exporting it to Latin America. No one could claim that *The Merchant of Venice* shows him at his most liberal-minded or clear-sighted.

Full of petty prejudices, both racial and religious, its characters are almost without exception the most irritating and irksome to be found in any major work. Time, re-reading and re-seeing only convince me more that William wasted a lot of very fine and quotable words on a pretty worthless bunch. Even fair Portia, one of the few meaty roles he wrote, lapses into quite unspeakable feminine double-think at times.

Look how she dismisses poor old Morocco in his moment of proud defeat: 'A gentle riddance... let all of his complexion choose me so.' As callous a touch of heartless colour prejudice as you'll find on this side of the Deep South.

As for the bright young men who cavort around this tightly woven narrative, their modern-day equivalent would undoubtedly be the debs' delights who dash around in E-Type Jags, depending on yet another cocktail party for their next meal and on marrying a rich wife for security in their old age.

Ironically, the centre of sympathy in this play these days, revolves around Shylock, originally the stock villain of the piece. Always good for a hiss on Monday matinées at the Globe was Shylock.

Thanks to Shakespeare's acute observation of this character, however, the text allows different interpreters to play it in a very different light. They invariably bestow on him the dignity of a wronged man, the right to revenge, and the hurt of a wounded father.

All these, in some measure, were caught by Sir Ralph Richardson, the latest in a long line of distinguished actors to don a false nose and grey beard and turn a terrifying countenance to Christian injustice. Richardson is not a great Shylock. But his performance has a power and majesty which make him almost so. He hovered on the brink of asking for sympathy but never quite stretched out for it. Yet when his eyes blazed across the footlights one scarcely bothered to notice the 'Christian fools' with their 'shallow fopperies' who tormented him.

Sir Ralph can command a stage as few other actors can. He never once allowed his Shylock to descend to caricature, either in gesture, accent or concept. By his control he gained his authority.

Barbara Jefford, on the other hand, is a great Portia – though Portia is not a great part. The muted quality of her mercy speech to the court was quite the most moving thing in the whole production. Elsewhere she gave Portia a strength of character which made one willingly turn a blind eye to some of the heroine's weaker moments of feminine stupidity.

I liked also Bernard Hopkins' gentle little Lorenzo. He had all the freshness of youth in love. So had Valerie Sarruf as Jessica, though why a nice lad like Lorenzo should waste himself on such a fly-by-night, turncoat little thief as Jessica I have never been able to comprehend.

David William provides a text-book direction of a very lavish prestige production, as indeed it must be considering its backing and its purpose. He tries no new-fangled tricks; just plain honest-to-goodness Shakespeare as-he-is-spoke. The settings, many and varied, were seldom inspired. The Venetian court room, however, had a quite splendid backdrop which redeemed the overall dullness – and all the scene changes were smoothly and speedily handled. When one is playing to audiences of shuffling English fifth-formers, or hot-tempered Latins, that is quite a consideration in a production of this kind!

A Midsummer Night's Dream
William Shakespeare
Theatre Royal, Brighton
Brighton *Evening Argus*, February 1964

Even a twist session blends with this 'Dream'

Wendy Toye has worked her own wonderful magic on Shakespeare's fairy fantasy *A Midsummer Night's Dream*. She has delicately embroidered on it fey lyrical qualities and adorned its comedy with jewels of humorous inventiveness. Miss Toye has, in fact, not merely captured the spirit of *The Dream*, she has enriched it most marvellously.

This play has always been a favourite of mine, but never did I hope to see it attain such spirited perfection. Miss Toye's hand never falters. Her woodland ballets, beautifully danced, her witty slapstick, rumbustiously played, are always perfectly in taste and directly in accord with her material. She can even introduce a cheeky moonlight twist session without striking a jarring note.

This is, of course, the second of the British Council prestige productions destined to honour the Bard abroad. And beside it, last week's plodding production of *The Merchant of Venice* pales into oblivion. This is undoubtedly the play which will wow the Latin Americans and conquer the capitals of Europe.

Everything echoes the tasteful subtlety of the direction. Carl Toms's costumes are a joy. His fairies wear colours which have been plucked from the forest. His mortals are attired in gentle good taste.

Sir Ralph Richardson, who fell short of target with his first shot at Shylock, scores a bull's eye by taking up once more with Bottom. There were times when Richardson was enjoying himself so immensely (and that can be very immense indeed) that he threatened to tip the intricately poised balance of Miss Toye's production. But he managed to remember that he was part of a larger pattern long enough not to rock the boat too energetically.

There were times, too, when he got quite carried away with all the tricky little strings which worked his ass's head (a truly lovely beast it was, too). By the time Bottom was restored to himself once more, we knew every puppeteer's trick in the donkey's head – Sir Ralph had displayed them all so blithely. But when an actor of Sir Ralph's command is enjoying himself on stage, an audience can't help but share his pleasure.

Barbara Jefford, a tall and graceful Helena had moments of the most endearing whimsy. A most elegantly lyrical performance. And the same might be said for Patsy Byrne if she hadn't been miscast.

Bernard Hopkins, who showed up so favourably as Lorenzo in *The Merchant*, couldn't quite manage all Puck's impish sprightliness. A pity. He has the face and the build for the part. He was spry and fleet on stage, but the youthful devilment, so essential to Puck, eluded him.

It is, perhaps ungracious to pick out such minor flaws in this gem of a production and hold them to the light. On the other hand, they are nothing that a little polishing here and there will not remove. The whole is a dazzling affair and you should let nothing stand in your way of seeing it.

Hamlet

William Shakespeare
RSC Stratford-upon-Avon
***Daily Mail*, 4th July 1980**

Hamlet... as Shakespeare meant it

When you have seen almost as many *Hamlets* as you have eaten omelettes, there is a definite danger of a jaded palate. Anything to give it fresh flavour is appreciated, especially as it can last up to four hours. So there I sat, waiting for John Barton's new Royal Shakespeare Company production to tickle my taste-buds with added new ingredients in the old favourite recipe.

At first, I felt rather let down that the ghost of the old king was all too solid flesh and Hamlet himself was neither lusting for his mother, nor thirsting for power. Could he really be suffering the melancholy depression of a normal devoted son whose mother has married his father's brother less than two months after the old man's death?

Then it struck me. This was *Hamlet* as it was written. Lines I had practically forgotten were resounding on the ear, as if for the first time. It was like discovering the play all over again.

I am more than grateful, therefore to Barton and his *Hamlet*. For Michael Pennington's brooding Dane points up all the logic in the text. His is, indeed, a crafty madness used to shield an all-too-vigorous and cynical mind. He is full of straightforward passion. Yet his self-torment at his treatment of Ophelia leads him to deliver her a terrible punch in the face – the battered-wife syndrome before he has even proposed.

There is simple vigour about the whole production, which makes the telling of the tale fresh to those who know it well and ideal for those who don't.

Derek Godfrey's usurping Claudius is a bluff and fearless soldier, whose love of power is patently obvious as his motive for poisoning his brother. Barbara Leigh-Hunt's socially impeccable Gertrude receives the news of his treachery for all the world as if she were Betty Kenwood finding herself at quite the wrong party to write up her *Jennifer's Diary*. A swoon is the only answer. And Carol Royle's pre-Raphaelite Ophelia is beautifully played as the luckless tool of all their machinations.

For once, we have a *Hamlet* which has got to the heart of the matter with no tricks, save that of playing it all on a makeshift stage as if it were itself the famous play-within-the-play.

Macbeth

William Shakespeare
Old Vic
Daily Mail, 4th September 1980

Baby Jane is playing Macbeth with laughs

It would be uncharitable to describe Peter O'Toole's long heralded return to the Old Vic stage as an unmitigated disaster. There is at least one thing to be said in mitigation: he is the first actor ever to set me off in fits of involuntary giggles throughout *Macbeth*.

Now that in itself is a sort of achievement. The performance is not so much downright bad as heroically ludicrous. What O'Toole conjures up may not be the tragedy of a brave man wrecked by a single flaw in his nature (the classic definition of tragedy, Mr O'Toole) but it is Hollywood at its most hilarious self-parody.

The voice is pure Bette Davis in her Baby Jane mood; the manner is Vincent Price hamming up a Hammer Horror. Never are we allowed to glimpse the mettle of the man destroyed by 'o'er vaulting' ambition. 'If ch-ahn-ss will haff me kingk!' rasps O'Toole on hearing the witches' prophecy. 'Ch-ahn-ss musst crown mi!' No wonder one has to suppress the urge to guffaw when such burlesque dignity is given its come-uppance.

It was, of course, the rottenest luck for him to run smack into a wall on his third bravura exit (so much of the play takes play in the dark). But it is surely the most hilarious miscalculation to totter out of Duncan's death chamber covered from head to toe in bright red gore, clutching two dripping swords and eventually gasp out the purely superfluous information: 'I have done the deed!'

That got a laugh. So did Queen Macbeth's endeavours to calm her singularly unsurprised guests at the banquet as Brian Blessed's massive Banquo sat larger than life dripping even more stage blood while Mr O'Toole went into yet another Baby Jane tirade.

Mind you, this Lady Macbeth's behaviour was calculated to cause gossip in the servants' hall from the outset. It takes only a serving maid to announce politely the arrival of King Duncan and his retinue for Frances Tomelty to grab the luckless wench by the throat and shake her like a rag doll. It is perfectly clear that she's not merely a hostess agitated by the lack of clean linen.

Yet this is all very typical of Bryan Forbes' British B-movie approach to the entire production. His three witches are transformed into glamorous extras from some abandoned *Brides of Dracula*...

'How goes the night?' Banquo asks his son. No one came forward with the expected cry 'Rubbish!' Instead, the lad meekly replies: 'The moon is dull...' The evening was not exactly that. Drear certainly. But when have you ever heard a critic come out of *Macbeth* claiming that his sides ached with laughter?

Richard III

William Shakespeare
RSC Stratford-upon-Avon
***Daily Mail*, 21st June 1984**

It's Sher genius...

There is little enough justice in the world and even less in the theatre. So I shall not waste time begging pardon of everyone from the humblest spear-carrier to the haughtiest noble, for riding rough-shod over their individual excellence in this extraordinary, exciting and tumultuously successful production. It must be enough for them to know they trod the same stage with an actor whose performance has scorched its mark in the annals of Stratford like a thunderbolt.

Richard III is, of course, a role which invites, even begs, lightning to strike over and over again. But it seldom does. Yet there is Antony Sher turning the crookback once again into the stuff of legend.

From his first appearance, he establishes himself as master of the role, the stage, the production and, if I am any judge, an era. All Richard's complex, cunning characteristics he manages to convey in that famous opening monologue.

First he surprises us with the unaccustomed sweetness of those opening lines. His crutches and deformity are concealed in an almost lyrical interpretation of the 'glorious summer' he prophesies.

Then suddenly two crutches are swung forward and his tiny, misshapen humpback body, dressed from neck to toe in shiny clinging black, propels itself forward with the speed of light to the edge of the stage to insist: 'I that am not shaped for sportive tricks...' Seldom have I seen an actor switch mood with such speed.

Bill Alexander's high-Gothic production makes great play of the thin, dangerous line between the religious piety and pagan superstitions that Richard exploits to his own heady ends. And Mr Sher gives us a creature that is almost supernatural in its ability to shed its skins at will.

Clearly he is a consummate actor. But he is also his own scriptwriter, brooding over the improbability of the plot – as when he wonders how he may marry a woman whose father and husband he has killed. And he is his own most cynical critic.

There are times, as in his inspired coronation where the crowns are borne in by the murderers and the orb and sceptre carried by dead Hastings' harlots, that he resembles nothing so much as those magnificent prints of Edmund Kean, at the peak of his prowess in this very role.

It is an amazing, outstanding bravura performance which catapults Mr Sher from the ranks of our most interesting actors to a plateau of a great and memorable triumph. We may have to wait an entire generation before we see anything so thrilling again.

ANTONY SHER

I have always been quite awkward in the company of critics. At Stratford it is interesting since you come face to face with them, whereas in other places they just dash in and out of shows. They come from the dark of the night and disappear back into the night. But at Stratford, where I worked with the Royal Shakespeare Company they all used to stay on at The Dirty Duck, the pub where all the actors eat and drink. That was my first contact with critics in the flesh. Jack was always particularly friendly, warm and easy to talk to. I enjoyed meeting him then and feeling relaxed in his company.

My professional attitude towards critics is ambiguous. I go through periods of not reading them at all, but they are like cigarettes, or any other addiction – you reject them and then you have a relapse and go back. Reading reviews is, as a rule, not good for an actor. I did find with Jack's enthusiasm very touching. What struck me was not just that he was a very canny and communicative writer, but that he conveyed the sense of actually having enjoyed sitting in the theatre. That is very rare, a critic making you feel that your work is enjoyable. It is inspiring and reminds you just why you do the job.

He struck to the heart of the experience, and wrote from the heart. I can only think of one and a half other critics, and I mean one and a half, who share that quality – too many of them are just walking brains. Often if one is in a very emotional piece, one expects bad reviews because a show which requires people to respond with their heart will pass over critics busy sitting there making up their phrases and doing what they think they have to do. Jack was an exception.

Henry V
William Shakespeare
RSC Barbican
Daily Mail, 17th May 1985

So moving – this king for today

There are few moments in English history when this most jingoistic of Shakespeare's plays sits easily on the conscience of the audience. In times of war or national strife it can rouse us to illusions of heroism. In moments of gross self-indulgence, we can afford to patronise it as a satire on the worst excesses of chauvinism. But these are times of deep divisions and self-doubt. There is no clear image with which to identify.

Yet it seems to me that Adrian Noble's lean and spare production has found something buried within the text that is altogether more inspiring and appealing than either of the two obvious alternatives. He shows us, in Hal's progress from a youthful, untried Kingling to the conqueror of France, an intensely personal journey – simple and moving in very human terms.

Which of course directs almost all the thrust of the play on the 24-year-old shoulders of Kenneth Branagh. Clearly here is an actor with a capacity to fulfil all the early promise he showed in his first roles on leaving drama school.

There is not a moment's wavering as he takes us from Hal's righteous anger at the Dauphin's insults through moments of self-doubt and painful self-knowledge, which inflict wounds quite as deep and deadly as any suffered on the field of battle. His death sentence on Lord Scroop is accompanied by an embrace which shows how great and unspeakable is the betrayal. When it comes to signal Bardolph's execution he cannot bear to look on the act of justice. And at Agincourt he can barely stand upright to deliver the speech of victory.

He is a man driven on by a sense of moral certainty that is no way blinkered to the awful possibilities of being wrong. And that, perhaps, is his appeal today.

The production is less sure-footed when called upon to be humorous, except where Mr Branagh is mocking himself. Patricia Routledge, for example, as Mistress Quickly is painted and rouged like some gross pantomime dame and acts accordingly.

Yet the heart of this play beats unexpectedly true.

The Winter's Tale
William Shakespeare
RSC Stratford-upon-Avon
Daily Mail, 5th May 1986

Irons shows his true fire

Having attained the status of a matinée idol on screens both large and small and silver, Jeremy Irons returns to the theatre to prove he has all the stature of a fine Shakespearean star as well.

The role of King Leontes, though nowhere near as deep as Hamlet or the heights of Lear, is as testing a middle ground as any. And Mr Irons comes to grips with its ambiguities in a commanding and commendable style. He also avoids its gaping pitfalls.

It is clear from the outset that he is in the grip of some emotional disturbance, for his manner is as distant and his smile as chilly as the remote white kingdom over which he rules, even while dispensing social pleasantries.

The jealousy which so unaccountably overwhelms him as he watches his wife and best friend exchange teasing familiarities is no sudden thing. From the way he eyes Paul Greenwood's open and easy-going King Polixenes or demands the attention of his own small son you understand he is gnawed by some unresolved anxiety buried deep in their far-off childhood.

Jealousy is, of course, as unedifying as it is corrosive and Mr Irons speedily gives his a physical eloquence. The eyes grow wild, his cheeks gaunt and chalky, and his speech slips into a scarcely controlled sibilant stutter.

All this accomplished with a dizzying speed demanded by Terry Hand's fleet-footed, if occasionally frenzied production. Yet beautifully paced and precise for all that. Mr Hands has thrown in a polar bear the size of King Kong, a feathered Father Time who wings in from on high and some distinctly unrustic dance routines.

It is, however, a ravishingly attractive production to behold. Penny Downie doubles as Queen Hermione, magnificent in her humiliation, and her lost daughter Perdita, a shepherd nymph delightful enough to capture the heart of any romantic Prince Florizel, and certainly worth the poetry she inspires from him.

Antony and Cleopatra
William Shakespeare
Theatre Royal, Haymarket
Daily Mail, 27th May 1986

Queen Vanessa more eloquent than the Bard

Vanessa Redgrave erupts into a setting that resembles nothing so much as a disused corn exchange in some run-down corner of Macclesfield. She is pushing a vast dressing-up trunk from which she coaxes her Antony – a Roman gone so native he resembles some fantasy prince from a Valentino movie.

But instantly the Haymarket Theatre is electrified. This is Egypt and we are her slaves for as long as she wishes to keep us in thrall.

Once more this remarkable actress proves that nothing, not even this unbelievably sluggish rendering of the greatest love story ever told, can stand in the way of her great talent or extinguish the brilliance of her dazzling technique.

Crop-haired and statuesque as a graceful Amazon, with a tiny dagger at her waist, this Cleopatra makes even Enobarbus' eulogy seem like unutterable understatement. Her moods are mercurial on a scale so magnificent and magisterial that no one could doubt how she came to captivate the two great Romans of the age. Her sharp and mischievous wit strikes even the most mundane lines with a thunderbolt of new meaning; her authority is never challenged. That dressing-up trunk is no empty device. This Queen of the Nile is a consummate actress, trying on and discarding roles as lesser women try on hats.

And although Timothy Dalton's Antony is only too happy to join in the romps, there are moments when you see by the tired way he discards a turbaned headdress or glumly regards his exotic costume that he knows – as all adults must learn – that the time for make-believe is brief.

In the end, he is called up to Cleopatra's mausoleum almost naked; all the disguises have gone and the game is not only over but up.

Miss Redgrave soaks her tunic in his blood and the grief etched on her face is even more eloquent than Shakespeare's words. However, when these two doomed creatures are not on the stage, we might indeed be at the Macclesfield Corn Exchange.

The Merchant of Venice

William Shakespeare
RSC Stratford-upon-Avon
***Daily Mail*, 30th April 1987**

Once again it's Sher genius

The shining star of Antony Sher's meteoric career continues to rise ever onward and upward. Returning to the RSC, scenes of such recently past glories, he now gives us a Shylock of mesmerising intensity. An Eastern tribal Jew, exotically turbaned and defiantly alien in a cruelly antisemitic city, he shrugs off verbal insults and even physical abuse with an indifference born of deep religious conviction, giving an occasional shark's smile which springs from the certainty of his moral superiority.

As with any actor of this rare quality, no gesture, no glance is unimportant enough to pass unnoticed by us and help us reach the nature of his character. So, when finally the news of his daughter's callous treachery sinks in, the wound is painfully visible, robbing him of breath and speech.

Slowly rocking back and forth with grief, his eyes take on the messianic madness which propels him to seek the terrible retribution on his enemy. This event he anticipates with almost devilish relish spitting on his knife and rhythmically sharpening while Antonio's friends, in turn drench him with their spittal and chant 'Jew! Jew! Jew!' like some mindless football mob.

As you might imagine, director Bill Alexander, who directed Sher in his brilliant *Richard III*, bravely spares us nothing of this deeply unpleasant play's darkest motivations. This is a Venice dankly shrouded in mists, with mouldering buildings where an ornate shrine to the Virgin and the Child is set in a crumbling piazza wall next to the daubed yellow Star of David...

The Tempest

William Shakespeare
The Playhouse, Edinburgh
***Daily Mail*, 18th August 1988**

Caught in a joyous storm

There have been farewell *Tempests* (Sir Peter from the National); there have been welcome back *Tempests* (John Wood to the RSC). But set against this theatrical thunder and lightening which has blown in from Japan and hit Edinburgh like a tornado, all the rest look like mere storms in cracked tea cups.

Even with Shakespeare's darkly lyrical text transformed to the alien sing-song of the Orient (translated in computerised captions above the stage), the essence of his final magnificent abandoning of the theatre's deep mysteries is distilled into stunning visual power.

Director, Yukio Ninagawa, and his company have become something of a talisman to the Edinburgh Festival in recent years, their resplendent *Macbeth* dominating the event in 1985 and their stark, rhythmical *Medea* taking up the torch again in 1987. This is the only chance you will have to see this third and most ambitious of their works anywhere in Europe this year.

Yet nothing they have delivered before could have prepared us for this radical re-thinking of the play. Prospero's island is at first full of life's circus. Clowns, musicians, casually-clad stage-hands roam the vast arena as we enter. In their midst is a rustic, raised pagoda, its thatched roof ruined by years of neglect.

It is here that Prospero (a commanding figure in Haruiko Jo's god-like interpretation) rules with a magic wand that can turn swords into paper fountains and conjure parades of gargoyled spirits. Miranda (Yuko Tanaka) appears halfway up a massive pine tree under which the musicians and stage-hands sit as spectators to the wonders Prospero performs. A strangely bisexual Ariel floats balletically above in changing skies that owe everything to the traditions of the Noh theatre.

And anything, from the massive ship that is wrecked to the thousand twangling instruments which are so much part of the action, is supplied in a trice from the strewn debris that lie at the base of the forest glade. It is, in fact, the most joyous celebration of this play's innate theatricality I have ever seen.

Do not hesitate. Even if you have to hitch to get here, sleep out on wet grass when you arrive and hang from the rafters to see the spectacle, you will find no richer crock of pure gold at any rainbow's end. They are here only till Sunday.

On your marks, get set... GO!

The Plantagenets

Adapted from Shakespeare
RSC Stratford-upon-Avon
Daily Mail, **24th October 1988**

Noble house of grim glory

The heady scent of success and achievement – an all-too-rare aroma here in recent seasons – hung once more around the RSC's Stratford stronghold. For over nine hours we had sat and watched the royal house of Plantagenet tear itself apart from the inside. Nothing yet conceived in television soap opera could match the accumulative fascination of Adrian

Noble's grand sweep through the quagmire of this epic of protracted death throes and their catastrophic consequences on the entire nation.

Played together from the rarely-performed *Henry VI parts I, II* and *III* and a rich slice of *Richard III*, it begins with the death of Henry V, and the final burst of Plantagenet glory, and leads us through a day-long labyrinth of internecine power struggle...

Ralph Fiennes' portrait of Henry VI as a raw, yet thoughtful and pious youth maturing into a remote but saintly martyr is one of the production's main glories. As indeed is Penny Downie's towering Margaret of Anjou. Her arrival in Henry's court, shimmering in a breathtaking gown of gold and exuding overheated appetites, both sensual and ambitious, stamps her place not only on the stage but in history. ...

We have waited over ten years for Anton Lesser to return to Stratford and fulfil the promise of his embryo Richard of Gloucester. But the most heartening aspect of all to emerge from the marathon pageant unfolding on Bob Crowley's evocative minimalist settings was the sound of applause which greeted the delivery of key speeches as if they were great arias in an opera. No-one can pretend the *Henrys* are among the Bard's finest works. But it was wonderful to hear fine verse speaking restored once more to the Stratford stage.

Richard II
William Shakespeare
Phoenix Theatre
Daily Mail, 29th November 1988

Iron King Derek gives the RSC a lesson in playing the Bard

Whereas once we flocked to the Barbican to see the finest Shakespeare in London, the Phoenix Theatre now seems the place to play homage to the Bard. First came Crown Prince Kenneth of Branagh with his retinue of fresh-faced followers. Now arrives King Derek of all Jacobi with as goodly a look of majesty as we poor, starved subjects have been allowed to gaze upon these many seasons past.

What doth this portend? Well for one thing, it means that the RSC must quickly build on the good work of its Stratford *Plantagenets* production if the despised commercial theatre is not to steal its crown and bring the spectre of further erosion to the subsidised sector. Mr Jacobi's company is, to a man and a woman, the calibre we used to take for granted at the RSC's high noon.

He himself sits among the great interpreters of this role. When we first meet him it is plain the notion of anyone's questioning his absolute authority has simply never occurred to him; in the imperious disdain is indeed the stamp of the last King of England to hold his throne in unbroken succession from the Conqueror.

What Jacobi goes on to convey so splendidly is the erratic whim of iron which is the seed of his destruction and the real core of his tragedy. 'MY earth!' he cries exultantly, childishly spreading himself upon it on his ill-fated return from Ireland. Yet, surrounded by his enemies in Flint Castle he can summon up such an awesome spirit of immovable majesty you doubt the need of any army to defend him.

Next minute he is spinning again with self-doubt. A king who never learned how to be a man...

I predict wild welcomes across the Atlantic when Jacobi moves this fine court there, as is the battle plan.

The Merchant of Venice
William Shakespeare
Phoenix Theatre
Daily Mail, **2nd June 1989**

Hoffman may not be great, but he's good

To put Dustin Hoffman's achievement in the land-mined role of Shylock at its very lowest, the wonder is not that he did it well but that he did it at all. Had he not risked his reputation in the attempt, how else would Sir Peter Hall's magnificently measured, clear and timely reading of this deeply uncomfortable play have attracted the presence of such leading Shakespearian scholars as Joan Collins, Billy Connolly, Paul McCartney or Lynsey de Paul to worship at the shrine of the Bard, or attract round-the-block queues of less exalted fans?

Without being great, he is most certainly good. While he neither plumbs the darker depths of the role nor scales its more prickly heights, he nevertheless brings a patent integrity that lays bare the quite dreadful implications of the play. Diminutive in his pigtails, skull-cap and plain gabardine, he stands in the middle of the marbled splendour of the market-hub of Venetian finances, smiling his wary, polite smile, his voice thick with the faintly-honeyed tones of the alien all too used to deflecting the worst indignities of racial persecution as an everyday matter.

Sir Peter's production seeks neither to disguise nor absolve the casually vile behaviour of almost everyone in this Rottweiler society. Shylock's hefty loan of 3,000 ducats to finance what amounts to Bassanio's arm-chancing fortune hunt of a rich heiress is brutally rewarded with a stream of spittle, voided not upon his beard but smack between the eyes by Leigh Lawson's deliberately dead-eyed Antonio.

Hoffman scarcely bothers to dab it away, so accustomed is he to the manners of these Christian merchants. For those who denounce this as an anti-semitic play, this brutish moment should give the lie. It is simply about anti-Semitism.

A difference clearly underlined by Mr Lawson as a man whose very look speaks of a lifetime chasing riches without the least idea of how to enrich his own life.

And Hoffman's cry for revenge as he wields his knife in preparation for his pound of that hated flesh is quite terrible in its direct simplicity.

But surely the real jewel in the crown of this production is Geraldine James's unsurpassable Portia. A woman whose shimmering intelligence is matched by a vibrant beauty that makes the quest of princes and potentates only too understandable. She speaks the verse as if it bubbled fresh-minted into her mind, and her command of the trial scene is touched with a rare tenderness as well as a quite awesome command.

In all, a production worth all the queuing and braving of the Tube-strike traffic.

Othello

William Shakespeare
RSC The Other Place, Stratford-upon-Avon
Daily Mail, 26th August 1989

Catching the soul of the eternal outsider

If there has been a more powerful, more eloquent, more emotionally shattering production of this great play, then I must have missed it. Director Trevor Nunn, returning from the green pastures of the musical theatre to the grass roots of his former glories and to the Royal Shakespeare Company's tiny tin studio, discovers a momentous domestic intimacy in the work which at times turns us into embarrassed eavesdroppers.

So deeply claustrophobic is the barrack-room and bedchamber atmosphere Nunn achieves that it becomes almost unbearable to watch. Yet its fatal fascination never for an instant palls throughout its entire four-hour unfolding...

The linchpin, as ever, is Iago. And in Ian McKellen, a sturdy buttoned-down, bottled-up redneck NCO, we are confronted by the hypnotic snake-stare of true paranoia. It is quite terrifying in its power, for not only does this plain, repressed man try to convince those around him of the justice in his poisonous scheming, he plainly convinces himself too.

With each twist and turn of his own ingenious plotting, McKellen seems to suck up some deadly life-force, becoming awkwardly animated beneath his stiff, soldierly discipline. And when finally Othello and his spirited Desdemona lie lifeless on the deathbed of his devising, the haunting image we are left with is of his pallid face staring down on their corpses with nothing more than blank curiosity in his dead eyes.

It takes Willard White, making his acting debut from the world of opera, some time to work his way from the base grandeur of Othello's noble verse and to catch the soul of this bedevilled man. But his power is cumulative and his final bedroom carnage with Imogen Stubbs's terrorised Desdemona is, in the true sense of the word, awful to behold. So real, one recoils...

This production's enduring triumph is in bringing all the discordant elements into such painful proximity and sharp focus.

Henry IV Part 2

William Shakespeare
RSC Barbican
Daily Mail, 8th May 1992

Stephens, truly a giant among Falstaffs

I know there is not an artist in the company, not even in the land, who will carp or complain if my enthusiasm for this commendable two-part production yields to the gargantuan achievement of one actor.

Falstaff is, of course, a gift of a role. Many fine and distinguished men have made their mark as 'yon fat knight', yet I have not seen one in 30 years' professional theatre-going who has given us a Falstaff the equal of Robert Stephens.

Stephens does not play the part as just a fat man. Or a foolish one. Or a vainglorious braggart. He gives us the whole human being. Lumbering in the obesity of his declining old age, his mind still dances in perpetual youth. Yet instead of being merely absurd – the butt of Prince Hal's mischief and the despair of the King's advisers – he shows us something much more complex and disturbing. Behind his hearty, ready laugh, Mr Stephens reveals his own self-knowledge; the ever-widening chasm between the gentleman he used to be and the buffoon to which fortune and self-indulgence have reduced him.

It is exquisitely expressed when Michael Maloney's calculating, watchful Hal catches his roistering with the low life of Eastcheap. And it fairly blazes through all the celebrated rural scenes with his bold acquaintance Justice Shallow.

Whereas David Bradley's croaky old husk lives only on inflamed memories of his misspent youth, Stephens exists solely in his own precarious present.

It is wonderful to watch this old rogue sweet-talk his way out of the tightest corner, summoning up well-worn and threadbare charm which had clearly been the hallmark of his own young days.

But what grapples him to our hearts is the genuine shudder of weariness with which he dredges up the old tricks and, in so doing, feels the chill of his own bleak future.

The relationship with Hal is underscored by subtle undercurrents. He sees in the Prince what he himself might have been while the Prince, in turn, recognises in Sir John what he, too, might become.

No one on that stage knows this Falstaff, however, better than he knows himself. That is both his comedy and his tragedy.

Mr Stephens encompasses all this and more with such effortless truth and ingenuity that it scarcely seems to be acting at all. I defy you even to see the performance. All you are aware of is Sir John Falstaff.

And this is art of the highest order.

Hamlet

William Shakespeare
RSC Barbican
Daily Mail, 19th December 1992

Masterful Branagh claims crown as the great Hamlet of our time

Kenneth Branagh comes back to the Royal Shakespeare Company where less than a decade ago we were all hailing him as the brightest new star of the age. And in doing so with this momentous Hamlet – his third stab at the role if you count the recent radio version – he reclaims the crown I had thought was all but lost. Those of us who prophesied that he had turned the shining promise of a career into a mass-marketing gold mine are having to digest a slice or two of humble pie.

When last I saw him disguised in the black robes of the Prince of Denmark I could not help but concur with the ghost: 'Oh Hamlet, what a falling off was there.'

Now, however, matured both emotionally and physically he is undoubtedly the great Hamlet of our time. I have seen none to match him in many a season.

The muffin face of his youth now has a commanding gravitas. The voice can soar the verse to the heavens or draw us into his innermost thoughts by its quiet confiding. The marvellous set speeches come as newly-invented; the dangerous mood-swings between the wintery grief of his earliest scenes to the tightrope journey he hazards between feigned madness, careful cunning and deeply felt wounds are expertly charted.

Yet, to dwell entirely on the splendours of his performance is to do a gross injustice to the man who made it possible. Director Adrian Noble's entire production – four hours long and set in a stiff Edwardian court – is so full of similar felicities the narrative fairly flies by on wings. Clear, true and totally comprehensible to the dullest soul.

Seldom have I understood so powerfully the deep family ties at the heart of his play; father and son, sister and brother, son and mother.

Nor is Mr Branagh alone in his personal triumph. The cast reads like a catalogue of excellence.

Jane Lapotaire's Gertrude, a sensuous elegant beauty, destroyed before our eyes by the terrible reality with which her son all but rapes her; John Shrapnel, a stocky, persuasive Claudius unafraid to put in the boot below the belt – even when Hamlet is strapped up in a strait-jacket; Joanne Pearce, a brightly eager Ophelia, tipped over into a crazed and vengeful transvestite by the enormity of all she has endured. The roll call goes on.

And Bob Crowley's simple yet splendid settings set the seal on this extraordinary powerful production which miraculously manages to marry inner-truth with the grand theatrical gesture.

As for Branagh's Hamlet, I cannot recommend its brave authority or emotional dexterity too highly or applaud it too loudly.

MORE FIRST NIGHTS

Gentle Jack
Robert Bolt
Theatre Royal, Brighton
Brighton *Evening Argus*, 8th November 1963

Too much for Aunt Edna, but not for me

Over and over again in *Gentle Jack* playwright Robert Bolt asks: 'Where is innocence? What has become of humanity?' And a hundred Aunt Ednas came away from the theatre bleating to each other in high pitched first night voices: 'What did he mean?'

They had watched Kenneth Williams, all decked out as a spry God of Nature, gaze across the footlights and ask in anguish and sorrow: 'Is there an animal in the house, a man who will stand up for what he wants?' The rows of sheeps' eyes stared blankly back at him from the cosy darkness.

'Don't you remember how the seagull's cry could lift you to the top of the highest cliffs?' asked the voice of Mr Williams' Pan. Still they asked: 'What does he mean?' Which all makes me think Harold Hobson was all too right when he lamented that we ask for playwrights who make us think, but what we really want are playwrights who tell us what to think.

Bolt is wise as well as confident and able. He is one of the few really exciting forces in the theatre at the present time. He understands the nature of theatre and comprehends the nature of man. What is more, his ability and confidence enable him to experiment boldly with both. This he does in *Gentle Jack* but admittedly his experimenting rather throws the book at the Aunt Ednas.

He shows us what man was and what he has become; he shows us his heart and his mind. We see the incomparable Dame Edith Evans, a virgin queen figure, magnificent and ageing, at the head of an empire of balance sheets, stocks and shares, gilt edged securities and hotel chains.

Dame Edith dominates the whole of the first half of this play (nothing so rigid and old-fashioned as acts for Mr Bolt).

Surrounded by her young men in smart city suits she stands for order. That voice, that presence are all used to their fullest effect, and her performance etches out all too clearly both the compensations and the yearnings which can come from such an ordered existence.

Every man has his place in her empire; every man is the suit he wears and the wage he is paid.

Person Unknown

Stanley Clayton
Theatre Royal, Brighton
Brighton *Evening Argus*, 17th December 1963

I have a confession... I very nearly confessed!

There was one moment, about halfway through the final scene of the third act, in *Person Unknown* when I thought I was going quite, quite mad.

A bout of hysteria swept over me. A mad impulse to leap to my feet and confess to murder most foul (if only to stop the nightmare before my eyes) was almost irresistible. And then the real culprit crumpled and confessed. He had been on stage all the time. The relief was indescribable – but then so was the play.

It wasn't the butler, although it could well have been, despite the fact that there wasn't one. Nor was it the innocent-looking pianist who lurked in the pit during both intervals, daintily playing at her piano and, no doubt, thinking to establish her alibi.

But with a play like this even an alibi like that counts for naught. In that final chaotic last scene we were whisked from suspect to suspect, from clue to clue, all the evidence laboriously laid during the past five and a half scenes forgotten, disregarded or shamelessly abandoned. And that's just not cricket, or any other game, chaps.

The play was billed as 'a new experience in suspense.' But there are some experiences even the most hardened of us must fight shy of. This was one.

Before the play (and I) went berserk in its closing stages – and you must understand I can only speak coherently about what passed before my sanity temporarily fled – it had all seemed so cosy, so uneventful.

There was Miss Anna Neagle presiding serenely as the warden of a ladies' college. Ronald Howard, moody and drinking a little too heavily (Hah, hah..!) as her lecturer brother about to break into the big-time egg-head circles. And Charles Tingwell, earnest and brisk as her police inspector boy friend.

Her idea of a dashing proposal of marriage, by the way, goes something like: 'One of these days I plan to take you into custody permanently.' At which the regal Miss Neagle blushes as though some mad-cap had whisked her off her feet.

During the first act a girl student at the college is missing; during the second she is found dead (suicide or murder, my friends, that is the question); and by the time we crawl into the third, her pregnancy is discovered and now we are faced not only with a murderer but a seducer of Scottish Catholic college girls. Are there no depths to the depravity of the British stage? ...

Busybody

Jack Popplewell
Theatre Royal, Brighton
Brighton *Evening Argus*, 13th July 1965

They know how to Handl a play with care – and if they didn't Irene would show them

Isn't it marvellous that some actresses are born scene-stealers who never rest until they have wrung the last ounce out of a part? For what would *Busybody* have been without that inveterate hard-working scene-snatcher Irene Handl?

As a detective yarn it doesn't begin to convince. But as an evening of riotous fun, with the humour of the same pale blue hue as Miss Handl's eagerly displayed bloomers, then it is good, if not always too clean, holiday fun.

The whole play, of course, is built around Miss Handl's peculiar stage talents, that cocky Cockney charlady's impudence which is so disarming even to an audience accustomed to all the tricks of her trade. And as the office cleaner who not only discovers a couple of bodies lying around the place, but goes on to outwit both the police and the murderer to solve the crime, Irene Handl holds the play together at its rather rough seams.

If it were not for her indefatigable clowning, surely we would have been irritated by the fact that the police officers who come to investigate the crime go around putting their own dabs all over every available object, including the chair in which the corpse was found. On that sort of showing any char in England could have outwitted them.

And, but for that hectic chase where the murderer all but throttles Irene in all sorts, wouldn't we have been only too aware of the implausibility of his guilt?

Perhaps. But with all the Handlisms coming thick and fast none of that seemed to matter. This was indeed a play which needed a Handl to its name.

The Party

Trevor Griffiths
National Theatre, Old Vic
Daily Mail, 21st December 1973

Hearts in all the right places

Trevor Griffiths' hero, Joe Shawcross, has his heart in the right place: just a little left of centre. Physiologically speaking, of course, there can be no more satisfactory condition. But politically, neither Mr Griffiths nor Joe is satisfied with this state of affairs.

Like hypochondriacs in a cardiac clinic, they have their hands constantly on the collective heart of revolutionary society.

Here diagnosing a treacherous shift to the Right; there fearing a sudden and fatal lurch to the Left.

The setting is well-heeled SW7 at the time of the abortive Paris student-worker uprising of 1968. And Mr Griffiths has gathered together a fairly gruesome, if typical array of enlightened Left-Wing opinion to debate his thesis. This is that all revolution is doomed bar that which springs eternal and natural from the human breast.

This is wrapped up in two huge and eloquent, if unwieldy speeches. One is delivered by Denis Quilley academically setting out the rise and change of socialist revolution. The other is delivered by Sir Laurence Olivier, attaining towering heights of working class anger in a rolling Glaswegian accent at the eunuch concert of the non-productive middle-class professionals.

Their host, Joe (Ronald Pickup) is a television drama producer. We see him first copulating naked with his wife – very conformist – under a mirrored canopy while Trotsky-Marxist texts are illuminated on enormous screens. I confess I glanced at these only after failing to find any better instruction from the bed.

John Dexter's smooth and neatly decorated production, however, effectively points out the doctrinal intricacies of the ensuing debate while minimising many of the work's dramatic faults.

And at least it all proves that the National Theatre's heart is also in the right place.

Destiny
David Edgar
Aldwych Theatre
Daily Mail, 13th May 1977

Today the Aldwych, tomorrow the world

The Royal Shakespeare Company bring David Edgar's remarkable political epic from the spit and sawdust atmosphere of Stratford's Other Place and expose it to full staging at the Aldwych. The timing could not be more apt; London should flock.

With evidence of our national dismay increasing daily, the play's vivid description of the rise of a neo-Right-Wing Party gathers even more strength to its already sharp elbow.

Against a Jubilee Year background of 20 per cent inflation and rising two-million unemployed, Edgar's theory looks even more like potent prophecy. He has gathered together the wildly disparate strands of dissatisfied post-war society – the disenfranchised, the disillusioned, the discontent and the plain disreputable – and woven them into a Union Jack design of patriotic backlash.

Starting with the hand-over of India, he marshals his characters through the years of change to focus the action on an obscure Midland by-election.

What makes this piece outstandingly mature is the way the author refuses to load his dice until after his Left-Wing game is won.

His view of the extreme Right remains comprehensible, understanding and not least authentic.

The little dealer squeezed out of his livelihood by flash speculators, the housewife isolated by an immigrant community – gradually all are pushed over the edge of fanaticism by an insidious process of tragedies, bewilderment, frustration and finally vested interest.

The form is lucid and formidable; the language potent; the message clear. If the ending seems contrived on second sight that is a forgivable end to the means.

Ron Daniels directs a fine cast with compelling clarity. The company contains many of the finest young character actors to be found, not least Ian McDiarmid as the manipulated candidate, and Michael Pennington as his erudite zealot manipulator.

My view that this is the most important political play of recent years remains unchanged.

Joking Apart

Alan Ayckbourn
Globe Theatre, Shaftesbury Avenue
Daily Mail, **8th March 1979**

How comedy has won back its good name

Comedy has become almost as dirty a word as refuse in the West End these days. Yet here is Alan Ayckbourn, perennial as the sweetest rose, to give it back its good name.

We must beware, however, of taking his annual success for granted. That would be to write him off as a laugh-machine, to diminish his courage as a playwright and dull the impact of his ideas.

Who, for instance, but Ayckbourn would – or could – fashion such an accurately observed discourse on the destructive elements of human perfection? He also examines, succinctly, the corroding effect time has merely by passing.

The instant he introduces us to his golden couple we recognise immediately the envy, insecurity and disillusion they spread beneath their dazzle. In fact Ayckbourn spreads it over twelve years of open house hospitality. Through the nightmare of a children's bonfire, the horrors of a colour supplement Sunday, the alcoholic haze of a wet Boxing Day tennis tournament, and finally their daughter's 18th birthday party, they seek only to find sunshine and cheer.

Their effortless grace and relentless charity reduce the vicar's nervous wife to a gibbering junkie, brings down their thrusting Finnish business partner to a trough of self-pity, while destroying his wife's illusions.

The humour is often low key and Chekhovian in its irony. Only one joke escapes from Ayckbourn's pen: 'I'd give my right arm to be able to draw.'

But the production – by Ayckbourn himself – is full of theatrical tricks. The unseen part of the outdoor tennis court is for ever alive with action be it a spectacular firework display (lit by Richard Pilbrow) or the fateful wet Christmas tennis match...

Alison Steadman and Christopher Cazenove in the seemingly thankless roles of the central couple actually manage to remain nice and recognisably lovely people. But the evening's key performance comes from Marcia Warren, who begins as a likeable vicar's mousewife and ends up a garish, redundant wreck.

Dogg's Hamlet, Cahoot's Macbeth
Tom Stoppard
Collegiate Theatre
Daily Mail, **20th July 1979**

Bad joke, Mr Stoppard

It is a testament to Tom Stoppard's versatility that after writing *Night and Day*, the best play in London last season, he should now lumber us with the two worst. I have long suspected that Mr Stoppard's love of a literary joke at any price might go too far one day. And it has.

Two main giggles attempt to gurgle along in *Dogg's Hamlet* and they burst each other's bubbles as they go. The first is that polite conversation in a boys' public school consists of insulting gibberish (the school's prize-day guest of honour begins her address: 'Scabs, Slobs, Black Yobs...'). We don't need to hear the rest to recall instantly those infantile Sixties sub-satire sketches once thought so smart by undergrads. The second – better – giggle is the school's 15-minute version of *Hamlet*, cut so close to the bone that the only remaining quotations are: 'Alas, poor Yorick', 'Get thee to a nunnery;' and 'To be or not to be'.

However, with *Cahoot's Macbeth* Stoppard is attempting something more profound while perpetrating the same paste-and-scissors gambit, which makes 'the jokes sit all the more heavily.' We are supposed to be witnessing a truncated version of *Macbeth* performed by banned Czechoslovakian actors at a friend's home – a sort of rent-a-dissident floor show.

But as we saw in Mr Stoppard's celebrated *Every Good Boy Deserves Favour*, his brand of political commentary needs André Previn and the LSO to merit serious attention.

Ed Berman's British American Repertory Company labours good-naturedly through it all. On this occasion, the BARC was much worse than its bite.

The Crucible
Arthur Miller
Comedy Theatre
Daily Mail, 6th March 1981

Parable for our times...

The fact that this stark parable stretches far beyond the specific times in which it was preached, and transfers to the West End by public demand, is as much a testimony to our continuing uneasy conscience as to Arthur Miller's undoubted skill.

For, in the story of the Salem witch hunt, he was mirroring the McCarthy era. Then, as in the setting of his play, good men and women suffered the persecution of bigots, blackguards and the spiritually blind. And all for an 'invisible crime', as Miller has it in his potent language.

Yet even with the shadow of those disgraceful anti-Communist purges behind us, the world looks scarcely safer for men of independent mind. Now, as then, the word of an informer is as much proof of guilt in many places as were the words of hysterical pubescent girls who opened the Pandora's Box of lies and suspicion in Puritan 16th century Salem.

I am not surprised, therefore, that this magnificent production by the National Theatre Company comes to the West End.

As a performance it is immaculate. The scent of simmering sexual frustration hangs in the air as a girlish fantasy escalates into the hysteria of mass execution.

But Miller has humanised his theme by concentrating on John and Elizabeth Proctor, an upright farming couple. And in Mark McManus and Lynn Farleigh (new to this production), we have the perfect picture of honour which stays steadfast despite its own blemishes and flaws.

McManus' performance speaks volumes of fleshly weakness while Miss Farleigh brings a frighteningly unbending virtue to their household. Yet, somehow, as in all the best morality tales, their basic goodness grows in direct proportion to their adversity.

It is heartening that London has room for excellence which preaches the Gospel of the individual. For if John Proctor's martyrdom means anything to a modern audience, it is that one man's small defence of his good name is also a giant step in the progress of the human spirit.

The Hypochondriac

Molière
RNT Olivier
Daily Mail, 23rd October 1981

The Hypochondriac who dies the death

The road to hell is paved with good intentions, which has the merit of being one well-known phrase or saying which Alan Drury's knockabout translation of Molière's last savage satire leaves tactfully alone.

For good intentions we have in plenty at the National. Director Michael Bogdanov has sought to marry the colourful *Commedia dell'Arte* style which so influenced the mordant French satirist with the 'natural style' Molière encouraged in his own players.

The result, for all I know, may well be an accurate approximation of what the play really looked like in 1673 – heaven knows the translation of the title from *Le Malade Imaginaire* can't be faulted for its modern accuracy. But it only hints at the graceless vulgarity of the result. At first I was prepared to welcome and enjoy the flood of carnival music, masks and movement spread over the Olivier stage. Here, I thought, was Molière's cruel eye for the grossness of human nature captured in the *Commedia dell'Arte* spirit.

However, it soon became embarrassingly clear that the performance was not going to match the purpose in any degree. All you can say in favour of a troupe of jugglers who can't juggle, tumblers who can't tumble, dancers who can only stamp and singers who shout is that it keeps a couple of dozen actors in gainful employment and off the streets at night when they might have been out enjoying themselves.

As for the attempt at the natural style the result is a textbook in coarse acting. It is one thing to satirise vulgarity but quite another to stoop to it. And fine actors such as Daniel Massey, cadaverous in the title-role, and Anna Carteret, as his wife, are called upon to indulge in prat falls and belly flops which have not even precision to recommend them...

All My Sons

Arthur Miller
Wyndhams Theatre
Daily Mail, 5th November 1981

Right in the gut by the guilty secret in an all-American home

Times have rendered guilt unfashionable and an all but obsolete commodity. The generation which taught itself that the thing to do was your own thing is hardly likely to sit around adding up the cost to others – let alone foot the bill. So let us hail this splendid play for reminding us so powerfully of a time when there was still time to warn of the consequences; of a time, too, when there was still time for the well-made stage play.

Miller wrote this when the world was still licking its wounds and burying the dead of the Second World War. When television had not conditioned us to shorthand drama. So he took an entire act to set out the landscape he then explodes beneath his audience.

The sun-drenched American back porch reeks of dowdy downcast neglect which even Midwest affluence cannot hide. And Hayden Griffin's setting for this superb revival captures the very flavour of the era.

Only gradually are we allowed to glimpse what hides behind the half-closed blinds of this all-American timber-framed home. The hysteria behind the mother's denial of her son's death, which throbs so insistently below the surface of the low-key first act, is a meticulous preparation for the high drama which follows...

As in so much of Miller's work, it is the father who is revealed as the hollow, worthless statue, with whom his son must come to terms. Colin Blakeley visibly shrinks when confronted with the consequences of unloading that fatal batch of faulty aircraft components, which sent 21 airmen to their deaths, and brought his own son's suicide to the very back doorstep of his home.

Mr Miller is not afraid to touch the air with melodrama, to make the point that we are all, in the end, our brothers' keepers; and our sons' too. The acting is uniformly of the highest order. Rosemary Harris' mother, hiding her fears behind sad, slow, stubborn smiles, while Garrick Hagon shields his with Boy Scout integrity.

Mr Miller's message is: we could be better. I doubt if that applies to this production.

The Oresteia

Aeschylus
RNT Olivier
Daily Mail, **2nd December 1981**

Losing face behind masks...

Some plays lie in an agent's bottom drawer longer than others waiting for a major London production. The *Oresteia* has the singular distinction of gathering dust for the past 2,439 years, which must be something of a record.

It has taken Sir Peter Hall and the combined resources of the National Theatre to pluck up courage to bring it to the English stage. No doubt heartened by the fact that his audience will suffer no over-familiarity

1. *42nd Street*: 'Finally it's here. The father and mother of all showbiz
musicals.' (p.16)

2. All the Evitas: Marti Webb, Jacquey Chappell, Stephanie Lawrence, Kathryn Evans, Siobhan McCarthy and Elaine Paige.

'In the unlikely event of my verdict having any effect whatsoever on its box office success, I must first report that *Evita* is a technical knockout, a magnificent earful, a visual triumph and a wow.' (p.2)

3. *Phantom of the Opera*: '...at heart, a simple tale of unrequited love.' (p.20)

4. *Barnum:* 'Crawford's own personal gospel: if it can't be done, try it. This, of course, is the urge that is the hope of the human race. It is why the Wright Brothers wanted to fly, why Michelangelo painted the ceiling of the Sistine Chapel.' (p.10)

5. *Oliver!*: Composer and lyricist Lionel Bart outside the Albery Theatre during the first run. (p.41)

6. Antony Sher as *Richard III*: 'Sher genius...' (p.57)

Ken Towner

7. Peter O'Toole as *Macbeth*: A performance 'heroically ludicrous.' (p.56)

Neville Marriner

The Daily Mail

8. *Above*: Jack would do anything to get a good story. Nell Dunn's *Steaming*.
9. *Below*: Patrick Hill, Jack Tinker, Charlie Catchpole and Dee Dee Wilde of 'Pan's People', performing together in a charity gala held at the Dome Theatre in Brighton, June 1994.

with Aeschylus' blood-soaked trilogy, Sir Peter has decided to go back to basic Greek origins for his inspiration.

Thus an all-male cast disguised in a variety of masks declaim Tony Harrison's crude Anglo-Saxon couplets on a vast steely arena to the hypnotic rhythms of Harrison Birtwistle's marvellously evocative music.

There are moments when this ritual approach works spectacularly well. The initial appearance of Orestes in the second play, *Cleophori*, for example, has the power to chill the blood. This is the youth returning from exile to find himself, like Hamlet, cast in the role of a son whose mother (Clytemnestra, for it is she with a butch baritone voice and gold *Beaux Arts* ball mask) has murdered his hero father Agamemnon and made her lover ruler in his place. But there are few such moments when the actor has the skill or technique to reveal to us the emotions behind his mask. It is all very well for Sir Peter to argue that this is how the Greeks would have done it. But they would also have done it without his sophisticated lighting and stage effects.

Why should he ask his audience to cope with the anonymity of masks when modern actors have not the training that the Greeks endured for this long, intensely religious calling.

Only Orestes as an actor manages to transcend completely the deliberately alienating limitations of this elementary technique. And only the final play – *Eumenides* – with its legal wrangling between the Gods and the Furies entirely justified the approach. Elsewhere one is left to fend off the beckoning arms of Morpheus.

Worzel Gummidge
Keith Waterhouse and Willis Hall, music by Denis King
Cambridge Theatre
***Daily Mail*, 23rd December 1981**

Borrow someone's child to see Worzel

Like most sentimental adults I believe children deserve the very best at Christmas time. Which explains the touch of frost crackling through this column of late. Quite frankly, the best is rarely on offer: not in several of the theatres I have been visiting recently, which is licensed lunacy on the part of managements. If you cannot touch a captive audience of children with the magic of live theatre at this time of the year, when in the name of Santa Claus can you? So without more delay, let me urge everyone who can beg or borrow a child to hurry along to the Cambridge Theatre.

There it all is, in the unlikely turnip-and-straw creation of the TV scarecrow *Worzel Gummidge*. A show sparkling with all the good things the spirit of theatre can heap upon you. An original story, a witty script, recognisable characters, a pace-packed production, first-rate cast, and yes, magic.

The aura is created the moment the curtain rises. A mystic ceremony which gives our scarecrow hero life is in itself, a piece of splendid theatrical illusion and the spell is never broken.

Not having seen Jon Pertwee's television incarnation, I was totally unprepared for the force of this wayward scarecrow's appealing personality. On stage those masters of the clever yarn, Waterhouse and Hall, have supplied him with a series of adventures in his unsuitable love-suit with a snooty wooden Aunt Sally who is given a performance by Una Stubbs which in my Christmas book ranks her alongside Mrs Malaprop, Lady Bracknell and Annie Walker as my favourite comic female creations.

To discover Miss Stubbs haughtily dismissing Worzel's declaration of love with a disdainful 'Ay 'ave 'ad wooden balls thrown at me by nobles, lords and dukes' puts her alongside the high camp of Edith Evans' finest Lady Bracknell social snobbery.

The evening is full of such moments as Mr Pertwee's splendid hay-stuffed anarchist disrupts the life around Scatterbrook Farm. Aiding and abetting him are two of the most enchanting children to be seen in many a season's Christmas Shows. Little Jonathan Byatt and Lucy Baker live every moment of Worzel's escapades with a refreshing blend of professional aplomb and unfeigned innocence.

The show deserves children like these and children of every age deserves a show like this.

Noises Off

Michael Frayn
Lyric, Hammersmith
***Daily Mail*, 1st March 1982**

The refined art of coarse acting

I am about to let you in on what is very nearly the best theatre joke of the decade. So while the cheap fares last, prepare to beat a track to Hammersmith and do yourself and this magical theatre a favour.

There you will find a set, the like of which you will not have seen since seaside rep. On to it will reel a comic char straight off a McGill postcard. By the time she has answered the ringing phone, the better to inform her audience that the house is empty, the estate agents are trying to let it and the master and mistress are tax exiles in Spain, you in turn will be nervously searching your programme.

Yes, the play IS by the brilliant Mr Michael Frayn. Yes, that terrible performance IS coming from the gifted Miss Patricia Routledge. No, this is NOT the wrong theatre. In the nick of time, Paul Eddington strolls sardonically through the stalls to redirect the entire scene.

What we are witnessing is Mr Frayn's cruel writer's eye focused unblinkingly on that most vulnerable theatrical institution: the last dress rehearsal. Under his ruthless examination the actor and his art are stripped naked in a dizzy accumulation of forgotten lines, missed cues and personal foibles.

Improbably – impossibly – Mr Frayn goes on to cap this *coup de théâtre* with a second act that is a sublime re-run of the first... only backstage this time... As the split-second bits of stage business they have laboured over are performed perfunctorily to some unseen audience beyond, the frustrations and private passions of the play's cast are acted out *sotto voce* or in dumb-show behind the scenes with ferocious zeal.

Such masters of the comic art as Michael Aldridge, Nicky Henson and Jan Waters work the miracle of offering a definitive lesson in coarse acting through the most finely judged performances.

The third act runs out of steam...

Captain Brassbound's Conversion

George Bernard Shaw
Theatre Royal, Haymarket
Daily Mail, 11th June 1982

For Penelope Keith, I'd cross the Sahara

For once I will not cavil at this revival of yet another minor Shavian pot-boiler. This glossy confection serves exactly the purpose Shaw himself intended. He wrote the play as a star vehicle for his adored Ellen Terry. And he also showed a most un-Fabian interest in the financial benefits to be reaped from a box office smash...

Alas, the great Terry turned out to be a disappointment as the redoubtable Lady Cicely Waynflete, whose forte is to subdue savages with a smile and a brisk 'How d'ye do' and freeze fiery tempers with the ice-cool charm known only to a certain class of English lady. Miss Terry's admirers could not stomach the thought.

Miss Penelope Keith's public, on the contrary, will have no such qualms. They will flock to the Haymarket to see Miss Keith add Lady Cicely's scalp to the beltful of formidable heroines she has made her own. It is no small test on her part.

And it makes an ideal addition to the repertory season at the Haymarket. For it provides Miss Keith with a splendid counterpart to her triumphant, loving, no-nonsense Maggie in *Hobson's Choice*.

Lady Cicely is all nonsense if you take her at face value, which Miss Keith cleverly does not... In her every gesture you read that here is the true daughter of that intrepid breed of women who got their own way in every corner of the Empire without raising so much as a starched lace handkerchief – the last sighting of which were the two rescued lady scientists who rescued cucumber from the Argentine invaders and itinerant penguins of South Georgia.

While her irascible brother-in-law Judge and his long-lost brigand nephew confront each other with all kind of Shavian tyrannies pertaining to law and order, Miss Keith calmly sews bandages and holds out for the kind of natural justice Shaw wistfully attributed to womanly wiles. It is a performance which shines with intelligence, bright good humour and the glow of common humanity.

John Turner, as Captain Brassbound, and Michael Denison bluster unconvincingly in her wake. But Miss Keith herself is worth braving the big Sahara to see even in a half-baked play.

Other Places
Harold Pinter
RNT Cottesloe
Daily Mail, 18th September 1982

The sleeper awakes with a real beauty

Two plays into this brief triple bill – and my mind had begun to drift to several other places I would rather be. It is no joy watching a writer of Pinter's early power dissipate his reputation on trifles which are remarkable only in the achievement of moving backwards while marking time.

But then, to complete the programme, came a most astonishing change of pace and vision called *A Kind of Alaska*. Instead of doodling around old familiar themes of characters locked in their own private twilights, he comes up with something so surprising that – for the first time in any Pinter play I can recall – he feels it necessary to provide a long programme note of explanation.

Back in 1916, an epidemic of sleeping sickness (encephalitis lethargica for those with a medical turn of phrase) froze vast numbers of Europe's population into a comatose state not unlike that of Sleeping Beauty. It took 50 years for scientists to produce a princely drug called L-Dopa to kiss the survivors back to life.

The enormity of the subject seems overwhelming. But inspired by Oliver Sacks' account of this bleak freak history in his book *Awakening*, Pinter has produced a world more personally emotional, more nakedly dramatic and certainly more accessible, than anything he has written before.

This is one girl's journey from the darkness of her lost past into the blazing light of a new and unknown world.

It offers Judi Dench an inspired opportunity to demonstrate that special blend of waif-like vulnerability and aggressive mental alertness which fills the theatre with moments of unforgettable, if ambiguous, emotions. True, with this new surge of realism it may be stretching the imagination more than somewhat to have Miss Dench gaze on the sister she last saw as a child of 12 and declare: 'You've put on weight!' For the sister happens to be Anna Massey and no comment could be more hugely inappropriate. But the play stands as a long-awaited landmark in Pinter's continuing career.

Of the other two, the first, *Family Voices*, was a radio play and still is. And the second, *Victoria Station*, gets nowhere fast: a mini-cab driver comes over all funny outside Crystal Palace. Unfortunately, the play did not come over funny enough to carry this passenger very far.

Heartbreak House

George Bernard Shaw
Theatre Royal, Haymarket
Daily Mail, **11th March 1983**

The stars shine on Shaw's classic night

Ask anyone except, perhaps, a true Shavian scholar what he can remember about this indestructible masterpiece and I doubt if he will be able to remember more than three scrambled scraps of information. That it is Shaw's finest play; that Captain Shotover's house is a symbol of Britain, the sinking ship of state; that it all ends, literally, with a bang since Shaw deluges the stage with falling bombs.

So why should I, at this late date, try to remedy the habits of several lifetimes and waste breath debating the merits of the action spread over three word-filled acts? It is, after all, copper-bottomed productions such as this which ensure that it remains afloat in the vanguard of modern classics.

The reason is not hard to find. Shaw, in order to tease, described it as a 'fantasia in Russian manner'. Its only brush with the spirit of Chekhov is that it is full of atmosphere and that every role is fit for a star.

Stars are what we have in plenty here. Not all of them in the roles the Good Lord intended, perhaps, but shining forth with undiminished splendour nonetheless. An all-seeing divinity, for example, created Miss Diana Rigg to bestow her cool intellectual elegance on parts which call for her comic assurance with high-class ladies. Lady Ariadne Utterword was made for her.

Rosemary Harris, on the other hand, is one of nature's free spirits: warm, impulsive and full of life. A God-sent gift to the Bohemian/Hesione Hushabye. It is testimony to the superb artistry of both these ladies that each should be so strikingly memorable in the role providence intended for the other. Rex Harrison, on the other hand, is exactly where both he and nature intended. Foursquare, centre-stage as the grizzled 88-year-old marine who can only see Armegeddon for his cargo of capitalism, crass snobberies and all the other impedimenta Shaw despised in modern society.

'Many men would be offended by your style of talking,' Mr Harrison is told. But only a fellow actor would object to his delivery, directed straight to the audience with seldom a glance for anyone else on stage. As for the rest of the stars, they shine out from their appointed place as they prattle their way towards the day of judgement with all the wit and wisdom no one ever quite recalls once the curtain has fallen.

When the Wind Blows

Raymond Briggs
Whitehall Theatre
Daily Mail, **22nd April 1983**

Blast it, I was bored to death

The kindest thing to be said about this misbegotten homily on the effects of a nuclear attack on Britain is that its heart is in the right place. Unfortunately the play is not. The power and charm of Raymond Briggs' original illustrated story, which worked so well on radio, is dissipated on stage throughout two hours of accumulated boredom which works on the audience in much the same way as the fall-out from the holocaust drains the life-force of the luckless couple on the stage.

By the end of the evening I felt my own hair had fallen out and that my gums were starting to bleed like the victims of the blast. Only in my case the first was through tearing and the second was through gnashing.

It is all very well to say that at its core the piece contains a vital message for our times, that its urgent intention is a savage satire on the uselessness of our ludicrously inadequate Civil Defence arrangements in the face of a nuclear attack. The fatal flaw in all its good intentions is that in order to demonstrate the stupidity of the Government's instructions to the populace – take off your doors to build an inner nuclear-free core; whitewash the windows; stock up with peanut butter – we have to put up for the entire evening with a couple of people asinine enough to take them seriously.

Twenty years ago the immortal *Beyond the Fringe* review team demolished the self-same safety instructions to jump into brown paper bags and point the feet towards the bomb in one quick, five minute sketch. Poor Patricia Routledge and Ken Jones have to wallow for two uninterrupted hours through dialogue which would patronise the IQ of an average white mouse.

'Don't you catch your death out there in the rain,' Miss Routledge enjoins hubby as he carefully gathers in the radium-polluted water to make a nice cup of tea. Miss Routledge's character is congenitally incapable of remembering that we are not at war with 'Jerry' while Mr Jones is saddled with a compliant buffoon who, even within the comic-strip approach of the piece, would happily eat razor-blades if bidden by an official leaflet.

By the time they are lying about stoically rationalising their bodies' hideous disintegration – 'Blue spots? Those are just vacuous veins. All people of our age get them' – I could happily have exploded a conventional bomb strategically placed close to their rears...

Private Lives

Noël Coward
Lunt-Fontanne Theatre, Broadway
Daily Mail, **9th May 1983**

Those not so private lives are a potent mix

So very little has ever been remotely private about the lives of Elizabeth Taylor and her sometime spouse Richard Burton. And while normally I would blush to base any critical opinion of a star's professional performance on what I know about their offstage shenanigans, it is impossible to impose such rules on this extraordinary twinning.

For the couple (all right, ex-couple?) know no such shame. Their single reason for being in Noël Coward's immortal comedy about post-divorce manners and two people who can't bear to live together yet cannot be apart is because of who they are and what they've done.

This is not being patronising. It is also not being strictly Coward. But it does explain the extraordinary potency of cheap music being made before one's very eyes.

'We are two violent acids bubbling around in a nasty little matrimonial bottle,' intones Mr Burton at one point. And the vast audience fairly catch their breath with the thrill of the utterance.

Now all this may say more for the Master's gift of clairvoyance beyond the grave than it does for Mr Burton's truly turgid delivery of his lines, but it is nonetheless a sort of theatre. Not my kind of theatre. Not, I suspect, Sir Noël's either. But that strange mystic chemistry between an audience and the artists on stage, which is the essence of live theatre, cannot be denied.

Miss Taylor's comedy style – to be as blunt as her salary published in the programme prompts me to be – is infantile. 'Ch-ah-nce roo-ools moi loif,' she drawls at one point in a tawdry attempt to be high tone. But who cares? She has only to stand there while Mr Burton exclaims: 'My God, Amanda, you look wonderful,' for someone in the preview audience

I joined to yell back, 'Yeah!' And the rest to break up in rapturous applause.

That fan was no slouch as a critic either. Miss Taylor does indeed look ravishing. A decade or more of care and indulgence seemed to have been removed since her unfortunate London appearance in *Little Foxes*.

And clearly she knows it. With dresses slashed up to her thighs and drops down practically to her navel she made good and sure that the glittering first-night audience, gathered not entirely without coincidence on America's celebration of sacred Mothering Sunday, did not miss the point.

This was no tired mother and granny having a last fling. She may be no gift to comedy, but on Broadway at least she is a star who can have them queuing around the block.

And in this town no one argues with success.

'What fools we were to ruin it all. What utter, utter fools,' says Burton whose tired way with Coward's lightning flashes of insight put a tortoise in the Seb Coe class of speed. Yet the line comes over as real and fresh as if he had minted it new and already won a *Tony* for its delivery.

The audience sighed with ecstasy, and if I sighed for Sir Noël, I was among a minority of agitators, as irrelevant to the experience as the other actors on stage and the director.

The Real Thing

Tom Stoppard
Strand Theatre
***Daily Mail*, 17th November 1983**

Nothing quite like The Real Thing

It is a rare and privileged experience to witness a writer of Stoppard's eminence take a bold and dangerous leap into unexplored territory. Until this moment, if Stoppard ever moved his audience, it was inevitably towards the *Oxford Dictionary of Quotations*, or perhaps just the *Oxford Dictionary*. The driving force behind his work has always been his undisguised joy in the literary reference. Enjoying his plays is akin to passing A level.

Well, here, he presents us with just such a writer as the central character for this extraordinarily personal and engrossing play. And to bring this story even closer to home, he begins the evening with an exquisitely-contrived comic scene about marital infidelity, typical of his own literate preoccupations. Only later does it dawn on us that this is, in fact, an excerpt from his hero's latest play – not the latest fictitious exercise in playwriting we shall see this night.

However what fills the rest of the evening with the glow of theatrical excitement is not the neatness of Stoppard's famed dramatic conceits. It is the unusual warmth of his understanding of human love, on all its levels. Infidelities, jealousies, companionship and finally a true union. He examines these from every angle, as if he himself were trying to comprehend their nature.

The beautifully crafted scene which opens the play, is immediately exploded, almost with self-disgust, as a hollow contrivance, when the actor performing it is faced with a virtually identical situation back home. For this man, the real thing offers no smart line to keep the hurt at bay or preserve his dignity intact. Then it is the turn of 'the Author himself'. We join him on his own private journey of discovery (no expense spared, by the way), as he tries to come to terms with emotions he had only conceived in others.

And if, occasionally, Stoppard seems to lead us up the occasional blind alley, for my part there was nowhere he led, I was not happy to follow. The extraordinary intensity, generated on-stage by Roger Rees, as the tormented literary figure up the creek without a metaphor and the wonderful Felicity Kendal, as the actress he runs off with and marries, leaves one with no alternative but to melt into a soggy heap and grab at superlatives.

At one point, Mr Rees compares the craft of writing to a perfectly-constructed cricket bat... with which to send ideas soaring over the boundary. If Mr Stoppard will forgive the cliché, I was knocked for six.

Man and Superman
George Bernard Shaw
Theatre Royal, Haymarket
***Daily Mail*, 19th November 1983**

Nobody sleeps while O'Toole the tornado is playing his part

Say what you will, nobody sleeps while Peter O'Toole is on. Which, in a play that has often acted as a cure for insomnia to me, is not a quality lightly to be dismissed. Mr O'Toole, showing no hint of shyness in facing a London audience with the memory of a historic *Macbeth* still comparatively fresh in their minds, tears on to the stage, an elegant tornado of energy in exquisite dove-grey morning clothes.

He then proceeds to adopt the entirely appropriate posture and tone of a distinctive street corner ranter. For, in fact, Jack Tanner, the loquacious hero of this play, is the man Shaw used as a repository for all his most puckish political broadsides.

And Mr O'Toole, his voice loud and sonorous liked the cracked bell of doom, declaims his speeches mainly to no one in particular and everyone in general, which in any other context would be a disastrous display of histrionics. But as the whole point of this man is that everyone concedes that he speaks well yet nobody listens to a word he says, O'Toole cannot be accused of being untrue to the text.

Indeed, he is just what the play needs. His immaculate appearance, hurtling on and off the stage in a lilac car, proves that at least the elementary lessons to be learned from his Old Vic debacle has been duly digested. He neither bumps into the scenery nor wears shoes that are totally alien to his costume. What is more, he keeps his audience laughing throughout – which is more than most actors can do through three and a quarter hours of Shaw (we are mercifully spared the *Don Juan in Hell* sequence)...

A Streetcar Named Desire
Tennessee Williams
Mermaid Theatre
Daily Mail, **13th March 1984**

All that one desires...

The forlorn Mermaid Theatre has come back to life – and with a great and glorious performance of one of the world's greatest and most glorious plays.

I have not seen *Streetcar* performed for almost ten years. Yet last night, it worked a magic so strong and potent that I was moved to the old tears in a new and splendid way. And my reason for rejoicing is the performance of Sheila Gish.

So many fine actresses have brought their talents to the legendary role of Blanche Dubois that you might suppose there was nothing left worth saying. But Miss Gish brings to this tortured, broken butterfly a range that is truly staggering. The beauty which Blanche is so terrified of losing is still undeniably there. But this is a woman who cannot bear to face daylight for more subtle reasons than mere vanity.

She is terrified the realities of her life will be revealed, along with a few wrinkles. You can see she has tried to use all her natural charm, sex appeal and a belief in life's joys to protect her from its cruelties. It is an all too fragile defence.

In this last dingy refuge at her sister's home, the world has finally ganged up against her, and Miss Gish shows us that deep down she is astute enough to know this is where it will all end. Even when the compliments she craves are finally paid by Duncan Preston's gangling Mitch, her femininity flickers only on automatic pilot, while her eyes cloud over with the knowledge that she's heard all this too often for it to hold out any hope. What also marks this production as definitive is the futile mental and physical battle Blanche wages against her brutish brother-in-law, played by Paul Herzberg in an impressive debut in the role which made Marlon Brando's name.

American Buffalo
David Mamet
Duke Of York's Theatre
Daily Mail, 3rd August 1984

Oh, Al! You almost made me swear

Both Al Pacino and his *American Buffalo* cross the Atlantic already covered in native glory. From where I was sitting, however, it was very difficult to guess why either should move any theatre audience of average sophistication to anything other than the distance between indifference and irritation.

Perhaps it helps to be an American, who would know that a buffalo on a nickel means it is worth planning a robbery.

In itself the play might make a mildly interesting short lunchtime exercise. Mr Mamet has a nice line in small-time despair, the natural mistrust of the underdog, and that litany of obscenities which is the patois of the back-street crook.

However, his technique often overwhelms his fragile theme, and the piece manages to stagger over two acts only through the endless repetition of each line and every known expletive. What is more he takes the least pretty route to his chosen destination and when we arrive all we learn is what we already knew: that in any jungle each creature must attend to its own survival.

But the tedium of the piece is a mere pinprick, a small vaccination, against the armoury of tricks, mannerisms and self-regard with which Mr Pacino bombards us throughout the evening.

There is no respite from the posturing that passes for energy, no shelter from the array of cynical quirks with which he guards the real nature of his character, Teach – a bantam cock loser with whom we are supposed to sympathise.

Thumbs pick at teeth, hands sweep the hair, fingers tug and re-adjust the waistband of his saggy trousers. It would take a hallucinating octopus to do credit to such an interpretation. And, of course, it does spell out the great divide between what the British believe to be fine acting and what passes for the same in the more undisciplined areas of Broadway.

May I beg Mr Pacino, for his own good, to hie him to Chichester during his brief stay and witness the wondrous Maggie Smith demonstrating how to contain natural stage energy and get her finest affects in deep repose. For every once in a while a sly, secret smile plays across Mr Pacino's unshaven features which, try as I might, I could not equate to any character motivation. I do hope it was not an involuntary sign of pleasure in his own performance. If so Mr Mamet would undoubtedly have a word for it. And it would be a four-letter word. Repeated many times.

Intimate Exchanges

Alan Ayckbourn
Ambassadors Theatre
Daily Mail, 14th August 1984

Ayckbourn's eight-some had me reeling

Alan Ayckbourn, a master gamesman in public and private, believes life is a series of random choices. The doorbell you leave unanswered, the sly cigarette you stop to smoke – each can rearrange the pattern of your existence as surely as jumping out of a 12th storey window. In a staggering *coup de théâtre*, Mr Ayckbourn not only demonstrates this enthralling theme to its limits but shows once more that no contemporary can touch him for bold stage invention.

Into the Ambassadors move not one but EIGHT variations on the same initial circumstances. For the next two months a different play each week will explore a totally different path dictated by a casual choice.

Each piece is complete in itself. In one the hyper-tensive wife of an alcoholic headmaster stops for a quick drag on a soothing ciggy and is plunged headlong into a chain of events which lead her, through a total nervous breakdown while dispensing tea on sports day, to a life of lonely tycoonery.

In another the same lady has to cope with a traumatised family friend who has selected her garden shed as the site for his terminal retreat to the womb – simply because she decided to answer the front door. The bitter internecine warfare which shrives middle-class English domestic life is, needless to say, thoroughly dissected.

But Mr Ayckbourn is not content with even this ambitious concept. For he calls upon the services of only two actors for the eight roles. Their marathon involves feats of memory equivalent to playing *Hamlet*, *Lear* and *Private Lives* at hourly intervals. Pure theatre in every sense of the word.

Mother Courage

Bertolt Brecht
RSC Barbican
Daily Mail, 8th November 1984

The miraculous Mother Judi

The fact that *Mother Courage* remains stubbornly one of the great potent forces of modern theatre, despite all its ruinously cumbersome trappings, is a testimony to Brecht's genius as an artist and his crass stupidity as a theorist.

Read the fellow's views on the subject of his own sprawling, episodic epic and he will insist we feel no sympathy, no empathy, no human compassion for the blatant opportunist, this profiteering camp follower who seeks only to line her pockets through the hungers and petty corruption of war. When he leaves her, childless and bereft, dragging her caravan in the wake of an unprofitable peace, he pretends we should care as little as if the woman had just lost her stake at bingo.

What blithering nonsense, when every other line leaps from the page and proclaims her a tigress protecting her cubs through naked cunning and the law of the jungle. What piffling rot, when up there on the stage is the glorious Miss Judi Dench, bringing tears unbidden to the eye merely by gazing dry-eyed herself on the body of her son.

With little hunched shrugs, as though used to warding off misfortune's slings and arrows, she exhibits that rough Cockney stoicism which, whatever Brecht may have thought, is the true badge of her namesake: courage. There is no miracle Miss Dench is not capable of performing on any stage. Hair spiky red and punk, she wheedles and waddles her way around the vast, smoke-ringed arena of the Barbican stage, trundling her caravan in a constant circle of increasing misery and misfortune.

Yet never once does she allow herself the luxury of self-pity – that least attractive of emotions. Her wit remains her sharpest ally. Whatever Brecht may have said to the contrary, it is impossible to sit through Howard Davies' thunderous production without knowing that Miss Dench has brought us face to face with the raw pain and humanity of motherhood.

JUDI DENCH

I entirely agree with Jack about Brecht's theories. I could never understand the playwright's idea of alienation. It is very difficult to stand back from a performance if you are in it, and yet make people appreciate the depth of your grief (in the case of *Mother Courage*). How can one do that? I do not know.

If Brecht intended his audience to clearly see his political points without becoming emotionally involved in the story, why did he put in the incredibly moving death of her son? No doubt there is a way to do it, but it is alien to me.

Old Times

Harold Pinter
Theatre Royal, Haymarket
Daily Mail, **25th April 1985**

Old Times from a new angle

By the time Pinter came to write *Old Times*, his reputation was made and his formula both familiar and set. It gave every sign of an artist trapped in the aspic of his own past glory with little to say and no fresh way of saying it.

The question marks which hang over almost every line of his dialogue no longer seemed in any urgent need of an answer...

The theme, as so often before, is territory. A married couple living in some nameless coastal retreat are visited by an old – indeed the only – friend of the wife. At first, our curiosity about her is stirred by the peculiar fact that they are discussing her impending arrival while she is plainly standing behind them gazing out of their drawing room window. Is she there or isn't she?

All we learn, however, is that the couple have lived their entire married life together without the wife ever mentioning she had shared a flat with her former friend. But then, as Nicola Pagett's whole existence seems to have been one of suspended animation, this ought not to surprise us.

The husband and their visitor engage in a complex jigsaw puzzle of random reminiscences, each designed to lay some personal and vaguely sexual claim on the lovely Miss Pagett's past. Yet since these impromptu memories are continually readjusted to meet the needs of the moment, we are never too sure whose old times were had by whom. Or indeed who was had by whom.

The husband is at great pains to assure his guest that he once spent an entire evening looking up her skirt. But was it her? And was it her skirt? (Miss Pagett insists the woman used to pinch her panties.)

Well, all we really need to know is that under the direction of David Jones, Liv Ullmann, Michael Gambon and Miss Pagett match the stylised pattern of the dialogue with playing that is both subtle and powerful.

Sweet Bird of Youth

Tennessee Williams
Theatre Royal, Haymarket
Daily Mail, **10th July 1985**

Vulnerable? Not you, Miss Bacall

Jaded past all recall is the palate that has lost its taste for the plays of Tennessee Williams. The florid grandeur of his language, the juicy richness of his characters, the flamboyant courage of his theatricality are, in themselves, a celebration of drama few writers can match.

Yet what keeps his work alive through all the spins of fashion's wheel, is his unqualified compassion for human frailty. And never more so than here, where few managements in this country have ever dared come to terms with his capacity to take enormous risks (not to mention enormous casts). So the fact that this glorious bloom is on display at all is a cause for cheering.

Of all his plays this one speaks most potently of our times. The story of an ageing film star holed up with her over-age toy boy in the Southern comfort of a luxury hotel is a remorseless portrait of all the false idols which our civilisation chooses to worship. Success, power, wealth, beauty – and youth. Both the star and her lover are fleeing failure and the heavy tread of time. Their pitiful partnership might have the stale odour of cheap perfume were not the author so astringent in his observation of human nature. For although it would appear that the handsome young stud has all the cards stacked in his favour, while 'Princess' hovers in a haze of drugs, sex and alcohol, when the chips are down he is revealed as one of life's all-round losers. It is the Princess who proves that merely surviving is an unbeatable victory.

And it is at this point that the play and the production make uneasy partners. To cast Miss Lauren Bacall in the part of the faded star may be a sure box office pleaser. She has presence and panache. But not for a moment is anyone going to believe that this lantern-jawed beauty with the eyes of a predatory tigress has ever suffered the vulnerability of a moment's blind panic or crippling self-doubt. Where her performance matches the mood of the play, therefore, is when she unsheathes her steel (if sheathed it ever be); where she contemptuously brushes aside her mate's pathetic attempt at blackmail, or drags herself upright from a drunken stumble to make a queenly exit.

Michael Beck's terror at his thinning blond hair and the tarnish on the promise of his golden youth are much more tangible.

But as with the casting of the star, the choice of Harold Pinter as director cuts curiously against the grain of the play. Where Williams writes with his heart on his sleeve, Pinter directs with everything up his sleeve. Where the dialogue turns deep purple, Mr Pinter strives to keep it ice blue. Instead of masking the brazen theatricality of the text, this merely points it out and tips it into self-parody.

Double Bill

The Real Inspector Hound
Tom Stoppard

The Critic
Richard Brinsley Sheridan
RNT Olivier
Daily Mail, 13th September 1985

The joke is on Inspector Hound

On the surface it seems the perfect double-bill – two plays, each a pleasure of critics and popular box-office, which mercilessly bite both the hands that feed them. Unfortunately, Tom Stoppard's modern variation on this old theatrical theme suffers sadly from the aptness of the coupling.

For whereas Sheila Hancock's full-blooded staging of Sheridan's acid vision of the hypocrisies and hyperbole which have always gone hand in hand with high artistic endeavour comes up fresh as an ingenue, Stoppard's *Real Inspector Hound* is unhappily exposed as a one joke nine-day wonder.

Sheridan was at pains to draw a careful line between the artful satire of his critics' offstage banter and his elaborate parody of Mr Puff's truly awful attempts to stage historic drama. And Miss Hancock's troupe of players do him proud on both counts.

Indeed, the carping of Roy Kinnear and Jonathan Hyde from the sidelines sounds like the sober voice of reason confronted with the wonderful comic excesses the company perpetrates. There is nothing feigned in the startling bewilderment of Ian McKellen's capering Mr Puff.

Where *The Real Inspector Hound* suffers by comparison is that Stoppard draws no such clear line between his deliberate parody of his two main characters – the dreaded critics – and the appalling play into which they are essentially drawn. I know that on one celebrated occasion when a telephone was left ringing interminably on stage Robert Benchley called out from his seat in the stalls: 'Will someone please answer that. It's probably for me!' But it is asking a great deal of our credulity to carry the joke to its logical conclusion and have one of the critics clamber on stage and take the call himself.

Yet despite this minor disappointment, the company Ian McKellen and Edward Petherbridge have assembled at the National obviously enjoyed the heaven-sent opportunity to show their versatility.

A Small Family Business

Alan Ayckbourn
RNT Olivier
Daily Mail, 6th June 1987

Innocent adrift in Big-Bang world

It was clear almost from the outset that here was a bold, new departure for Alan Ayckbourn, perhaps the boldest of his outstanding career. For at a time of creative output when other prolific playwrights have either dried up or become atrophied in their ways, he seems to have struck an even richer vein of invention.

True, we are lulled into a false sense of security at first. There are all his favourite characters indulging their favourite pastime – enduring a cocktail party. This is, however, the worst manifestation of this meaningless game – the surprise gathering. And although the surprise inevitably is humiliatingly on the very person it is intended to cheer, the real shock of the evening is yet to come.

For Ayckbourn is not trotting out another black comedy of the aspiring classes contemplating their navels. He is writing with a deep and convincing venom about the new British malaise – which appears to affect an entire generation.

It is the story of one good man, a mildly successful businessman, desperately trying to keep faith with his ideals in the post-Big-Bang world grown sick with greed, where even the well-off want more than they need, and manufacturers become consumer junkies. From one seemingly-minor incident of shoplifting the plot unravels in a dizzy descent through industrial espionage in the family firm through a thousand-and-one moral compromises into big hush-money and finally to murder and drug-peddling.

Michael Gambon – an actor whose range has become even more prolific and impressive than the author's – is the lynch-pin of this extraordinarily complex yet smoothly ordered production. His earnest trust, billowing into bewildered rage and eventually total surrender is the stuff of comic tragedy. This is a man obeying every best instinct, yet betrayed on all sides.

Wonderful performances of the same stamp from the likes of Polly Adams as the adoring wife, Simon Cadell as the insidious investigator whose inquiries start off the mayhem, from Michael Simkins as the sinister Italian connection and from Elizabeth Bell, the very symbol of the painted face of Eve.

For, make no mistake, although it is a piece of uproarious fun it has about it the look of Ben Jonson – a comic mirror of a corrupt society into which no one dare look and laugh without seeing his or her own reflection.

ALAN AYCKBOURN

As a writer you have a choice. You can either find a formula and stick to it, which is finally self-defeating, or try to evolve. I was pleased that, because of the continuity of our relationship, Jack was able to see the directions in which my work gradually moved – from manically plot-driven works to explorations of characters, from studies of adultery to rather wider social issues. Working in my own theatre in Scarborough, out of the public eye to a degree, I am able to take risks which I could not take if, say, I had an annual spot to fill at the National Theatre.

Jack was also perceptive in his support for regional theatres. In recent years the big London companies and the West End have not originated much new work. They have been reliant on a supply from the regional theatres. New writers have to be nurtured over a number of years, and the West End sees the end product of that. In my case, it was not until I had written my seventh or eighth play that one wafted into London. So when people then hail an overnight success, it is rarely true.

Jack noted in my work a wafer-thin line between comedy and tragedy. It has always fascinated me that audiences are often unsure with my work on which side they are standing. Often they are divided. To be able to do that to an audience is a great feeling, a wonderful power. More important, it offers them a rich meal with a main course as well as a trifle. And why not run the two alongside each other?

A View from the Bridge
Arthur Miller
Aldwych Theatre
Daily Mail, **4th November 1987**

A magnificent view from the stalls

There is now in the West End a production, a play and above all a performance of such abundant richness that to miss them is to be the poorer. No praise can be too high or too fulsome for the wonders Alan Ayckbourn's subtle and spare direction brings to Arthur Miller's deeply disturbing family tragedy.

He delivers a company and a concept which fulfils everything Miller himself promised when he described this play as: 'a high, visible arc moving in full view to a single explosion.' That arc, which we can all plainly see mounting to its terrible conclusion, is the dark, unspoken – and unspeakable – the love his swaggering longshoreman, Eddie, feels for his nubile niece.

What reveals it to us, and seals Eddie's fate, is the arrival of the girl's illegal immigrant cousins from Sicily. From then on, Miller's tale takes on the aspect of classic tragedy.

But what brands this version into the mind and burns it into the heart is the stature Michael Gambon brings to the central role. He has about him the true stamp of heroism which wrings the emotions of all reason. A simple-hearted bull of a man with the bow-legged strut of an eager toiler, we see his jaunty spirit drained by forces inside him which only he, in his bewildered innocence, cannot comprehend.

Miller may be dealing with the instincts of incest; but Gambon becomes as much the victim as those lives he so deeply scars...

Around this Everest summit of a portrayal are ranged equally towering performances. Suzan Sylvester takes the girl through carefree ebullience to a steely resolution only the young in love can display. Elizabeth Bell breaks your heart as the wife who can only stand by and watch. My admiration for both Michael Simkins as the silent, brooding avenger and Adrian Rawlings as his blond, high-octane brother only intensifies after seeing them at the National. These are actors of whom high achievements can be confidently predicted.

After all who, 10 years ago would have credited Mr Gambon with a *tour de force* of such shattering power?

The Best of Friends
Hugh Whitemore
Apollo, Shaftesbury Avenue
***Daily Mail*, 11th February 1988**

The Old Master taps a rich vein of friendship

The presence on any stage of Sir John Gielgud at the age of 83 is a cause for unconfined rejoicing. But the upright figure, the proud and noble profile and that familiar flutingly clear voice bestow their own intensely personal dimension to Hugh Whitemore's mellow, autumnal celebration of friendship, fame and fate's unpredictable whim.

What he brings to the theatre today is not the mere demonstration of a great actor's technique, surviving into venerable old age. It is something above and beyond this. Like the unique friendships depicted in the play, tried and trusted, Sir John himself has acquired the rich patina of a valued friend. To him the audience responds instinctively with genuine affection, admiration and warmth. He is, in fact, the very embodiment of all the play has to say. Without him – and indeed without the sterling performances of his two co-stars, the radiant Rosemary Harris and the indomitable Ray McAnally – it passes as a sentimental oddity.

Mr Whitemore has alighted on the unlikely ties that bound together three forceful characters in a long, yet loosely tied, knot of mutual esteem and concern. Sir Sydney Cockerell (Sir John), the literary scholar who happily admits: 'No man ever possessed such a galaxy of distinguished friends,' George Bernard Shaw, who needs no introduction to anybody, and the saintly Dame Laurentia McLachlan, Abbess of Stanbrook Abbey until her death in 1953.

Mercifully for Mr Whitemore, the advent of Mr Alexander Graham Bell's infernal gadget was apparently no impediment to this ill-assorted trio's prolific correspondence. Perhaps because Dame Laurentia, being a member of a strict closed order of nuns, could not be running to pick up the telephone every five minutes and GBS wrote letters like other people blink, their discourse is charged with authentic humour, spontaneous response and studied wisdom.

In James Roose-Evans' discreet production they roam at will through Julia Trevelyan Oman's book-laden set, which reeks of associations with William Morris and collected treasures from a full, rich life. Each has a fate to tell, a trust to impart, a homily to bestow. Naturally Shaw falls temporarily foul of the Sister's manifold tolerance; naturally he amply redeems himself. But it is Sir Sydney, the inveterate collector of writers and their writings, who binds them together for our appreciation. With twinkling eyes above that imperious Roman nose, a grizzled goatee beard wreathing his sly smiles as he delivers a confidence or happily name-drops (Thomas Hardy, Walter de la Mare, William Morris, Tolstoy, Ouida are scattered indiscriminately into his conversation with the same skill as Sir John himself drops his celebrated bricks), he takes us through the journey of their intertwined lives...

Here is a man who radiates the joy of one who has indeed walked with the great and good yet been true to himself; a man who can look back with benign satisfaction on a life that has known both pain and achievement yet marvel at his own little worth. A man, in short, who would readily find himself befriended by a strong-minded nun and a self-willed man of letters.

If I have lauded Sir John to the exclusion of his fellow cast, then I trust from the generosity of their performances that his distinguished co-stars will not begrudge a word. Miss Harris is incandescent with the stuff of true sainthood, Mr McAnally explosive with the mischief of devil's advocate. A truly impressive team.

But more. A humanising evening made memorable, even historic, by the great grandee of British Theatre.

Ghetto

Joshua Sobol, adapted by David Lan
RNT Olivier
Daily Mail, 28th April 1989

So heartbreaking, it's almost an impertinence to applaud

The survival of the human spirit against insuperable odds is being triumphantly celebrated at the National Theatre. I can only urge you to go and drink deeply of this powerful, if unpalatable, antidote to the smugness and self-satisfaction of our winner-takes-all society.

But first, apologies are in order. There is no way I have ever been able to maintain objective critical faculties sharp and defensive when confronted by such historical facts as presented here by Joshua Sobol. The distinguished Israeli playwright has researched the appalling history of the Vilna Ghetto in Nazi-held Lithuania and come up with a moral conundrum that will perplex theorists and those who deal in the dogma of social certainties for the rest of time.

For while the Nazis were decimating the population of Vilna in all manner of brutal, humiliating cruelties, a defiant musical theatre flourished. Musicians, actors, singers, acrobats practised their arts as the population of the ghetto dwindled from 60,000 to a mere 16,000. Mr Sobol's argument is that while the population of men and women in Vilna perished, the soul of their community, their race and their culture survived as much through their art as through their strength.

Nicholas Hytner's rich, sprawling pageant can be counted part of that continuing process. For while bringing this ambitious work of the Yiddish theatre to this stage, he manages to transcend all barriers of race, creed and language.

Just to see that remarkable singer-actress Maria Friedman being forced to gratify her persecutor's desire to hear decadent American jazz by singing *Swanee* is itself a sermon on the survival of human dignity. Miss Friedman turns it into a defiant anthem for dispossessed aliens everywhere. And when the ragged company end their elaborately-choreographed routine, the effect is so heroic, so heart-breaking, it seems an impertinence to applaud.

John Woodvine carries the play's crucial dilemma on stern, unyielding shoulders. As the ghetto's Jewish police chief, he has to balance the weight of idealism and pragmatism that is the key to all survival.

Whether the play can be counted great art or simply an effectively-researched documentary brilliantly played, I am at a loss to say. I can only add that the issues and images it evokes will live in my mind and conscience for many years.

Shirley Valentine
Willy Russell
Duke of York's Theatre
***Daily Mail*, 29th June 1989**

Scottish or Scouse, this kitchen sink St Joan is still a universal heroine

It may be that Willy Russell has been lucky enough to know some remarkable women. Or even that some remarkable women have been lucky enough to know Willy Russell. Or simply that in his days as a Liverpool hairdresser, the perfect repository for so many female confidences, he had the courtesy, the kindness and the wit to listen to all his customers cared to impart – and understand it.

For there is not a playwright in the land who touches the female psyche more powerfully or accurately than he. Don't take my word for it, a mere male theatre critic. Listen to the response this extraordinary one-woman play provokes wherever or however it is played.

The first, and for me the definitive Shirley Valentine, Pauline Collins, took it from the West End to Broadway gathering awards and nightly standing ovations all along the way.

Re-directed by Richard Olivier, the play took to the road here with Paula Wilcox giving a vivid account of the Liverpool housewife who found that she had simply run out of life in the prison of her pristine kitchen, with nothing but the wall to talk to all day. Now Hannah Gordon, hijacking the accent and the setting to suburban Glasgow, brings Shirley back once more to the West End, living proof that this St Joan of the fitted units is a universal heroine. She is every woman who has ever found her identity disappearing under the layers of domestic trivia that life dumps on her, once the only shine she can bring to her existence is by applying Vim to a stainless steel sink.

Miss Gordon is not one of nature's instinctive comic ladies on a stage. So she misses some of the irreverent swagger that clearly marked Shirley Valentine out as a school cynic long before she submerged herself into the humdrum life of Mrs Joe Bradshaw, the stranger she has become. Nevertheless, she makes Shirley's dramatic bolt for freedom just as heroic, just as touching, just as triumphant as ever. And again, as ever, the audience roars its approval.

Shirley's spell is unbreakable. It reaches out and touches you – men, women, husbands, wives, lovers, sons and daughters – with a common understanding. You leave the theatre not with the smugness of feeling a better person, but fired with the determination to become a better person. That is the key to Willy Russell's rare humanity.

Look Back in Anger
John Osborne
Lyric, Shaftesbury Avenue
***Daily Mail*, 10th August 1989**

Looking back... with tantrums

'Dreadful! Dreadful! The most terrible performance I have ever seen!' bawled a woman from the stalls, clearly the angriest person in the theatre and only a quarter of an hour into this historic play. So saying, she made her noisy exit.

It just so happened that her astonishing outburst erupted in the middle of one of John Osborne's most virulently misogynist soliloquies. So whether it represented a back-handed compliment to the author on his power still to outrage and disturb across the distance of three decades in this his first play, or an overstated reaction to Kenneth Branagh's rather humdrum impersonation of our most notorious post war anti-hero, we will sadly never know.

Certainly it seemed to provoke Branagh into one truly believable moment of anger throughout the entire evening. 'Female!' he yelled after her retreating form, flinging Osborne's fortuitously scripted insult with something like true conviction.

Of the play's enduring qualities there can be no doubt. It has a fascination quite beyond its place in the history of modern drama. Written in flames a mile high – to quote Jimmy Porter, its rebel protagonist – it also has an unexpected beauty, a nobility of language that raises it above its period, beyond its narrow class bickerings and sustains it as an indelible love story between two scarcely reconcilable forces.

The trouble with Judi Dench's meticulous revival lies in its central performance, however. While Mr Branagh is by no means deserving of the abuse hurled at him so rudely from the stalls, it must be admitted that, in spite of popular legend, as an actor he has his limitations. The chief of those is that which flawed his Hamlet and his Romeo: namely his inability to convey an inner conflict, to convince us of a darker, deeper life below the surface of his technique and expertise as an actor.

While Emma Thompson as Jimmy's long-suffering middle class wife reveals all the provocative passivity of a rabbit hypnotised by a snake, Branagh responds with tantrums instead of rages, bad mannered petulance instead of bleeding wounds.

It must occur to us that if Jimmy were not so eloquent, so in command of his newly-minted language, he would assuredly be a wife-beater.

Mr Branagh never suggests this knife-edge of danger.

The Price

Arthur Miller
Young Vic
Daily Mail, 22nd February 1990

Power that's beyond price

The Arthur Miller bandwagon rolls on apace. Given a shine as clear as in this stunning Young Vic production by David Thacker, his reputation among the vanguard of 20th century playwrights is in no doubt. It is a mystery why his popularity in his native America should lag behind the acclaim he inspires elsewhere, most recently on these shores. For wherever he is tackling major themes of modern morality, as in *The Crucible*, or as here addressing himself to the personal struggles of everyday life, he is a dramatist of undeniable power, insight, intellect and no mean wit.

As in his initial 1947 success, *All My Sons*, Miller explores the simmering sibling rivalry a dead father bequeathed his offspring. Now, in middle-age, they confront each other among the clutter of their parents' past, just as it is to be sold off to a 90-year-old Jewish antique dealer.

Nostalgia and recrimination fight an unequal duel and Miller exploits the possibilities with innate skill and timing, the inevitable meeting being postponed until the very moment of the first act curtain. By the time the brothers begin to peel back the layers of their complex relationship, Miller has established his claim on your hearts, minds and compassion.

David Calder and Bob Peck give wonderful performances as the two men whom fate appears to have dealt with so differently. Calder, the disappointed cop nursing the resentment of having sacrificed a medical career to take care of his shattered parent and his younger brother's education, Peck the successful doctor who sent home only $5 a week to help the family out of penury.

On the sidelines Alan MacNaughtan's rumpled Jewish dealer is the keeper of the play's conscience as well as the joker in the pack, and the marvellous Marjorie Yates, barely concealing the disappointments of life with an essentially good man bent on self-sacrifice, gives the story its underlying emotional tug.

If the Young Vic does not immediately yield itself to the atmosphere of a claustrophobic attic, this quartet soon dispels any doubts on that score. The intensity of their performances is all-embracing.

Henry IV

Pirandello
Wyndham's Theatre
Daily Mail, 25th May 1990

Richard, king of the West End

We heard the rumours. We read the signs of early mortality. We intoned the roll-call of the dear departed directors, designers and co-stars. Yet the news this morning is that Mr Richard Harris and company look as live, as well and as triumphant as any proclaimed disaster has a right to be. This is a performance of mesmerising charisma which stalks danger and holds us spellbound.

Pirandello's hero is, for those many who have never seen the play performed, a study in that fine line between madness and bleak reality. Taking part in a carnival, dressed as the obscure Holy Roman Emperor Henry IV, the man's horse threw him and cracked his skull. For 20 years he has lived as the despotic 11th Century monarch. And only when the ghosts of his real past appear to try to confront his obsession and draw him from the comfort of madness does Pirandello strip away the many masks which hide the true face beneath.

Harris embraces all these difficult concepts with a rare attack which makes each complexity painfully clear. Rouged, painted and raddled like a carved clown, he nevertheless reveals exactly who pulls the strings at his puppet court – while all the time allowing us to glimpse the innate watchfulness lurking behind the hollow eyes.

Isla Blair, Ian Hogg and Harold Innocent are consummate in their support. But Harris holds the stage. His sudden weary acceptance of his own charade is a blinding moment of theatrical magic, making us long to see his Lear and regret his years away from the London stage.

Valley Song
Athol Fugard
Royal Court Theatre
***Daily Mail*, 7th September 1990**

A deceptively potent play

For one, no for several stricken moments, I feared that Athol Fugard, for so long the voice of South African Liberal Conscience, had lost his sure, unerring touch.

This newest play from his pioneering Market Theatre of Johannesburg started in so simple a fashion it began to seem uncomfortably simplistic.

A black township boy and a visiting bright white girl confront each other in a school debate. Their arguments, impassioned with youth, are confined to the usual awkward conventions of the issue under discussion.

The uncertain realities of the melting pot future into which their country is now plunging headlong appeared far removed from the joy with which the boy's benign teacher brings them together to join forces – poor black and privileged white – in a national school quiz on English literature.

Byron, Wordsworth, Shelley and Masefield are all blithely quoted at length. Indeed, it takes practically all of one act before a single note of racial confusion has been struck.

Yet this is, of course, all part of Fugard's masterly master plan. A vivid means to illustrate in one easy lesson, on the one hand, the irrelevance of high-flown, far-off English education for a people struggling to find an identity of their own, and, on the other, the magic potency of the English language without which their cause could well be lost.

Starkly staged, and with three vivid performances to illuminate its theme, the play becomes a fascinating see-saw debate in itself. And one of almost unbearable poignancy and perception.

That marvellous actor John Kani has seldom been seen to better effect than as the good-hearted township teacher hoping to heal wounds with words but finding human passions too strong to be turned aside with speeches.

When he burns the flyleaf in the book that has been the cornerstone of his lifelong creed and goes out to meet his accusers and certain death, it is a moment of heart-stopping theatre. For it contains all the cruel contradictions and complexities which have turned black against black and white against white in that poor, benighted country.

Sterling support comes from Fugard's own daughter Lisa and Rapulana Seiphemo as the bewildered pupils caught up in the crossfire of racial conflicts in this deceptively potent play.

The Madness of George III

Alan Bennett
RNT Lyttelton
Daily Mail, **29th November 1991**

Long live this king, brought to life by our prince among playwrights

Obviously encouraged by his exquisite miniature portrait of the present Queen in his previous stage play, Mr Bennett now applies his sense of artistic and historical insight to a far larger canvas. And, to my mind, scores a proportionately greater dramatic success.

The madness of George III has hitherto been one of the enduring popular jokes of British history. We are inclined to remember only that he lost America as well as his mind.

What Mr Bennett achieves with a consummate sense of theatre is in making this remote, ambiguous monarch a character totally accessible to a modern audience. At once a fascinating figure of both tragedy and heroism. True, his tragedy is not on the scale of King Lear's – in spite of the parallels neatly pointed up as he recuperates from this, his first crippling bout of illness.

George III suffered neither from self-induced madness nor any abandonment of his duties. His tragedy was brought about by the accidents of genes and the cruel quackery of his doctors.

His heroism was in enduring the barbaric treatment inflicted upon him by medical ignorance and political expediency. Porphyria, as we now know, and here Mr Bennett imparts with his only clumsy move of the entire evening, is a hereditary metabolic imbalance which induces symptoms of madness.

Yet we hardly needed to know even this, so vividly does director Nicholas Hytner in this masterly production draw all the strands of this confusing history together in one brilliant tapestry.

Moreover, Nigel Hawthorne's performance shines out as its focal point like the light and dark sides of the Moon. We watch this upright, bluff and dutiful sovereign crumble physically and mentally, and with the loss of his own sense of identity and dignity so the whole fabric of the State begins to unravel. He takes us on a painful and piteous journey to the other side of human endurance.

Of course, being a piece by Mr Bennett, comedy is never far away. There is much to chortle over. The miracle and the humanity of the evening is, however, that we do not laugh at poor mad George.

Our laughter is directed at the opportunists and idiots sucked into the vacuum he threatens to leave. Not least of these, of course, is the posturing Prinny (Michael Fitzgerald) about who I suspect no play of this depth will ever be written. There are, too, sympathetic and telling roles, notably from Janet Dale as his devoted queen and Daniel Flynn as his equally concerned equerry.

The Sea
Edward Bond
RNT Lyttelton
Daily Mail, **13th December 1991**

At last, kiss of life for comedy gem saved from a watery grave

Almost 20 years ago – it seems only two decades – I hailed Edward Bond's first foray into comic drama as 'a lasting achievement.' Such is the power of the pen, such is the awe in which we pundits are held by craven producers that the play has not seen the inside of a major London theatre since.

Not only did *The Sea* sink without trace, but one now feels obliged to explain exactly who Edward Bond is to the youngsters of today – i.e. anyone under forty. So imagine how grateful one is to the infant Sam Mendes (a gurgling child of 25) for so speedily jumping on to the bandwagon I feared had got stuck in the mud of time.

Although his production is occasionally a little uncertain and unfocused, and some of his cast show signs of being themselves slightly at sea, the play has a life force all its own. It is bold, bizarre and yet for all its wildness oddly benign.

To describe it as a comedy, of course, is to wrong-foot the unwary. Mr Bond, as has always been his humour, is dealing with such rib-tickling subjects as death, madness and the class system.

The play begins with a drowning and ends with the healing benediction of two young people making a new life. Behind them, among the flotsam of wrecked dreams and a nightmare funeral, they leave a murderously crazed haberdasher (Ken Stott) who would rather believe his life is ruled by aliens from outer space than by the real enemy within the gate – the crushing hierarchy of small town life.

At its formidable pinnacle is Dame Judi Dench, strangely uncomfortable in a role which calls out for hauteur of unassailably high camp. It should be as unthinkable as the rape of a nun that the draper should raise his shears in anger against her. However, when called upon to show this impossible matron's human face, Dame Judi is matchless. And as the two innocents who redeem everything she presides over simply by falling in love, Sam West, with his *Boys' Own* profile, and Sarah Woodward, with her brave dimpling smile, shine out with honest truth. Everything Mr Bond and we could wish, even if we had to wait so long.

An Inspector Calls

J B Priestley
RNT Lyttelton
Daily Mail, **12th September 1992**

Case of the play that came back to life

This is how a Royal National Theatre earns its laurels. This is how a musty, dust-laden classic is polished and reset to blaze like a new gem in the crown of our cultural heritage.

You may gather from this that I cannot speak too highly of Stephen Daldry's monumental expressionist reworking of the play so many of us had come to view as a cosy pot-boiler, a sop to the conscience.

What this timely production does so superbly is to restore the savage heart of its rage against social injustice. When it was first produced (in Moscow in 1945) it needed no such help. The world was already seething with the desire to right wrongs and trample the old class barriers. Gradually, however, the play has dwindled into a curio.

Until now.

Five members of one smug, middle-class family are confronted by a mysterious inspector about their involvement in the death of a working class girl who, by the standards of the day, was no better than she should be.

Director Daldry makes us look on all this with fresh eyes. There is an altogether filmic quality even in the ragged little lad trying vainly to raise the heavy plush red curtains to get inside the play itself. When they rise they reveal a wasteland of gas-lit cobbled streets surrounding an ornate Edwardian mansion of doll's-house dimensions.

Inside are the family congratulating their own good fortune while the boy peers in and the rain pours down.

It is this sense of Them and Us which illuminates the whole play. Kenneth Cranham's angry, antagonistic inspector never sets foot in that opulent haven. Instead, the house splits apart and the family are forced to descend on to the wet streets for their grilling.

When all their pretences are stripped away and they are utterly humiliated, the house itself tips up, spilling all its valuables on to the street around them. It is at this moment, I suspect, Jack Priestley himself would have stood up in the stalls and shouted Hosanna to the echo. For I do not think Ian MacNeil's setting swamps the play's strong characters. This splendid cast, with Richard Pasco and Barbara Leigh-Hunt heading the fallible family with the kind of pride that searches out its own fall, does not miss one heartbeat of the play's human dilemmas.

I had thought never again to see this play with a feeling other than sufferance. Now I simply want to rush back as if to rediscover a masterpiece.

No Man's Land
Harold Pinter
Almeida Theatre
Daily Mail, **3rd November 1992**

What a flop in Pinter land

To have Harold Pinter step into one of the two leading roles in his own play can be counted a resounding coup, even by the standards of the tiny Almeida Theatre, which seems to deal only in this theatrical currency. Unfortunately coups, like fireworks on Guy Fawkes Night, have a nasty habit of exploding in the hand. Certainly, Mr Pinter's presence here has the effect of singeing a great many hitherto raised highbrows.

I have long suspected that there was a great deal less to this play than met the ear. And here is the author himself to prove so.

It was written almost 20 years ago, just before we all realised that Pinter had pitched headlong into self-parody.

The justly celebrated duet between those two matchless knights, Gielgud and Richardson, swept the piece along at such a dizzying pace.

By contrast, Mr Pinter in the role of the rich, inebriate man of letters which Sir Ralph made so memorable, perversely reveals nothing of the mercurial mood changes, mystery or menace on which the piece must fly or die... he pile-drives his own ambiguities into the ground. It is left to the mellifluous Paul Eddington, that most delicately subtle of actors and a worthy successor to Sir John, to breathe much-needed real life into this jaded old joke. To see him like some crumpled, startled eaglet testing out the territory into which he has unaccountably strayed is a joy.

Arcadia
Tom Stoppard
RNT Lyttelton
Daily Mail, **14th April 1993**

Another lesson in whining and conceit at the knee of too clever Mr Stoppard

Mr Tom Stoppard is a man who has never worn diligence lightly. If he knows it, then we must learn it. So it is no surprise to those of us who have sat previously at his knee, so to speak, for the mysteries of quantum physics or the minutiae of Lenin's journey back to Russia to be revealed unto us, that he should now turn his avid attention to a subject on which he is amply qualified to occupy over three hours of our time: research.

Nominally, his latest work revolves around two of the more thrustingly arrogant academics (Felicity Kendal and Bill Nighy) locking egos in rival theories on Byron. The self-seeking Mr Nighy imagines he has unearthed some hitherto undiscovered love letters from the noble poet – a notion any literary scholar who has glanced through Henry James's *Aspern Papers* will recognise as by no means new.

However, Stoppard's story unravels on two levels – at once giving the true dramatic account of what occurred in the stately home in Byron's time and who actually wrote those letters, and also showing modern literary sleuths mistaking most of the evidence in the archives. A clever enough device. But, alas, Mr Stoppard cannot resist making it too clever by about two-and-three-quarters.

One comes away instructed by more than one can usefully wish to know on the theories of advanced 'mathematics of deterministic chaos,' which apparently have smashed Isaac Newton's poor fumblings to smithereens.

They have something to do with us all ending up at room temperature. But don't quote me on this.

However, it is Mr Stoppard's whim to have an 18th century aristocratic girl hit upon this revolutionary theory and then disprove it by being incinerated in her room. I forgive him this conceit only because of the dazzling performance it produces from Emma Fielding.

There is, it must be said, some equally fine acting to match it. Rufus Sewell's smouldering sexuality alone is a good reason why this forward young lady's libidinous tutor should have his antics confused with Byron's. Harriet Walter's imperious Regency *Grande Dame*, too, is a marvellous creation. Kendal and Nighy are joined by the impressive Samuel West in trying to fathom out their tangled lives.

Trevor Nunn directs with great reverence yet skilfully manages not to let the generations bump into each other when they share the stage.

David Hare's Trilogy: Racing Demon, Murmuring Judges, An Absence of War
RNT Olivier
Daily Mail, 8th October 1993

Awesome experience in this sad old world

David Hare's marathon three-part basilisk eye-view on the British establishment as it moves through the Nineties may not be the most important watershed some have claimed in terms simply of theatre.

Only the first piece, *Racing Demon* is, to my mind, a truly moving and important drama in its own right. Yet, taken as a whole, it is a profoundly bleak and disturbing chronicle of our times. For it paints an all too cogent picture of a society spiritually lost, morally bankrupt and politically bereft.

Like Shaw, Hare is more concerned with issues and ideas, sometimes at the expense of character. He is also, at times, overly concerned with hard facts, often to the detriment of pace. But these are flaws which should not blind us to the powerful message contained in its entirety.

It is, for example, a pause for grim thought that, despite the chronic overloading of our hard-pressed judicial system, only three per cent of all crimes actually reach the courts. Or so we are informed in *Murmuring Judges*, the second play. The ironic conclusion being that if the police were doing their jobs efficiently, the courts could not conceivably do theirs.

Personally, I doubt whether a High Court judge would be teasing a Tory Home Secretary with such damning statistics at a banquet for leading lawyers. But still it makes you think. I believe the argument, even if I can't credit the context.

Likewise, it is chilling to learn that if all those who died since 1914 fighting for this country were to parade past the Cenotaph on Remembrance Day, while the procession's head entered Whitehall, its tail would still be in Edinburgh. This is gleaned from the opening scene of his intriguing, if flawed, final work in *An Absence of War* – not as you might expect an investigation into our military but into the Body Politic.

Who knows how he arrived at this remarkable fact. No matter. It is a powerful image when used at the Remembrance Service with the Queen, her Church, her Government and loyal Opposition solemnly in attendance. It is also a potent reminder that politics is not a game played out by two or three competing teams to see who gets past the winning post first. It is, quite literally, a matter of life and death – yours and mine.

For this reason I approved of *An Absence of War* more than I liked it, just as I had with *Murmuring Judges*. There is something deeply troubling, even rotten, eating away at both our systems of law and order and of government. As with the established Church, the subject of *Racing Demon*, they are each suffering a crisis of conscience – or lack of it.

And these three plays are at pains to make us sit up and take heed of what, in our hearts, most of us are already aware.

Yet, curiously, it is in the area of religion, about which I suspect he is least concerned, that he moves us most. In the battle between Richard Pasco's autocratic bishop, vainly trying to shore up the old standards, and Oliver Ford Davies' beleaguered, ineffectual rector battling with his faith, he shows an even-handed, even haunting compassion, which is sadly missing from the remaining two despite his robust commitment.

Of these, the last is the most humane and dramatically believable. It is a virtual re-run of the Labour Party's last election campaign, with only the names changed to protect the vanquished. With victory in sight, Hare's Left-Wing hero is finally deemed unelectable.

Not on his policies. Certainly not on the popularity of the tired and tottering Tory Government. But, finally, because of a marketing cock-up. A failure of the human spirit to match the packaged image.

John Thaw, cocky, loquacious, overprotected by well-meaning sycophants, betrayed by over-ambitious colleagues, gives a memorably touching account of a good man at bay. A decent man in a profession which has ceased to know the very meaning of the word.

Director Richard Eyre has marshalled all three into an impressive stage epic, visually enriched by Bob Crowley's splendid cinematic sets. And a cast as fine as any to appear on the stage of the Royal National Theatre give the plays an added gravitas and spice.

As usual, each one contains a Hare heroine whose presence is the keynote of the drama – variously Saskia Wickham as the agnostic voice of conscience in *Demon*, Alphonsia Emmanuel as the radical barrister in *Judges* and Clare Higgins as the acceptable face of PR in *Absence*.

But it is the combatants who win the plaudits – most notably Richard Pasco and Michael Bryant in all three and John Thaw in the last.

A brave day in a sad old world.

Medea

Euripides
Wyndham's Theatre
***Daily Mail*, 21st October, 1993**

Watch it! This majestic Medea will curl the toes

Here is the crowning role of Diana Rigg's career thus far, the performance which has restored her to the very summit of her own hyper-achieving generation of actresses. You have not seen a wife's pain at her husband's faithlessness, nor a mother's love turned to the most unnatural act by insupportable grief, nor even a woman's lust for revenge, until you have witnessed Miss Rigg's towering, unsurpassable Medea. It is at once both awesomely majestic in its classical control and terrifyingly moving in its raw modernity. Which is exactly as it should be.

For although Euripides' play is more than 2,000 years old, and his heroine comes from the mists of even more ancient mythology, he gave both it and her a subversive subtext which 20th century feminists have eagerly embraced.

Not to put too fine a point on it, her two-timing husband (Tim Woodward) is nothing better than a smug schmuck. He may be Jason of the Argonauts, the shining captor of the Golden Fleece. But she knows – and we know – that he wouldn't have made it around the nearest fish pond if she hadn't committed the most ruthless acts of family treachery to save his Greek bacon. When he proposes to cast her aside to marry the bimbo daughter of Corinth's king, Miss Rigg takes us through all the emotional somersaults of a woman scorned – but on a scale so heightened it fairly curls the toes.

We first see her on Peter J Davison's massive set of rusting steel plates, 'slumping into grief' as her faithful nurse (Madge Ryan) puts it in Alistair Elliot's sparklingly colloquial new translation. Her back towards us, she nevertheless radiates a force gathering strength to erupt like a volcano.

And though we are always apprised of her terrible blood-letting schemes to kill her rival and murder her own children, the manner in which Miss Rigg cajoles, wheedles and dupes her way behind her enemies' macho self-regard is breathtaking to behold.

Hers is no idle boast when she admits to being clever. It is a lethal intelligence at work, and when she claims supernatural powers from her grandfather, the sun – boy, you'd better believe her.

Jonathan Kent's production transfers from the tiny Almeida stage to fill Wyndham's with resounding splendour. Even the scenery reverberates with the sound of her fury.

Playing a mere one and a half hour without interval, it pins you to your seat by its power and leaves you wrung out with pity, horror and wonder when you leave.

When the play was first performed, it was voted, by popular voice, last of the twelve plays on offer. I can only think it lacked Miss Rigg to make its message clear.

DIANA RIGG

I was very fond of Jack. I think it was very important to him that the theatre reached people, that it was not considered an intellectual pursuit by an elite who could afford the tickets. His writing, for the most part, bore that out.

Years ago I compiled a book of bad reviews, entitled *No Turn Unstoned*. I read the work of a large number of critics and subsequently, out of sheer interest, I have continued to look at reviews.

Jack's writing was highly accessible. It communicated his excitement about theatre wonderfully well. For perhaps the first time, the person emerged, it was less Olympian than critics had been hitherto. In that sense Jack pioneered a whole school of criticism, largely single-handed.

When Jack wrote bad notices, it was never perverse. I speak for all actresses when I say that any bad review is devastating, because it is a public dressing-down, which millions of people read. Yet Jack always stayed true to the performance he had seen, one never felt that he brought personal prejudices to bear.

Moonlight

Harold Pinter
Comedy Theatre
Daily Mail, **5th November 1993**

I called it great. Now I second that emotion

A daunting thing, to walk into a West End theatre and see, suspended below the title, the judgement: 'A Great Play.' Even more daunting to recognise your own name as that uncompromising arbiter.

Well, yes. I did say *Moonlight* was a great play when first seen at the little Almeida Theatre in Islington. And now, having seen it again, I insist it is still so, only more so. No other Pinter play has moved me so much. No play he has written has come so close to the raw knuckle of human emotion.

If you miss this, then you miss the entire heartbeat of the first full-length work he has penned in over 15 years.

To be honest, it moved me to tears. Nothing you ever expect to confess at a Pinter play. A second viewing does not stem the emotion, but it gives one the chance to analyse why it smacks so close to home.

Basically it is about something I find utterly inexplicable yet disturbingly understandable: the total rejection of a parent by its offspring.

It is, in fact, a searing heartcry from a dying father to his family, and particularly to his sons. They, in their turn, have already made their judgement on him. They have rejected everything he has ever upheld.

This you know by the contrast, simply, of the two beds set side by side on an otherwise bare stage. One, pristine and antiseptic, is the deathbed on which Ian Holm lies ranting.

Beside him sits Anna Massey, cool enough to give cucumbers a bad name for overheating.

Between them, these two extraordinary actors stake out the retrospective ground rules of a marriage which has given neither joy, but both an interest.

In the other, rumpled, bed lies one of the absent dropped-out sons (Michael Sheen) playing elaborate word games with his protective yet combative brother (Douglas Hodge).

The formula is pure Pinter. Yet the undertow is genuine heartbreak. What you clamour to know is what Pinter is saying about that dark chasm which so often divides father and son.

David Leveaux's direction of this superlative cast loses none of its mysterious acerbity in transferring to a larger, more formal theatre. And both Ian Holm and Anna Massey convey inner hurts it is impossible to describe.

Only go and you will see.

The Skriker

Caryl Churchill
RNT Cottesloe
Daily Mail, **4th February 1994**

Deadly tug-of-war between evil and innocence

There are fairies at the bottom of Caryl Churchill's garden. This must come as a profound shock to those who have come to admire her for such down-to-earth works as *Cloud Nine*, *Top Girls* or *Serious Money*.

But there has always been a kind of sensuous spirituality about Ms Churchill's writing. And by golly, does she give it full rein in this strange, hypnotic and almost wilfully obtuse concoction of dance and drama.

She seems to be warning us that the evil in the world springs from ancient spirits who hang about trying to gain possession of our souls. Rather like scruffy squatters, but a great deal more troublesome to evict.

To anyone who comes from Lancashire a skriker is someone who cries a great deal. To my amazement this is not entirely unrelated to the ominous presence at the heart of Ms Churchill's play. For we learn that a skriker is a shape-shifter, the elusive portent of death wandering the woods and uttering piercing shrieks.

A role seized upon by that most febrile and shape-shifting actress, the award-winning Kathryn Hunter who stalks her hapless human prey in various guises of an ancient lunatic crone, a svelte Californian bar-fly, a clamorous lost child, or an importunate bag lady.

Her victim is a sad woman (Sandy McDade) already incarcerated in an asylum for murdering her own baby and a skriker's natural prey. Into the frame comes her gentle friend (Jacqueline Defferary) innocently awaiting the birth of her own child.

Against a background of eerily insistent music (Judith Weir) and movement (Ian Spink) the piece becomes a deadly tug-of-war between evil and innocence.

The Editing Process

Meredith Oakes
Royal Court Theatre
Daily Mail, **3rd November 1994**

From Sixties roots, Oakes grows mighty

Fashions, be they in clothes, writing or politics, tend to go in 30-year cycles. And while we are busy heaping blame for all the sickness of today's society on the Sixties, kids are wearing the clothes of the era, writers are echoing its pre-occupations, and an overtired, discredited Government is sinking up to its backside in sleaze.

Meredith Oakes, a new writer with a powerful voice, sounds to me to be beginning almost exactly where such dissimilar writers of the Sixties as Joe Orton and Edward Bond left off.

Hers is a savage satirical world where the meek inherit nothing and are even tricked out of their redundancy pay.

Her polished and eloquent play is set in the fast-disappearing world of the small literary magazine, a symbol, surely, of that eccentric English enterprise and national identity which has been all but crushed under the accountants' jackboot of the market economy.

Abruptly relocated from the faded grandeur of their old home, the small, fractious team which produced the idiosyncratic *Footnotes in History* are swallowed up in the giant march of corporate takeover.

Ian MacNeil's revolving set of curved post-modernist glass creates its own impact of alienation. It is, however, director Stephen Daldry and his superlative cast who bring Miss Oakes' intriguing, if slightly unfocused work to such strong and vibrant life.

As did Orton, she has her figure of unimpeachable moral integrity, the splendid Prunella Scales. A figure of dowdy heroism, she represents the last vestige of loyalty and decency in their beleaguered little world. And she is its first victim.

Alan Howard, reinventing the impressive authority which made him such a force in the RSC, gives the tinpot tyrant a saving note of humanity when he, too, is crushed underfoot by unworthy foes.

Chief of these is the Ortonesque Tom Hollander, a wonderfully unlikely sex object who exploits his ambidexterity in this department with a combination of knowing innocence and rapacious ambition.

A heartening sign that social passion is once more alive and kicking where it is best served and seen.

Three Tall Women

Edward Albee
Wyndham's Theatre
***Daily Mail*, 16th November 1994**

Enriched by Dame Maggie's old age tension

Edward Albee's new play has rightly re-established him at the forefront of contemporary American drama. At its diamond-hard and multifaceted heart, it has a searing glimpse of old age in all its many raw humiliations, its defiant outrage and its wasted regrets.

It is written from Albee's own bitterness at the domineering society beauty who adopted him, never hid her disappointment in that bargain, and disowned him. It also has, in this lavishly staged production, a towering central performance from one of our greatest actresses, whose talents have never burned brighter. And when one considers that we are talking Dame Maggie Smith here, this is no light claim.

She dominates the entire first half of the play, which is as it should be and in no way prepares us for the *coup de théâtre* Mr Albee has in store for the second. In this preparatory act, Dame Maggie delivers herself of a blow-by-blow account of the indignities heaped upon the aged as one by one their senses slip away... Head darting like a sparrow in search of worms, Dame Maggie captures all that birdlike energy which surprisingly comes with extreme frailty.

Watched over by a kind companion (Frances de la Tour) and wasp-tongued young legal assistant (Anastasia Hille), she rages against the dying of the light as the old have every right to do. It is a performance of immeasurable magnificence and great humour. Without asking for our sympathy, she moves one to admiration, laughter and profound pity.

The second act is much more evenly balanced. With the matron struck down by a stroke, the three tall women gather at the bedside to check on their collective memories.

Miss de la Tour, at 52, is the ghost of her prime. Disillusion has hardened her into an elegant cynicism. Here, she comes into her distinctive own and gives the Dame a good run for the honours. The glitter of her sharp wit is already preparing us for the lethal-tongued matriarch who lies in bed waiting for death.

Dame Maggie, meanwhile, released from the physical strictures of extreme old age, conducts the case for the defence. How did these women come to be the unloved old crones so cruelly cheated of a decent ending? 'I will never become either of you!' cries Miss Hille, aghast at their revelations... I wish the performance carried some hope that she might not. It is, ironically, Dame Maggie who absolves this unhappy creature from our damnation with a second-act performance of subtlety and human understanding. This she does without ever once compromising Albee's unforgiving view of a life which was basically meaningless, yet which he renders endlessly fascinating.

What The Butler Saw

Joe Orton
RNT Lyttelton
***Daily Mail*, 3rd March 1995**

Orton's timeless tour de farce

The early loss of Joe Orton to the British theatre, almost 30 years ago now, must be mourned whenever one of his sublime, subversive comedies is revived. He was a unique comic voice which has never been replaced. Yet mourning is the very last of one's inclinations as the Royal

National Theatre turns this, his last completed masterwork, into an exhilarating, celebratory hallelujah to the art of high comic farce.

Phyllida Lloyd's fast and furiously-paced production demonstrates Orton has mastered the art of packing more polished gems of genuine wit into one fleeting exchange than any other writer of his age, or since.

The plot is astonishingly crafted, the dialogue glitters with malevolent glee. This is Wilde on speed, Coward on cocaine, Sheridan on a trip. Yet he obeys all the rules of classic farce.

'There is a perfectly rational explanation for all that has taken place,' the unctuous John Alderton tells his would-be secretary after she has had all her hair cut off and clothes removed and been declared insane subsequent to the innocent admission of her shorthand proficiency.

And indeed there is. Orton was taking the psycho-babble of modern psychiatry and – there always being method in any madness he chose to perpetrate – wickedly proving that every human act can be given an ominous Freudian diagnosis.

The result, played here by Ms Lloyd's splendidly fortissimo cast, is hilarious mayhem.

Alderton's descent from assured social smugness to crumpled and crazed incoherence as Richard Wilson's barking (literally) mad Inspector of Insane Establishments runs amok in his asylum is an object lesson to any farceur. So too is Wilson's utter, unblinking belief in his own sanity against all evidence.

But every character on stage being equally convinced of his, or her, own story as the world proceeds to go mad around them is the central joy of this glorious revival.

Nicola Pagett as the predatory wife, Debra Gillett as the hapless typist, David Tennant's beanpole bellboy of rapaciously ambivalent sexuality, Jeremy Swift as the solid constable, all have their marvellous moments as the confusion of cross-dressing and mistaken identity dizzy into the play's artfully classic denouement.

Taking Sides
Ronald Harwood
Criterion Theatre
Daily Mail, 4th July 1995

A taut and timely tug-of-war with the mental muscle to pull us apart

To say that the West End today is devoid of plays which challenge the heart, fuel the intellect or strike a blow for humanity is to ignore the evidence. And high among this contemporary roll of honour must come Ronald Harwood's most marvellous human tug-of-war with our collective conscience. Mr Harwood's play flexes intellectual muscle in every other line. It fizzes with the passion of intrinsic human justice.

And it poses questions which will reverberate in the mind for a great deal longer than it took to give this splendid company their due ovations.

The play itself deals with the post-war interrogation of the internationally-acclaimed German conductor, Wilhelm Furtwangler.

His crime was that he stayed on in Nazi Germany while other artists left. And though he undoubtedly helped Jewish colleagues to escape, the simple and damning question, repeatedly hurled at him throughout this fascinatingly constructed character analysis, is: why did he remain an honoured and protected citizen of Hitler's abhorrent regime – though never a party member?

Harwood holds the scales of justice with considerable and commendable dexterity. And Harold Pinter's extraordinary, taut and compelling production gives all his arguments full value.

Indeed, Daniel Massey's extraordinarily hypnotic performance as the harangued maestro is a master class in the art of shifting an audience's emotions. His face, from the moment he enters, is etched with every line of his character's history. A great autocrat, a great artist, a great intellect and yet a man of human frailty.

It is on this latter weakness that Michael Pennington's gloatingly philistine inquisitor plays. And while all our cultural refinement is claimed by Massey, the gnawing gut doubts which prejudice breeds are insidiously fed by Pennington's justifiable passion.

There are exquisitely observed subsidiary roles used to build up the conflict from Christopher Simon, Gawn Grainger and Geno Lechner.

And there is one thing I promise you: whichever side of the argument you come out believing, you will have revised it a dozen times by the time you reach home. A powerful and provoking piece at a time when we are all re-examining our attitudes to the last war.

The Hothouse
Harold Pinter
Chichester Festival Theatre
Daily Mail, 23rd August 1995

Suddenly it all ends, not with a bang but a Pinter

When an author wheels on a totally new character in the dying moments of any play simply to resolve its tangled events, two things inevitably occur to me.

First, he must have become quite desperate to end the thing. Secondly, what on earth has the poor actor been doing for the preceding two acts?

Certainly not sitting down in this case, judging by the immaculate cut and press of Mr Peter Blythe's business suit.

But, there you are; see how distracting these superfluous entrances can be. Already it threatens to eclipse serious consideration of this curious venture into black comedy thriller-writing by Harold Pinter. An event made even more auspicious by his own appearance in the leading role. So, one assumes, he must have been quite proud of the result.

Well, even that is open to debate, for he wrote the play in 1958 and kept it locked away for 22 years. It was produced at Hampstead 15 years ago, transferred briefly to the West End and has never been heard of since in mainstream theatre.

One can see why, despite Peter Jones's polished, taut and immaculate direction and some perfectly splendid performances, not least by Mr Pinter himself as the strutting manic military chappie in charge of some mysterious clinic.

We are present on the brink of an unnamed cataclysmic event. One patient has died; another become pregnant. Mr Roote, Pinter's tetchily insecure medical director, is plainly unbalanced.

Strangely, however, for a play written at the very flowering of Pinter's gift for combining menace with black comedy, these two forces emerge only intermittently with real conviction.

Undoubtedly the mood of comic terror works best when played out between Pinter's own increasingly barking-mad colonel and Tony Haygarth's shamelessly insouciant know-all lush.

But as I said, having tossed them all into the melting pot of subliminal violence, Pinter seems at a curious loss as to how or why to fish them out. The audience also seemed quite astonished that the play had ended so abruptly. So, I suspect, was the author.

John Gabriel Borkman
Ibsen
RNT Lyttelton
Daily Mail, 12th July 1996

Talented trio who turn farce into a gripping family affair

The conflict of emotions which brought me to the theatre last night can only be imagined by a recovering schizophrenic. There was, on the one hand, the prospect of seeing three of the most admired actors on the stage of the Royal National Theatre from which their prolonged absence can only be counted a national scandal.

But then to see them in a play which, from the time I first discovered its rabid preposterousness, thanks to the actorly histrionics of the late

Sir Donald Wolfit, I have beheld like Oscar Wilde contemplating the death of Little Nell.

Could such confusions be born? Well, thanks to director Richard Eyre and the uncompromising talents of Vanessa Redgrave, Paul Scofield and Eileen Atkins, yes. It most resoundingly could.

Possibly for the first time, I gazed on this fractured, dysfunctional family of the unbelievable old fraudster, J G Borkman, and instead of stifling giggles I fought back tears.

Scofield gives Borkman's monstrous self-absorption a very human face. The believable son of a miner, his voice has a sepulchral tone, at once coarse yet carefully modulated as if speaking an alien tongue. While he paces the ballroom above, Vanessa Redgrave and Eileen Atkins fight out a bitter sibling battle over the past and the future down below.

Miss Atkins' arid, drained need to possess is pitted against Miss Redgrave's implacable capacity for understanding. It is a play in itself. But it is when Redgrave confronts Scofield with his greatest betrayal that I knew any resistance was breached.

'To enter a human heart and then destroy it!' she cries out, appalled at his betrayal of her. And then the tears came unbidden. You know you are defeated.

The entire production is on this high plateau of performance. Not least Felicity Dean's seductive Mrs Wilton, the exotic bird of paradise in the nest. For an actor to dominate a scene in such company is a personal triumph indeed.

Shopping and F£££king

Mark Ravenhill
Royal Court Theatre Upstairs, Ambassadors Theatre
Daily Mail, 4th October 1996

A compelling new voice to be heard...

Speaking of blood and guts, those blessed with iron-lined stomachs and a strong social conscience should hurry to the Royal Court's Theatre Upstairs, in exile at the Ambassadors. There, a compelling new voice is to be heard. Mark Ravenhill's debut play may bear the seemingly frivolous title *Shopping and F£££ing*, but there is nothing trivial about its intent or its impact. It hits you like a punch in the solar plexus – or even lower below the belt.

It is a shocker in every sense of the word. But whereas I led the chorus of disapproval when the Royal Court staged Sarah Kane's now notorious *Blasted*, I can only applaud its courage in staging this dangerous and to some, offensive work. For the explicit (simulated) sexual acts, the pungency of the language, the darkness of the theme or the on-stage (equally simulated) vomiting cannot be found guilty of being gratuitous. Their purpose is to underline the bleak despair and the futility of the lives of the trio of lost youngsters blighted by their gnawing sense of inadequacy and displacement. They are at the mercy of a world which brutalises and blinds them to any moral imperative.

Ravenhill writes with a vivid comic undercurrent. His scenes where, in order to pay off a £3,000 drug debt, all they can think of selling is sex-line phone-ins, are both wickedly witty and shrewd. Yet he discloses an odd compassion for those whom life has abused and who, in turn, become abusers themselves, or self-selected victims.

His portrait of the doomed rent boy (a startlingly moving performance from Antony Ryding) is an extraordinarily judged insight into the appalling consequences of child abuse and, as such, raises the piece to a high moral tone.

Max Stafford-Clark's production explores all the play's contrasting moods and tones with a confident assurance; likewise, his excellent and convincing cast – Kate Ashfield, Andrew Clover, James Kennedy and a menacingly slimy Robin Soans, who, like Antony Ryding, touch their blurred, unfocused characters with a startling clarity.

Following its London staging, the production will tour extensively. Watch out for it.

STEPHEN DALDRY

Jack Tinker's relationship with the Royal Court was a long and loyal one; through many years he reported on work from the cutting edge to a readership not naturally suited to that work.

However, during my specific time as Artistic Director of the Royal Court, Jack, characteristically, was responsible for two very differing responses to new work.

In the case of Sarah Kane's *Blasted* (January 1995) Jack set off one of the most violent furores which a work of fiction has ever inspired. His now famous *This Disgusting Feast of Filth* piece, telephoned in to the *Daily Mail* from the call box in front of the theatre in Sloane Square, set off a Sarah Kane witch-hunt which took us all by surprise. We were quite literally besieged for about two weeks, with newsmen camped on the doorstep, invading our offices and telephoning at the rate of one a minute.

One year later, in January 1996, Jack attended Mark Ravenhill's *Shopping and Fucking* in the new Theatre Upstairs in the West End. It was a late night show beginning at 9.30; someone at the *Mail* had forgotten to tell him, so he turned up at 7pm sharp and had to wait around for two and a half hours before undergoing another two hours plus in the small theatre.

With a trip to Brighton still ahead of him, he waited for the actors to emerge to assure them that he had loved the play. The blaster of *Blasted* became one of the great admirers and supporters of *Shopping and Fucking*.

This turned out to be the last thing he ever reviewed at the Royal Court, and indeed one of the last plays he reviewed. Mark Ravenhill, its author, fittingly spoke at Jack's funeral. None of us will ever forget this unique critic, both larger and smaller than life.

4

THE BATTLE OF EDINBURGH

Leaflet lunacy on the frenetic Fringe

Daily Mail, 16th August 1985

Russell Harty is beckoning conspiratorially. 'Get a look at this,' he hisses, hardly daring to look himself. 'This' turns out to be a six-foot giantess, dressed in a genteel blue two-piece and gazing at us with the disapproving mask of a matronly Edinbourgoisie. Bolder inspection reveals it is indeed a mask – worn by some huge bloke in yet another desperate attempt to lure naive souls like Mr Harty and myself to savour the 101 delights nightly offered on the Edinburgh Fringe.

There are around 600 of them and only about half a dozen of us as the ritual *Meet the Media* party gets underway to plug another annual jamboree of youth and optimism in search of fame and fortune.

The heat of the chase is at flashpoint from the outset. Anyone who looks like a media person is pounced on, handed a leaflet and delivered of a line in sales talk.

The giantess is out of luck. Hampered by her plastic disguise and high heels she has neither the fast talk nor the fleet foot needed to make her kill. A girl with a purple straw hat and a winsome gap in her teeth is in first. 'We're a feminist group doing a show on the theme of patriarchy and capitalism and really letting them have it,' she informs me.

Mercifully, before a sudden rush of sympathy persuades me to ask for a ticket, Dr Jonathan Miller is paraded before us as living proof that one appearance at the Edinburgh Fringe can lead to a life of artistic and material fulfilment.

I don't get to hear his words of encouragement, however. A man representing a new Anglo-Canadian comic duo is earnestly assuring me that if I get to see their show a free bottle of beer awaits. I demur that it all sounds rather like payola. 'No. Straight bribery,' he beams.

Next an elfin-sized student tells me her group is putting on a play all about the experience of childbirth. She is followed by a nicely mannered young man here to promote a 'medieval fantasy set in an ordinary suburban house.'

I begin to feel very dizzy, although only one glass of wine has passed my lips during the whole two hours, mainly because both hands are full of leaflets. 'We are too poor to have leaflets,' a pretty girl tells me as if reading the thoughts behind my glazed eyes. 'But if you've got a pen, I've got a piece of paper you could write it all down on.' I point out that with both hands full I, unhappily, am in no position to write down even my own name.

Outside, the rain is sheeting down as I head for my hotel to try to make some sense out of all the information and the invitations. From the doorway a gaunt youth emerges to push yet another leaflet into my hands. 'The King, and Our Lord is here!' he whispers. Automatically I hear myself asking: 'Where and at what time?'

He is mortified. Sorry. But this is the Fringe. There are 600 shows and no time to be born again.

Fringe goes straight – now all the shocks and sensations have gone official

Daily Mail, 17th August 1989

On the surface, nothing seems to have changed. The streets are thronged with bizarrely-painted beings who, behind the carefully-coloured make-up, spend the rest of the year greyly studying law, shorthand or accountancy, like as not. Meanwhile, pavement artists watch their latest showers dribble away beneath the rivers of the latest shower.

This is Edinburgh and this is its annual festival. The three weeks of the year when John Knox gives way to the rule of Dionysus, Bacchus and the queues of patient tourists anxious to join the pagan rituals of outrageous arts. Two dogs mating in the street seem quite likely to qualify for an Arts Council grant.

Mr Steven Berkoff, that life-long baiter of Establishment bulls and smasher of sacred cows, is in typically fine lunchtime form. Rave reviews for his sensational, sensual production of Oscar Wilde's taunting tease stripper, *Salome*, a play banned from Britain's theatres in more corseted times, have in no way slaked his thirst for critics' blood.

Yes, he declares, he had meant his death threat to the *Guardian*'s acerbic Nicholas de Jongh 'very seriously indeed'. The hapless critic, we might recall, had to be given police protection when he innocently reviewed one of Mr Berkoff's plays with the ill-fated phrase 'fatally miscast.' Mr Berkoff now moderates his murderous impulses sufficiently to compare the breed to 'toilet rolls, sadists and faded old tarts'. Mr de Jongh, his host in this diverting public debate, gives as good as he gets.

We all agree that Edinburgh can still cut the mustard when it comes to controversy. Ah, but here's the rub. In other years, in other times, Mr Berkoff would have been the power in the very elbow of the Fringe, that mish-mash of a thousand unknown companies carpet-bagging their way to this Celtic capital in the hope of fame, fortune or, at least, a mention in the *Scotsman*. Berkoff was their champion, seen by prim insiders as Attila at the gates of theatrical respectability and by artistic rebels everywhere as their John the Baptist. More than their elbow, he was their knee in the groin of respectability.

The Fringe was always where the action was. But no, Mr Berkoff's vivid and erotically-stylised production of *Salome* for Dublin's talented Gate Theatre Company is today the hottest ticket of the Official Festival, not the Fringe. So hot that not even Joan Bakewell, surely no toilet roll, sadist or faded tart she, could come by a first-night ticket.

Likewise, that Brueghelesque Catalan company, Els Comediants, rending the city's crisp night air with astounding firework vision of exploding phalli and Spanish devil worship in *Dimones*, they too belong to the official Festival. The same with Glaswegian dramatist Iain Heggie, another born-again shocker whose battle cry against the corruptions of a market force economy ensure his latest play, *Clyde Nouveau*, is calculated to send the matrons of Morningside fleeing for refuge. This too is part of festival director Frank Dunlop's Official fare.

Mr Dunlop, it seems, has out-fringed the Fringe. Unthinkable 25 years ago when the sight of a nude woman at a student 'happening' brought Fringe and Festival to the verge of civil war. Now, it seems, the Cavaliers and Roundheads have reversed their roles.

Two factors have played into Dunlop's clever hands in achieving this small miracle. The first, of course, is the long-standing rivalry between Edinburgh and neighbouring Glasgow. The good burghers of Edinburgh have, in the past, made no secret of their mistrust of the likes of Mr Dunlop and his predecessors and have matched their feelings with grudgingly-mean grants.

For around half-a-million pounds investment they have enjoyed profits of between £30 million and £70 million, depending on whose analysis you rely on. Edinburgh grows fat on these three weeks when the eyes of the artistic world turn towards the Athens of the North. But now, with Glasgow having last month been designated by the European Commission as its Culture Capital of the World in 1990, they look to the festival to restore their glory. To this end they have upped the grant to £650,000 and given Mr Dunlop a three-year guarantee to enable ambitious forward planning.

Secondly, the Fringe itself has become victim to the market force economy so reviled by Iain Heggie. It now costs some £5,000 merely to rent two hours' prime acting space per day for the duration of the Fringe. To qualify for a place in the official Fringe brochure you will pay the best part of £200. Even if you are a one-person show, you still have to foot the bills for transport, publicity, costumes, scenery, plus food and shelter for you and your crew.

It is no carefree jaunt be assured. Not only are young dreams broken, bank balances take a hammering too. Small wonder then, that the Fringe is now a highly-competitive, highly-commercialised set-up. Where once aspiring young actors looked on the Fringe as an addition for London, it would seem today that London is simply the audition hall for the

Fringe. Established favourites are rewarded by the best spots and the longest queues.

In the quest for fresh discoveries I was drawn to an exotically-named trio, the Fabulous Singlettes, with upright beehive hairdos that looked as if they were permanently plugged into the mains. Just in time I saw blazoned across their advertising poster: 'Simply Unforgettable' – *News of the World*. Simply forget it.

Fringe stalwarts like Jeremy Hardy, Simon Fanshawe, the Frank Chickens, Roy Hutchins with Heathcote Williams' beautifully-delivered prose poems, et al, are by now all seasoned media figures. The Hull Truck Company, once the innovators of the Fringe, now the darlings of the West End, have this year settled for quantity rather than quality with, among many old standbys, the worst production of *Twelfth Night* I have ever seen.

This year the Fringe's only real headline grabber to cause the authorities any alarm is an amazing avant-garde French circus called, appropriately, *Archaos*, whose juggling with chainsaws has left a trail of their members dismembered throughout Europe. Predictably, their troupe of leather-thonged motorcyclists, bare-breasted high-wire artistes, and the demonstrative antics by men in tutus have left them open to indignant accusations of flagrant homosexuality and sado-masochism. But, in fact, their on-stage demeanour – disciplined and death-defying – makes the habits of the average goal-scoring soccer player look like an open incitement to Mary Whitehouse, by comparison.

Of course, the Fringe has always been a place where you will hear more obscene language in one week's pursuit of art than you will in a season following Millwall FC. Yet I defy you to find anywhere any more erotic or disturbing an experience than the scene Steven Berkoff has dreamt up for *Salome*'s fabled dance of the seven veils. Without removing so much as a shoe, actress Olwen Fouere mimes a climactic masterclass on the art of seduction. Only in Edinburgh, in August, could the act of keeping your clothes on seem so new and daring.

A rollicking week in the life of Auld Reekie
Daily Mail, 22nd August 1992

Truly I had no intention of featuring in the Festival's first – and to date only – public sex scandal. But I would like to put my side of the story. Indeed, I had resolved before leaving Gatwick to dip a toe ever so gently into the turbulent waters of the frantic Fringe instead of diving in at the deep end as in previous years.

A little light supper at the Café Royal with the redoubtable Liz Smith, den mother to the Press hordes who gather at the bustling Assembly

Rooms to catch up on first-day gossip and arrange my schedule. Then perhaps a late-night cabaret. That should keep me out of harm's way.

Alas, for such modest ambitions. You don't have to be the Duchess of York to discover toe dipping can lead to big trouble. The night had hardly begun before I had not only received (and refused) a highly compromising proposal from the largest black lady I have ever set eyes on, but also been shopped in the gossip column of a rival paper.

Shopped, furthermore, by the Old Harrovian son of a former Conservative minister. This, I like to think, says everything we have always known about ex-public schoolboys and proves that politicians really should spend more time with their family.

Unhappily, I cannot deny his account of the affair. It is as reported. Yes, Ms Thea Vidale, the outrageous No.1 hit of Festival 1992, did indeed espy me across a crowded room. Yes, she most certainly did unaccountably announce a graphically phrased desire to know me a great deal better. Yes, too, she is most definitely built like a cross between a Sherman tank and Tina Turner.

And emphatically Yes, I did decline her generous offer with the words:

'But my dear if you did that, I'd disappear.' I was however merely pointing out that the pairing would have been akin to Mr Magoo meeting King Kong's sister. It was not an example of lofty *sangfroid* as the *Independent* newspaper would have the world believe. Those words were uttered out of sheer terror.

Besides, we hadn't even been introduced.

Monday

Yesterday's events prove several things. Not least how slow news is up here this year. Already the cry has gone up among the hungry hacks: 'Come back Frank Dunlop – we are in serious need of a story.' The pixie-like Mr Dunlop was always good for a snappy quote. Indeed, he ended his stint as Festival Director making front page news and blasting the Fringe with a machine gun fire of headline grabbing epithets. This, I must add, came about after he had roused himself from his sick bed to entertain half a dozen of us to a lavish lunch at his home. It has now become Festival folklore. The champagne flowed, so did the director's tongue and our pens. Ah, those were the days.

No fear of that with his self-effacing successor, Mr Brian McMaster. He appeared this morning at his first official Press conference and managed to say nothing about almost everything the journalists wished to know.

What did he think about Richard de Marco – one of the Fringe's mega impresarios – describing his first official programme as the dullest in years? 'We'll just have to wait and see,' smiled Mr McMaster mildly. Clearly he needs a crash course in newshound handling.

Livelier by far is his conference co-star, the exotic American dancer and choreographer Mr Mark Morris. Mr Morris looks like a member of a heavy metal band but talks like the late Truman Capote. He is here to plug his latest dance creation *Dido and Aeneas*. It turns out that he himself will be dancing the two leading female roles.

'Why?' asks one puzzled female ballet critic. 'Because they have the best parts,' primps Mr Morris unashamedly.

It is pointed out that as he choreographed the piece, why couldn't he have beefed up *Aeneas* a bit? Mr Morris dismisses such conventional views with airy disdain.

'*Aeneas* is – you know – just a visiting cad,' he assures us.

Next he is pressed to give his views on being described as the '*enfant terrible* of American dance'. On this matter his language becomes quite as colourful as his compatriot Ms Vidale's – the colour being blue. 'Besides,' he adds huffily, 'I'm 35 and regard the description as most insulting.'

In order to recover a sense of civilised decorum I spend the afternoon at the Chaplaincy where Gwyneth Powell – formerly the upright headmistress in BBC TV's *Grange Hill* – is performing one of the best-kept secrets of the Fringe, *The Diary of a Provincial Lady*. It is adapted from E M Dellafield's best seller of the 1920s and brought to astonishing stage life.

This one-woman show deserves to be preserved as one of those shining gems and polished into a cult. It is, to my mind, *Shirley Valentine* played in a minor key.

The day ends with the Festival's inaugural production attended by so many familiar London faces it is almost like dining in The Ivy and Joe Allen's simultaneously. Susannah York is dressed entirely in interesting black, more in mourning for the actors on the stage, one suspects, than for her debut as the director of her own Fringe production.

Mr McMaster's attempts to resurrect the reputation of his two chosen playwrights, Harley Granville Barker and C P Taylor, seem on this showing doomed to bear out Richard de Marco's dire prophecies.

By midnight I am in desperate need of alternative comedy and discover an act called *Flacco*, which seems to have landed from another planet entirely.

Tuesday

Ms Vidale's vivid proposals by now have become notorious. People call out in the street, quoting her with embarrassing accuracy. I am asked to broadcast on Radio 4. The subject? What artistes will do to get a review in the Press. Even more than they will to find decent accommodation is the short answer to that.

There are 560 companies and more than 10,000 hopeful performers on the Fringe alone. Many a prudent resident makes a fine financial killing simply by moving out for the duration and surrendering their home for a fat profit.

Eleanor Bron, here for her delicious anthology, *Desdemona – If Only You Had Spoken*, was explaining to friends that she was actually staying in the house where John Knox lived.

She swears she was asked in all seriousness if he had moved out, too.

I take in five shows during the day. At one, named *The Misogynist*, six women walk out. At another called *Below the Belt* one woman vomits. In spite of this, I enjoy both hugely. Am I becoming play-dead so early in the week?

Wednesday

By now every surface of my hotel room is covered with leaflets. I try not to worry about the rainforests which must have been felled in the forlorn hope of trying to attract audiences to yet another student production of *Macbeth* or a one-woman show by a right-on Australian lesbian.

Mhairi Mackenzie-Robinson, the tirelessly cheerful administrator of the entire Fringe, tells me of the struggle they've just had trying to get the solitary Yugoslavian theatre company here intact.

They made it just in time for their opening night. But such matters are fairly routine in her busy schedule. And she is already deeply involved in planning next year's Fringe.

In the Festival Club I spy another willing refugee from the upheavals in Eastern Europe – no less a person than Ion Caramitrov, who for a brief time following the downfall of the Ceaucescus was Vice-President of Romania.

A dodgy career move, one would think, even for an actor. But he seems happier here with his company of eager young students and is pressing the Royal National Theatre's brilliant young director Declan Donnellan to visit his country and direct him in *Cyrano de Bergerac*. Mr Donnellan demurs modestly. 'You will sleep in the same bed the Ceausescus slept in!' the former Vice-President offers grandly.

Mr Donnellan is suddenly interested. I wonder if Mr Caramitrov has seen the astonishing production of the play at the Traverse, where audiences are being reduced to tears. But I do not voice this.

It would be churlish to do the chirpy Mr Donnellan out of his king-sized bed, especially when his production of *Fuente Ovejuna* enjoyed such a successful opening night the previous evening. Am I learning discretion at last? Only four shows to go before bedtime.

Thursday

Outside the Fringe office, a leaflet for the *National Youth Theatre*'s ambitious production of the musical *Billy* is pushed into my hand. 'If you come tonight, I think you might get to see Prince Edward,' the courteous young man promises. I figure the Royal Family have enough problems without me and my newly soiled reputation.

So I tell him that I have already promised the show's lyricist, Don Black, and its biggest fan, my friend Marti Webb, that I will pop in before the week is out. He seems satisfied.

I am beginning to look like the picture in the attic, I notice as I go into the Radio Forth studios to do a live link-up with Frank Bough of LBC. The phone calls are wall-to-wall about the Duchess of York. Frank has the nerve to ask me about Ms Vidale. It is a trifle difficult to do full justice to the full-frontal attack of her late-night show at the Dream Tent without getting us cut off the air. But I struggle through. I had plucked up courage to see her robustly explicit act last night – but skulked timidly behind a pillar. She is definitely worth every inch of her considerable cult status.

Friday

Even the Dorian Gray's picture in the attic could not look as I feel. These midnight cabarets are addictive, but like most such things, not wise. Especially after a day dodging from venue to venue, attic to cellar. Nor would I describe Lily Savage last night as exactly a cup of calming cocoa.

An improbable drag act, she is to Liverpool what Ms Vidale is to the Deep South. I was always brought up to believe in laughter as a healing, healthy thing. But these two on consecutive nights have done nothing to halt the ageing process.

Somehow, I have been persuaded to appear on radio this morning to confront an Australian woman who impersonates a bag lady on this vexed question of how artists get critics to review their shows. Am I to be haunted by this for the rest of my days?

Then, late in the day, I am booked for a TV spot to explain why I have said I feel that if the Fringe were suddenly to vanish there would be very little reason left to visit the Edinburgh Festival as it rumbles on to its 50th anniversary.

With a bit of luck I'll live long enough to catch the first plane out in the morning.

NICHOLAS DE JONGH

At one time I had the worst job in theatre criticism, being number two at the *Guardian*, which meant that I had to seek out some rather obscure shows. Jack loved to tell the story of one play that we attended in Edinburgh, when I was being very difficult and kept moving seats. Finally, when I got the one I wanted it collapsed.

However, that story was in retaliation for another time, also in Edinburgh. We were waiting for a production to begin, and there were two old ladies sitting just in front of us. I leaned forward to them and asked,

'Do you know who is sitting behind you?' This was when Jack was very famous. They looked, and demurely said, 'No.'

'Jack Tinker,' I told them grandly, 'The *Daily Mail* theatre critic is here. If you want, I could get you his autograph. Would you like it?'

Bemused, they repeated, 'No.'

I turned to Jack and loudly complained, "Did you hear that Jack? They don't even want your autograph!" He was not pleased.

Rare joys in such a soulless Festival

Daily Mail, 23rd August 1996

Professor George Steiner came in for a great deal of stick at the start of Edinburgh's annual arts jamboree. He dared to suggest in his opening lecture that after 50 years, the world's oldest and largest festival should think about re-inventing itself.

Truth to tell, as golden jubilees go, this year's festival could hardly be judged as glistening. There is an air of stagnation and self-satisfaction that is distinctly unhealthy.

As for drama, the official programme devised by Brian McMaster hardly smacks of exciting innovation, which should be the watchword – indeed the very reason – for any festival worthy of the name.

True, the works of Robert Lepage, Robert Wilson, Mark Morris and Peter Stein are never less than interesting. But they have become almost as permanent a fixture of the Edinburgh scene as the grandiose monument to Sir Walter Scott.

Discouragingly, it was the much publicised and disgraceful non-appearance of M. Lepage's one-man homage to *Hamlet* – 'for technical reasons' – that proved the most newsworthy event of the entire collection so far.

The Fringe, too, seems to have lost the plot somewhat. It can be argued that it is so slickly organised that the chances of sitting through total dross for a couple of hours – as one frequently did in the more freewheeling days of yore – are mercifully reduced.

Each of the main Fringe venues – the Assembly Rooms, the Pleasance, the Gilded Balloon and the ever redoubtable Traverse – scrupulously vet the productions to which they lease out their space, expertise and publicity machines. Stay within their orbit and you are pretty safe.

But is safe what the Fringe should be? Even the most dangerous of artists appearing here are commercially pretty sound, professionally polished and up at the Fringe merely as a showcase for acts they have spent the year perfecting elsewhere.

Which is why I left as I arrived, with the sinking feeling of *déjà vu*; of being a helpless cog in a mammoth machine that has somehow taken over the spirit of the festival. What has gone is the sense of adventure; the right to strive and fail. This is what Professor Steiner is bemoaning.

Nowadays, the Fringe has become little more than a rather cut-throat annual competition for the *Perrier Comedy Award* and a series on Channel 4.

This said, there are magic moments to treasure. In the case of Slava Polunin's utterly breathtaking *Snowshow*, the magic is the kind we used to know as children. Slava is a clown in the age-old tradition of Grock, with a Chaplinesque love for the little man. He has his capacity audiences in the palm of his imagination from the moment he appears. And his stage effects are dazzling.

Dolorous yet sharp-witted, slow and remote yet balletically fragile, his charm wraps itself around the audience like a warm comfort blanket – literally at one point. For he envelops his entire, vast and doting audience in a gauze-like substance which stretches endlessly across our upraised hands like some giant cobweb and then disappears as instantly and mysteriously as the morning dew.

As a finale, he deluges everyone with a gentle snowstorm. The entire auditorium is transformed into a winter wonderland. Suddenly they are young, innocent and transported with delight.

A more adult delight is Sandi Toksvig, making a genuine debut with a solo show. Ms Toksvig's rapport with an audience is engaging and instant. *Rambling* (Edinburgh Suite) is deceptively titled. For although she does lead us up some extremely diverting personal paths of confessional, this is an elegantly structured piece.

Centred on the one-sided correspondence ('Rather like St Paul and the Corinthians, I suppose') from an old school chum called Margaret, Ms Toksvig brings her subjects to vibrantly believable, comic, yet ultimately moving life. Margaret's is a sad and unfulfilled existence until her husband's obsession with Shirley Bassey gradually manifests itself into full transvestism.

Ms Toksvig's breezy conviviality provides the telling counterpoint to these fascinatingly introspective domestic outpourings. Yet a serious spiritual purpose underpins the entire piece. It is tellingly revealed when, right at the end, she blasts St Paul and his brutal bracketing of homosexuals with thieves, murderers and all the scum of mankind, with all guns firing. And she can only be applauded her for it.

Over at the Pleasance 2, punk gets a comic retrospective with Paul Hodson's mega-decibel *Pretty Vacant*. It is an in-your-face appraisal of how far we have travelled since Sid Vicious first gobbed in the face of authority. And it more than underlines the irony of Johnny Rotten's recent sad attempt at a punk revival.

Johnny Commune has stayed true to punk's outsider ethos, while his one-time partner, Sammi, has thrived under Mrs Thatcher's grab-and-run economics. Their reunion is raw, explosive, noisy, politically opinionated and highly entertaining.

Even more disturbing in the power of its playing, and following *Pretty Vacant* at the same venue, is *Poe*, George Dillon's hypnotically surreal portrait of that master of spook, Edgar Allen. Dillon is an electrifying performer, a Berkoff babe and a perennial festival favourite.

His power to subsume himself in his subject marks him out as a stylist of distinction.

BENEDICT NIGHTINGALE

Edinburgh is extremely erratic these days. Jack was probably right to be despondent. There is nothing inherently wrong with the Fringe being the main focus of attention, except that it is impossible to predict the sort of work it will throw up. When it consists of endless lines of alternative comedians using it as a way of getting their careers launched there is reason for worry. On the other hand, there are people bringing some interesting oddballs from Hungary and Poland to the Fringe. The real problem is that the Fringe is just too big. There is a feverishly large amount of events, most of which are not good, some of which are actually exploitative. The Festival proper has become submerged. You come back year after year and everyone asks you what you have discovered and time and again the answer is nothing. It was never exactly a treasure trove of talent, but it was smaller and one could be more discriminating. Jack's worries are very widely shared.

5

BROADWAY vs THE WEST END

Bacall... so little to give but her name
Daily Mail, 18th January 1982

No industry sells itself so confidently, so brashly or so remorselessly as Broadway. Hype is the name of its game. Show business over there is precisely what it says. All show and big business.

It is a technique which won Lauren Bacall her *Tony Award* for the best performance in a musical. And it is what has turned another so-so show – this one is called *Dream Girls* – into the hottest ticket in town.

Bacall is enjoying something of an artistic sinecure in a relentless trifle called *Woman of the Year*, based precariously on the delightful old Hepburn-Tracy movie. Giving us scant evidence that she can act, or sing or dance, Miss Bacall is nevertheless presiding over a solid gold hit merely by the loan of her name. Over here she wouldn't win a vote for the title *Woman of the Week*.

Probably you have been urged already to swim the Atlantic if necessary to catch Michael Bennett's latest creation, *Dream Girls*. Don't waste the water wings.

The man who gave us *A Chorus Line* has given us nothing new and little that is exciting in this blatant white-wash of black music. Alleged to be the story of the Supremes' struggle to the top, its book (by Tom Eyen) is so sugar-coated with clumsy show business clichés that the spoofy, bracing escapism of its arch rival *42nd Street* hums with torrid social comment by comparison.

How is this sleight of hand achieved? By hype of course. By hype you contrive, as best you can, to send an audience into a show whistling the tunes. Anticipating the spectacle. Primed to applaud on cue. They arrive knowing they are going to love it – because they've been told so; long, loud and without pause for breath.

You must remember New York is Theatre City. Almost everyone you meet has some slice of the action. There isn't a cab driver who can't – and won't – freely offer you his views on any show or star he's driving you to see. There is not a hairdresser who does not boast a client who is either in showbiz or 'very friendly with a big producer.' There's not a matinée afternoon (Sundays included) when the streets around 8th Avenue are not clogged with out-of-towners jostling to see a show.

And you can seldom pass the cheap-price ticket booth in Times Square when the queues are not a block long. Even the unfriendly neighbourhood cop probably has a brother-in-law who's writing a play.

But above all, you cannot escape the TV advertisements. Whole chunks of the shows are filmed especially for screening alongside the soap commercials. To this end *Woman of the Year* is sold to the viewers on almost every channel with a ravishing production number. The fact that neither this routine nor these costumes ever materialise on the stage of the Palace Theatre would appear to bother no one.

True this advertisement has the distinct merit of demanding little more of the star than she sways silently to and fro while an energetic row of tuxedoed chorus boys take the strain. When she does deign to dance in the ad, the cameras speed up and cover any inadequacies.

It is purest hype. A manufactured hymn to a programmed star who is visibly succumbing to the trampling of time. Only a rave review in the *New York Times* could more speedily disarm this gullible public of their critical faculties.

Which is exactly what *Dream Girls* was fortunate enough to receive, in the nick of time. Frank Rich, the *New York Times*' newish theatre critic threw every superlative over the moon in a loud, lone bout of hysterics. And *Dream Girls* was home and dry.

In vain did the New York *Daily News*' vituperatively witty Rex Reed warn that some brave and mystified punters had been yelling for their money back. 'To me,' wrote Rex, 'it's like spending three hours at the dinner show at Caesar's Palace in Las Vegas with all the exits locked and no way to get out.'

In vain did my friend Clive Barnes, now of the *New York Post*, warn sagely against the show's shortcomings. As the saying goes on Broadway: if you employed a monkey to write the *New York Times* reviews it could still make or break a show.

Personally I found nothing bright or innovative in the waltzing towers of light which occasionally stabbed the auditorium. Nor was I astounded when the lead Dream Girl's costume changed from glittering green to shimmering whit (as I was promised it would be).

As for the show being a hard-hitting history of the Supremes, baloney! The real-life lead singer the group's manager dumped on the way up in order to promote the middle-of-the-road sound of Diana Ross in fact died in agony and squalor. Jennifer Holliday, who essays the dropped Dream Girl in the show, survives to stage a glittering comeback for the finale.

Just as well: Miss Holliday is the evening's one big bonus. Her heart-rending soul sound which brings the first half to a close is the stuff to stop any show. But one song and one singer does not make the greatest show in town. The same goes for *Woman of the Year*. The book is lousy, the routines are routine and Miss Bacall is less than both.

But from all the hype, you'd never know until you'd paid your money. That is an average cost of £25 per seat. So hang on to your dimes because I'll be telling you what's biggest, best and most beautiful on Broadway.

MELVYN BRAGG

The good writing for theatre in New York has moved to off-Broadway. And this has been noted by their leading playwrights, Arthur Miller for example. The conditions are no longer suitable for good new plays – although Broadway can still do the big musicals. The trouble now, though, is that the place has been overrun with what I call 'conference delegate theatre,' big standardised musicals where companies can dump conference delegates *en masse*. And this breed of theatre has multiplied across the world. You can find the same shows in New York as in Japan. There is some good work emerging, but it is the minority.

Great escape at its pinnacle of perfection

Daily Mail, 19th January 1982

After eight days and eleven shows on New York's Great White Way, what is the first news to greet me as I set foot back on British soil? Broadway has bought its first slice of London's West End, that's what everyone can hardly wait to tell me.

Frankly my little *I Love New York* badge fairly lit up at the prospect. If Mr James Nederlander, one of America's most impressive impresarios, has indeed purchased London's Aldwych Theatre as an aftermath of the Royal Shakespeare Company's imminent removal to its new base in the Barbican, then look out for flying sparks to set the town alight.

I speak as one who in the space of one week managed to be mugged by an enraged usherette in mid-show and terrorised by Katharine Hepburn in mid-play; two unlooked for firsts in 20 years' professional theatre-going.

But the mood of Broadway is neither so angry nor so wayward. It is girls, it is glamour, it is dancing. It is dazzling escapism, the sort that only money can buy. Broadway does it best. And it is summed up in one eye-zonking show which, if it could be transported to these shores intact, would keep Drury Lane ablaze with life for the next 10 years.

42nd Street is the musical. Our own magnificent Millicent Martin is its current star – which should bring one tap-step closer. And if you think you've seen it all on the movies back in the Thirties you ain't, as they never tire of telling you over there, seen nothing yet, mister.

The curtain rises slowly to reveal 40 pairs of feet tapping in unison fit to bust the stage. The rest gets better and better. The old story of the hick kid who arrives with nothing but a pair of tap shoes to be told: 'You're going out there a young girl; you've got to come back a star,' is what the Great American Dream is all about. This is every Broadway baby's lullaby to the life.

It is also Broadway peddling its own myth, magic and expertise with such opulence that only seeing is believing. While the latest Sondheim musical *Merrily We Roll Along* flops ignominiously and the intellectual *Book* musical takes two steps backwards, this frenzied desire to escape into our own rose-tinted past has never been more potent on both sides of the Atlantic.

Which is why *Sugar Babies* could do for London's Victoria Palace what *42nd Street* must do for Drury Lane. This wonderful wallow into the best of old time Vaudeville has its own in-built instant nostalgia in its two stars, Ann Miller and Mickey Rooney. Enthroned in the old VP it would be as if the Crazy Gang themselves had returned in triumph.

Middle-aged matinée matrons gasp and applause in glee the moment Miss Miller makes her first entrance, flashing those fable Hollywood legs, sitting atop a mountainous pile of zebra-skin luggage and trailing memories of her old dancing partners, Astaire, Kelly and all the other MGM names from her 40 Hollywood movies. The fact that she can still smack 500 tap-steps into one minute without pausing for breath while admitting to a 56-year age tag (despite being labelled 63 by ungentlemanly reference books) only enhances her glory in their eyes.

She endures. And they are buying a stake in her undiminished survival. The same goes for Mickey Rooney. This rotund, balding India rubber ball bouncing through those sharp, suggestive burlesque routines is Andy Hardy come home after seven marriages and countless battles with the taxman. They ooh and they aah his every move. At $40 a seat, this living evidence of immortality comes cheap, and they've been buying it for the past three years.

With a string of our own best music-hall turns to back up the magic of the Miller-Rooney partnership this would be just the thing when Elizabeth Taylor has finished burnishing her own legend at the VP.

Hot on the homage trail is *Sophisticated Ladies*, a high-tone tribute to the music of Duke Ellington that is everything its title implies. Given the success over here of the comparatively self-effacing *One Mo' Time!* I would guess this glittering, glossy almost all-black revue should be next in line for a transfer.

Its Ritzy neon-streaked settings, its slinky, seductively stylish star Judith Jamison and its exhilarating precision dancing transport us right back to the hey-day of Flo Ziegfield's *Follies* or Josephine Baker's legendary *Blackbirds* extravaganza.

The other long-runner with nothing but its own artistry to offer is Bob Fosse's *Dancin'*. Sadly this bow and curtsy to great choreography has all but danced itself into oblivion; with the dazzle removed, its hollow centre is all too clearly revealed. Why do we need *Dancin'* when we have our own ephemeral magic in *Cats*, the nearest thing to any of these shows I can think of?

What we do not have is the ripe, irreverent blast of fresh air Joseph Papp has blown into *The Pirates of Penzance*. Michael White, praise be, has already secured the British option on this bag full of Broadway tricks perpetuated exuberantly on the old Gilbert and Sullivan piece of nonsense.

Kay Ballard had undertaken the funny business when I got to see it and Maureen McGovern (she of The Continental hit parade fame), was warbling wittily and surprisingly true as the principal of *Ward in Chancery*. Leading her an exceedingly merry dance is a 19-year-old blond six-footer making his Broadway debut.

He is Joseph Cassidy, half-brother of pop star David, son of producer Jack and movie-star Shirley Jones. His effect on the audience is devastating. 'That,' prophesied the redoubtable Broadway veteran Miss Ballard to me after the show, 'is going to be our next big star.' Young master Joseph certainly appears to have run off with the lion's share of the family talent.

Perhaps what I have described is a great deal more of less and less. No innovative book, no tunes you don't know. But it is escapism at its pinnacle of perfection and in tune with the needs of the moments. Which is the way things go whenever a society finds itself wondering where next to go.

Quickly snuffed out, the whiff of failure!

Daily Mail, 20th January 1982

There is no insider in the business of show business, who will not assure you confidentially that you have just witnessed the worst season in Broadway memory. It's like asking a farmer how his harvest has been this year.

Of course, they speak no more than the living truth. The musicals I have drooled over were all the products of other seasons, kept lovingly honed and polished to new perfection by a culture that holds success as the highest and most visible of its virtues.

The outsider sniffs scarcely a whiff of failure as he scours the Great White Way on pleasure bent. A show is either a smash or it is off faster than it takes to book your seat after the stinkeroo reviews. And a smash means standing room only most of the time. To keep it that way Liza Minnelli once cheerfully stepped into the shoes of Gwen Verdon, Millicent Martin has taken over from Tammy Grimes, just as Raquel Welch relieved Lauren Bacall. The stars are always the brightest.

Only one theatre I visited in an eleven-hour show of duty bore any similarity to the average West End house halfway through a run. In Max Wall's memorable phrase, you could have shot a stag in the gallery and no one would have been any the wiser. But it was a matinée. And it was a straight play.

In this department, it seems, Broadway has been forced to buy British and they see the visitors walk off with all the laurels. Although Ian McKellen has returned to these shores clutching his *Tony Award*, the National Theatre's production of Peter Shaffer's *Amadeus* enters its second season in bountiful good health.

At the Brooks Atkinson Theatre, Tom Courtenay has teamed up with Paul Rogers for a replay of *The Dresser*, which of course started its life in Manchester's Royal Exchange theatre before taking London by storm. It is still one of the most full-bodied comedies about theatre life you are likely to see. The New York audiences devour it and Mr Courtenay like parched travellers stumbling across a desert oasis.

Still they talk about Jane Lapotaire's shattering performance in *Piaf*. And already the advance hype has begun for her Broadway return later in the year in the title role of Edna O'Brien's *Virginia*, a searing study of Virginia Woolf.

To escape the success of *Nicholas Nickleby* you would have had to have been a blind, deaf hermit these last few months. It closed the night I arrived – and no opening was ever so starry as this closing.

Yet for me the wonder was not so much that tickets which cost around $100 (about £50) at the box office were changing hands at $1,000 a piece. It was the night which struck me as ridiculous – a Sunday. Broadway, being in the city of the Big Sell and recognising its wares as a service industry, is happy to make itself available to customers whenever they choose to come.

In London, by sad contrast, we send them to the Zoo and then home to bed with an early cup of cocoa.

This, sadly, is the *Tale of Two Cities* I bring home. What we have to teach them is Class with a capital C. What they have to show us, is how to sell it. At $1,000 a throw if it's classy enough. No trouble.

Ian McKellen has already returned to expound his relief at being back in an environment which produces actors of a range that is as broad as it is deep. The Lapotaires, the McKellens, the Courtenays and of course Nicholas Nickleby himself, Roger Rees, are the product of a system which in America is inconceivable... The huge repertory company kept alive and vital by subsidies, often inadequate to their needs, but ensuring their development as artists.

Compared to their stature, most of what I saw of Broadway drama was merely slick and routine. Jules Feiffer's new play *Grown Ups*, directed by Mike Nichols, harps on the American neurosis of family ambition. But all it really amounts to is that its star Bob Dishy throws in his job at the *New York Times*. 'Big deal,' murmured my companion by way of a review. There seemed little more to say.

Katharine Hepburn is the driving force keeping a piece of schmaltzy trivia entitled *The West Side Waltz* twirling gaily at the top of the box office ratings. It was a non-star vehicle by an (to me) unknown playwright called *Crimes of the Heart* which stole mine. I would love to see this demented modern black comedy version of *The Three Sisters* brought to London if only to see the Royal Shakespeare Company's fine comic actress Jane Carr as its centrepiece.

Set in deepest Mississippi, the sister who has made the good marriage has shot her husband because she can't stand the sound of his voice; the sister who has escaped to the big city has had a nervous collapse, and the sister who stays at home is rewarded by having her horse drop dead on her birthday.

It is young Mia Dillon who put me in mind of Miss Carr. Playing the part of the sister who shot her man, she is cast irrepressibly in the mould of the late Judy Holliday.

Only when I read the programme did I discover that this was the lady who won Broadway notoriety in *Once a Catholic* playing the role Miss Carr originated here in London. So it would be the fairest exchange for Jane to return the compliment.

There you are, then. With our class, and their commercial flair, these two cities have a lot to offer each other. Equity, the ball is in your court. Fair exchange, as they say, is no robbery.

Let's stop knocking our great West End

Daily Mail, 18th February 1983

About this time every year someone dons the hair shirt on behalf of London's commercial theatre and rings its death knell. This week it was the turn of Melvyn Bragg, in his role of Keeper of the Nation's Cultural Conscience, to prophesy that the end is nigh for live entertainment as we know it.

The refrain was old hat even when Shakespeare and Burbage were tearing their hair over falling receipts at the Globe. Now it has come to Mr Bragg's attention that there are no fewer than 16 theatres in the West End with their lights dark and their doors closed.

It cannot be denied that if you walked down Shaftesbury Avenue you might feel the doom-and-gloom brigade were a little late in uttering the last rites over the corpse of the West End.

That old grey ribbon of real estate which runs from the vast Shaftesbury Theatre at its Northern tip down to the pretty Lyric at the Piccadilly Circus end is indeed a sad sight.

Where once the best (and quite a bit of the worst) of our theatre talent saw their names blazed in neon lights, only one solitary theatre was lit up last night, but I submit that Mr Bragg has based his calculations on a Never-Mind-the-Quality-Feel-the-Pinch basis.

He blatantly ignores the fact that even with 16 theatres dark – incidentally what he does not reveal is that four of them are about to open with new shows – London can still boast a wealth of more live entertainment than Paris, Berlin or even Broadway.

We have over 40 major theatres, and of those that are still open for business I could reel off more than a dozen shows I would gladly cough up good money to sit through for a second, third and even fourth time.

The irony of Mr Bragg's timing is that, for all the belt-tightening and streamlining in line with every other British industry, the commercial theatre has never had more cause to pat itself on the back for the sheer range, enterprise and daring of its offerings...

The producer, Michael White, who put the hit production of *Pirates of Penzance* into Drury Lane has just sunk £1.5 million into breathing a similar sort of life into the old Piccadilly theatre. Glamour and spectacle by the bucketful is the format for his new extravaganza, *I*, which opens there next month. But even he seems infected by the prevailing despondency.

'The West End is finished as we know it,' he sighs. 'In future there is going to be only room for the extremely small cheap two-man shows and for the lavish spectacular. All traditional theatre in the middle will disappear.'

Now well as I wish Mr White's enterprise and admire his desire to play Canute, I would beg to differ. Plays like Tom Stoppard's latest and best work, *The Real Thing*, Michael Frayn's farce, *Noises Off*, and the charming *84 Charing Cross Road* * all belie this trend...

All may not be well with the heart of our theatre. But it is by no means *in extremis*. It is still one of our greatest tourist attractions, one of our most prestigious dollar exports.

* *84 Charing Cross Road*, adapted from Helene Hanff's novel by James Roose-Evans.

MELVYN BRAGG

I wrote a piece pointing out the parlous state of the West End, and predicting that the situation would probably worsen. Jack then went into print dismissing my claims as rubbish – he pointed out that people say the same thing every year, and still the West End flourishes.

Well, I thought I had a point at the time, but Jack was absolutely right.

Because Jack wrote for the *Daily Mail*, some people were inclined to think that he was a less weighty critic than, say, the reviewer on the *Observer*. That was never true, but Jack worked very hard to spice up his articles to counteract that feeling. In the end, the *Mail* carried more theatre coverage than most of the broadsheets.

Curtains for Broadway

Daily Mail, 27th June 1988

B roadway looks exactly what it has become. A shabby mess. Two vast excavations yawn where once theatre lights twinkled – visual testimony to the commercial greed which has, since its fabled heyday, sapped its vitality and drained its daring.

How rosy the West End seems from this distance. There, every mood is pandered to, every reasonable taste is gratified, from Shakespeare, Chekhov through Rattigan and on to the modern diversities of Stoppard, Berkoff, Cooney, Gray and the glories of Barry Humphries' inspired public humiliations.

Note that I don't even bother to mention the musical. The best of what you can see at home is over here, representing the mainstay of its dwindling fare and increasingly resented by the old die-hards who remember when the very name Broadway was synonymous with all that was most innovative in song and dance. Now even the old Palace Theatre, once the great flagship of New York's show business glamour, is shrouded with scaffolding as if in symbolic mourning.

I read, blazoned from every trade paper and gloated over in the *New York Times*, that the season just brought to its climactic finale by the glittering *Tony Award* presentation and ball, has been the biggest box office bonanza on record – total gross receipts of well over $253 million and attendances topping eight million. 'You can't buck the market' is a phrase which leaps to mind.

You look closely behind those figures and you will discover that, as ever, there are lies, damned lies and statistics. Only 31 new productions have opened on Broadway in the year just past, the lowest output since its very worst crisis year, when the death of the stricken patient was confidently predicted on all sides.

Why, back home that paltry tally could almost be equalled by the National Theatre, the Royal Shakespeare Company and the Old Vic alone. In London, well over 40 theatres are open and being added to with the Playhouse and the Cambridge both recently reclaimed from the dark.

Look more carefully at what has taken the giant slice of Broadway's billion dollar cake, and there is even more cause for alarm along the Great White Way. Six sell-out shows accounted for almost half the box office receipts, and if I named the town's top earners you would wonder why bother to cross the Atlantic.

Phantom of the Opera heads the list, opening to an unprecedented box office sale and grossing over $1/2 million a week, besides virtually making a clean sweep at the *Tonys*. Close behind comes *Les Miserables*, last year's *Tony* wipe-out; *Cats*, which cleaned up several seasons back;

Me and My Girl; and *Starlight Express*. These are the ones that are putting bottoms on seats that are now costing upwards of $100 a pair.

'UK Tuners Toot Broadway to $mashing Box-office High', Variety screamed in a headline that is the hallmark of its own distinctive patois. And of course it is the soaring cost of everything connected with putting on a show in New York which is rapidly killing off the goose that once laid such golden eggs among the stinkers.

From the cut-throat cost of a square foot of real estate to the hiring of a stage-hand and the rental of space for a poster, nothing comes at affordable prices any more. No one is willing to take risks where one bad review from Frank Rich in the *New York Times* can close a show overnight. As a result, any playwright with a hope of getting a new work performed on Broadway must seemingly confine his imagination to a maximum of three characters on one set-preferably with only two chairs.

I saw two of this years' straight play contenders in one day and my stint in the stalls netted me a grand total of five performers on two Spartan sets. Moreover, as one of those actors was Madonna in *Speed the Plow*, giving a performance indistinguishable from the stage furniture, I felt distinctly underwhelmed. So did the plays.

Curiously, however, Broadway cannot wait to bite the hands that are currently feeding it. With crazed logic and not a small amount of political malice it, too, could not buck the market by denying *Phantom* the Best Musical trophy. It withheld the laurels for Best Score and Lyrics. Best Book and Best Choreography – the very elements which must combine to make a musical supreme.

And with the catastrophic failure of the disastrously misconceived *Carrie* (didn't we all warn them anyway?) and the critical mauling of *Chess*, there was much ill-disguised glee at the discomfiture of what Broadway persists in seeing as British interlopers. 'That much ballyhooed phenomenon, the English musical, is a bubble that has burst,' crowed Frank Rich, the man whose poisoned pen has done most to prick it.

Named the Butcher of Broadway it is Rich's reviews in the *New York Times* which virtually seal the fate of most shows. And no doubt a trifle irked that *Phantom*'s pre-sale box office rendered it virtually critic proof, he provided the mouthpiece for the anti-Lloyd Webber faction which so unjustly withheld even a Tony nomination for his wife Sarah Brightman.

Rich was clearly rooting for *Phantom*'s only real home-grown challenger for the Tony crown, Stephen Sondheim's beautifully scored but ultimately flawed fairy tale fable *Into the Woods*. Beauty versus the Beast is how the cynics viewed the battle so crushingly won by the Beast. It is some measure of the confusion produced by the current crisis of confidence.

This surly reluctance to give the contribution of the Lloyd Webbers anything but the most grudging critical acclaim can only be construed as a version of what used to called The British Disease: a deep mistrust of anything that smacks of commercial success.

No one would ever accuse Lloyd Webber's rival Sondheim of the taint of commercialism, of course. And this is one of Broadway's many troubles. As its sole surviving native giant, Sondheim's latest offering too often gives every sign of disappearing up its own artifice and only a bag full of *Tony Awards* could have guaranteed it a financial killing.

For the rest of New York's home-grown hit makers, George Strausse has not had a winner since *Annie* (1977), Marvin Hamlisch has not found favour since *A Chorus Line* (1975), while Jerry Herman's last success was *La Cage aux Folles* (1983).

The legendary director Hal Prince, who won his first *Tony* 35 years ago and has notched up 17 since – the latest being for *Phantom* – sums up the sickness with an insider's eye: 'These are poisonous times on Broadway. Musicals are coming over from England because it still has a flourishing theatre community. For every hit musical there is a bunch of flops – but we don't get the chance to experiment any more. The body of my work would not have lasted beyond Saturday night in a Broadway that functions the way it does. It's all about money, not about art.'

Back home, of course, the commercial theatre is enriched and broadened by the cross-fertilisation which is generated from the subsidised sector, *Les Miserables* itself being the joint venture of the RSC and producer Cameron Mackintosh, who also has three shows playing on Broadway – with *Cats* and *Phantom*.

'It is foolish to talk about the British invasion – especially as *Phantom* was directed by an American and designed by a Scandinavian,' he says. 'But it just so happens that in London we have found our musical voice at the same moment that America appears to have lost its. What we look on as the great American Musical, in which people like me were brought up, is now a thing of the past. And as sure as I stand here, we too will be a thing of the past eventually. Not because we start to do things wrong, but merely because in the nature of things, people's taste moves on. They want something different.'

'What America needs to do is to find some way of answering that need, of finding a new voice. Originally they took all the ingredients from their immigrant population – the Viennese Operetta, the rich Jewish sentiment, the British sense of drama – and turned them into something that was uniquely American. But the days of *Oklahoma*, *Annie Get Your Gun*, *West Side Story* and *South Pacific* are over. They stand as monuments of their time and will go on being revived just as I am sure shows like ours will be revived wherever musicals are played.'

Meanwhile one can only endorse the epitaph that Ian McKellen delivered when his Broadway stay in the National Theatre's lavish and exquisite version of Chekhov's *Wild Honey* was brought to an abrupt and premature end with some brutal critical mauling.

'On Broadway, drama is dead.' he said.

CAMERON MACKINTOSH

When Jack wrote about the lack of good new work on Broadway, he was right. For the past fifteen years, the writing that has caught the public imagination in the United States, at least in musical theatre, has been largely European-based.

There are signs now, though, of a new school of American writers beginning to find their own voice. It will take time, the process is very gradual. Even Jonathan Larson's *Rent* is a flukey show. It is not perfect, but it displays great talent.

If you look at the 1997 Broadway season, it is still powered by the vestiges of the old writers. The only one who is vaguely contemporary is Maury Yeston with *Titanic*. He is probably in his late forties, whereas the others are over sixty.

Having said that, there is a far greater excitement about going to the theatre on Broadway than is the case in London at present. Even with the shows that are not doing that well, the audiences are keen to see them to have an opinion. That only happens here when you have a smash-hit. It happened with *Art*, it will happen with the next big musical. But when will that be? London has not had a smash musical since *Miss Saigon*, eight years ago.

That's rich!

Daily Mail, 29th May 1992

The Broadway season is in full swing. Even now the *Tony Awards* are being polished ready for Sunday's yearly orgy of euphoria and despair. Which means, in terms of backstage chatter, so is the annual Rich bitch. Bitching about Frank Rich, the *New York Times*'s all-powerful drama critic, has been a ritual Broadway pastime for the 11 years he has held this uniquely influential post.

The term Butcher of Broadway was coined not for him but for a long-ago predecessor. However, it is most often used about him. He can, with one swipe of his pen, close a show overnight – as many producers know to their cost. No single critic in London, thank heaven, wields so much omnipotent clout.

So when the Harvard-educated Mr Rich hails the current season as one of the most healthy signs of recovery from a long and ailing decline, we must flock to see.

Having flocked, however, I confess I am deeply perplexed by the august arbiter's pronouncements on almost every stage.

For example, his well-known mistrust of the British takeover of the Broadway musical has led him into some wild critical convolutions. He offers the smash hit musical *Crazy for You* as a sure sign that the home-grown American product has at last re-asserted its rightful supremacy.

Well, *Crazy for You* is indeed a show to shout and sing about. It would undoubtedly be a huge hit in London. But as for re-establishing the American musical dominance, let us not overlook the fact that the songs, by the unbeatable Gershwins, were first heard 60 years ago when Ethel Merman took the town by storm, belting out *I Got Rhythm*.

Without wishing to echo Mr Rich's xenophobia, let us not forget that its present success is in no small measure due to the wickedly witty rewriting and inventive staging of its British director, Mike Ockrent. For me, the main pleasure of the evening, aside from a score which manages to introduce hitherto unknown Gershwin numbers into a parade of immortal standards, is Ockrent's mischievous send-up of almost every Broadway cliché.

The only British production contending for this year's Tony line-up is, ironically, the show which has so far created the most spectacular Rich row. *Five Guys Named Mo*, that joyous party tribute to the music of American Louis Jordan, caught the critic on the raw. Almost alone among his peers, he flailed producer Cameron Mackintosh for attempting to teach his American grandmothers to suck eggs and indulged in some gratuitous Brit-bashing along the way.

I attended the rapturous New York first night. The audience was in ecstasy mode and had I been reviewing, I would have rushed out to join Mr Rich's colleagues with a tribute even more glowing than the superlatives I heaped upon it here.

The next morning a crestfallen Cameron confessed: 'Had I got a batch of reviews like this back home, I would have considered I had been dealt a full house. But things here are different.'

However, being able to out-rich Mr Rich financially, he threw down the gauntlet the following day, taking a full page advertisement in the dreaded *New York Times* with every rave quote from its rivals generously displayed. At the lowest edge of the page was a balloon containing Rich's final line: 'Bottoms up!'

So far this enjoyable show has survived. But then few producers on Broadway have the resources left, after the monstrous production costs, to withstand the financial freeze a panning in the *New York Times* usually brings.

The other musical which has taken the Great White Way by storm, and provoked another eulogy on the supremacy of Americana from Mr Rich, is Frank Loesser's perennial *Guys and Dolls*.

It is, of course, a classic monument to Broadway's art form and skilfully revived. But to claim that a 40-year-old fireproof veteran is a living symbol of Broadway's renewed musical vitality seems to me like us re-staging *The Boyfriend* to point the way forward in the West End.

Elsewhere this has been the season the film celebs have taken to the boards – either through boredom with what is on offer in Hollywood, or in desperation about what has not been offered.

Beauteous Jessica Lange and hunky Alec Baldwin supply the biggest disappointment of this stellar exchange. Their performances in Tennessee Williams' combustible passion-rouser *A Streetcar Named Desire* was, for me, the dampest of squibs. Miss Lange's performance flickered intermittently as she chased the shadows of the legends who had preceded her into the gossamer dreams of Blanche Du Bois. But she can sustain no real grasp on the emotional turmoil of the role.

As for Mr Baldwin, his faltering reputation as a bodice-ripper guaranteed to inflame the box office can only have been further diminished by the 40-watt sexual glow he emanates from the stage of the Ethel Barrymore Theatre.

In the old Marlon Brando role he radiates about as much heat as a five-bar gate. Never did I think to be so underwhelmed by anything written by Tennessee Williams, certainly not this landmark opus. Yet, by and large, the critics have been rapturous in their reception and a *Tony* nomination is Mr Baldwin's inexplicable reward.

Glenn Close has also been nominated in the role she snitched from our own Juliet Stevenson in *Death and the Maiden*. I'm sure Miss Close, headlining with those equally illustrious Hollywood names Richard Dreyfuss and Gene Hackman, is a huge box office draw. All three acquit themselves admirably in Ariel Dorfman's nerve-edged picture of a torture victim's revenge. But whereas Ms Stevenson's torment was almost tangible and a terrible, unbearable thing, Miss Close is disposed to display her surface skills as an actress more than burrow beneath the skin and into the bones of her character.

The same might be said of her co-stars. Maybe it is just a question of an alien technique. But I was less convinced by the play itself as a result.

Speaking of which brings me to Neil Simon's terrible turkey of domestic gobbledegook played in contrived flashbacks. *Jake's Women* stars Alan Alda, another movie refugee, giving a superb impression of a man involved in something meaningful and worthwhile. For this alone he earns his *Tony* nomination, showing heroism above and beyond the call of duty.

Sunday's *Tony* celebrations are being canvassed as Broadway's comeback. True, there have been more openings in New York this season than for a decade.

But if these are the eventual winners of the awards, I fear that Broadway still has a long way to go. And remember, Mr Rich is still directing the traffic.

DAVID ENGLISH

Jack and I both loved Broadway very much. I worked in New York for many years, and one of my responsibilities was to cover the theatre. When Jack began working for me, one of his first requests was to be sent to report on Broadway once a year. I was extremely enthusiastic – indeed, sometimes I would try to arrange to be there at the same time and we would visit the theatres together.

We were both fascinated by the power of the *New York Times* and Frank Rich in particular. Jack would return from his trips to America seething with rage at what he saw, justly or otherwise, as very egocentric criticism. However, taking a broader view, the *New York Times* had an immense and in my view an unhealthy power across the whole spectrum of American life, not just in theatre. There is a reason for this. When I lived in New York there were about eight main papers. They were then hit by the same union problems that we experienced in Britain. There was a whole series of strikes which decimated the newspaper industry. Finally, the only survivors were the *New York Times*, the *Daily News* which was a tabloid, plus the *New York Post* which was an afternoon tabloid. Neither of those two tabloids had any great authority.

Therefore, the *New York Times* had a tremendous say in business, politics, sport. It could make or break anybody. Nowhere more so than in theatre, because Americans are so susceptible to being influenced by the word from a powerful organisation. The situation was out of all proportion.

That power was eventually broken with Andrew Lloyd Webber's *Evita*. I covered stories in Argentina at the time in which the musical is set, and I thought that to use the subject in this way was genius. The Americans, however, felt almost the same way about Peron as Europeans do about Hitler (though clearly there is no comparison). The *New York Times* announced before the show opened, that the very idea was vulgar and shocking. They ran a campaign which decreed that *Evita* would not succeed on Broadway.

Lloyd Webber was very upset at the opening night, and the review was harsh. Such was the emotional power of the show, though, that it over-rode that criticism. In a way, that was the first production to break the influence of the *New York Times*.

BENEDICT NIGHTINGALE

I worked with Frank Rich for a time, and he himself thought that the degree of influence which he had was worrying. The *New York Times* critic has as much power over the box office, probably more, than all twelve London critics combined. They have, however, chosen very responsible reviewers. These people are in an extremely delicate position, if you really hate something you must say so. However, so far they have all seemed to be well aware of their stature and have been at pains to write carefully considered pieces.

It's sheer Broadway butchery

Daily Mail, 30th April 1993

The Broadway audience had gone wild. Wilder than I can remember any First Night audience going since Judy Garland made a comeback.

They brought the elated cast back from their dressing rooms, standing and cheering, refusing to leave the theatre even though the houselights had gone up and the exit doors were open wide.

For a time Willy Russell must have thought the gravy train had once more pulled into his own private station. He is fabled among New Yorkers for writing *Shirley Valentine*.

Now, it seemed, he had done an Andrew Lloyd Webber and conquered the Great White Way with a musical, *Blood Brothers*; his compassionate, passionate piece which back home is celebrating the tenth anniversary of its arrival in the West End.

Then, halfway through the euphoric celebration party, thrown by director-producer Bill Kenwright, the review arrived. Not *a* review. *The* review. The only say-so that matters in this one review town.

All the British contingent felt personally slapped down. And I cannot pretend to be an impartial referee. Haven't I been extolling the virtues of this magnificent and gritty slice of social comment for the past decade? And hadn't its British stars, Stephanie Lawrence and Con O'Neill, moved me to tears once more?

However, Willy Russell was Liverpool-cool itself in the face of such a put-down. 'As the writer I can't say I have been compromised in any way by the production we've brought here. It's everything I ever wanted the show to be. If Frank Rich doesn't like it, then all I can say is: tough. We obviously don't have the same taste in theatre.'

Nevertheless, you could see the hurt he felt not only for himself but for everybody else. Bill Kenwright immediately rallied. 'I don't close shows because of reviewers, as you should know. I only close them when no one comes to see them and we have a huge word-of-mouth advance from our preview audiences.'

Nevertheless it was a sizeable skeleton at what first appeared to be an epic feast. For Willy Russell is a writer you wish to see win all the prizes on the shelf.

No one writes female characters like he does. *Educating Rita*, *Shirley Valentine* and this, their leather-lunged musical counterpart, are all roles every actress dreams of playing.

148

'I suppose I write about women from their own point of view because I actually like them better than I like men,' he admits a bit sheepishly.

'This may sound wimpish and I know that coming from Liverpool you're not supposed to say things like that. But quite honestly, I only have one or two close male friends. I love the company of women. All male society of any kind appals me. If I'm in a room and there is a woman there I find myself responding in a way I never do if it's just the lads. I'm not hoping to resolve any sexual charge. It's just that I come alive when they're around.'

And he does. So do they. Even though he is now approaching 50 and the shoulder-length unreconstructed Beatles' haircut is iron grey and his taste in clothes verges on adolescent naff you can see normally mature and self-possessed women go girly in his presence. Even when he says something as openly blokeish as: 'That's a sexy skirt.'

Tennessee Williams, Alan Ayckbourn and other writers have written well for women too,' he says. 'But I suppose my view is different in that I actually celebrate women. In my plays they're not victims, I see them as heroes. I admire their courage. That's what I say and I suppose that's why it strikes chords.'

He has always been the same. Steadfastly married to the same woman, Annie, whom he met as a student, and staying faithful to his Liverpool roots in spite of all the wealth that his heroines have heaped upon him.

I was the first Fleet Street journalist he ever met back in 1974 when he and Annie came to London with their tiny baby for the opening of his first big hit, *John, Paul, George, Ringo and Bert*.

'I think if I'd had that sort of success before we'd been married and had the baby, I might have come to London and moved on. Don't forget, I was a £30-a-week teacher who suddenly went to earning £1,000 a week in the West End. I think I was very lucky it happened as it did, when I at least had my feet on the floor.

'I live in Liverpool now because, although there are a lot of things wrong with it, it is like wearing an old coat. You feel the collar warming your neck and it's very comfortable.'

Also he had two very strong and caring women to take the strain of that first flush of new-found fame. One, of course, was his wife. The other was the celebrated literary agent, the late Peggy Ramsay, who had also nursed such talents as Alan Ayckbourn from obscurity to success.

'She taught me to behave,' he says. 'She was remarkable, the only agent I know who would side with a producer or director if she thought you, the writer, were not doing the decent thing.

'My wife does that now. I don't even have to ask her if she thinks what I'm doing is wrong. One look is enough. But, of course, you don't admit that sort of thing if you come from Liverpool.'

And sure enough, into the small hours of the morning after he behaved as impeccably as any native Liverpudlian could, holding together a party which Frank Rich had done his best to turn into a wake.

It is one of Broadway's unfathomable mysteries how Frank Rich can heap columns of undiluted praise on the intellectual cutting edge of *Tommy*, The Who's pinball wizardry rock opera, while dismissing Willy Russell's infinitely more moving and socially-aware musical *Blood Brothers* as simplistic and melodramatic.

But as a result of this quirky reviewing, Broadway's biggest box office bonanza on record is *Tommy*. Tickets are selling at the phenomenal rate of 1,000 an hour. The show failed dismally to light up the West End when it was staged in London in 1972.

But its runaway success on Broadway is due in no small measure to the pulling power of critic Rich, who shed his Butcher of Broadway image to enter his second adolescence with a paean of praise for the piece.

Such is his influence that the review was carried in part on the front page of his paper. He hailed the show as: 'The stunning new stage adaptation of the 1969 rock opera by the British group The Who is, at long last, the authentic rock musical that has eluded Broadway for two generations.'

Advanced takings had been slow until its Thursday opening last week. Rock operas are no longer the taste of Broadway's ageing theatre-going public, especially with top priced tickets at $67 (around £43) a time.

However, immediately Rich's review hit the streets the box office takings soared to $494,897 (more than £317,000) for the day, beating New York's previous 'day after' record held by the revival of *Guys and Dolls* by more than $100,000.

Visually the show is an eye-zonking techno-wonder with Pete Townshend's pounding music and searingly simple lyrics as its driving force. Along with its director, Des McAnuff, he has reshaped the book considerably.

Even so, intellectually it would not challenge a lollipop, being the quirky and explicitly unsavoury story of a boy, played by young star Michael Cerveris, who goes deaf, dumb and blind on seeing his father return from World War II and shoot his mother's lover. The lad, having suffered sexual abuse from his uncle and mental torture from his cousin, grows up to express himself as the unchallenged wizard of the pinball machines.

For reasons which have always escaped me, he becomes the icon of his generation, reigning imperiously over his fans like a cross between the early Elvis Presley and the Pope.

Mr Rich reads startlingly deep social statements into this unlikely taradiddle and has deemed it to be 'a poster-simple political statement reflecting the stark rage of the Vietnam era'.

WILLY RUSSELL

Jack was the one critic with whom I felt I had a relationship beyond that of theatre practitioners. That may in part be because he was the first national journalist who ever interviewed me. The circumstances of that meeting were rather out of the ordinary. It was when I was doing my first play, *John, Paul, George, Ringo and Bert*. I had arranged to meet Jack in a house which I was borrowing in London. I was late, he had to hang around, then I had no milk for the baby so he accompanied me to the shops and we just got on as human beings.

He wrote this terrific feature based upon this hunt for milk in Barnes and the surrounding areas. Then, three weeks later, he wrote the most damning review of the play.

Once I had got over the shock, I respected the fact that the little time we had spent together had not in any way diminished or affected his reaction to it. From then on whenever I saw Jack, we would always greet each other as friends.

He called me out of the blue one day because he had been in Athens to do some work for the British Council. He knew that I was going out there, and he had been to see a production of *Educating Rita* starring an amazing Greek actress. Jack was just full of this extraordinary woman, who must have been sixty when she played the part, but was perfectly convincing as a twenty-six year old. Jack had been doing some workshop on *Blood Brothers*, and wanted me to know about it. I was thrilled – you tend to forget praise, and this meant a lot.

It was lovely to be in New York with Jack at the time *Blood Brothers* opened. I spent a fair amount of time with him, at lunches and in bars in the evening. He made one realise that he was there, not merely as a columnist and critic, he passionately wanted the show to be a success – almost as much as the producer, Bill Kenwright. The night that he writes about in the article, there was no doubt that Frank Rich's review affected Jack far worse than it affected me. He was really battered by it.

6

TAKING THE TEMPERATURE

When the first night is before the wedding!
Daily Mail, 31st July 1978

It was the brightest, biggest, flashiest, most glittering first night of the year. The stalls were awash in a sea of celebrated faces. The show was *Evita* and the reviews it won were as remarkable as the scenes on that first night. But *Evita* had already had three Royal gala previews before that triumphant opening. It is part of the pattern of West End openings, these days. For, like modern marriage, the first night no longer takes place after the wedding.

It all started ten years ago with a play from the then little-known author Tom Stoppard. Everyone remembers him now. Mr Stoppard became the darling of the critics with his *The Real Inspector Hound*, a wickedly contrived parody of their craft. But the acclaim which followed *The Real Inspector Hound* was nothing compared to the furore that preceded it. For it ushered in the new phenomenon of Public Previews. For the first time the public were able to see a play at a reduced price before the official opening night. And it was here to stay.

West End producers embraced it euphorically. No more long, unprofitable out-of-town try-outs; productions' teething troubles could be ironed out in front of a paying West End audience before the critics sharpened their pens on opening night. Actors welcomed it with joy. No more living out of a suitcase and playing to unpredictable regional audiences for weeks on end before the West End opening. It was like having a week of full-scale public dress-rehearsals to steady the nerves and pace a performance before the fashionable first-nighters.

And, of course, the more sophisticated fans welcomed the idea of a cut-price preview so that they could jump the gun and spread the word before the papers had their say. So who was hurt? The provincial theatres, that's who.

They knew what was coming the moment producer Michael Codron announced his plan for *The Real Inspector Hound* experimental previews. And the past decade has proved them depressingly right. The big musicals which used to open out of town to run themselves in, now play to packed preview audiences instead.

At the time spokesmen from both Howard and Wyndham and Moss Empires – the then great twin chain of major touring theatres – were highly vocal in their horror. 'It will mean almost certain death to many provincial theatres. Stars are already reluctant to tour, but now that there is no necessity for them to leave London, their provincial appearances will become even rarer,' lamented a spokesman for Moss Empires when Codron announced his plan. He prophesied no more than the truth. Today the Moss Empires and Howard and Wyndham are shadows of their former glory.

The last major West End musical to launch itself in Manchester – once the provincial capital of the big scale musical try-outs – was *Billy*. Managers of provincial theatres faced with finding major attractions week in and week out, have found the task harder and harder as the London preview habit grows.

'We have to face it that there just are not 52 major productions on tour in any year for theatres which change their bills virtually weekly as we do,' says Melville Gillam, the managing director of Brighton's elegant Theatre Royal, still among the doyens of the try-out towns. 'Luckily subsidised companies like the Royal Shakespeare Company and Prospect Theatre Company tour as part of their policy. And companies like Triumph Productions put on specially mounted touring productions which, if they are successful, are brought into the West End. But it remains a headache.'

The crisis has reached such a pitch that the Arts Council only this week stepped in with a £45,000 investment in a lavish commercial touring revival of *My Fair Lady*. Not exactly the sort of venture one associates with the Arts Council, whose purse is already stretched to capacity by the demands of the prestige theatres such as the National and the RSC and by the struggling experimental fringe. But it shows how seriously they view the starvation of the major regional theatres for this sort of musical.

Nor is it any coincidence that one of the prime forces behind the £500,000 venture is Louis Benjamin, the present managing director of Moss Empires. Mr Benjamin has been in close negotiations with the Arts Council in recent years in their joint efforts to keep open such theatres as the Nottingham Theatre Royal, the Manchester Palace, the Liverpool Empire, the Bristol Hippodrome and the Birmingham Hippodrome.

'Having promised local authorities and trusts in the areas concerned that by entering into booking arrangements with Moss Empires they would get first-class service and value, I think it only right and proper that my company should invest in touring productions to keep our side of the bargain – even at this very early stage in what I hope to be a new lease of life for provincial theatres.'

So while *My Fair Lady* goes out tailor-made for the road, current hit shows like *Evita*, *Annie* and *Bubbling Brown Sugar* take advantage of Michael Codron's ten-year-old brain child and come straight into town from the rehearsal room, safe in the knowledge that with a regulation week of previews in front of a London audience, there is just as much chance that everything will be all right on the night.

The night, of course, for both audience and performance is still the First Night. And there are still many lower-cost productions of straight plays which stick to the old-tryout tradition.

Either the play has to wait for a West End theatre to become available or it is careering around the country on a wing and a prayer that some West End management will bring it out of the cold.

ANDREW LLOYD WEBBER

The problem is that it is so expensive to stage musicals now, that a big production could never carry the cost of out-of-town touring. We did *Whistle Down the Wind* in Washington recently. It was not right and I aborted it there. That is an example of an out-of-town run being a good thing, preventing an unsatisfactory show from reaching Broadway. However, I did it because I am in the position that I can afford to do something like that. All the investors were paid back in full. We must now consider that a total loss.

I was misquoted somewhat recently, when the papers reported my statement that 'the day of the big musical is dead'. I did not actually say that. What I said was that if we do not get the costs of these big musicals right then we will enter very dangerous times. That is different, and I think that Jack would agree with me. The last time I spoke to him, we were discussing exactly that point.

My company's best estimate of the cost of mounting *Cats* today is that it would be anything between three and five times as much. But ticket prices have only doubled, approximately. I find it very hard to see how, in the end, the very big musicals can stay commercially viable.

I am planning to do *Whistle Down the Wind* in London. If I find that come November, when all the sets and the costumes have gone out to bid, the figures come in at an unreasonable amount, then I will have to seriously reconsider whether I go forward with it. I cannot with that show put it in a bigger theatre to sustain it, because I do not think that would be right for it. Things have got to that point now, and Jack realised that.

It would be wonderful to go out of town – I wish we could, but it is impractical. Mind you, Larry Gelbart once quipped that if Hitler was alive, he hoped he would be out of town working on a musical.

PETER HALL

Jack was on the Brighton *Evening Argus* in the early Sixties, where we used to tour and which was when I first met him. Brighton at that time was a watering-hole for prospective West End managers. It was generally thought that the Brighton audience was as close as one could get to a West End audience. Hence it was an important chance to gauge the likely London reactions - if only in terms of depression or elation, since by that time it was usually too late to change anything.

The throw-away theatre

Daily Mail, 12th August 1978

When the National Theatre staged its first new play in its brand new building, the theme was a revolutionary workers' sit-in. The Royal Shakespeare Company was showered with critical acclaim when it presented a terrifying documentary about the rise of the National Front. And recently the Royal Court won sheaves of laurels with a vivid picture of aimless, unemployed teenagers.

All of them themes plucked straight from yesterday's headlines. All of them written by the new breed of playwrights. A tough politically committed group of young men whose plays are rooted in the issues of the day.

I am all for them. They are turning the theatre into a stimulating arena of morals and intellectual debate that has not been seen since the heyday of George Bernard Shaw. But will their plays survive the issues which inspired them? Or have we heralded the advent of the School of Disposable Drama? Playing the Posterity Stakes is always a mug's game. Nevertheless it is still my bet that when our grandchildren go to the theatre (if indeed they do still go to the theatre) to find the definitive life-style of the Seventies, they will not look to the works of these serious and talented young men.

Heresy as it may be to say so in the face of so much political awareness and social conscience on the London stage today, but I would still put my money on Alan Ayckbourn's totally apolitical picture of middle-class life in the suburbs to supply the audience of a 100 years hence with their Seventies classics.

For today's news all too quickly becomes yesterday's fish and chip wrappings, as those of us who write it know well enough. Like fashion, the burning issues of the day becomes the discarded curio of tomorrow.

What remains constant and universally recognisable from generation to generation is the unchanging quality of human nature itself. Mr Ayckbourn, with his bitter, commercial comedies, supplies this in full measure.

Shakespeare himself survives, not only through the shining supremacy of his language, but for his unyielding insight into the human soul. The political necessities of Tudor and Jacobean dynasties which forced him to bend history to suit his masters are totally forgotten. Yet his *Richard III*, *Macbeth* and *Henry V* endure as lasting studies of human nature coping with fate.

Does David Edgar's quite brilliantly documented drama, *Destiny*, do this in dealing with the rise of Fascism in middle-class Britain at the RSC? Did Howard Brenton illuminate the human soul of his revolutionary factory-workers in *Weapons of Happiness* for the National? And will Barrie Keeffe's horrendously sharp picture of aimless youth in

Gimme Shelter survive the great debate about comprehensive schools and punk violence? Will other generations with other economic climates be able to relate to David Hare's parable of a nation in decline with *Plenty* at the National?

Messrs Edgar, Brenton, Keeffe and Hare are the children of the Mass Media Era. Their plays are an immediate response to the news of the day. Uncompromising and hard-hitting. Without doubt they are supplying us with the most stimulating theatre to be seen in London.

Yet I wonder, sincerely, what conclusions an audience would arrive at if some as yet unborn producer put Mr Keeffe's punk heroes or Mr Hare's disillusioned heroines into the costumes of a century hence.

Even now, John Osborne's *The Entertainer* lives on more as a highly compassionate portrayal of Archie Rice's capacity for self-delusion than as a satirical analogy on the state of England. It fairly rings with the stuff of common humanity. And this is the quality of which lasting theatre is made.

If the theatre is a mirror of life – as I believe it to be – then its audience wants to see a recognisable reflection when they look into it. And ultimately The School of Disposable Drama is in the business of persuasion, not reflection.

A showdown that could close the show down..!

Daily Mail, 30th October 1979

With ITV back on the air, it's one crisis down and one to go for the acting profession. For Equity, the actors' trade union, has decided to imitate the actions of a tiger. By stiffening already rheumatic sinews and summoning up some of its hotter young bloods, it is set to call the first strike in the 50 years of its own history.

As a demonstration of the art of timing, the gesture could hardly be more inept. As an example of industrial courage their call to arms has the resounding ring of kamikaze pig-headedness. For the enemy under attack is the already embattled commercial provincial theatre. And the plan to bring the actors out on strike during November is designed to hit these hard-pressed theatre managements where it most hurts – in the box office takings of their Christmas shows.

Yet who, apart from the dwindling circuit of provincial palaces of fun, will be the main casualties? Equity's own hard-up members, of course.

This has been one of the worst years in most living memories, so far as earnings and opportunities for actors are concerned. The West End has trembled to its foundations through lack of tourist spending-power during the dog days of summer; then there was the ITV strike.

Seldom have actors had a leaner time. The postponement of prestige ITV series, the drying-up of highly paid commercials (there is scarcely an actor in the world too proud to withstand the lure of such lucrative remunerations nowadays) have made disastrous inroads in even the most secure monetary calculations.

A dwindling film industry shuts the door on yet another source of income. And the Arts Council's recent revelations that 12 leading regional theatres may well lose their subsidies due to Government cutbacks cannot have brought any comfort to this most notoriously insecure profession. To the actor with his opportunities disappearing the Christmas panto and the touring show are the last sure source of revenue which might enable him to face his bank manager with something approaching confidence.

Are we to believe that Equity seriously propose to snatch this last remaining crumb of Christmas cake from the needy hands of its very own members? They are doing it, they say, to raise the living standards of the profession. Yet from where I sit it looks just like handing a glass of water to a sea of drowning men.

Vincent Burke, the newly appointed Development Officer for the Society of West End Theatres, is in no doubt about the outcome of such industrial action. 'It could cause closure, certainly,' he says. Which begs the sobering question: why shrink an already shrunken industry – especially when over two-thirds of your members are on Social Security at any one time?

In the heyday of the provincial theatre there were 1,500 playhouses offering employment to Thespians and entertainers. They were the breeding ground of tomorrow's stars. That was 1914. Today there are just 320 offering employment and apprenticeships.

If the managements of these do not agree to a 40 per cent rise on actors' salaries, as Equity demands, November 5th is the day set aside to see more fireworks. The jobs of 4,000 theatre folk could also go up in flames. Should the strike last, the Christmas shows will be blacked out, too.

It is, of course, the very reason for their existence that Equity should struggle to give members reasonable remuneration for their talents. As its General Secretary, Peter Plouviez, points out, the £56-66 minimum wage being offered by the managements is £14-24 less than the basic pay of an 18-year-old London postman. 'If managements are thinking in these terms, there won't be a commercial theatre in this country,' he warns. The managements wryly retort that if Mr Plouviez's claims for a £70-75 minimum wage is met, there still won't be any commercial theatre in this country. How can there be when to stage even a half-decent Christmas pantomime the lowliest chorus girl, scene shifter or gauche young ASM is being paid between £70 and £75 per week? Time was when panto, summer seasons and touring shows were where artists were only too grateful to learn about their craft, no matter what the privations for the privilege.

Gary Bond, who plays Che Guevara in *Evita* in the West End spoke for all of his fellow actors when he said: 'There is a feeling of fear and desperation among us all today. Those in work realise how lucky they are and are determined to stay in their job no matter what, for they know that if they leave a production it could be ages before they get another part.'

So where do tomorrow's stars win their spurs if Equity deals this body blow to their last remaining training ground? Moreover where are Equity and its members to find the funds to finance a protracted struggle if the provincial managements dig in their heels and decide to fight for their lives? Equity had to set up a £20,000 emergency fund to help its impoverished members through the ITV dispute while their royalties were frozen.

This is not, of course, the first time Equity has threatened strike action at this vulnerable time. In 1974, shortly after voting themselves back the right to strike (they gave it up in 1934 in order to ensure a closed shop in the West End) they rattled their sabres at the provincial theatres during this vulnerable time of the year.

Commonsense and compromise prevailed eventually and the shows went on in the old show-biz tradition. Since then, however, they have been shrieking at the Government to save endangered out-of-town touring circuits with grants and take-overs. They have paraded – justly – through the streets of London to persuade Mrs Thatcher to remove crippling VAT.

I wonder just how many of the actors and actresses who joined those laudable protests in order to preserve what is left of live theatre in this country would actually risk a whole chunk of it dying by withholding their labours this Christmas time.

It is my guess that Equity's tiger will prove to be merely paper.

Is there a new playwright in the house?
Daily Mail, 21st November 1980

Can Shaftesbury Avenue be saved by the Freddie Laker-style standby ticket scheme which was announced earlier this week? West End theatre chiefs are hoping that the brightly painted booth they are erecting in Leicester Square will help to bring back audiences. But is it all window dressing? Have they looked deep enough into what they are selling in their theatres today?

There is a popular fallacy – though I may be crucified for saying so – that theatre is the mirror of its time. That it is the voice and heartbeat of its generation. On this sacred assumption, huge sums of public money are consumed in keeping it alive, virtually sustained on the life-support machine of Government subsidies. Pull out that particular plug and, everyone agrees, theatre as we know it in this country would be a goner.

Yet even with its Arts Council grants, its local government subsidies and the care and concern of the finest artistic administrators, it continues to give every sign of expiring from chronic anaemia.

As Alan Bennett's latest play, *Enjoy*, flops ignominiously after only two months, the panic cry goes up: where is the new blood? Where indeed? The fact that the question is asked gives the biggest lie to the assertion that our theatre is the truest barometer of the moment.

Could our times possibly provide more in the way of dramatic possibilities? Lengthening dole queues, though not a new phenomenon, are uniquely distinguished by the numbers of highly educated, articulate youngsters in their midst.

A dreadful civil war rages on in Northern Ireland. Class barriers are being reinforced. Law and order is set against civil rights.

Yet the West End is in the grip of galloping nostalgia. Instead of new blood, the National Theatre is serving up the gore and gristle of Howard Brenton's now notorious *The Romans in Britain*. In defence of the lavish spectacle of Druids being raped on the stage of the Olivier, of course, it can be claimed that Mr Brenton intended this to be symbolic of the violation of the Celtic race – and thus was contributing to the Ulster debate.

But it is nonsense to pass Brenton off as an up-and-coming playwright whose work needs a showcase to bring his talent to our attention. Like all his generation, he has been up-and-coming for the past 15 years. Back in the Fifties, I was among those who first hailed him as one of the vanguard of interesting new British writers. The promise goes on without ever being fully redeemed.

In the late Fifties, Britain was just stepping out of its post-war austerity into the sunshine of Macmillan's much-maligned You've Never Had It So Good economy. John Osborne marked the moment with *Look Back In Anger*, and we all thought nothing in the theatre would ever be the same again. Yet do we look back in anger at the Fifties? On the contrary. We look back with something akin to affection.

And what of the Sixties which brought us not only Mr Brenton but an explosion of earnest revolutionary theatre heavily laden with the nudity and shock tactics employed in *Romans in Britain*?

Well, what a silly, time-wasting interlude that decadent decade now appears, set against the grim realities of the Eighties. The sole representative of those Sacred-Cow punching days currently represented on the commercial West End stage is Bennett.

Of the other giants-in-their-time, Harold Pinter has become a self-conscious self-parody. Arnold Wesker has all but disappeared from view. And Mr Osborne himself gives every indication of having nothing left to say about anything.

159

Even that one-man writing machine, Alan Ayckbourn, has shown signs of engine fatigue with his last London play *Season's Greetings* – though his is hardly the stuff that cries out for subsidies to keep it before the public. Like Coward, at best it is timeless.

The absence of fresh blood running through the arteries of the London theatre is, I fear, a sign that television has siphoned off the supply at source. Certainly, exciting creative writers like Dennis Potter and Trevor Griffiths confine themselves chiefly to television.

Perhaps that is the root of the trouble. It is no use blaming West End managements for failing to discover a new generation of playwrights. The scripts are simply not dropping on their desks.

Occasionally a new gem emerges. Willy Russell's *Educating Rita* at the Piccadilly was first staged by the Royal Shakespeare Company at their small studio theatre – one of the few new plays by a promising playwright which can claim to mirror our modern dilemmas. Recently, too, Andrew Davies' *Rose* gave Glenda Jackson a rare chance to create a truly contemporary role, showing the frustrations of the liberated woman. For the rest, each visit to the theatre reinforces my irrepressible urge to stand up in the audience and shout: 'Is there a living playwright in the house?' Too often, the answer is – 'No.'

A royal flush – five winning plays that balanced the RSC's books

Daily Mail, 4th December 1980

The prospect of a disastrous £250,000 deficit was facing the Royal Shakespeare Company when it announced its plans to stage virtually the entire saga of *The Life and Adventures of Nicholas Nickleby*. On the face of it the project seemed to bear all the signs of Kamikaze madness – two evenings of dramatised Dickens, siphoning off an enormous proportion of the company's collective talent, energy and resources. The enterprise was greeted by the resounding silence of bated breath while the pundits stood by awaiting the inevitable crash.

Yet, hey presto! The scoffers were once again left with egg on their egos, and the RSC had produced a fat rabbit from an apparently empty hat. They completed the trick by turning into the hottest family Christmas entertainment since pantomime. It is the perfect antidote to the usual tired fare of TV refugees in disguise and business has never been brisker at the Aldwych.

Nicholas Nickleby reopened at the Aldwych Theatre for a Christmas run to practically a pre-production sell-out... Already, by last October, the books were showing that the expected deficit had been reduced to around £60,000, thanks entirely to the box-office returns on such other hits as *Once in a Lifetime*, *Educating Rita*, *Piaf*, and the televising of their sensational Dench-McKellen *Macbeth*.

'They must be mad!' was the cry which greeted the news that the RSC were to splurge 45 of its choicest actors on a revival of the old Hecht-Kaufmann slickie, *Once in a Lifetime*. It was so popular you couldn't beg a ticket to see it at the Aldwych or when it transferred to the West End.

'They must be crazy,' was the word when Trevor Nunn let it be known that he was putting two of his biggest box-office attractions into a bleak, no-scenery, small-studio version of *Macbeth*. It carried off all the plaudits and awards in sight, and TV ensured it would be seen by millions in all its original intimacy.

'They've taken leave of their senses,' was about the kindest sentiment to welcome the plan to put the legend of Edith Piaf on to the stage. *Piaf*, with Jane Lapotaire poised to repeat her award-winning role, is about to burst upon Broadway and is eagerly awaited there. And have you tried getting a ticket for Willy Russell's *Educating Rita*, the marvellous two-hander now transferred to the Piccadilly?

Trevor Nunn, the artistic director of the RSC, thrives on this go-for-broke philosophy. The Society of West End Theatres themselves have to recognise that while London Theatre in general is in full panic retreat, the RSC's spirit of adventure is a 'treasure trove of outstanding merit'. Their own Theatre Awards, announced with Oscar-like ceremony on Sunday night, are crammed full of nominations from the subsidised Royal Shakespeare Company.

And it is difficult to find a single category which does not feature one nominee from the runaway hit of the festive season – *Nicholas Nickleby*.

Even the disasters were sensational..!
A look back at 1980

Daily Mail, **30th December 1980**

Having lived all year with cries of doom and despondency echoing like the cries of the Trojan women around the West End, let me put the record for 1980 straight as a Roman Road.

It was a damned good year at the theatre. Almost a vintage one. Given the state of the country in general, London's theatres have just cause to be proud of the year just flown. Even the disasters were sensational. May I offer, for instance, a festive haggis to Mr Peter O'Toole in recognition for his heroic efforts in making drama front-page news all around the world. That's good. *Macbeth* was bad.

But how can I speak grudgingly of a production which gave me so much innocent fun? O'Toole, the only leading man I have ever seen run full tilt into the scenery, dubbed the fated production Harry Lauder – and surely that grand old man was never so funny?

It is sad that the escapade, having filled theatres wherever it went, should end on such a sour note. O'Toole removed himself from the Old Vic, and the Arts Council have removed the Old Vic from their list of subsidised endeavours.

On a similar theme, we were blessed by the hugely rewarding spectacle of Sir Horace Cutler making an absolute chump of himself by threatening to cut the National Theatre's GLC grant. The sight of Druids being violated on the stage of the Olivier Theatre convinced Sir Horace that *The Romans in Britain* would encourage the spread of legionnaires' disease throughout the island.

All he succeeded in doing was to turn a mild miscalculation on the part of the National into an even greater hit than *Macbeth*. A recipe for instant success, therefore, might be to have Peter O'Toole playing a naked Druid and encourage Sir Horace Cutler to stomp out of every first night.

But there were more positive and enduring achievements to 1980. It was the year of *Nicholas Nickleby*, the eight-hour marathon mounted by the RSC in the teeth of financial crisis and no small chorus of scoffers. It proved to be one of the most magical two nights of theatre – laughter, tears... the lot.

The fact that *Nickleby* won every prize it was eligible for at the recent Society of West End Theatres Awards should not blind us to the sterling work elsewhere. Frances de la Tour made an all-too-rare appearance in a most moving two-hander *Duet For One* written by her husband, Tom Kempinski. David Schofield repeated his extraordinarily powerful performance as *The Elephant Man*, the role he created in the play which had to find fame on Broadway before its audience potential was recognised over here.

The Royal Shakespeare Company's small studio theatre also provided the West End with yet another hit to follow *Piaf* – this year it was Willy Russell's brilliant and penetrating comedy, *Educating Rita*, now thriving mightily at the Piccadilly Theatre.

Perhaps this growing pattern of collaboration between the subsidised companies and the commercial theatre is the way the West End will eventually survive the cold economic climate

At the National Theatre, Paul Scofield's magnificent *Amadeus* was partnered by the emergence of Michael Gambon as an actor of weight and distinction in *Galileo*.

Jonathan Pryce kept his claim to future greatness open with a fine *Hamlet* at the Royal Court; Judi Dench gave the decade's definitive Juno in *Juno and the Paycock* at the RSC; Maria Aitken became a classic Amanda in Noël Coward's perennial *Private Lives*; and Tom Courtenay, with Freddie Jones, kept the provincial flag flying at the Queens with *The Dresser* – which began its life at the Manchester Royal Exchange.

Of course, you can't win 'em all, even in a fat year like this. Alan Bennett's remarkably strained and lacklustre new play, ill-advisedly entitled *Enjoy* did not draw the town, as they say, despite the presence of Joan Plowright and Colin Blakeley, two artists with impeccable West End track records in commercial offerings.

Ayckbourn's *Sisterly Feelings* found its way into the National at a time when commercial managements are crying out for commercial plays. But rather there than nowhere.

Certainly my prophecy that, despite all the early scepticism, Norman St John Stevas would come up roses on behalf of the Arts has been conspicuously fulfilled. At a time of swingeing Cabinet cuts in every department from Health and Social Security to Education, the bedrock of our future, he alone has come up with a 14 per cent increase in Government spending.

On the musical scene there has been more that is charming than blockbusting. The collapse of *Sweeney Todd* at Drury Lane may seem to bode badly for the lavish show. But I think *Sweeney* will live to sharpen his razors another day. Stephen Sondheim's score is too literate, too fine, too enduring to languish in obscurity.

The trouble with the show was the staging. It was New York's notion of Victorian London. Had it been given the authentic flavour of *Nicholas Nickleby*, then I suspect we might have been writing a much happier chapter.

Meanwhile, *They're Playing Our Song* is packing 'em in (another virtual two-hander) at the Shaftesbury on behalf of the Broadway brigade and the charming *Biograph Girl* is carrying the honours of the British musical.

All this in 12 short months does not speak to me of a dying industry.

A pilgrim's progress to cultural Oldham
Daily Mail, 19th March 1981

The posters on the London Underground make a brave attempt to sell Oldham as a cross between a booming town and a rural idyll. 'Oldham, The Town In The Country' I see emblazoned every day on my way to work. And I have to smile.

The object is to lure light industry to a town that, in the past decade, has seen the collapse of its very reason for being on the map at all. Cotton is King no longer. But try as they will, the name remains to most folks a persistent music-hall joke. The unemployment figure hovers around 11 per cent of the population, which is no joke at all.

To me Oldham is the grim and grimy mill town where I received the most formative part of my education – and my first taste of theatre.

Plays like *Peg o' My Heart* and *Ten Little Niggers* (later tactfully retitled *Ten Little Indians*) were the uninspired mainstay of our theatrical diet.

All of which will explain my own astonishment at finding myself back at that very theatre on a cultural pilgrimage. Never in my wildest fantasies about this dour industrial wilderness did I imagine I would be proclaiming theatre among Oldham's most thriving assets.

The Coliseum stands at the end of Fairbottom St. The entrance framed unglamorously by the Artisan's Friend and The Old Mess House pubs.

Posses of West End theatre critics and managements are now constantly finding their way to Oldham and the other day a whole party of MPs arrived there to see a world premiere of fellow MP Joe Ashton's bleak view of the workings of Westminster in his controversial new play *A Majority of One*. Mr Ashton has taken the lid off the Parliamentary Whip's office and revealed a rather nasty can of worms at the heart of our democratic system.

The town has become quite used to theatrical bombshells of this kind. They gave standing ovations – and they're not a demonstrative lot in Oldham – to the first regional performance of *Bent*, the play which even the West End fought shy of when it first opened at the Royal Court. Homosexuality in a Nazi concentration camp is indeed a far cry from *Peg o' My Heart*.

The next world premiere to follow *A Majority of One* is a black farce set in a vasectomy clinic complete with male nude, *Having a Ball*. It is by the talented TV and radio playwright, Alan Bleasedale, and after sitting in at rehearsals, I can promise Oldham a further rich helping of strong meat to digest and more visiting theatre impresarios looking for likely West End fodder.

Yet only three years ago the little theatre was closed... like so many more enterprises in this unlovely town. Against all the prevailing trends of the time, maybe even against their better judgement, the local council bought the theatre. And the man they appointed Artistic Administrator, Kenneth Alan Taylor, has become to the Oldham Coliseum what Henry Ford was to the car.

A Londoner, long ago adopted by the North, he immediately embarked on an ambitious programme of specially commissioned plays and controversial revivals which have put many West End managements to shame. He says 'We've found that by not playing safe, we've attracted an entirely new and predominantly young audience. I know the West End has met the recession with musicals, revivals and escapism. But I'm afraid that simply doesn't work here. Our audiences want something they can recognise as real.'

All of which goes to prove that theatre will flourish despite recession, depression and dole. All it needs is flair.

Hear! Hear!

Daily Mail, 22nd April 1981

When Michael Crawford last appeared at Drury Lane, he insisted on having two identical costumes – one waiting in the wings in case of technical problems – so he could be heard.

When Broadway star Gwen Verdon last appeared on The Great White Way, she wore a metal-lined wig on her head – so she could be heard.

When Carol Channing came to London with her own production of _Hello Dolly_, she carried a bustful of transistorised radio equipment – so she could be heard.

And when Dame Anna Neagle stepped on to the stage one night, confident that she would be heard at the back of the gallery – all the audience received was a string of taxi cab messages...!

Each of these stars owes something to the radio microphone, now here to stay in the modern theatre. Time was when the first requirement of any artist was to be heard at the back of the hall; talent took second place to volume.

But we live in a hi-fi era. Audiences do not expect to leave the comfort of their quadraphonic homes and pay West End prices to hear sounds that are inferior to their own basic stereos.

So when Andrew Lloyd Webber's forthcoming £400,000 musical, _Cats_, takes the stage at the New London, no less than £90,000 worth of sound equipment will have been installed in a theatre for a super-surround sound effect. It is a prime priority.

In the old days, artists like Ethel Merman used to seem to hit the back row with nothing more but their naked voice. But even that was really an illusion. 'A kind of fake,' says Abe Jacobs, the pioneer American sound designer (yes, they actually design sounds these days). 'Ethel used to be standing right down from centre stage and all the orchestration she would have, a flute and a violin underpinning those great big notes.'

'That just isn't good enough now. Many people have already heard the LPs of _Jesus Christ Superstar_, _Evita_, _A Chorus Line_ or _Sweeney Todd_ before they even see the show. And they expect that exact sound to be reproduced in the theatre. Otherwise they feel cheated.'

Of course he's right. A pop group or a solo singer today would no more dream of facing an audience without the sort of equipment that could give their fans the next best thing to a studio-session sound than sweeping the stage after their act. So it seems rather flat-earth of theatre purists to turn up their noses and scorn the plethora of sound equipment needed to mount even the smallest musical production nowadays.

'Sound,' asserts Mr Jacobs, 'has become the theatre's fourth creative element.' And to accommodate its high technology, artists and directors are having to learn a whole new range of techniques. Where to stack the radio mike and transmitter is the first of the hurdles. How to use them effectively, the second.

Even in the West End's most intimate current revue, *Tomfoolery*, for instance, a highly sophisticated sound system has been installed by Paul Farrah, at 22 the youngest of the new Sound System impresarios who hire their expertise – and more important, their valuable equipment – to various productions. He also has *Oklahoma!*, *Dangerous Corner* and the new production of *Tonight at 8.30* to his credit.

'In a small show like *Tomfoolery* the best compliment you can pay me is that you do not notice there is any added sound,' said Farrah. 'On a show like this, the whole aim is to make the artists sound as natural as possible.'

To this end he has designed special speakers, gold coloured to match the interior of the theatre. And his sound-technician, the very elegant Helen DuFeu, presides nightly over the complex keyboard of levers and knobs balancing the voices of the cast and orchestra to his approved concept.

Tricia George, the only female in the four-handed show, has solved the problem of disguising the bulky equipment beneath her revealing costumes by having the small button radio mike strapped inside her bra, winding the conducting wires neatly round her waist and stashing the transmitter in a glamorous garter on her thigh.

'I hope all I show is a flash of frilly garter. But the actual harness which holds it in place is about as appealing as a truss,' she says.

Which is precisely why the veteran Broadway star, Gwen Verdon, insisted on having all the transistorised radio equipment sewn into her wig when she oomphed her way through the recent New York production of *Chicago*. When a lady of Miss Verdon's age has a figure as trim as hers she is not going to add an inch to it with unsightly mechanics. She'd rather balance them on her head.

'We do our very best to give the actors confidence in their sound equipment. But things can go wrong. That terrible screech you still sometimes get, even with the very latest sound systems, can happen when they have gone too close to the speaker with their radio mike,' says Helen, who nightly double-checks all her artists' microphones before each show to minimise the risks.

Of course accidents still happen. The radio frequency band used by the various London shows is extremely limited by law (and it is not unknown for some big productions to supplement their allotment with a few illicit transmissions). The same goes for London taxis.

No wonder artists are still nervous. Michael Crawford in his marathon run at Drury Lane had identical costumes made to house spare mikes so he could rush off stage and change his transmitter the moment anything went wrong.

Carol Channing went further. She had two spare microphones stitched into the bodice of her *Hello Dolly* gowns.

'But you know these living legends simply could not go on working in today's conditions without our new sound techniques,' says Mr Jacobs with more truth than gallantry.

MICHAEL CRAWFORD

I have just finished a show in Las Vegas called *EFX*. The level of technology in that production is beyond what man can deal with. It proved to me once and for all that the human is more consistent than the machine.

The amount of times that technology broke down far outweighed the times I have worked with humans that have made mistakes. And with machines, everything just comes to a grinding halt, there is nothing that you can do.

People are hard on new technology – it has limitations, but one goes forward. There was a critic who moaned about the use of radio mikes on stage. He complained that I would walk to the back of the stage, turn my back to the audience and could still be heard. I was very tempted to write back and ask him whether he wrote that review with a fountain pen or on a word processor!

Of course you do not use that microphone to act, you use every fibre of your being. The technology is merely an aid, and occasionally a hindrance. Jack understood that. It is rare to find a critic who will understand all the aspects of theatre, as he did.

It's set wars on the West End stage

Daily Mail, 27th May 1986

C liff Richard finally achieved his long-cherished ambition to star in a West End musical. He woke up to the morning after the glittering first night of *Time* to find that a man called John Napier had stolen all the notices. Mr Napier was the designer responsible for the 15-foot high speaking head of Laurence Olivier and the breathtaking laser light show which captured the audience instead of the times.

David Essex should have warned him how it would feel. He, too, chased his dream; staging and starring in the bumper-budget musical version of the Bounty's famous mutiny. Yet even with that fine actor Frank Finlay playing Captain Bligh to his Fletcher Christian, the critics handed all their sparing bouquets to the ship – a miracle of technology designed by William Dudley.

So it was when *Chess* opened at the Prince Edward Theatre. Even the super-decibel lung power of Elaine Paige (not to mention the creative endeavours of writer Tim Rice and director Trevor Nunn) played second fiddle to the banks of high-tech equipment surrounding a stage which waltzed and floated beneath her feet as she sang.

In short, we are in the age of the mega-mechanised, hyper-merchandised musical – the high-gloss product of the Eighties where packaging is every bit as important as the product. Indeed, so worried have many actors become by the current Set Wars situation in the West End that they recently called a seminar to thrash out the issues with designers like Messrs Napier and Dudley.

But then, where do you find an actor who does not resent being upstaged by his props, let alone his colleagues? Both Napier and Dudley, two refreshingly self-effacing and engagingly level-headed men, find themselves deeply embarrassed by their unaccustomed super-star status. And they were not a little startled by some performers' attitudes to their work.

Mr Napier (*Cats*, *Starlight Express* and *Les Miserables* currently running) thinks it is simply part of the in-built British resistance to anything that interferes with our justifiable pride in the literary tradition. 'At last in this country we have learned to do what they are still doing in Broadway and that is constantly looking back over its own shoulder, and wallowing in nostalgia,' he says. 'I love nostalgia, but in the theatre there is room for everything.'

Mr Napier, it must be added, is the man who, two days after the opening of the now legendary Judi Dench-Ian McKellen *Macbeth*, begged director Trevor Nunn to throw out the sets and stage the piece simply with the actors sitting in a circle on crates. The simplicity of the sceneless production was hailed as a *coup de théâtre* everywhere. Mr Napier's name was hardly mentioned.

'So I don't think you can say I am insensitive to what actors produce. I was so overwhelmed by those performances in rehearsal that I knew my sets were superfluous.'

Yet even while the hyper-tech brand of musicals continue to rake in the shekels, there is a sign of a move back to the old familiar values. It comes from, of all people, Andrew Lloyd Webber, the man who started it all with his concept-musical *Cats*. His latest project *Phantom of the Opera* will break the Set Wars trend and rely on its music and its star to sell the story like Rodgers and Hammerstein, like Irving Berlin, like Cole Porter and all the other old masters of the musical before him. Meanwhile, as John Napier points out in his own defence, it has been the skill and imagination of the British designer which has tempted producers to raise big money on big shows.

ANDREW LLOYD WEBBER

Phantom is a great, strong story. Despite appearances, it is not actually a physically big musical. There is a lot of illusion, drapes, curtaining and so on. The movement of the show is very fluid. It is a series of brilliantly executed stage tricks. Go backstage, and you would be very surprised at how little scenery there is. Just two main pieces that come on at the side, a couple of things that come on for the operas. But nothing that is particularly vast. Nevertheless, its scale comes over as big.

Having done something like *Starlight Express*, *The Phantom*, my Requiem Mass and various others, I did then feel that I wanted to do something quite different. So *Aspects of Love* was never intended be anything other than a chamber piece. That was far more effectively realised in the second London production than in the first, which somehow became overblown. Then, both *Sunset Boulevard* and *Whistle Down the Wind* have a very strong premise.

Shows have always got to be mostly story-driven. However great the songs are in a musical, they cannot work without the correct dramatic situation. I have always tried to place emphasis through the music, through the story. Besides which, when the size and costs of the sets and costumes spiral, it becomes self-defeating. Something has got to change. That is why I have returned to hands-on producing – something that I have not done for about twelve years.

CAMERON MACKINTOSH

The big musical has always been with us. What the Victorians did makes *Phantom* and *Miss Saigon* look puny. *Ben Hur*, *Cavalcade*, these shows were absolutely enormous extravaganzas with thousands of people backstage. Those kind of shows go back to the Romans in the Circus Maximus. The public has always had an appetite to see something spectacular. They are part of what the theatre is.

What prompted Jack to remark on the emergence of the 'mega-musical' was that an extraordinary thing had happened in the Eighties. First of all, four shows within the space of ten years became great classic musicals. In terms of scale of achievement nothing has ever happened like it before. True, in the Fifties extremely popular musicals emerged every couple of years, but there are crucial differences. From the late Seventies onwards, air travel changed people's notion of the world. The Earth shrunk and it was no longer extraordinary dinner-conversation to say that you had been to Thailand or wherever. Therefore word of mouth suddenly accelerated. With cheaper air fares, you did not have to be terribly rich to see a show in New York and London, expand your scope for comparison and become a more discerning theatregoer. Now local productions had to measure up to their cousins in the West End or Broadway because audiences had learned to expect certain standards. The challenge which I faced during the Eighties was to reproduce shows around the world which were as good as or better than the original.

Also, the maintenance of shows has completely changed. Now they are made to last and have to be kept fresh five, ten years on. That never used to happen.

Spotlight on the new man at the National: Eyre to a theatre of problems

Daily Mail, 20th January 1987

It is the most precarious balancing act since they last threw a high wire across Niagara Falls. And as Sir Peter Hall, one of nature's high fliers prepares to step off the tightrope as overlord of the National Theatre, the focus falls on Richard Eyre, the deceptively self-effacing man almost unknown outside the profession, but universally liked within it.

The combination is rare in an industry fuelled by ego and in-fighting. But Eyre will need all the nerve and willpower at his disposal if he is to steer the National through the next five or six crucial years when the subsidised arts are threatened as seldom before.

The problems he inherits are motley: filling and financing a money-hungry building, promoting new talent while pleasing a fickle public; and keeping the bureaucrats at bay while controlling an administrative nightmare.

It was the cruellest irony that Sir Peter's successor should be announced this week so scorchingly hot on the heels of the critical drubbing his latest prestige production received at the grey, concrete flagship of our subsidised arts. Of course, the two events were in no way connected. But it serves as a warning to Eyre.

Sir Peter miscalculated badly. He raised all the old accusations of profligate public spending by using Stephen Poliakoff's weak and empty *Coming in to Land* as a main-house vehicle worthy of the South Bank debut of Maggie Smith, joined by hot properties Anthony Andrews and Tim Pigott-Smith.

Eyre will learn from the debacle if he has not already done so. Now 43, Eyre built his early reputation championing that very generation of British writers, like Poliakoff, whose reputation springs almost entirely from within the subsidised theatre. Writers whose plays seldom survive the hurly-burly of the commercial sector.

Eyre has consolidated his standing in the cut-throat world of TV drama, where respectively he commissioned Alan Bennett to write about Kafka, and in the movies where he was acclaimed for *The Ploughman's Lunch*.

At a time when critics will be gunning for him, all this can only bode well for his stewardship of the National Theatre, especially at a time when the funding of the arts is under stringent attack.

'Nobody gives money without expecting something in return, and I think that always has to be borne in mind,' he declared significantly, shortly after his appointment.

RICHARD EYRE

Having been directing for quite a long time, I got to know Jack at first nights over the last fifteen years or so. The odd thing with critics is that most of them at the moment have been reviewing for about the same time that I have been directing. So I have got to know their literary persona, their exact tastes, and then formed odd relationships with them, based on mutual respect.

Jack clearly loved the theatreness of theatre. He liked all things theatrical. That word is generally used in a pejorative sense, to denote something overblown, camp and superficial. In the sense I am using it, it belongs to a description of the properties of the medium of theatre that make it different from everything else. Jack liked the liveness of the theatre and its humanity.

All critics have to travel hopefully, because more often than not they are disappointed. Jack could be harsh – but when one has a high expectation of the medium of theatre, the corollary of that is high disappointment. When Jack felt short-changed he did not disguise it.

That article, *Eyre to a Theatre of Problems*, was prophetic. Certainly then, I would have agreed with every word. It is easier for me now in 1997, with the comfort of hindsight and having in a sense succeeded in confounding his worst fears, to say that he was exaggerating.

It is certainly true that the critics 'were gunning for me.' There is a double standard. You can do a piece of work outside of the National Theatre and get very highly praised for it. Do the same piece inside the National Theatre and you are likely to get damned with faint praise. Having said that, it is right that the standards that critics apply to the National are extremely high. One of the *raisons d'être* of the company is that you aspire to the highest possible standards consistently, and ask to be judged by the highest possible standards.

Sir Peter's Hall of fame

Daily Mail, 17th May 1988

It is the lot of powerful men to be engulfed in an aura of mystery, misunderstandings and not a small touch of menace. How else would they hold us lesser mortals in their sway? So it comes as no surprise that Sir Peter Hall leaves the National Theatre on the same high fever pitch of rumour, speculation and controversy as he arrived.

Lord Olivier never made any secret of his resentment of his take-over of the South Bank bunker 15 years ago. And Miss Sarah Miles has done a stoker's job in shovelling coals to fuel the fires he ignited with her abrupt sacking as a prelude to his departure. Hell hath no fury like leading ladies scorned, nor leading lords usurped.

In between times, even ever-impartial I have not escaped the magisterial wrath of Sir Peter's hair-trigger sensitivity to well-meant criticism.

Only someone in desperate need of a job would deny that this mandarin impresario is a highly combative, politically motivated high-flyer who can combine the charm of a pussycat with the teeth of a tiger to get his way. 'Ruthless and power-loving,' he has been called and no doubt will be called so again. Yet, passions apart, Sir Peter's 15-year reign at the National Theatre must be judged as one of the great unsung miracles of modern theatre.

The task he faced was Herculean. That vast fortress, conceived in the give-away optimism of the Sixties and executed in the worst of that era's monolithic civic styles, needed a man who could somehow make it viable artistically, economically and administratively.

In short, it required the talents of a visionary theatrical entrepreneur, the political savvy of a tough captain of industry and the sensitivity of a true man of the arts. Ultimately, whatever false starts and occasional stops, Sir Peter has proved himself not wanting in any of these demanding departments. He has turned a white elephant into a racing thoroughbred.

Look only at the glittering prizes it has garnered on the way. While not forgetting the mistakes and disasters that are the in-built risks of any artistic endeavour (Jean Seberg, will your ghost ever rest easy?), they make formidable reading.

The least stage-struck of laymen must be impressed by the unrivalled tally of 131 major awards his company has collected during his stewardship. More than any other management in the land. And the most cynical commercial producer would count himself a fruitful man to have presided over 15 West End transfers in as many years.

Indeed, the two seasons just passed have upped the average impressively with no fewer than 22 awards and six transferred productions. The West End would have been a mightily poorer place recently without such varied delights as Miller's *A View from the Bridge*, Neil Simon's *Brighton Beach Memoirs*, Ayckbourn's *A Chorus of Disapproval*, and the quirky *Glengarry, Glen Ross* (charity forbids me mentioning *The Petition*). All of them mounted with the eye to detailed perfection that only subsidised theatres can now really afford.

It was Peter Hall's oft-misunderstood vision, when he took over the sprawling grey empire south of the Thames, to turn it into a platform for the rich kaleidoscope of performers, directors, writers and designers who form the cream on the top of British theatre, instead of a permanent inward-looking, select company (he had already accomplished this at the RSC).

Thus it was that Michael Gambon was triumphantly transformed overnight from an accomplished boulevard light comedy actor into a towering *Galileo* in the first league of his craft; that the under-used Dora Bryan was revealed as the consummate Restoration *Grande Dame*; that the likes of Frances de la Tour, Beryl Reid and Julie Walters were able to rank alongside such establishment favourites as John Gielgud, Judi Dench and Albert Finney as star attractions in roles few commercial managements would dared have risked. Even now John Alderton can be seen transposed from telly sitcom and West End gloss into one of Beckett's immortal tramps opposite the impeccable Alec McCowen.

All this Sir Peter Hall has accomplished with a clutch of the country's most imaginative directors and writers working with their own chosen groups – Alan Ayckbourn, Michael Rudman et al.

And this is what Sir Peter hands over to his successor Richard Eyre, himself a Hall-marked appointee. It is truly a National theatre. And with the added benefit of Thelma Holt's inspired international input from Germany, Japan and Russia, the South Bank has become an exciting place to be these past few seasons.

With a single seat now topping £27 at the cradle of Shakespearean drama, I think a detailed enquiry into falling standards there is due. Watch, as Mr (Nigel) Dempster loves to say, this space.

PETER HALL

Jack and I had a row once. Before the National moved from the Old Vic to the new building on the South Bank there was a tremendous faction in the press which was hostile to the new building. That was largely because it was so late arriving. It had been trumpeted all through the Sixties and when it was finally ready in the early Seventies people had got bored with the idea, there was less money about for the arts, and it became a scandal. Jack was very responsive to such changes of fashion – he would probably have said that it was part of his job, and indeed he often contributed to the emergence of these trends. Anyway, he was part of the anti-South Bank faction. We argued, I shouted at him and he shouted back. I know that he never forgot, and mentioned it in his writing nearly twenty years later.

Jack is not quite right when he says that I deliberately made the RSC 'inward-looking, select' and the NT high-profile, filled with stars. The RSC was based on an ensemble, but you had some very big and mainstream stars – Peter O'Toole, Janet Suzman, Glenda Jackson.

The main job of the RSC was to find ways of doing Shakespeare. I always wanted it to become expert in Shakespeare and also very alive to modern drama. That was the whole aesthetic, to some extent it still is.

The National was another matter – three theatres with a remit to do the best of drama from Aeschylus to David Hare. How do you make a company to do that? The National was and is about diversity and excellence, not about concentration, because the spectrum is much wider.

I did not consciously think about the policy of either, I responded to what I believed was the right way to run a particular theatre at a particular time.

My bouquets and brickbats

Daily Mail, 28th December 1988

The annual orgy of Awards, Honours and Wretched Recriminations is upon us. May I swell the armfuls of hideous statuettes and malevolent brickbats with two new accolades of my own – the self-explanatory Tinkies and Stinkies.

As we have a Prime Minister whose grasp of the Arts extends no further than *Charley's Aunt Meets the Enterprise Culture*, and a monarch whose interest in the entertainment industry is soured each year by having to endure the *Royal Variety Show*, they are awarded not to individual actors and actresses, but in personal gratitude for services rendered to (or in the case of the Stinkies, withheld from) the theatre.

No doubt, the call will come eventually: arise Sir Kenneth. But we cannot wait for Mr Branagh to hang around behaving himself for vetting and veneration, even with Prince Charles as his patron.

Being a friend of The Family is no shortcut to a knighthood (Noël Coward did not bend the knee until he was a creaking 70 and he counted the Queen Mother and Princess Margaret among his close chums). So the first Tinky goes to young Ken – as he matily signs his Christmas cards to fans and critics alike.

This is not necessarily for his acting; his *Hamlet* was at best an adequate addition to that distinguished gallery of vacillators. But his itinerant Renaissance Theatre Company worked a miracle this year not seen in the West End since Sir John Gielgud's legendary seasons at the New Theatre, which even I am too young to remember.

And though Renaissance is a collective, it is undoubtedly the charisma and chutzpah of Kenneth Branagh which put it on the theatre map. It had young and eager theatregoers queuing for return tickets for Shakespeare in the West End as if for a pop concert. And it encouraged Dame Judi Dench, Geraldine McEwan and Derek Jacobi to make their debuts as directors.

It served notice that Sophie Thompson and Samantha Bond are the stuff dreams of stardom are made on. And it lifted the jinx of the Phoenix Theatre and paved the way for Derek Jacobi to bring both *Richard II* and *III* to that forsaken place, safe in the knowledge that an entire new generation of theatregoers knew their way to its doors.

All of which must give some pause for thought to the subsidised RSC, where once such radical experiments reigned. Instead, Terry Hands, its newly incumbent overlord, becomes the distinguished recipient of the

M. Courtney-Clarke

Alan Davidson

10. *Above*: Tennessee Williams: '...an unqualified compassion for human frailty.' (p.92)

11. *Below*: Alan Ayckbourn's *A Small Family Business*:'...make no mistake, although it is a piece of uproarious fun it has about it the look of Ben Jonson – a comic mirror of a corrupt society into which no one dare look and laugh without seeing his or her own reflection.' (p.95)

Ivan Kyncl

Ken Towner

12. *Above*: Harold Pinter: Jack was not always a Pinter fan, but he was certainly a fan of *Moonlight* – '...a great play... No other Pinter play has moved me so much. No play he has written has come so close to the raw knuckle of human emotion.' (p.112)

13. *Below*: Tom Stoppard: 'It is a testament to Stoppard's versatility that after writing *Night and Day*, the best play in London last season, he should now lumber us with the two worst.' (*Dogg's Hamlet* and *Cahoot's Macbeth*.) (p.75)

John Swannell

John Haynes

14. *Above*: Lord Andrew Lloyd-Webber '...has proved there is nothing
you cannot write a musical about...' (p.50)

15. *Below*: *Shopping and Fucking* at the Royal Court Theatre:
'...whereas I led the chorus of disapproval when the Royal Court
staged Sarah Kane's now notorious *Blasted*, I can only applaud its
courage in staging this dangerous and to some, offensive work.' (p.119)

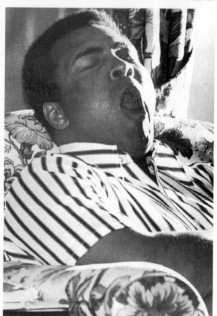

16. *Above*: Frank Sinatra at the Royal Festival Hall: '...holding a couple of notes so long and loud they draw applause. That is to demonstrate that the voice box is in good trim, of course. And of course it isn't.' (p.203)

17. *Left*: Lauren Bacall in *Woman of the Year*: '...presiding over a solid gold hit merely by the loan of her name.' (p.133)

18. *Right*: Muhammad Ali, of whom Jack writes: '...the man who not only walks with kings and presidents, but has pictures of them gazing up at him admiringly to prove it.' (p.207)

James Gray

ATV Photo

19. *Above*: 'Are you buying or selling?' Lew Grade (p.209)
20. *Below*: Bob Hope: 'Mr Hope may not believe this but I still say thanks for the
memory. But I would have been happy to have lived with the memory I treasure
and not had to sit worrying about his.' (p.206)

Dave Bennett

21. Michael Barrymore: '...most definitely, most triumphantly, most enduringly "Back in Business"' (p.240)

Alastair Muir

22. Steven Berkoff: '...life-long baiter of Establishment bulls and smasher of sacred cows.' (p.123)

SOLO   *David Rice-Evans*

Dave Cromd

23. *Above left*: Jack Tinker and Ian Adams, voice coach, the 'miracle worker'. (p.192)
24. *Above right*: 'My own mercifully brief career in late-night cabaret...' Partnering with
the redoubtable Libby Morris in a tribute to Ethel Merman at the Old Donmar.
25. *Below*: Jack Tinker and John Timpson, *Any Questions*.

Neville Marriner

Alan Davidson

26. *Above*: 'Seeing eye to eye...' Jack Tinker and Wayne Sleep, 1990. (p.227)
27. *Below*: Tribute to Jack Tinker at the London Palladium, 28 February 1997.

very first Stinky. *Carrie*, which should remain nameless on both sides of the Atlantic, was far and away the worst musical offering in a year when the British musical all but sank without trace after its decade of glory.

True, *Ziegfeld* (first with the anonymous Len Cariou, then with the unctuous Topol), *Winnie* and *Nite Club Continental* were all ignominious kitsch and sink disasters, but at least they did not tie up the time and resources of one of our major subsidised theatres.

Long and loud have I clamoured for Mr Alan Ayckbourn to receive an overdue knighthood. A mysterious conspiracy of deafness greets his assured scaling of ever dizzier heights. So a Tinky will have to suffice to put alongside all the other awards that mark his truly remarkable impact on the contemporary theatre, both commercial and subsidised. Time may well judge him to have been the Chekhov of our age, but 1988 was certainly another milestone.

With his 35th play, *Henceforward*, he again explored new territory, giving us the bleak glimpse into the near future that contained all the vigour and anxieties usually the preserve of new voices with reputations to make, yet touched with the unmistakable wit of a master.

Moreover he lately completed a triumphant two year season directing at the National Theatre with a production of *A View from the Bridge* which can be counted as a landmark.

In the New Year he will be 50. He will spend it guiding the fortunes of the Stephen Joseph Theatre up in Scarborough. May the grocer's daughter of Grantham recognise the uniqueness of this enterprise; meanwhile the Tinky must do.

One of the reasons for seeing *Henceforward* is the return of Ian McKellen to the West End stage. A Tinky goes to him for the tireless and selfless inspiration he has been on behalf of the AIDS charities with the fund-raising series of Sunday star concerts at the newly restored Playhouse Theatre.

The time and energy he has devoted to marshalling opposition to the infamous Clause 28 since its dangers were first perceived will not have endeared him to Downing St, so it is not advisable to hold one's breath to see his name ennobled in the New Year's Honours List.

Another equally political *tour de force* is Sir Peter Hall. It would be a churlish man who did not acknowledge the formidable achievement he accomplished in turning the now Royal National Theatre from a white elephant into a thoroughbred racehorse. A coveted Tinky must certainly grace his sideboard, along with the rose-bowls and testimonials which accrued to mark his exit from the South Bank bunker after a turbulent reign and a year of singularly mixed fortunes, both professional and private.

Finally, a fusillade of Stinkies to every MP who voted in the appalling Clause 28. It took decades to rid the theatre of the burden of censorship.

When Sir Peter Hall first directed Tennessee Williams' *Cat on a Hot Tin Roof* in London 30 years ago, they had to turn the theatre into a club to avoid the wrath of the Lord Chamberlain and his red pen. It is now hailed as a masterpiece and rightly 1988 saw it grace the repertoire of our Royal National Theatre.

Yet should some local authority give it house-room, or have it performed in their schools as a subject for open discussion, this catch-all Act now opens the door for any piddling self-proclaimed guardian of public morality to step in and invoke the might of the law against it.

Compassion for our fellows can so easily be represented as 'promoting' a cause.

ALAN AYCKBOURN

Being awarded the Tinky by Jack was great. Any award is wonderful. I have not won an Oscar yet, so the Tinky will do just as well.

Note: Sir Alan Ayckbourn received his knighthood in 1997.

A promising pair to manage the monster

Daily Mail, 10th February 1990

Whichever way they slice the hot potato they have been handed, (Adrian) Noble and (Michael) Attenborough will be lucky if only their fingers get burned. The RSC is in crisis. Both are men of proven talent and vision... But the task facing them at Stratford and, more particularly, in London is almost as daunting as bailing out the NHS.

Quite simply, the company has become an unmanageable monster, fed on its own past glories and needing ever more fodder and funding merely to stand still. Given the Government's present harsh economic treatment of the arts, severe retrenchment would seem to be the only way forward. (Terry) Hands, retiring captain of the beleaguered fleet, said as much when he announced this week that its London flagship, the Barbican theatre and its studio off-shoot, was to go into dry dock for a spell.

This was the first hint that Adrian Noble was one of those picked to step into the breach. It was openly rumoured by those with a vested interest in the choice of Hands's successor that the Barbican was Noble's main objection to accepting what amounts to the poisoned chalice that goes with the job.

According to the faction that backed him for the post, he would prefer to abandon it altogether. It eats both cash and resources; moreover, the concrete wasteland which provides its setting is viewed without much affection by actors and audiences alike.

However, the RSC is committed to the City of London to stay in residence for the next 17 years. So Hands's shock-announcement of its part-closure, besides firing off an SOS to the Arts Council on the state of the company's £3 million deficit, also effectively created the compromise which enabled Noble to take up the offer...

Alas, poor Kenneth

Daily Mail, 9th May 1992

As great actors go, Kenneth Branagh still has far to come. Last week on radio, however, he gave a truly impressive reading of *Hamlet*. Admirable in ever way. But did you hear this said?

No. As usual, the event turned into a media circus, this time hijacked by the fact that Sir John Gielgud, one of the great Hamlets of the century, was now playing the ghost to Branagh's Prince. A great deal of nonsense was talked about pretenders to the throne and heirs apparent, which Sir John treated with his customary Olympian loftiness.

Only once did he give way to his penchant for deadly aimed tactlessness. On hearing that his young co-star was about to give us his *Coriolanus* at Chichester next week, the knight was less than encouraging. '*Coriolanus!*' he chortled. 'I hate the play! And at Chichester? A nasty theatre!'

The story was gleefully passed around, the implication being that the upstart had once again been slapped down. Alas, poor Ken. But I do not propose to declare the ritual Branagh-baiting season open. It is this mean-minded trait in our national character which interests me far more.

As a race we find approval an almost painful process. Unlike our Continental cousins, even our language of praise has dried up and withered since the flowering of the fulsome flattery of the first Elizabethan age – an otherwise cruel and brutal era.

By contrast, although we no longer flock to see live bears tear themselves apart and even cock-fighting is illegal, our vocabulary of invective grows ever more barbed and quotable in its infinite variety.

Search my mind for some random remark I can bring forth from the tens of thousands penned and pronounced on Our Ken, I am ashamed I can recall only one. It is utterly trivial and demeaning. Yet it clings to the memory like Velcro and it clamours to get out.

I will not embarrass the perpetrator who first whispered to me: 'If you smeared Germolene over those lips, his mouth would heal over.' But its destructiveness is out of all proportion to its shameless pettiness. The wound – if Mr Branagh will ever forgive the expression – lies in the fact that we all know exactly what was meant.

Ask any actor to repeat the review which, like Calais on the heart of Mary Tudor, they will carry to the grave. Inevitably it will be equally bitchy, horribly apt and instantly quotable. Not a single paean of praise will they recall.

That most consummate artist Diana Rigg has excited more eulogies than your average Greek goddess. Yet she felt compelled to compile an entire volume of critical vitriol – the highly readable *No Turn Unstoned* – to exorcise the scar-tissue to the soul that even Germolene could not cure.

And who can blame her? No girl would ever forget her debut in a tasteful nude scene – strictly in the cause of Higher Art, you understand – being greeted with the epithet: 'Diana Rigg is built like a brick mausoleum with insufficient flying buttresses.'

Against this, all the superlatives in the dictionary will not sweeten that little hand, nor wipe the man who dealt it, from Diana's memory bank. There she was again at those interminable *Olivier Awards*, picking at the scab and reminding us of it all over again.

None of us is immune. I promise myself never again publicly to admit that my best friend, Nicholas de Jongh, once wrote in the *Guardian* on my modest attempts at late-night cabaret: 'He sings and he dances, and his tiny talent should take him as far as the end of the nearest pier – or just beyond. But there, like the aching tooth, the tongue simply has to seek it out.'

I come from that part of the country where overt joy of any kind is considered an affront to manliness. The highest accolade you could hope to aspire to in Oldham was: 'Well, I couldn't fault it.' 'It'll do' passed for a compliment. More than that would be considered an incitement to 'get above yourself'. Getting above yourself was the most heinous of all crimes. Hence the expression 'to put down'.

So it is doubly dispiriting to know that, while I may spend my entire working week attempting to communicate enthusiasm for what is best and finest in the theatre, only the brickbats stand any chance of an after-life.

Sir Peter Hall once accused me of writing nothing good about the National Theatre. I sent him a dozen recent reviews, only three of which could be considered downright damning. The rest ranged from fair to rave. It did not change his mind.

The bouquets? They either shrivel on the page or are exhibited on theatre hoardings for all to see the poverty of our power to applaud in print. 'Thrilling', 'Hypnotic', 'Stunning'. Clichés all. The heartfelt, passionate plaudits may survive, but only as objects of derision in Pseuds' Corner of *Private Eye*. Sadly, as a nation our innate instinct is to come to bury Caesar, never to praise him. We have simply lost the art.

NICHOLAS DE JONGH

I do not think that critics have remotely lost the art of praising. Quite the reverse. Often critics are too extravagant in their admiration. There are quite a few people trying in ridiculous terms to emulate Jack's style of sometimes hyperbolic, always eloquent praise. I used to mock Jack to his face about this. Once I went up to him and said, 'I would gladly crawl over a mile of broken glass just for a glimpse of Dame Maggie Smith,' which he very much enjoyed. The absence of self-importance was one of his endearing characteristics. Jack was very happy to mock himself.

A hot shot in the dark

Daily Mail, 20th June 1992

Pardon my ploughing an old furrow so soon after the topsoil has been thoroughly tilled. But I am finding it hard to go through the annual ritual of donning sackcloth and ashes for the demise of the West End.

I am still glowing from a theatrical shot in the arm that is a lesson to those producers busy blaming the recession, the heatwave, the lack of tourists and their Great Aunt Fannies for their dismal business. Admittedly six theatres threatened with sudden darkness is enough to set alarm bells ringing. But instead of looking for scapegoats, I would pack them off without delay to the Royal National Theatre – where the unobtrusive Richard Eyre has been giving masterclasses in the art of balancing market forces with inspired risk taking.

If they are not very quick about it, the National will have totally taken over their domain, leaving the West End with nothing but blockbuster musicals on which to survive.

Particularly I would direct them to the tiny Cottesloe studio where, as I have mentioned elsewhere, there is a production generating enough energy and imagination to keep the lights of the West End blazing for an entire year.

In spite of its ungainly title and raucous language, Jim Cartwright's *The Rise and Fall of Little Voice* is a piece of original theatre worth leaving home for. It has a story of such intense domestic power, you could measure it against the best Tennessee Williams... it has performances big and bold enough to fill the Palladium – not least from Jane Horrocks, who produces from her skinny, frightened frame a series of impersonations of such eerie accuracy that several of my colleagues were balefully debating in the interval whether or not the lady was miming.

Garland, Piaf, Monroe, Holiday, Bassey and Our Gracie all belted out from her frail frame. This – plus Alison Steadman creating another collectable grotesque for her indelible gallery – was a theatrical feast indeed.

Expect it to help resuscitate the lifeless West End any time now. For that wiliest of producers, Michael Codron had the foresight to co-produce this daring piece of pyrotechnics with the National.

Once it would have been the West End alone giving us the likes of Alan Bennett's finest, most glorious play *The Madness of George III*. It would have been along Shaftesbury Avenue that we found Tennessee

Williams' *The Night of the Iguana*. But the commercial managements can't forever be gnashing their gums and moaning that the subsidised theatre is unfairly snatching all the bread from their baskets.

Let them only remember the story of *Joseph*, even as told by Tim Rice and Sir Andrew Lloyd Webber. There have been at least seven years of fat and plenty in the West End, not all of it corn. What did they set aside from this rich harvest to see them through the lean years? Which new playwrights did they encourage? What innovations did they risk?...

To PC, or not PC?

What political correctness would mean to Shakespeare

Daily Mail, 21st January 1994

Yesterday it emerged that a headmistress in the East London borough of Hackney had stopped the pupils going to see a production of *Romeo and Juliet* because she felt the story wasn't Politically Correct. Here, the *Daily Mail*'s theatre critic wonders what Shakespeare would have done if some of his other great plays had been forced to meet the same ideological standards.

MACBETH

The Shakespeare version: Macbeth, a Scottish general, meets three witches who predict, among other things, that he will one day be King of Scotland. Half-maddened by ambition he is persuaded by his wife, Lady Macbeth, to murder the present King Duncan and take the throne. This sets him off on a great killing spree in which he gets rid of all his rivals – including at one stage Lady Macduff and her children. Thereafter, he is haunted by guilt and Lady Macbeth has terrifying visions. Macbeth is finally killed by Macduff after a battle in which another prophecy is fulfilled when his enemies disguise themselves as trees and use the camouflage to creep up on his castle.

The PC version: Macbeth's three witches pose problems. Not only do they represent quite unfounded propaganda for the occult, but being old and ugly are both ageist and what you might call 'repellentist'. Instead, three winsome social workers will help Macbeth sort out his politically unsound ambition. For, as we know, all competition is a crime.

King Duncan would still have to go, of course, for monarchy is the very symbol of elitism. But a humbling constitutional abdication would soon put that right – no need for violent murder in bed in the middle of the night.

And Ms Macbeth – as we must now call the infamous Lady Macbeth – will of course have to be the live-in partner of Glamis's sitting tenant rather than lady of the castle. To get over her nervous fits following the abdication, she will have to be sent away on a long therapeutic trip to India at the ratepayers' expense, where the repeated chanting of mantras and a course of aromatherapy will soon calm the symptoms of her unfortunate breakdown.

Child-battering is definitely out. Lady Macduff will employ the self-defence karate techniques she has acquired at the council's confidence-crisis centre to overcome the socially maladjusted intruders who have come to kill her children.

Having thoroughly humiliated them, she will then, naturally, put in a call to the three wise social workers who will set about rehabilitating the misguided youths into society with a three-month skiing holiday in Gstaad.

And if grown men want to go out and dress up as trees, then that is their choice. By all means let them. But swords must be made of papier-mâché and there must be no fighting in the castle yard afterwards, mind.

They will simply elect the socially rehabilitated Macbeth as their chairperson – which will greatly help the figures on delinquent re-offending.

OTHELLO

The Shakespeare version: Othello, the Moor and governor of Venice, secretly marries the beautiful (white) Desdemona. Her father is furious. One of Othello's soldiers, Iago, who harbours a deep grudge, spreads the rumour that Desdemona is having an affair. In a fit of jealousy, Othello kills her, then, when he finds out she was innocent, kills himself, too.

The PC version: this play is most certainly tainted. Some parts of the plot are fine but Desdemona's dad will have to welcome his new son-in-law into the family circle with open arms and blessings.

Until Iago's insidious suggestions get to work, our black brothers could not wish for a finer icon than Othello. What an achiever! Perhaps he should have married a nice black girl, but then mixed marriages are frowned upon by the politically pristine only if they want to adopt a child.

So with an Equity agreement that only genuine black males or females should play black roles (Frank Bruno or Jessye Norman, perhaps), so far so good. However, to absolve the plot from any hint of racist propaganda and to eradicate the suggestion that Othello, being black, is a jealous fool, the Moor has a master plan.

He will merely pretend to go along with Iago's perfidy, thus testing the loyalty of his men, unmasking his lieutenant's fiendish envy and demonstrating the superiority of his noble nature.

Desdemona will at all times be her loving husband's loyal accomplice in this clever scheme, but act the part of the battered wife so effectively that the local women's refuge offers her instant accommodation.

Iago, being white, lower-middle class and in full-time employment, will, of course, be sentenced to life imprisonment, there being no excuse for his behaviour. Otherwise he would have got away with 100 hours community service.

RICHARD III

The Shakespeare version: the evil and deformed Richard of Gloucester murders the princes in the tower in order to become King. In the end, of course, he comes to grief when he falls off his horse and though he pleads 'A horse, a horse, my kingdom for a horse,' he is mercilessly killed by the Duke of Richmond, who then becomes Henry VII.

The PC version: this play of course is an intolerable affront to the physically challenged. Richard's character is to be totally changed to the sort of role the late Errol Flynn could have played. He must indeed be given a horse in exchange for his kingdom, as he quite reasonably demands, and finally be allowed to ride off into the sunset with all the dignity that befits a person with an impaired right shoulder and left foot, as a lesson in compassion to us all.

The play would then become a classic celebration for all those 'not made for sportive tricks nor made to court an amorous looking-glass.' Certain personal habits would need working on, of course, if the piece is not to offend.

Richard's treatment of the little princes, or indeed any of his relatives, is a direct insult to the good name of deformity – sorry, physical inexactitude. Radical re-writes required here.

KING LEAR

The Shakespeare version: King Lear decides to divide his kingdom among his three daughters, Goneril, Regan and Cordelia on condition they tell him how much they love him. The honest Cordelia won't be bribed and Lear cuts her off. He lives on the other two until they tire of his noisy retinue and throw him out. The Earl of Gloucester, who loves his bastard son Edmund, is punished for his loyalty to the King by having his eyes pulled out. Lear loses his wits and wanders around with Gloucester's other son Edgar, who disguises himself as a lunatic. Lear ends up dying of grief.

The PC version: this violent play will be the toughest assignment for the stampers of those politically correct seals of approval. Gloucester's eyes must not leave his head. A man who is in the vanguard of informed opinion on the matter of his son's illegitimacy must not have even an ear tweaked.

The monarch is in dire need of a brisk lesson in PC. Does he think he's living in the Dark Ages, living off inherited wealth, taking early retirement, and bossing grown women as if he owned the place?

But there can be no suggestion that when Edgar disguises himself as Poor Tom that his wits are impaired. This is degrading to the poor and the witless – sorry, economically disadvantaged and intellectually impaired. He will become a strolling youth worker.

Goneril and Regan are simply victims of their upper-class upbringing, so the more evil they are and the more terrible their fates, the more children will learn.

THE MERCHANT OF VENICE

The Shakespeare version: Antonio, a merchant, gets into financial difficulties and borrows cash from Jewish moneylender Shylock. When he can't pay it back, Shylock demands the price – a pound of flesh. Antonio's fiancée Portia dresses up as a lawyer and pleads eloquently for mercy. But Shylock will not give way and finally is forced to turn Christian and give all his money away.

The PC version: Shylock's role will have to be totally re-written. He will be that despised thing, the Venetian equivalent of an Old Etonian Lloyd's Name whose ancient family was heaped with titles.

There can be no objection whatsoever in children laughing uproariously at any discomfiture he might suffer thereafter. Portia's trial scene can definitely stay, with her speech extended to include the Guildford Four, the Birmingham Six, the Magnificent Seven and the Ten Commandments.

John the giant killer

Daily Mail, 16th April 1994

The *Today* Programme, that early morning pace-setter for the informed classes, rang me the day prior to Sir John Gielgud's 90th birthday. Those who tuned in to the subsequent broadcast might even have heard me sounding a trifle astounded that at this great age Sir John had disclosed to that organ of scholarly research, *Hello!* magazine, a terrible secret. Namely that he had very little understanding of, and even less taste for, much of Shakespeare. And he never read poetry if he could help it.

Shock, horror and heresy was the tone of the item.

Of course, the greatest speaker of Shakespearean verse this century boldly admitting 'I'm able to bolt down a cheap thriller, but I couldn't read *Troilus and Cressida* or *Coriolanus* with any great pleasure' was bound to send tremors of consternation wherever academics or intellectual directors make fat reputations and loadsamoney theorising about the Bard.

I was merely concurring that Sir John's accustomed frankness might stand on its big egghead much of the received wisdom on which our students are ritualistically force-fed. 'And about time too!' is what I *didn't* say.

Truth to tell, given the choice between setting down with a mug of steaming cocoa and a copy of *Titus Andronicus* or a good Ruth Rendell mystery, I'm with Sir John all the way. Aren't you?

Shakespeare wrote for actors to act and audiences to watch. He did not sit down to consider the dusty debates of generations of dried-up professors down the ages.

When Sir John, from the lofty pinnacles of his 90 years, says 'I don't like examining much how I act. I find all the discussion very boring, I want colour, beauty, drama and magic,' he is only telling it like it really is. He is speaking up for actors who have not forgotten there is an audience out there – and also for audiences who still believe in the miracle of theatre to transport them to other worlds.

All great acting is in part intuitive. That is what sets it above the rest of the herd. This stamp of genius cannot be learned by rote or dinned in through diligence. Nor does it come simply by practice, though all these disciplines may go into honing its techniques.

If it could be taught, we would all be standing up there spouting Hamlet's soliloquy, with no one left to do the grave-digging, carry the spears, act the Players or lead the applause.

No. I think that Sir John was simply bored to his silver larynx by all the birthday brouhaha and decided, mischievously, to blow the gaff – then sit and watch the sparks fly.

True, I would have been less astonished to learn that the late Laurence Olivier had little comprehension of the subtext in Shakespeare's plays. He was always more concerned with the shape of the nose or the thickness of the thigh before he could bring meaning to the lines. But then Olivier would never have been the man to admit such a thing.

There is a salutary lesson to be learned in comparing the latter years of these two titans of 20th century theatre. Whereas Olivier, the arch-competitor, the athletic usurper of Gielgud's pre-war throne, the jealous custodian of his reputation's crown, endured a painful winter of discontent towards his own final curtain – the faculties more or less flown on ahead – Gielgud has been left to bask in a glorious golden autumn.

Anyone who heard his wondrous *Lear* on Radio 3 last weekend will know just how much in command of his unique vocal powers he still is. The voice James Agate once described as a silver trumpet wrapped in silk is as mellifluous as ever. Age has merely added its own haunting timbre. And if that was an actor who understood only half of what he was saying, then give me actors of so much understanding any night of the week.

Should Sir John have a malicious bone in his body, which I seriously doubt, as such serenity does not flourish alongside malice, he might well be forgiven a sly chuckle behind the hand. Yet perhaps he has not even noticed how time has come subtly to reverse the verdict on these two giants of the British stage.

It was Olivier who appeared to out-pace and outsmart the established Gielgud with his brash modernity at every turn after their early careers reached the high plateau at the Old Vic, where they famously alternated the roles of Hamlet and Mercutio! Gielgud the creature of light and air, Olivier the man of fire and action.

To discerning modern eyes and ears, it is Olivier's past performances which would appear old-fashioned and hammily declamatory, while Gielgud still excites the devotion of the young school.

Whereas Olivier always chose to hide behind a rich disguise, exhibiting an unerring instinct for each new fashion, Gielgud doggedly channelled his art through his own truths, his own fully-rounded personality.

So it was that when great age began, inevitably, to whittle away the tricks and techniques of their art, it was Gielgud, the older of the two, who had the infinite resources remaining to carry him on from one professional glory to another.

To a new, hip generation, it was Sir John, not Larry, who excited the critics and pleased the crowd. Olivier quite literally shuffled off this mortal coil reflecting, perhaps, that he who weds the times today is a widower tomorrow.

Apart from the bother of the birthday hysteria, I don't suppose there is an actor of this or any other age Sir John would have changed places with when he woke up on Thursday to his anniversary morn. Adored, acclaimed, still working – and with the licence of venerability to say any damned thing he likes. Even to *Hello!*

Who among us could ask for more?

Theatre is dead, long live theatre...

Daily Mail, 2nd September 1994

The words seemed so ominously familiar. They could have been taken straight out of any current report of West End woe-making. 'Last weekend there were eight shows closed in the London theatre. Audiences are dwindling to the merest trickle... it is all so frightening that the London theatre managers have appealed to the owners to reduce the theatre rents. I predict the closing of a lot of theatres. Soon there will be a coterie audience for the serious play – and theatres will house only musicals and light stuff.'

In fact, these words were written exactly 30 years ago, not long after the advent of the era we now look back on as the Golden Age of the serious play. In 1964 the dust had scarcely settled from the violent eruption of such volcanic talents as Osborne, Pinter, Beckett and Wesker. The New Wave writers were in their glory at the Royal Court. These, and other Young Turks were news as no new writer is today.

Yet Kenneth Williams (for it is he) was moved to this lament as he wandered through the streets of London after witnessing his dear friend Maggie Smith (now Dame) perform her seminal vision of Desdemona to Olivier's potent *Othello* at The National (now Royal). I came upon it this week while reading Russell Davies' enthralling new collection of Williams' letters, which are just as stringently revealing as his best-selling diaries – and provide an equally acerbic vision not only of himself and his friendships, but of the times in which he found himself so increasingly alienated.

Were he alive and walking around the West End today, he might well have felt his doleful conclusions only too prophetic. There are, in truth, no fewer than 17 musicals on display competing for the punters' increasingly hard-earned and unwillingly relinquished spare cash. And there are only four or five mainstream commercial theatres offering significant new writing. It all depends on what you call serious, of course. But I resolutely include Terry Johnson's killingly comic yet achingly painful *Dead Funny* at The Vaudeville in my collection of best new plays of the present decade. There is also David Baird's fascinatingly fetid hothouse flower, *900 Oneonta*. A splendid piece of hyper-poetic vision incorporating the over-wrought style of Tennessee Williams and the grim morality of Eugene O'Neill.

There is yet another new David Mamet play, *The Cryptogram*, at The Ambassadors, acclaimed by some of my colleagues but distinguished for me by the shining performances of Lindsay Duncan and Eddie Izzard. Tom Stoppard's latest play, *Arcadia*, transferred from the Royal National with a new and splendid cast, is the set piece at The Haymarket. And, lest we forget, *The Woman in Black* at The Fortune and now in its sixth year, adapted from Susan Hill's novel, has brought new distinction to the much maligned genre of the thriller.

Yet take these alongside impressive and, in some cases, landmark revivals of such classics as Priestley's *An Inspector Calls*, Rattigan's *The Winslow Boy*, plus impeccable versions of Wilde's *Lady Windermere's Fan* and Shaw's *St Joan* – which gave Kenneth Williams his first taste in the Fifties of West End fame as the Dauphin and in which now Imogen Stubbs is worth the price of any ticket in the house. And to me, the West End today looks a far healthier and more adventurous place than it did in 1964 when KW made his dismal prediction.

For new serious writing he could choose Iris Murdoch's rather worthy *The Severed Head*, Edward Albee's black domestic battleground *Who's Afraid of Virginia Woolf?*, Anouilh's *Poor Bitos* and Joe Orton's blackly brilliant *Entertaining Mr Sloane*. Ironically, for light relief, there was *Beyond the Fringe* – the revue which all but killed off the genre which was Kenneth Williams' theatrical forte.

Personally, I would match *Dead Funny* with *Mr Sloane* – or *900 Oneonta* against *Virginia Woolf* in any of posterity's listings. And certainly

Arcadia is streets ahead of *A Severed Head* for intellectual dramatic impact. As for sheer theatrical imagination, dare one say that *The Woman in Black* is every bit as fascinating as the ageing Anouilh's *Bitos*?

Interestingly enough, of the musicals Williams so despairs of, *She Loves Me*, now so enchantingly revived at the Savoy, was among that season's Broadway imports.

However there was a marked absence of Shaw, Chekhov, Wilde or any of the classics we now see so regularly and stylishly revived along Shaftesbury Avenue, particularly by the Peter Hall company. (Even in his Fifties production of *St Joan*, Williams himself had to creep into the West End via a triumphant run in the tiny Arts Theatre Club.)

Strangely enough it was this eternal question of the impending death of the West End and 'serious' new writing which stitched itself like a theme through question time during my one-man Edinburgh Fringe appearance last week – which went better than I had ever hoped, thanks for asking.

I felt suddenly very old, having to explain that the death of British drama as we know it has been actively under discussion since at least a century before the Puritans closed down all the theatres.

We are, it is true, coming to a crisis point. Public largesse, which enabled new writing to flourish through the subsidised channels, is drying up. And this can be nothing but a damning shame on any government which counts the cultural needs of its people as part of a nation's spiritual well-being.

Yet the thirst for a vital theatre in the capital persists, as it has done throughout the times of persecution, censorship and recession. It flourishes in places of experiment and excellence like the Bush Theatre in Shepherd's Bush where *900 Oneonta* was first staged, at the Almeida in Islington and the Hampstead Theatre, all of which have supplied an unending series of important transfers to the West End.

Independent producers such as Michael Codron, Bill Kenwright and Woji and Frank Gero, have forged vital links with subsidised and experimental theatres large and small. The Geros, indeed, have gone even further to form a ten-strong group of independent producers to combat the spiralling costs of putting on a straight new play. Their combined resources were responsible for giving *900 Oneonta* its opulent West End production. Meanwhile *Dead Funny* took a similar route from Hampstead and *Arcadia* originated full blown at the Royal National.

As for the dominance of the musical, well I even find some cheer in that. Most children gain their first taste for theatre via the despised pantomimes, which is why I demand so much of them come Christmas. Likewise, many adults return to the theatre through the 'event' musical – *Phantom*, *Saigon*, *Les Miserables* etc. And if London is still supplying these in a profligate fashion which would have appalled Kenneth

Williams, it is at least giving its potential new audience a touch of populist class which the likes of *Oliver!*, *A Funny Thing Happened on the Way to the Forum*, and *The Sound of Music* were generating back in 1964.

Heaven knows, it was *Salad Days* which first awakened a love of theatre in the young Cameron Mackintosh. And it was seeing Kenneth Williams and Maggie Smith in the light-hearted revue *Share My Lettuce* which gave me my first inklings of sophistication.

Nothing changes.

Blasted

Sarah Kane
Royal Court Theatre Upstairs
Daily Mail, 19th January 1995

This disgusting feast of filth

Until last night I thought I was immune from shock in any theatre. I am not. Finally I have been driven into the arms of Disgusted of Tunbridge Wells. For utterly and entirely disgusted I was by a play which appears to know no bounds of decency, yet has no message to convey by way of excuse. Why the 23-year-old Sarah Kane chose to write it is her affair. Presumably because she was given a grant by the hitherto admirable Jerwood Foundation in their quest to help new talent.

Some will undoubtedly say the money might have been better spent on a course of remedial therapy. But the real question is why, with the co-operation of our Royal National Theatre, the Royal Court saw fit to stage it. As a piece of drama, it is utterly without dramatic merit. Ms Kane merely creates her own lawless environment, and then allows her three characters to behave with utmost bestiality to each other as a result of it.

We begin with a journalist indulging in all manner of graphic sexual activity with an underaged and mentally retarded girl in his hotel room somewhere in England. Then we regress, by various implausible stages, from mere unlawful indecency to vividly enacted male rape, through to the barbaric cannibalism of a dead baby and on to simple defecation on stage. Just for those academics who seek to justify any stage violence with the example of Gloucester having his eyes put out in *King Lear*, Ms Kane has stern news for them.

Here our hero not only loses his eyes after being severely raped, his torturer munches them before our own eyes which by now are standing out unbidden on stalks.

Only one person left the arena during all these gratuitous acts, which must say a great deal for the politeness or stoicism of British audiences. Controversy is naturally always part of the deal when pushing forward the boundaries of art. But with the hounds of repression snapping at the heels of sex and violence wherever they sniff it out, the Royal Court have surely fed them a feast of it with this. Luckily for all of us, the play becomes so risible the only thing to do is laugh.

Our own theatre of the absurd

Daily Mail, 27th April 1996

Whatever it is that the world is coming to, I devoutly wish it wouldn't. It was surely the end of civilisation as we know it when I was forced to listen to a male acquaintance this week eagerly detailing elaborate plans for a face-lift and tummy tuck.

Gruesome. Truly gruesome – especially in view of the raw material in question. Women anxious to preserve their youth and beauty are perfectly understandable. But saggy men chiselling away at years of debauchery and beer bellies are a wholly unwarranted intrusion on any self-respecting surgeon's time or talent.

I simply couldn't help myself. 'Why throw good money after bad habits?' I wanted to know. After all, they're spending £41 million of Lottery loot on the Royal National Theatre but it will never be anything other than a hideous monstrosity.

Now, why did I have to go and bring up that horrible subject? If there is one topic guaranteed to turn my temper from risible contempt to blind fury in one sentence, it is that squat, blind concrete car park which Sir Denys Lasdun has been passing off as a palace of the arts for almost 30 years.

The very fact that the place needs a prince's ransom to tart it up so soon in its history speaks volumes. It was madness for anyone to have taken a riverside site and built a giant crustacean on it, which neither reflects the water in its windows nor affords any decent vistas across the passing tides. But to call a place like that a theatre is virtually a contradiction in terms.

A nation which cares anything about its culture should rightly have deported the culprits for such a scheme.

Theatres, whatever their period or style, should be instantly recognisable as places which hold out an invitation to the passing throng. They must be buildings which sing out the message that to be outside on the pavement is to be the wrong side of the door.

Stand in front of the gloriously restored Old Vic Theatre – the National's former home – with all its lights ablaze. Without a ticket to go inside you feel like Cinderella longing to go to the ball – and that is before you have even glanced at the posters advertising the play and its players.

Sir Denys' dismal dump, on the contrary, puts forth all the warm allure of an army barracks. Come the privatisation of our prisons he could easily flog off the blueprint for its grim exterior as the ideal role model for the long-term incarceration of the worst kind of miscreant.

Only the artistic vision of the two artistic directors of that brutal bunker glowering away on the South Bank – Sir Peter Hall and Richard Eyre – have stopped my spirits sinking whenever I have approached it.

Inside, of course, the play's the thing. You don't have to give a thought to the hideousness of the precast cladding into which you have been swallowed.

The new plans to open up the foyers connecting the Olivier Theatre's meeting place with Lyttelton's and putting plates of glass along the building's outer extremities may be considered an improvement. But really the expense is as futile as that poor bald, fat and forty something's facelift.

By all means replace the worn-out technical equipment. Get that notoriously temperamental drum stage working properly. Fork out for the latest lighting computers.

Do everything you can to make the internal workings of the place worthy of the greatest talents the country has to offer.

And while you are about it, make backstage life a lot easier for the actors. Dashing from some urgent shopping to rehearsals there one day, poor Dora Bryan – a National treasure in every sense – got hopelessly lost in the warren of corridors which link dressing rooms to the various theatres. Seeing a group of fellow actors on stage, she gratefully rushed up to ask directions – only to find herself, still with her plastic carrier bags, in the middle of someone else's matinée performance.

The audience seemed not to notice. Perhaps they were still recovering from trying to find their own way in; for among the building's manifold shortcomings, Sir Denys has designed an entrance which is as difficult for the casual caller to detect as the secrets of Paul Daniels' magic box. Even brick supermarkets say: come in and buy.

Why do I fume on so about this miserable excrescence? It is there and it will take more than a few sharp words to shift. After all, the easiest way to treat an eyesore is to look the other way.

Yet what makes me so mad about this building – and the millions soon to be lavished trying to make it look presentable and not show its age – is that it represents so much of what has happened to this country over the decades.

Only a nation in terminal decline could imagine that an edifice like this represents all that is best in our arts.

In the past century we have not erected a single civic, cultural or religious building which we can bequeath to future generations knowing that people in centuries to come will stop to marvel at it. Other countries have and do so. The Sydney Opera House is one of the wonders of the modern world. It appears to float just off the famous harbour like a flock of iridescent giant sea birds or a fleet of sailing ships, their sails lit by the sun.

It is no fanciful thing to trace Australia's new-found spirit of national pride and independence to the building of that inspired creation. Aussies who know as much about opera as I know of sheep-shearing will point you there with unflagging enthusiasm at its presence.

Can we show any similar glimmer of national pride in the building which houses our National Theatre? And isn't it indicative of a country which has lost its visions, its aspirations as well as its way that we have as the 20th century's temple to one of our greatest glories, drama, a monument to everything which is at best boring and uninspired and at worst brutal and ugly?

And unless we demand something better, that's us, folks.

RICHARD EYRE

I do not agree that the building is truly gruesome. I think that it has a certain nobility. The truth is that, demonstrably, people enjoy coming to the building and the foyers have a fantastic feeling of life about them. Consistently, two and a half thousand people visit the building most nights in the year. So I think that the audiences and the people who work here in a sense colonised the territory. It is irrelevant whether it looks ugly or not, essentially what goes on here is an activity that more often than not lifts people's hearts.

Peter Hall had the more difficult job. He opened the building and had to get the public used to the idea that this is a place that they should use. The construction work that we are doing now will make it even more accessible.

To say that we should just start from scratch is pointless. This is it. I did not decide to build this building, the people who did are long past taking responsibility for it. This is what we have got. Let us now make it as vigorous as possible.

7

THERE'S NO BUSINESS...

So you think you just can't sing!

Daily Mail, 26th September 1980

When Siân Phillips landed the star role in the revival of *Pal Joey*, there was only one doubt about her suitability. And it was an overwhelming one. Miss Phillips had never sung a note on stage in any major musical. It was much the same with Tom Conti when he was asked to star in the forthcoming West End production of the Broadway musical hit *They're Playing Our Song*.

Like Miss Phillips his singing had been confined largely to the bathroom, which caused them both separately to tear round in a state of gibbering panic to the side of Ian Adams' grand piano. For Mr Adams has acquired the reputation of a miracle worker among the West End acting fraternity. He finds the voices buried beneath the worst corncrake croaks and he can polish them until they shine with the best.

Which is why actors suddenly called upon to sustain long musical roles beat a trail to his front door in the nicer part of Chelsea. Miss Phillips, for instance, opened in *Pal Joey* after only three months intensive tutelage, to rave reviews for her deep, sensual Dietrich tones. And the word is that Conti is giving a fine account of the score for *They're Playing Our Song*, in a rich dark tenor voice.

Ah well, Siân's Welsh, says Mr Adams modestly. 'They have music in them.' And Mr Conti? 'Oh, he's Italian. They're just the same.'

Anyone, he maintains, can sing. It was precisely to test this theory that I was standing where the likes of Miss Phillips, Mr Conti, Michael Crawford, Cheryl Kennedy and Wayne Sleep – not to mention eleven members of the original West End cast of *A Chorus Line* – had stood before me.

I have not sung a note in public, unless drunk or in extreme agony, since the age of ten. Not since the choirmaster of the local church tested each boy in turn to discover the culprit responsible for ruining the descant section every Sunday. It was me.

Mr Adams was not one wit dismayed. 'When Michael Crawford came to me to prepare for his part in *Billy* at Drury Lane he was wildly embarrassed. He came here making what he describes as very small, unfortunate noises. But he had a very pretty quality to his voice. It was a tiny voice but it just needed bringing out.'

Brought out it was. Crawford sustained the role of Billy Liar for a hugely successful run at the Lane. 'He is,' says his mentor, 'a perfectionist in everything he does.'

Mr Adams works on the refreshing principle that everyone has a singing voice before ever one learns to speak. 'The sounds children make when they laugh or cry are the basic sounds we use to sing. They may not sound very pleasant at times, but that all comes with technique.'

And so we started. After a detailed explanation of how to use the entire body as a sound box, starting with the base of the diaphragm and the back muscles, we got down to the breathing exercises. Then I had to master the trick of panting rapidly like a dog, using stomach muscles I only suspected were there. 'That gets the oxygen supply quickly into the blood stream. Marvellous for calming nerves. All my pupils use it.'

By now we had progressed to producing actual sound and it was, as Mr Adams had warned, a terrifying moment. For both of us. An arpeggio on the grand piano way above middle 'C' was followed by a weak humming noise.

'Excellent! We start at the top and work down. You don't start weight training lifting two tons straight off.'

With Cheryl Kennedy, of course, he had worked in reverse. Years of singing in pop musicals before she won the coveted Eliza Doolittle role opposite Rex Harrison in the States had deepened her voice considerably. 'I just had to lift it a little. It's quite exquisite now. She's my third Eliza in succession.' He has also notched up four Evitas during the run, although Elaine Paige came only after she had played the role.

By now we were humming away like mad. 'You've got a very good light tenor!' he exclaimed. Easy to see why so many non-singing actors run here in their hour of crisis. He knows the art of communicating his teaching enthusiasm. I was in full hum and willing to tackle anything from *Figaro* to *Superstar*.

'I never try to change a voice,' he told me. 'Even with Grand Opera singers, its their individual quality you remember, not their technique – that's what makes a star. It's no good simply sounding just like anyone else.'

As someone who has not sounded like anyone else since the age of ten, I filled my diaphragm with air and scarcely a second thought and used my entire body as a sound box just as he had told me. 'You've just hit top 'C' perfectly,' he announced. To my amazement, when we played the tape back, I had.

JUDI DENCH

I cannot sing. But I know how to put over a song. The director Hal Prince once told me 'The secret of singing is that you only start to sing when you have exhausted all that there is to say.' The song is an extension of those feelings, and if a song does not fit the story, there is no point to it. The two people who can teach us an enormous amount about presenting something to an audience are John Gielgud and Frank Sinatra. Gielgud begins a soliloquy, Sinatra starts a song, and they both traverse an arc of absolute communication, with no interruptions or jolts. That is a wonderful facility, in speech and song.

Bring back the bird

Daily Mail, 11th August 1989

We could hardly believe our ears. We thought the species was extinct. But no, there it was, the unmistakable cry of the Lesser First Night Bird. Not one has been spotted in the wilds of the West End these ten years past. Not even Peter O'Toole could tempt so much as an audible hiss or boo with his historic demolition of *Macbeth*, so polite and acquiescent have modern audiences become.

To be fair, Sir Ralph Richardson did march out of that particular piece of theatrical ineptitude at half-time, declaring contemptuously in tones far more penetrating than O'Toole's: 'Its like having a duff operation at the Middlesex.'

But it was not the Bird. Not the full verbal assault publicly flung like a squashed tomato across the footlights, and just as humiliating when it strikes home. Any actor who has been the object of its attention will not forget in a hurry the terror it can strike in the guts.

Yesterday morning Kenneth Branagh woke up with its chilling echo still ringing in his ears and no doubt burnt into his soul. My guess is that he also awoke a finer actor.

There he was, happily declaiming one of John Osborne's finest speeches from the stage of the Lyric, when the creature rose from her perch in the stalls and let fly. Branagh visibly blanched and faltered. 'Dreadful! Dreadful!' she squawked. 'The most dreadful performance I have seen.' ... it had a salutary effect on the luckless Mr Branagh. The moment her noisy exit was affected he blazed back to life, hurling Osborne's virulent misogynism 'female!' at her retreating form with a gusto he had not hitherto displayed, and winning a round of applause for his sudden burst of fire. Which only goes to prove a suspicion I have long held. That the theatre is a poorer place without the Bird.

I do not, of course, advocate the slide of theatre audiences into the habitual hooliganism of the football mob. Heaven forfend. Nor am I urging a return to the bear-baiting habits of earlier London theatregoers who were separated from the players, not by an orchestra and a strip of crimson carpet but by a row of spikes and a couple of burly armed guards. Nightclub bouncers today have a tranquil life compared with the guardians of law and order engaged to keep the groundlings of The Rose or The Globe under control on a rough night.

It is simply that, with knighthoods now handed out like Smarties to anyone who has managed to stay billed above the title in a series of fairly respectable plays for an equally respectable amount of time, the theatre has become... well, respectable.

Mr Branagh is, perhaps, its most typical victim. A few early successes on leaving drama school followed by an indifferent *Hamlet*, a fairly average *Romeo* and one or two memorable comic turns, and people are already hailing him as the new Olivier.

Prince Charles becomes the benefactor of his company. And everyone sits back to await his knighthood. Until now no one has dared to stand up and declare that the Emperor has no clothes. Yet at the opera, at the ballet and certainly on the Continent in the theatre, such heresies are uttered all the time. A performance of *Aida* was all but booed off the stage at Covent Garden. And is this so strange after all?

Of course, such traffic is two-way, which is how it should be to create that essential knife-edge of danger if the dead hand of terminal dullness is not to descend forever on the dramatic muse. Will anyone who was there ever forget the sight of the redoubtable Miss Rachel Kempson, wife of the late Sir Michael Redgrave, descending from the stage of the Royal Court to set about two hecklers who had dared to disrupt the action, if that is the word, of a particularly unthrilling thriller which she was gracing with her talent?

In the old days actors were honed on the threat of such indignities. Even Sir Donald Wolfit, that great rabble rouser of old, did not escape the ripest of raspberries. After a suitably awe-inspiring rendering of *Othello* he stepped forward to announce his next production, expecting nothing but rapture from his audience.

'Next week we shall be performing *Hamlet,*' he boomed, 'I myself will play the irresolute Dane and my wife, Miss Rosalind Iden, will play Ophelia.' Into the pregnant pause he left for the applause burst a solitary voice from the Gods. 'Your wife's a rat bag!' it yelled ungallantly. 'Nevertheless,' replied Sir Donald after a moment's thought, 'she will still be playing Ophelia.'

And probably even this most egocentric of all Thespians never took audience approval quite so much for granted ever again.

Of course, Mr Branagh's partner, David Parfitt, has a valid point when he says that such behaviour is at best distracting to the cast. It does put them off and it does prick the illusion on which the magic of theatre depends. But if it also pricks the prevailing bubble of smugness that keeps so many actors happy with delusions of mediocrity, then the return of the Bird to the West End is a truly welcome sound.

KENNETH BRANAGH

I never met Jack Tinker. But perhaps like many actors, I feel as though I did. His personality shone through his reviews. His chief characteristic on the page, was passion.

I had come to regret this on more than one occasion. In a performance he had witnessed of mine, I was heckled. The next day he wrote an impassioned support of the heckler and suggested that I and the other actors on terrible form should be roundly booed.

This did not help me during the rest of the run, but it certainly toughened me up. When he disliked my work (as he often did) it was never through a pose of cynicism or weariness, he was angry and annoyed, hurt almost. In short, he seemed to care about what I did.

When he approved, as he did with my last stage Hamlet, it was generous and unsullied by previous disappointments. I was grateful for it. You couldn't hold things against him, because he judged each performance on its own merits. There was no schoolmarm quality.

Infuriating though he could be, he was never cruel, and though I was on the end of a few stinging one-liners, they did make me laugh. What I liked was that he was on the same team. He thought the theatre was important and exciting. Not in a pretentious way, he just loved live entertainment (and didn't mind using the word entertainment). His (genuinely) overnight reports had a breathlessness about them which seemed part of an older fierier tradition.

Yes, life is a bitch in the theatre
Daily Mail, 8th November 1989

How many actors does it take to change a light bulb? So runs the West End's latest jibe. Answer: twenty-one to put it in the socket and nineteen to stand around saying: 'That could have been me!'

Behind the self-mocking satire of the gag, however, lies a vital clue to the cauldron of theatrical bitchery set boiling this week by a scholarly report on the need for better training for theatre directors. In a profession where egos are often as fragile as egg-shells and where the unemployment figures would shock and shame the most deprived Third World economy, only the gullible or gag are fooled by the 'Dahlings' and 'Loveys' lavished so freely wherever two or three are gathered.

To survive in the arts world you have to be talented, tough, resourceful and resilient as well as sensitive and eager to learn. Outsiders, unfamiliar with the ways of this complex, competitive world, have no doubt been shocked by the candour of some contributions to the report by the great and good of British theatre.

'I have worked with so few directors worthy of the name that I don't have sufficient experience to help the enquiry, ' snaps Glenda Jackson, 'I have worked with a great many who have no right to the name of director.' Sir Peter Hall, at whose back Miss Jackson's unsheathed dagger could surely not have been aimed, speaking on behalf of directors, retorts: 'I have had to teach the actors for six weeks before we started rehearsing. That's not uncommon.'

Even Sir Richard Eyre, Sir Peter's successor at the Royal National Theatre, admits for all to read: 'Sometimes when you sit down with a group of actors and hear them talking about directors, it's like hearing the camp guards of Buchenwald being discussed.'

Overheated stuff, perhaps. And, of course, outsiders will again mistake this latest box of theatrical fireworks as further proof of the jealous rivalries and back-stabbing treacheries which are supposed to distinguish the thespian art. That is the public's favourite image of the entire inflammatory business. But the bitchery is even better in reality. As inquiry chairman Professor Edward Braun, the head of drama at Bristol University, points out: 'Critics and audiences only witness the end product. They don't see the carnage on the way.'

For those, like myself, who have experienced first-hand the particular blend of reckless daring, rigid discipline, and sheer terror that so often propels any performer onto any stage, our only amazement should be in the moderation of their outbursts.

In a profession where 97 per cent of its members are out of work at any one time, security is not in plentiful supply. Almost every working actor knows in his or her secret heart that there are a thousand others who would willingly give their expensively capped teeth to play that part – and probably 1,000 who would do it as well if not better. Their relationship with their directors, on whom their job and performance so crucially depend, is therefore not always the easiest.

Simon Callow famously denounced the director's powers in the first of his biographies, attacking the 'directocracy' for undermining the initiative and responsibility of the actors. More recently Kenneth Branagh has entered the fray with a scathing public denunciation of Trevor Nunn, his former mentor at the Royal Shakespeare Company.

Only last week David Mamet's new play, *A Life in the Theatre*, opened in the West End examining the precarious relationships between performers themselves. Lovingly acted by Denholm Elliott, it is at its best when revealing the havoc one well-meant word of criticism can wreak on even the most experienced actor's self-esteem.

'Brittle?' demands a devastated Mr Elliott, having pressed the eager young Mr West for an opinion on a particular scene. 'You thought my performance was brittle!' Wisely, the embarrassed innocent blames it all on the absent leading lady. This is not creeping cowardice. It is, let me assure you, a form of gracious tact.

Few performers are impervious to comments, however innocently intentioned, that seem to strike at the foundations of their technique and status. Being by and large a quick-witted, creative and volatile race, their reaction can often seem out of all proportion to the offence committed. But I don't believe it is.

There is the famous story of Maggie Smith's inventive vengeance on the late Laurence Olivier during their celebrated partnership in *Othello*. The memorable perfection they achieved each night on stage masked a sometimes less than harmonious backstage state-of-the-art. Olivier took to dispatching notes to Miss Smith on the subject of her fabled vowels. Mortified, it is said she took careful note of the time it took for the great man to transform himself into his thick-lipped black Othello, then struck her mortal blow.

It was his habit, having carefully applied full body make-up, to sit totally naked in his dressing-room and go through the elaborate vocal exercises which lowered his speech almost an octave. Alerted by the mooing sounds Miss Smith flung open the door on the astonished nude legend and enunciated with impeccable diction: 'How now brown cow!'

Yet at the awesome Westminster Abbey memorial to Olivier's incomparable genius, she was there to carry a silver model of the Chichester Festival Theatre where they shared so many triumphs – including that of her Desdemona to his Othello. Hypocrisy? Never. Simply one great talent honouring another and putting what Professor Braun calls 'the carnage along the way' into perspective.

RICHARD EYRE

By the standards of other professions I do not think that theatre is particularly bitchy. Spend some time with politicians, or journalists, or novelists. I cannot substantiate this, but my experience is that actors tend to be unusually generous about each other.

Part of the reason for this myth is the growth of the celebrity interview. The past few years have seen a huge expansion of coverage in the press and they have nothing to print. There is not very much arts news and yet they all have enormous arts supplements. So what do they fill it with? Celebrity interviews, which inevitably means that people want to know the sex lives of the stars. Then, when that subject is exhausted they want to know about their work. Well you cannot talk about acting properly. You just have to do it. It crumbles when you try to speak about it. So actors start talking bollocks – and the public have correspondingly developed this idea of actors as self-advertising creatures talking bollocks. The fact is that most of the time, they are pressured by the theatre, film or television company who want the publicity. There is a vicious circle of the product needing to be pushed and the newspaper wanting the star interview.

Every night's a first night

Daily Mail, 17th July 1993

Yes, frankly I do feel a genuine and, until now, secret smugness in the superiority of theatre over its newer, more blasé bastard competitor, the cinema.

Early in my career, so long ago you still automatically spelt Beatles with two ee's, I combined reviewing both these tantalising art forms.

The reason I gave up utterly on the movies was nothing to do with the generally loutish behaviour of their audiences, or the lack of staying power of their latter-day stars, nor even the take-over of special effects above human interest.

It was the sterile dehumanising quality of the critic's task which drove me away. You can shout obscenities at a bad movie, you can throw bad tomatoes at it, or rush up and kick the screen – as I have often been tempted, and on one occasion actually seen, others do. Or you can stand and cheer as the credits roll.

But what's the use? At the end of the night it is still just a moving piece of celluloid and nothing you or I can say about it, either in praise or contempt, is going to make it any better or any worse. Film is a film is a film.

Theatre, by miraculous contrast, is a living thing. People use the words synonymously: Live Theatre. And like all living organisms, each night is a changing, developing entity in its own right.

After the opening gala, when the reviews are in, no director, actor or even author in his right mind shouts: 'Right. It's in the can!' and goes home to loll by a pool until the next script plops onto the welcome mat.

Each evening is a new first night. Each audience brings its own new challenge. And each night their response subtly retunes the actors' performances.

There is no more thrilling or life-affirming sound than that of an audience rising to its feet and roaring its approval at the end of an unforgettable evening in a theatre, be it at the end of Olivier's *Othello*, Michael Crawford's *Phantom*, the latest Ayckbourn tragi-comedy or the newest Ray Cooney farce.

And you were there. Uniquely you were part of it.

On the other hand is there any more chilling or ugly sound than the catcall, slow hand-clap or rumble of booing?

Why? Because this is not the mindless mob knee-jerk of a soccer crowd on Saturday. It is because the very nature of the art has transformed and transported a gathering of total strangers into a uniquely shared experience.

At its best theatre is an almost mystic act of communion. By some inexplicable magic of ritual and art, almost as old as civilisation itself, we allow ourselves to be unified into a single entity and persuaded that the handful of men and women up there in the brightly lit arena are not what we know them to be – actors speaking other people's lines.

They are characters we believe we know, whose comedy and tragedy we are invited to share on the most intimate basis. We were there when they did it. We saw it happen. And we talk about it for ever.

At its worst, of course, it is none of this. We become all too uncomfortably aware that those mummers are merely mortals mouthing lines you would shame yourself to utter. So, yes, there is the gladiatorial element about it, too. I readily admit.

And yet even here there is a kind of humanity in our feeling of embarrassment or fury at their inadequacies. A kind of satisfaction in knowing that they, too, are only too acutely aware our disbelief has been anything other than suspended.

This is live flesh and blood up there on stage. And if we prick them, do they not bleed?

For theatre is a two-way traffic. Both actor and audience are givers as well as receivers. Movies are but a one-way cul-de-sac. If you don't like what you find at the end, all you can do is back off and go home.

RICHARD EYRE

I did a play about twenty years ago called *Comedians*, by Trevor Griffiths. At the time, I ran the Nottingham Playhouse and we premiered the play there. The second act is set in a club where all of the characters, would-be comedians, do their acts. One role, played then by Jonathan Pryce, is a bitter, bleak, anti-comic indictment of class. It ends extremely chillingly, with him just looking at the audience and saying, 'Well I made the buggers laugh.' And this woman shouted out, 'You didn't! You didn't make me laugh!' It was very frightening, because in some way she had been deeply disturbed by this character. The audience were collectively white-faced. Peter Hall was in that night and he thought that I had actually planted the woman.

So theatre is an interactive experience, and audience reaction can participate in that. However, if people just heckle, then it is merely a measure of how you have failed to grasp the audience. I always think that coughing is an indication of dissent.

What has theatre got? It is live, and its proportions are always human. With film, you are always changing the scale – long-shot, close-up, whatever. Theatre is all in wide-shot, so you just have the scale of the human body and the scale of the human voice, which does not vary. So as long as people want to hear stories told by other people, live, it is a medium that will survive. Jack felt that very strongly, he was a passionate propagandist for theatre.

JUDI DENCH

Jack had a great bias for the theatre, which is terrific. Theatre is a total interactive experience. As an actor, you react to the presence of the audience. And your performance changes every single night. At present I am in David Hare's play, *Amy's View* – tonight I might get it better! Tomorrow I have got two shows and who knows what might happen?

That is what is so exciting about theatre and television, say, cannot match it. As my character in this play says when asked if she likes television acting: 'No I don't. Working your guts out while people do something else. There you are working, what are they doing? They're eating and talking. Great. Being taken no notice of in ten million homes.' It is there in the lines.

The audience comprise a great part of any performance. Last night, for instance, they laughed very hard, and then fell extremely quiet. The level of communication was intense, and we responded to that.

Jack realised the importance of the audience, he often brought their reaction into his writing.

8

STAR QUALITY

Marlene Dietrich

Theatre Royal, Brighton
Brighton *Evening Argus*, 1966

At her feet her slaves would wait forever

How do you describe a living legend? The words have all been used before, and somehow that fact alone counterfeits them. The red velvet curtains part and there, caught in the spotlight, she stands. White furs cascade lazily from those superb shoulders and settle around her feet. Beneath them shimmers a flesh coloured gown too severe to be sexy, too sexy for anyone's piece of mind.

Last night at the Theatre Royal, Brighton, she showed just what it is that makes the legend that is Marlene live. Here, above and beyond the glamour, the mystery and the mystique, is an exquisite economy of stage movement combined with a stage craft which few can have equalled and none has bettered.

For a moment she pauses like some ageless goddess of beauty waiting for the homage she acknowledges by rights to be hers. She is, of course, Marlene Dietrich. Who else?

Here, amazingly, is an artist who could make a performance out of taking off her wrap and still send her audience away richly satisfied. What is more she does. A majestic glide to the wings to discard her furs had the celebrity decked first nighters practically on their feet imploring her to return.

Her curtain calls were, in themselves, an act to be cherished and relished, and only by appearing with her dress fastenings hanging loose could she convince her adoring fans that it really was time to call it a night. But oh, such a night it was.

For in between that first imperious appearance and that last, impish dismissal Marlene had proved herself a queen who could entertain her slaves right royally. She does it simply, and miraculously, by never being anything less than perfection.

The songs, all of them familiar favourites for any Dietrich fan, and all splendidly arranged by Burt Bacharach, come in a kaleidoscope of sophisticated moods. To them all she brings this illusive majesty.

One can only gaze at this honey-coloured creature with a voice at times more honeyed than honey and at others more deadly than the deadliest nightshade, and marvel that it is given to the human race to call such a being its own. It is not the unbelievable loveliness of her face. Nor is it the statuesque pride of her body. It is simply that when she sings or breathes, one feels instinctively that here is a woman who knows what life is all about.

And in the end, when reluctantly you have to accept that she has vanished behind the velvet drapes for the last time, she leaves her whole audience panting for more.

It is as it should be, for this is how goddesses are worshipped at their temples. And this week the Theatre Royal is surely such a temple.

Frank Sinatra
Royal Festival Hall
***Daily Mail*, 12th September 1978**

An old dog's tricks but the kick is no longer there!

The small, top-heavy man with the grey velvet hair looks fleetingly pleased at the ovation 3,000 people give him from their £20 seats. It might be relief, for he comes on after a first half that is so middle of the road it would pass for a white line in broad daylight. His suit is so well constructed you cannot tell where it stops and he starts and it tapers down to two dainty elevator shoes.

Mr Sinatra is showing the nice side of his nature to an audience that has bribed, grafted or queued its way into the Royal Festival Hall. And for four bars of *Night and Day* he shows them the best side of his voice, too – holding a couple of notes so long and loud they draw applause. That is to demonstrate that the voice box is in good trim, of course.

And of course it isn't. A lifetime of booze and brawls now lodges in that formidable throat. There are times when he makes the descent into his lower register with all the grace of a corncrake mating.

This would not matter – it would even lend an added dimension to his repertoire if only Mr S were any respecter of a great lyric. But he is not. He drives through them like a Cadillac scorching up a country road on a quiet Sunday. Larry Hart must rotate in his grave every time Sinatra pitches into *The Lady Is a Tramp*, assuring us that *She'll never bother with some bum she hates...*

He is, naturally after all these years, fitting those carefully assembled rhymes into his own tricksy interpretation. Everyone from the Gershwins to George Harrison gets the same cavalier treatment (Harrison's haunting *Something* is apparently sung to a girl calling herself Jack).

In his more generous moments Sinatra has acknowledged the influence on his phrasing of a great lady named Mabel Mercer. I heard Miss Mercer at the age of 80 recently. Her voice is nowhere near the fettle of Sinatra's but her way with a lyric could still make an audience laugh or cry at will. This Sinatra never does. Though he never attempts anything he can't reach, either, the impression remains of an old dog going through old tricks for the laughs and the kick that are no longer there...

Bette Davis once defined a star as someone who, when his name goes up in lights, a crowd forms beneath it. On that definition Mr Sinatra is, I suppose, still up there with the greats.

And two years later at the same venue...
Daily Mail, 9th September 1980

Sinatra's melody lingers on

The immaculate blonde lady of uncertain years in front of me burst unbidden into discreet tears the moment The Living Legend strode out on to the concert platform.

Nothing about the object of her temporary breakdown could have prepared a stranger from Mars, anyone under 25, or an unsuspecting amnesiac for this outburst of emotion. The man in the spotlight looked as benignly solid, and even less prepossessing, than this season's crop of Presidential candidates.

The welcoming standing ovation had about it the formality of an adoption meeting. It was a foregone conclusion, considering the entire audience had indicated the mood of the house by applauding the delegate of The Clan – Sammy Davis Junior – just for walking to his seat and sitting down.

But this was Sinatra. Ol' Blue Eyes. Not some jumped up senator running for office, though he did kiss the girls who gave him flowers and warm-handed the man who interrupted his act with a gift.

Sinatra's claim on our collective vote goes back over 40 years. Anyone who has sat alone in a bar and played _In the Wee Small Hours of the Morning_ on the jukebox holds him in irrational affection. Almost any one of the predominantly middle-aged, middle-class capacity audience had only to hear one note from those distinctive tonsils for memories to come flooding back, pre-programmed by melodies like _I've Got a Crush on You_ or _I've Got You under My Skin_.

And I must say Mr Sinatra seemed in mellow enough mood to take on the role of unrivalled master of nostalgia with sunny good grace without feeling the necessity to put one over on any Johnny-Come-Lately in the business. Nor had he any need to. He was sounding on better form than I have heard him in an age. The lungs defiantly demonstrating they could sustain any note he aimed at – and he had the good sense never to try for any that they couldn't...

I must say I'm still irritated by the liberties he takes with lyrics he is bored with. Larry Hart's pen would have jumped up and stabbed him in the eye had he had the bad form to write that the lady 'loves the groovy, super wind in her hair,' tramp though she may have been. And Sinatra's rewriting of Cole Porter on the stage as he sang was little short of an impertinence.

But to see him so back on form, one could forgive him anything. Not that his adoring audience considered that there was anything to forgive.

Bob Hope
London Palladium
Daily Mail, 27th March 1979

Thanks for the memory – but not this show

What makes an artist chase his fame long after the flame which fed it has gone is as much a sad mystery to me as the power which keeps a chicken running around after its head has been cut off. I have admired Bob Hope's sardonic, wise-cracking style since before I knew there was such a thing as style. But this personal appearance does little to keep that legend alive for this ardent fan.

He hits his innate gift for throw-away timing only infrequently. For the greater part of his act he relies on a prompt card the size of an advertisement hoarding, hidden (but not so hidden) in the orchestra pit. Now any comic with both eyes on his next line must suffer a crisis of timing, however practised his art and however fast his accomplice at changing the joke cues.

So, sadly, it was not until he engaged in eye-to-eye fun with two slow-moving stage-hands carrying a peach-coloured *chaise longue* that he really eased into the shadow of his old form. As he relaxed on the sofa, singing an old self-mocking routine, he cracked up the audience, as he has for generations of film and vaudeville fans.

The jokes, of course, are as topical as a highly-paid bunch of gag smiths can deliver... 'I haven't seen so much garbage since I played vaudeville.' But as Mr Hope reads them now, at a youthful 75, that is as far as they go. He has removed the essence of his own personality from them. And, as he himself admitted, someone should have researched our British brand names before selling him at least a couple of the stories.

So he found a new echo of his *Road* picture roles in a duet with the talented Leslie Uggams (a young Lena Horne look-alike, with more style than her name allows) who occupies the first half of the bill to stunning effect. But then he botches each build-up. First with embarrassing parodies of *Thanks for the Memory* in pop song style. Then, introducing every celebrity in the audience, he almost overlooked the very noticeable Raquel Welch and was saved from the *faux pas*, only by his wife Dolores.

How did she get into the act? Inexplicably he invited her from the royal box to sing a number on stage. Mr Hope may not believe this but I still say thanks for the memory. But I would have been happy to have lived with those I treasure and not had to sit worrying about his.

Bruce Forsyth
Fairfield Halls, Croydon
***Daily Mail*, 10th January 1980**

Brucie's back, taking the world by storm

Like a champion jockey who has taken a mighty tumble, Bruce Forsyth has taken no time getting back into the saddle. His first West End musical may have stumbled at the first fence, his TV series collapsed beneath him, and his Broadway debut taken a crucial fall. But at the moment he is galloping around far from the bright lights, taking his familiar one-man show to such spots as Bolton and Slough, wooing back the fans, getting back his nerve in preparation for the new ITV series.

Last night he was back among the grassroots of his following at Croydon and the Fairfield Halls were packed to capacity with the faithful. Into the applause he strutted, airbag defiantly slung across his shoulders to remind us he had been away. And if he was bloodied, he was certainly not bowed.

The chin was out, the ego apparently undented and the only sign of any injury was the wrist plaster on broken bones he'd sustained in a real life slip-up in Slough. The inevitable *Generation* couples, who came on stage to go through the ritual humiliation of performing the *Laughing Policeman* song and several dances, were sent away basking in the warm assurance that they had not made fools of themselves but had helped to spread happiness all around the audience.

He could do no wrong. Not withstanding the memories from Broadway, he went into the showbizzy routine of *New York, New York* until his audience cheered him as they would a returning conqueror. One can only report, in all honesty, that this is exactly what he looked like.

Mr Forsyth is serving notice out in the sticks that anyone who has written him off had better get himself a different pen.

BRUCE FORSYTH

Critically Jack and I were on the same sort of wavelength. I rated him because he could be relied upon to give a very fair review. With some critics you know that if they love it you will hate it, if they hate it you will love it. Not Jack. With him you always knew where you stood.

He wrote some lovely things about me. At one point he hailed my comeback, but my trip to America was not as big a flop as he had written. I went over there, and outside the theatre were two reviews on placards, one saying how awful I was, and another saying just the opposite. It was a mixed bag. When I arrived back in England the press interest was phenomenal, and Jack hailed my return. He liked performers in a way that too many critics do not, and the performer's point of view informed his writing. We did not meet often, but when we did we always had a bit of a laugh.

Victor Borge
London Palladium
Daily Mail, 12th November 1980

A clown prince

There is something of the great W C Fields in Victor Borge's comic lineage. His slow-burn delivery, his ballooning sense of dignity, inflated until it bursts under the pressure of its own hot air, are the hallmarks of the greatest clowns. And as he grows older, there is much more of the music-hall and less of the musical in Borge's act.

He strides onto the stage of the Palladium with all the old-fashioned grandeur of Harold Macmillan in his prime. What, in fact, he has come to discuss are his reasons for missing the 7 o'clock lift at his hotel. The one going down, of course, he adds after a suitably grave pause.

He then proceeds to tangle with the English language as only a brilliant foreigner can, confiding that he was a child prodigy at eight – or possibly one minute past. But nothing, it seems, will persuade him to sit down at the piano and play as we know he can.

Whatever energy he saves, however, is expended in the violent response of his willing dupes, the audience. Time and again he leads us up one garden path after another and still has us begging for more.

Muhammad Ali
Daily Mail, 15th December 1980

Ali – major new world role for the fallen champ

'I don't need boxing,' announced Muhammad Ali, suddenly rousing himself from what seemed like an overwhelming and permanent weariness. 'I might not fight after all.'

His eyes flashed that famous saucer stare for just a moment. The one he used to blaze across a ring to intimidate an opponent or startle a cameraman. He used it now to make sure I understood the importance of what he was saying.

Ever since his ignominious battering beneath the gloves of Larry Holmes last October in Las Vegas he has kept the boxing federation on tenterhooks with his MacArthur-like promise: 'I shall return!' Universally, the experts prayed that at 38, he would call it a day while the glory remained.

Maybe he sensed my interest was not in boxing, a futile and cruel occupation it has always seemed to me, but in the phenomenon it produced. Muhammad Ali, the man who not only walks with kings and presidents, but has pictures of them gazing up at him admiringly to prove it.

'What you thought you needed yesterday you are sometimes shown you don't need tomorrow,' he murmured, nodding sadly to himself. 'I wanted to make history. To be the first man to come back four times. The only man on the planet to have done so. I wanted to do that for myself.'

It sounded almost childlike, coming from this big, brown man. The warrior-instinct to go down fighting and not merely be put out to pasture. Now that, I understood.

There was something of the old stag-at-bay about this still baby-faced ex-champion slouched deep into one of the Dorchester's floral armchairs, his speech slightly blurred. Compared with the crisp, rapid-fire repartee which once marked him out among his fellow fighters, there is a measured monotone about his delivery these days. One joke only. 'I shaved off my moustache because someone called me Dark Gable!'

Except, that is, when the talk turns to religion. This is his consuming passion. He rattled off for me, on tape, a 30-minute lecture he had just prepared on the power of prayer. It was fire and brimstone stuff and when he'd finished, he played the tape back to himself, listening with his eyes closed and a beatific smile on the face which now shows no visible signs that Holmes's gloves had ever come near it.

I had come to discuss his new starring role in the film *Freedom Road*. From the excerpt I had seen, his performance was full of dignity, fire, conviction and no small technical ability.

'I've been acting for 20 years, so why shouldn't I know a thing or two?' he smiled, something of the old mischief surfacing. 'Besides, I don't think too much of acting. Acting is exactly what it says. It's about pretending to be something else.' The words were rapid, the voice had cleared the way through the fog of fatigue.

'The people who go down in history are the people who dared to dare. I dared. I dared to come back again and again. You know I'm the only superstar you could ever talk to like this?' he demanded suddenly, and daring me to contradict through sulky, lowered eyebrows. 'You can stay right into the night and talk if you want to. Shall I tell you why? Because I fought for my freedom. No one says to me: it's time, Champ.'

It took more courage than I thought I possessed to bring him down to the practicalities of religion and his profession. If God spoke so clearly to him, I ventured, did it not perhaps follow that there might have been a message to be learned in that ring with Larry Holmes?

He didn't get angry. He didn't even counter or feint. 'Maybe,' he mumbled. 'But you know boxing was the bait God gave me to do my work. We all have two missions in life: one major, one minor. I have completed my minor mission. And that was boxing.'

Perhaps it was the mood of the moment speaking. But the fire for trading punches seemed to have gone out of his belly to me. And in its place was a formidable black preacher planning to conquer the world with something quite different.

Lew Grade
Daily Mail, 15th January 1982

The last tycoon

It is part of Showbiz mythology that someone, somewhere, asked Lew Grade: 'Hey Lew, what's two and two?' 'Are you buying or selling?' came the reply from behind the seven-inch cigar.

True or false, it's a story Lew loved to hear told against himself. It typified the man. It typified his style. He was the sharp operator. The wise guy who could send himself up higher than anyone else and still be there to tell the tale. Only of the biggest of moguls do they tell stories like that, and Lew Grade was the sort of mogul only one of his own fantasy scripts could have invented.

When I was researching my book on the Silver Jubilee of commercial television in Britain a couple of years ago, it was clear from the outset that this egg-shaped caricature of old-style Hollywood movie mogul was indeed the force that had created our modern mass culture.

Before Grade there was the cut-glass all-British BBC. It was this little ex-Charleston champion who got the nation hooked on give-away quiz games, on *Sunday Night at the London Palladium*, on an endless variety of variety shows. His taste became our taste, for a time anyway.

'My policy is to offend the least and sell to the most,' he was fond of saying. It was a proud boast. His own television consumption was no richer or more daring than that he sold to his customers. 'Education is not entertainment,' he once snapped.

'An ideal evening for me to watch at home would be *The Persuaders*, *The Saint* or *Danger Man*. Then a good half-hour comedy like *On the Buses*. Throw in the news and, for me, that would be a lovely evening. I could go to bed at 11 feeling great,' he once said.

What is more he would be up again at 5.30 the next morning and on his way to his vast desk to begin another day producing just such fare. It made him a multi-millionaire, though he always said that money was the last thing which interested him. The deal was the thing. 'Are you buying or selling?' pumped the adrenaline.

The image he had of himself was of an avuncular man who knew all his staff by their first names and kept his office door open to everyone from the office boy upward. Of course it was not so. No man knows that many names; no door is ever so open. Nor was Lew.

Employees who fell foul of him had a saying: 'You don't know you've broken your leg until you've reached the end of the carpet.'

It was this streak of ruthlessness which he kept closely hidden. No one to this day tells the real story about how his co-founder of ATV television, Val Parnell, came to tumble from the chairman's chair. Nominally Lew was then, as Managing Director, his junior. But a call from Lew to the Parnell home during dinner one night put paid to Val Parnell's reign.

And it was a pattern to be repeated throughout the years; a technique which culminated in the golden handshake to his own crown prince Jack Gill and the events which finally toppled him from the seat of power he had guarded so jealously for so long.

The trouble was that the inspired old war-horse had come to believe all the legends that surrounded him. He had survived so many slings and arrows from so much outrageous fortune, that I am sure it was inconceivable to him that he could not pull one more trick out of the bag – even when the bag was being rapidly emptied by misjudgements on a scale even more colossal than his triumphs.

'He is a pedlar of dreams,' Shirley MacLaine gasped after Lew had sold her the idea of the worst TV series she ever imagined in her worst nightmares. 'It's not until you've stepped into them that you find that you are up to your behind in manure, artistically speaking.'

And it was, indeed, this artistic blind spot which finally brought the old showman low. He believed implicitly that if you could put 12 stars into one movie and spend more dollars on it than anyone else had ever done, you must come up with a great product. It didn't work out that way. And he was always plaintively puzzled why.

Of the movie disaster *Raise the Titanic*, he muttered in disbelief: 'It would have been cheaper to have lowered the ocean. With all those stars, how could it fail?'

He was indeed a movie mogul in the old Goldwyn-Mayer mould. They don't make movies like that any more – because they don't need them. But how do you tell a man like Lew that his day is done? That his taste is no longer what the public are buying?

This was the man who single-handedly built an empire in his own image; a man who left Rochelle Street school, East London, at 14 and a half to work in a gown firm called Tew and Raymond and worked his way non-stop to the House of Lords. He and his brothers Bernard and

Leslie had woven their influence into every corner of British show business. Theatres: they owned them. Artists: they controlled them. Music: they bought up the rights and the musicians.

Yet his philosophy was always that his word was his bond and even his enemies would agree on that. In vain the Monopolies Commission fretted and fumed about the Winogradski brothers' habit of producing their shows with artists and musicians for whom they paid themselves commission in theatres where they paid themselves rent. Lew shrugged his way through all the criticism. 'Are you buying or selling?'

The bonhomie was unending until he was crossed or it was hinted that he should leave the decision to someone else. 'When they get too big for their boots,' he would say, 'let them go walk on someone else's carpet.'

Well, now he is walking on his own carpet only by the grace of a take-over company. He says that he is 75, but the records aren't so sure. He could be into his eighties. All reliable documents were lost in the Winogradski's flight from their native Russia during the terrible anti-Jewish pogroms.

Either way he was still getting into his office before the cleaners in the morning. Still watching videos of his own shows for late-night relaxation. Still wheeling and dealing on a dozen different telephones all around the world. Until the very end.

'All my life I've liked to work. Why do I do it? Not the power, who needs it? Not the money, how do you spend it? Look, is it fair to ask a man who is having so much fun to stop?'

Then he said that he was, of course, joking. Lew being Lew. Now he's been told to stop. And where do proud workaholics go when they take their work away?

An Evening's Intercourse with Barry Humphries
Drury Lane
Daily Mail, 5th February 1982

Dame Edna, firing on all outrageous cannons

Curiously, it is becoming a part of Anglo-Australian folklore that Dame Edna Everage and I had a slight falling-out. Or, in her case, a slight falling off for anyone who remembers her ill-advised concert at the Albert Hall last year.

Her 'husband,' Leslie Colin Patterson, 'The Australian Cultural Attaché to the Court of St James, was moved to write a poem about it; unfortunately the relevant stanza was totally unprintable both in sentiment and scan. And last night Dame Edna herself wove a fresh chapter of revelations about our rocky relationship into her evening's intercourse.

What can one say? If words could be eaten, we would both be having a banquet this morning. For my part she is back on the highest pedestal show business can provide. The best stand-up-and-sock-it-to-'em entertainer London has seen in years.

There is not a comedian who can belabour an audience so dangerously, so outrageously or so remorselessly as this garrulous creation of outraged middle-class morality on a good night.

Anyone who can compare Drury Lane to a bathroom at the Dorchester and then proceed to treat it more intimately than a shared shower at the YMCA, is nothing short of a phenomenon.

The whiplash mind and matching tongue are never still. 'I'll bet you were an attractive woman once,' she beams at the luckless Ruth from Kensington. While poor Beverley, all the way from Toronto, only paused in astonishment at being asked to describe her house back home for Edna to command impatiently: 'Oh, cast your mind back, Bev!'

Somehow the audience adores this voluntary mortification. And this was Dame Edna firing on all guns. Quite literally, as it turned out, for four huge high-tech cannons deafened the 2,000 adoring fans in a vain attempt to fire gladioli up to the Gods where Dame Edna claims her pauper followers lurk.

If I personally ever wounded her by the suggestion that Barry Humphries was allowing his creation to become remote from her fans, she was clearly determined to spare herself nothing in audience contact last night. Shoes were gathered up in an over-sized shrimp net (the Dame ever sees herself as a fisher of soles) and reluctant shoe-less innocents were herded up on stage to cook, eat and serve up a gargantuan barbecue.

However the real surprise from Barry Humphries' stable of grotesques is Sir Les Patterson, the Australian Poet Laureate. He has become to taste, delicacy and finer feelings what a steamroller is to tarmacadam. Irresistible.

The Little Foxes

Lillian Hellman
Victoria Palace
Daily Mail, 12th March 1982

You can call this theatre – but I certainly wouldn't call it acting

You call this theatre?, sneered a despondent colleague in the first interval. Indeed I do, I told him. I certainly don't call it acting. To imagine there was a person in the stalls last night who had paid £25 a seat to see Elizabeth Taylor act is as foolish a notion as pretending anyone had gone there just to see Lillian Hellman's creaking old classic.

No. They came to see a star in the flesh. There were investing their money in the mythology of that dumpy little lady up there on the stage, stomping her way through a lot of kind lighting. It was a stake in her seven husbands, fabled beauty, wealth, diamonds, and successful tracheotomy they had paid for.

A star, according to the Bette Davis barometer, is someone who, when their name goes up above a theatre, can cause the crowds to queue below. And the beano created by Miss Taylor's mere presence at the VP is the dictionary definition of Miss Taylor's contribution to living art.

More she does not, or cannot, offer. Although truth to tell even judging her on these ephemeral standards I found her somewhat wanting.

Her first appearance in a cottage loaf wig and matching figure (had she by some mischance put on her bustle back to front?) was less than pre-possessing. Not a woman in the place could have missed that the beaded burgundy dress was woefully unflattering to a lady of her generous girth and lack of height and the lacquered seaside wig only served to emphasise her generous helping of chin.

Of course, none of this would have mattered a jot had Miss Taylor been here in the business of bringing new life to Lillian Hellman's complex heroine, Regina, the Southern Belle who personifies the turn of the century decay of everything good and decent in the Deep South. But sadly this is way beyond the range of any stage technique she has acquired in her long and glorious career in films.

For the most part, as an actress, she teeters on the brink of competence. Her accent slides from South Fork to South London and encompasses more vowels in one word than anyone would have thought possible.

Her reactions for the most part are signalled with a machete. 'The rich don't have to be subtle,' she squeals at one point. And on this philosophy she has clearly based her entire performance. Even when she sees her sick husband dying she stifles our amazement at the enormity of her callousness well in advance.

Occasionally she reaches out for something splendid from her film past. A whiplash retort from *Who's Afraid of Virginia Woolf?* A spit of fire from *The Taming of the Shrew* or the rage against misfortune from *Butterfield 8*. These she explodes in our face like a flash bulb of a camera. Dazzling for an instant, then gone.

Somewhere in her wake, a play is struggling for attention. It is a decent, old-fashioned production by any standards but illuminated by some fine supporting performances. Notable among these is Sada Thompson as her high-born brow-beaten sister-in-law and Ann Palman as the daughter who sees through all her wiles.

When Sam Goldwyn was warned when he bought *Little Foxes* for Bette Davis that it was a caustic play, his retort was: 'I don't care about the cost – get it.' I rather feel that the same maxim went into the getting of Miss Taylor.

Shirley Bassey

Royal Albert Hall
Daily Mail, **28th September 1982**

Hey big spenders, is this the real thing?

If being a star means that you can fill the Royal Albert Hall with adoring fans, big spenders all at £17.50 a seat, then there is no arguing that Miss Shirley Bassey must rank with the biggest. But for a lady who obviously has a great deal going for her – vivid glamour, arresting good looks and a voice that finds the pitch of the hall with the first belting note – she seems to me to have an awful lot still to get right. Miss Bassey's act now so closely resembles those grotesque drag impersonations of her which crop up in tired seaside reviews that it is difficult to tell who is parodying whom.

She strides into the stage in a glittering puce harem ensemble, arms outstretched like some exotic oriental princess presiding over an ancient rite. Her subjects yell their relief to see her fully delivered from the jaws of death fully recovered from the serious illness which caused the postponement of her current national tour.

So far, so good. Stars must inevitably trail their private dramas and griefs into the spotlight. And at this Miss Bassey is certainly no slouch. She rebukes her record company for failing to call her album *All By Myself* – which is what she happened to be when she recorded it. And when a plump fan invades the stage and pushes a bottle of champagne and glass into her hand after only two number she coos: 'Oh, such a reputation!' – and instantly there is triggered off the reflex memory of the night she celebrated more than wisely and ended up on a highly publicised drunk charge.

It is now we reach the rocky seas of self-parody. For Miss Bassey proceeds to mangle a whole string of numbers which at times you can make intelligible only by relying on memory and listening carefully to the band. Songs of loneliness, survival and hope, which are the staple diet of any act such as this, are rendered equally resistible by the wilful absurdity of her vocal eccentricities and the armour plating of her synthetic mannerisms.

George Harrison's 'favourite city' turns out to be New York with a crazed assurance that she is in 'a New York state of mind'. Which must inevitably prompt the question in any probing mind: 'Well what the heck are you doing in the Albert Hall?'

But for the procession of youngish gentlemen who glided up between numbers to interrupt the flow and present her with personalised bouquets and kiss her hand it was clearly enough that she was here at all. All of which may be a kind of style. But it is not real Style.

Shirley MacLaine

Apollo Victoria
Daily Mail, 1st October 1982

The long running show that is simply and wonderfully Shirley MacLaine

It is virtually impossible to pinpoint accurately the chief appeal of Shirley MacLaine's barnstorming, two-hour show. At the age of 48 she is a lady who shows no signs of settling into the legend of her own screen mythology. No cosy 'Remember when' for this one.

She still does it the hard way. And her screen image is the very first thing to have a ripe raspberry blown full in its face (Miss MacLaine is a great girl for raspberry-blowing and tongue-pulling). 'Thirty-seven pictures and 11 hookers!' she declares, contemptuously, her marmalade hair spread anyhow across her neat head and a grin splitting her face from ear to ear, 'I once got to play a nun and even she got to be a hooker by the end of the movie!"

No, this is definitely not your average evening of showbiz glitz. But despite her matey, girl-next-door entrance – from the front of the stalls, and leaning nonchalantly against the stage for her introductory remarks – nor is she your average girl-next-door.

No girl-next-door to anywhere I've ever lived has flashed legs like those in unison with four of the slickest zingiest dancers the London stage has seen since the last time she was here. And no legs fast approaching half-a-century of relentless workouts deserve to look in such good shape either, even if she doesn't mind letting you know that it is getting a little tough kicking them past the ears these days.

No, despite all the quick changes, this is not a night of artificial glamour. It is the real thing, take it or leave it. The star will sweat, burp, wisecrack and insist that she is merely showing you how you put a show like this together. Gleefully, she will explain and demonstrate the wilder techniques of choreography. Wickedly, she will wisecrack her way through the entire Royal Family, and most of the world's political figures. 'I understand Mrs Thatcher fell down some stairs in Peking and broke her hair.' 'I wish Reagan would do to Nancy one night what he's doing to the rest of the world every day.'

Yet this raucous good-timer can drink a toast to 'the peace of the world' with a glass of water, and render her audience as still and reverent as the Pope delivering a blessing. She can preach a little sermon on positive thinking and bring her tremulous voice into a wistful rendering of *Cockeyed Optimist* that is neither mawkish or coy but as moving as a whole act of Chekhov.

She can sit at a typewriter and negotiate a melody of songs that take you into matrimony at one side and out again at the other end, with the sure touch of a true, creative writer (which she also is). And by the end of the evening, her hair matted with the excesses of her labours, and wielding a hairbrush into it, she swears she feels like Michael Foot looks and the audience rise to their feet to cheer her to the echo, like a victorious champ.

At £20 a top seat there is no-one who will say Miss MacLaine's stint has short-changed them in any way. Yet what is she selling? Talent, surely. Energy by the bucketful, no arguing. But the real answer is originality. Miss MacLaine's is a one-off model. These do not come cheap, but boy, do they give value for money and last the distance.

Ralph Richardson
Daily Mail, 18th December 1982

Sir Ralph – knight in impenetrable armour

If only I could have warned Bernard Levin in advance. There is simply no way of interviewing Sir Ralph Richardson unless you are prepared to end up ignominiously hoisted by your own petard.

This is a man who has taken the art of self-concealment to the heights of compulsive viewing. There are no lengths he will not go to – short of rape, pillage or murder, perhaps – to deflect a probing question or avoid a direct compliment.

Yet, being the most consummate actor ever, he has developed the unique knack of remaining four-square in the spotlight while giving nothing of himself away, as you will see only too clearly tonight, when poor Bernard ties himself benevolently in knots trying to guide Sir Ralph through an 80th birthday tribute.

Next to the Queen Mum, Sir Ralph must be the most genuinely loved of our mortal institutions. Indeed, he conducts his own interview knowing that he has a blank cheque on the affections of the interviewer – and cashing in on it for all its worth.

My first meeting with him had all the hallmarks of the confrontation which tonight leaves even the wily Levin literally flat on his back. 'Dear boy!' declaimed Sir Ralph, bounding through the door of his elegant first-floor drawing-room overlooking Regent's Park, where I nervously waited for our introduction. 'I've always wanted to meet you!' Now that was my line, I had always wanted to meet him.

But no time to demur. Before a suitable reply can form on lips that are gaping widely, he embarks on a résumé of my career as a theatre reviewer some 12 years ago in Brighton. 'Go to Brighton, I used to tell them', he cried, pointing dramatically in the general direction of the Thames, 'and you will find a poet waiting to review you! Tell me candidly, what happened to you since?'

Well, of course, there is no rescuing an interview from an opening like that. He tries the self-same tricks on Mr Levin, who is far more experienced than I in netting slippery customers. And he reduces this most acerbic communicator to schoolgirlish 'Ahhs' with his own rapid (and honest) assessment of the Levin talent to amuse and instruct.

The technique never fails. A former colleague of mine once returned from an encounter with this charismatic but indefinable presence able to remember little of what had passed between them save for the fact that Sir Ralph had insisted on draining his tea from his saucer in the Savoy. 'It wants a lot of air in it', he announced as if imparting a nugget of ancient wisdom. And proceeded to slurp down two saucerfuls of well-aired beverage.

The fact that he lives cosily with his wife Meriel, that he has a son called Charlie and an unabated love affair with high-powered motorcycles (which he still rides) are well chronicled. But that is all one ever knows about his private life. If Sir Ralph had not been an actor he would have been a superb illusionist. For his speciality is surely the most spectacular disappearing trick ever to hypnotise an audience and keep us all on the edge of our seats. Now you see him – now you don't!

Tennessee Williams
Daily Mail, 26th February 1983

Tennessee Williams – master of decadence

'Don't look forward to the day when you stop suffering,' Tennessee Williams was fond of warning anyone who would listen to him. 'Because when it comes – you'll KNOW you're dead.'

He would look you straight in the eye as he said it, then laugh an explosive, infectious laugh and go on giggling until everyone had joined in. Just as though he's told the greatest joke. And in a way he had. It was the joke life played on him.

He was famous for his suffering. His plays were full of it. All those tortured Southern Belles like Blanche Dubois in *A Streetcar Named Desire* were either women he had adored, like his own mad mother, or reflections of himself seen through a distorting mirror.

The first time we met, he told me a story about the woman he claimed had been his inspiration for Blanche – perhaps his most definitive heroine. It was horrific in its detail and culminated in them both being turned away from a five-star hotel because the lady in question was incapable of recognising the ladies loo from the potted palms.

'She was,' he would add conspiratorially, 'quite mad.' And then he would laugh all over again.

Madness loomed large on his domestic horizon. And you did not have

217

to stay long in his company to find out why. He would happily regale perfect strangers with intimate accounts of his mother's lunacy. And having spent most of the sixties in an alcoholic stupor, he would confide to even the least curious interviewer how his own brother had him committed to a long-term asylum. 'I was very, very angry with him', Tennessee told me, still braying with laughter.

Yet from all this largely self-induced torment came some of the most sensitive and brilliantly observed dramas of post-war theatre. From the landmark dramas like *A Streetcar Named Desire*, *The Glass Menagerie*, *Cat on a Hot Tin Roof*, *Night of the Iguana*, to his later works such as *Vieux Carré*, these all depict inadequate people in some sort of terminal crisis. And yet, whenever you tried to discuss them he would deflect you with a stream of anecdotes and gossip.

'I once told Gore Vidal that I thought I must have slept through the sixties,' he confided to explain away any lack of literary momentum after his initial impact. 'He said I hadn't missed anything.' He used this to disguise the years of pills and less-than-distinguished companions that so often distracted him from his writing.

Yet from all this sprang a succession of characters which have become established classics. Marlon Brando owes his career directly to Williams' brutal anti-hero in *A Streetcar*. 'I have always depended on the kindness of strangers,' is a line even Woody Allen borrows for one of his own movies and assumes everyone will understand the reference.

Just how much Tennessee Williams depended on the kindness of strangers, David Frost tried to discover in a TV interview when he asked Williams if he was a homosexual. 'I covered the waterfront!' shrieked the most famous living American playwright.

And seldom could you push past these defensive barriers of wit. One day he would tell you Vivien Leigh was the definitive Blanche Dubois, the single actress who could bring everything he intended to the role. The next he would regale you with scurrilous stories about her inadequacies both on and off the set, and you would wonder if he were talking of the same woman.

Yet even at his most mischievous he was never less than surprising company. When Sylvia Miles, the star of *Vieux Carré*, was out walking with him they came across a painfully thin woman. 'That's anorexia nervosa I'm sure', Miss Miles informed him, knowing of his morbid curiosity with disease and death. 'Oh Sylvia!' he crowed, 'you know just everyone.'

He found almost everything painfully funny. Even Blanche, he insisted, was full of humour.

'Life is a terrifying experience,' he once declared laughing loudly as usual, 'but oblivion is even sadder.' However terrifying his own life may have been from his viewpoint, his work has ensured his permanent escape from oblivion.

Liza Minnelli

Apollo, Victoria
Daily Mail, 17th May 1983

Liza – in a class of her own and she's spine-tingling!

It has to be said at the outset that what Tiffany's is to the jewellery business, what Rolls Royce is to the car trade, Miss Liza Minnelli is to the concert stage. A polished, solid investment. Bankable, gleaming class. Guaranteed never to give you a moment's worry or let you down in times of need.

She returns to London with her new one-woman (plus 12 musicians and two dancers) show which is a lesson to all in precision professionalism. Not a mood is struck, not a moment let go without the lady being in total control of the proceedings.

If this sounds a mite too formidable should you be made of soggier stuff, let me say here and now that technique is only a fingernail measure of her achievement.

The surprises she springs along the way, just to keep her celebrity packed audience on their toes, are to have her orchestra stroll on casually one by one while she begins her opening number, unannounced, unaccompanied in the wings. And then to bring on her dancers as if they were fans who had just strolled in from the street and interrupted a rather flashy dream sequence dance.

All this she conveys with an air of bewildered surprise and wicked delight. She asks us to believe, and we do, that she is really just the girl from next door letting her hair down and having a ball. But whoever lived next door to a girl like this?

She can show you the inside of heartbreak with a simple Charles Aznavour ballad. She can lift you off the ground with *Some People*, that belter of an anthem for everyone who has had the courage to get up and go, no matter where. And she can stop you in your tracks with a medley of her own hit numbers from the Broadway show *The Act*, in an encore which is as mesmerisingly stage-managed as those of the great Dietrich.

But the outstanding accolade of this appearance is her spine-tingling tribute to her father, in his 80th birthday year. As she shimmers her way through a whole haze of musicals memories from the great movies of Vincente Minnelli, she is, you can plainly see, making an enormous personal statement. The title song from his Oscar winning *Gigi* – the *Gandhi* of 1958! – might well be her own story, for example.

But when she arrives, gleaming with the perspiration of her exertions, at the medley from *Meet Me in St Louis*, the immortal film which first brought her exquisitely tasteful father into the orbit of her wildly talented mother, then she really lets rip.

Her version of *The Trolley Song* may not have all that vulnerable Garland sense of rising panic behind its glitzy delivery. But what she is really saying, as she slyly reminds us of her own Hollywood triumphs, is that she stands there, a person sufficiently secure in her own fixed star never to be overshadowed by the sun or moon of her amazing parentage.

It is, I promise you, a moment which makes the hair on the back of your neck rise with emotional recognition. This is a pedigree in which, if you have ever been to the movies, ever played an old standard record or tuned into the radio, you have somehow shared.

If this sort of class costs dear, it is worth every last penny of the price. It is a class of its own, one off, and unrepeatable.

The Way of the World

William Congreve
Chichester Festival Theatre
Daily Mail, **2nd August 1984**

Marvellous Miss Smith takes over

Every so often – once in a lifetime if we are lucky – there arrives a performance of a great role in a great play which obliterates all that has gone before and sets its stamp on everything which may follow. It is now 60 years since Dame Edith Evans put her own personal hallmark on the pure gold of Congreve's wayward heroine, Millamant. And until this moment, every actress since has been judged against this rare currency.

Now, let me waste no time in telling, till the end of this century and far beyond, whenever Millamant is played they will speak of Maggie Smith. Miss Smith has minted this role afresh. One can only marvel how impoverished the British stage is whenever she is absent, which sad to say is all too often.

In William Gaskill's mega-stellar production, Miss Smith streams on, ribbons flying, fans flailing, in full sail just as Congreve describes. 'I have denied myself airs today!' she confides, her eyes wide with mock innocence and lips pursed in pretended propriety.

It is all she does deny anyone. From that moment until she vows her famed declaration to dwindle into a wife, she is a creature of sudden teasing laughter, sharp intellectual wit and quicksilver delivery. Mercurial moods scutter across the small fine-boned face as light and quick as clouds on a fine spring day.

Yet beneath all, there is a trembling vulnerability. When she finally succumbs to her love for Mirabell, she sits on a bench utterly shaken, stunned and drained by the force of her own passions.

Of course, in Congreve's famous brick wall of a plot which shelters a society built on intrigues, inter-relationships and the indignities of the vanities of age versus the lust of youth, these two lovers are surrounded by gargantuan scoundrels, knaves and fools. It is therefore only shortage of space and the everlasting dazzle of Miss Smith which makes me skate over the individual joys of Joan Plowright's teetering Lady Wishfort, Sara Kestelman's predatory Marwood, John Moffat's precious Witwoud, Geoffrey Hutching's farm-booted Sir Wilfull, Jane Carr's impish Foible, or indeed Michael Jayston's laconic Mirabell.

Suffice it to say that as a grand finale to Patrick Garland's last and finest season as overlord of Chichester, this production is one for the history books. Miss Smith herself is already the stuff of theatre legend. I do honestly believe there is scarcely the part written she could not encompass at the height of her genius or depth of her ability to move us to tears. I am once more at her feet.

LINDA LEE-POTTER

When Jack went to Stratford, he always stayed at the same hotel, and they gave him the best room, and treated him like a star. He always recommended the place to everybody, so Maggie Smith decided to act on his advice. She booked in under her married name of Maggie Cross, and was allotted a tiny, poky little back-bedroom. Jack was absolutely appalled by this. He marched up to the reception, demanding an explanation. The hotel staff stammered that they did not know who she was, since she had booked as Maggie Cross. 'Well now she is Maggie very cross.' retorted Jack, without skipping a beat. The next time Jack paid a visit to the hotel, he found himself in that same back-bedroom. Upon complaining, he was informed that he had been beaten to the best room - by one Maggie Smith.

Jack could have been an actor, but he never wanted to be. He sang and danced and did his one-man show, but I don't think he ever had any regrets. He was incredibly visual and wore the most outrageous clothes. The first time I saw him was in the old *Daily Mail* building in Fleet Street, and he had on a full-length fur coat - in the days when a full-length fur coat on a man was dazzling, to say the least.

Jack's daughters used to come into work sometimes, and sit absolutely quietly, waiting for him. Then, as soon as he had finished he would whisk them off to some glamorous occasion. He thought that glamour was terribly important in people's lives. Whenever we had lunch, there was always champagne. He sent glamorous presents. And this showed in the tribute in his honour at the Palladium - the cast was so full of stars that nobody could ever have afforded to put them all on the same stage together under normal circumstances.

Kenneth Williams
Daily Mail, 16th April 1988

The Carry On Clown Prince who could raise laughs from the least likely lines

Kenneth Williams was one of the most loved, best known and least understood men in the world of modern entertainment. The public warmed to the campy, gossipy persona that enlivened a thousand chat shows, quiz programmes and countless *Carry On* films.

Show business professionals marvelled at his intuitive comic instinct; no one could conjure a laugh from the least likely line of dialogue with such practised artistry as he could.

Indeed Maggie Smith, one of his oldest friends from their collaborations in long gone yet still legendary stage revues, has always vouched that it was Williams who helped turn her into the most consummate comic actress of her generation.

'Kenneth taught me how to recognise the one word in a sentence which would turn it from a commonplace statement into something wildly funny,' she once told me when we were discussing the art of comedy.

It was this ability to invest everything he said with a high gloss of shimmering delivery which made him instantly one of the most celebrated voices on radio in its heyday. From *Hancock's Half Hour* – where his immediate cult following caused the show's deeply insecure star, Tony Hancock, to have him dropped from the series – through the memorable *Round the Horn* years to being the linchpin of the enduring *Just a Minute*, he created a gallery of comic characters that were institutions in themselves.

Yet his career, and his life, were both curiously unfulfilled. He was by temperament both ascetic intellectual and instant clown, and the two never sat easily together. It was a discerning headmaster who long ago warned him: 'Jokes will make you popular, but you won't be taken seriously when you want to be sincere.'

And he himself confessed: 'My exhibitionism always concealed a sense of inadequacy.' Perhaps it was this inadequacy that drove him to a constant quest for self-improvement of the mind and a voracious appetite for knowledge.

Yet from his unprepossessing origins as the son of a humdrum suburban hairdresser, he armed himself with an almost encyclopaedic recall that would daunt the average professor – only to find its main outlet was as a panellist on the long-running *Just a Minute* radio game where he specialised in outrageous outbursts, largely directed at the show's long-suffering chairman, Nicholas Parsons.

222

Likewise his deep and far-ranging insight into the art of acting was confined largely in the public's memory to the arch character roles of the *Carry On* films.

That he was a memorable Dauphin in Shaw's *St Joan*, or that he was one of the first to encourage and promote the writing of the late Joe Orton are today largely forgotten, his potential never fully realised, even by his peers.

When Dame Edith Evans heard that he was to appear with her in the ill-fated Robert Bolt play, *Gentle Jack*, she exclaimed in horror: 'But he has such a peculiar voice!' – an anecdote he never tired of telling, giving Dame Edith's own peculiar voice the full benefit of his own unerring mimicry.

True his gifts as a raconteur, which made him every chat-show host's favourite guest, found more lasting worth in his best-selling autobiographies, each one a masterpiece of comic insight and descriptive observation. But the Spartan quality of his private life – Joe Orton in his published diaries came to the conclusion that by nature Williams was probably totally asexual – was more suited to that of an Oxbridge don or a contemplative guru than the flamboyant show business personality which was how his adoring public perceived him.

To them, middle-aged and highly-respectable as likely as not, he represented the acceptable face of high camp. It was, in fact, his celebrated partnership with Hugh Paddick as Jules and Sandy, the unrepentantly gay couple in *Round the Horn*, which turned the then illegal homosexual world into safe family entertainment, and probably prepared the way for the subsequent enlightened legislation, insist some.

He owned few possessions, formed no long-term relationships, though he was possibly the personality most people would put top of their definitive guest list.

Michael Jackson
Daily Mail, 24th May 1988

Emperor of Rock shakes old Rome to its foundation

Rome, we know, was not built in a day. But it took a slip of a rebuilt man-child going on 30 to knock it flat in less than two hours. Here, where mighty Caesars once strutted before their triumphant legions, where the ancient gods were not lightly mocked, Michael Jackson began his own personal conquest of Europe.

He was most definitely in gladiatorial form. The giant Stadio Flaminio was ablaze with flicking lighters, held aloft like candles in some time-honoured ritual by his adoring fans like some latter-day deity emerged from behind a wall of headlamp glare.

What on earth did we expect of him? A prancing plastic Peter Pan, perhaps?

Well, the countless changes of costume, certainly owed a great deal to the child's love of dressing-up. But this aggressive, thrusting figure in his metal encrusted leather trousers pounding the stage with the haughty, raunchy vigour of a matador was as much a creature of earth as air.

Some Peter Pan. 'Was he really still a virgin?' some eager journalist had asked his mentor, Frank Dileo. Well, here he was, thrusting his pelvis arrogantly in the most explicit way possible. Some virgin.

What we had on stage was an act that was as full of fascinating contradictions as the myths that preceded it. A chiselled, androgynous face plastered with tendrils of hair sneered and leered, pouted and preened, simpered and seduced.

The voice, too, took on many thrilling disguises. The high, haunting wail of a man in love (*I Just Can't Stop Loving You*) the harsh, mocking sound of a guy who walks away.

But what, to me, was the most astounding part of this incredible evening, was the sheer electric power of the persona on stage.

He is a modern Mephistopheles. In an astounding transformation, he was one minute shrouded by a silver tent, which collapsed to reveal thin air – only for Jackson to appear borne astride a giant lift high above his fans, a wind machine blowing a black satin cape around him.

A Wiz of Showbiz, if ever I saw one. This was only a prelude to the gravity defying, backsliding slither he had perfected for *Billie Jean*, a number which had the hills of spectators ring their delight. This was a dance step the great Fred Astaire would have given a year's salary to have brought off to such adored acclaim.

It is this multi-array of talent which raises this strange, enigmatic creature above and beyond the range of mere Rock Stars.

The less reputable Italian papers have already been printing stories claiming he is actually an alien from Mars.

Well the answer is surely more simple than that. Jackson is a star – a star with a self-mocking sense of humour who can come out on stage dressed as a baboon before going into his multi-million seller, *Thriller*.

But he is not the boy-next-door. Look only at the women he adores, Jackie Onassis, Liz Taylor, Diana Ross. Hardly the sort of girls you'd find yourself living next to – unless you happened to inhabit that unique Never Never land.

No. Like all true stars, this one is unique in his field. A law unto himself. And every step he strutted on that stage last night said three things: *veni, vidi, vici*.

Samantha Fox
Daily Mail, 15th February 1989

The night that finally exposed Samantha Fox

By any calculations Miss Samantha Fox has been a very lucky lady in her short, but scarcely uneventful, life. Of course, everybody loves a winner. And everybody loved our Sam. Indeed, there is only one thing the British warm to more readily... the successful nobody.

Again, Miss Fox has filled this quaintly Anglo-Saxon role with such spectacular distinction that there is scarcely a Tesco check-out girl in the land who does not now imagine that, with a D-cup bra, a bottle of peroxide and an introduction to one of Rupert Murdoch's lackeys, she too could make forgettable records and end up on the *Terry Wogan Show* being probed for her thoughts on the state of the arts.

But this week, the adorable little Fox's luck ran out. Worse, it ran out in front of several million television viewers – and what passes for the cream of Britain's record industry. Shock, horror.

Scores of angry viewers bombarded the BBC with protests as she stood like a lamb delivered for slaughter among the blood-curdling chaos of the annual Brits award ceremony.

The bubble had burst, if you'll pardon the expression in the context of an ex-Page Three pin-up. To the apparent astonishment of all concerned, not least the great British public, it became embarrassingly clear that any cute looker cannot, after all, become a Sue Lawley in as little time as it takes to read the news.

The spectacular shambles of the event was not, of course, Samantha's fault. Nor was the decision to emphasise her unfortunate resemblance to a pouter pigeon dressed for dinner by dwarfing her alongside drummer Mick Fleetwood's gangling impersonation of Dr Death. But quite clearly the hapless Miss Fox simply had none of the resources needed to cope with the debacle surrounding her, much less rise above it.

Eyes slithering from side to side in blind panic, gloss-coated lips sticking to her teeth and her pretty little face frozen with terror, she could scarcely put together two coherent rehearsed sentences, let alone ad lib her way out of the engulfing mire. Never has Miss Fox seemed more vulnerably naked in her headline-hunting career than she did, though fully dressed, at the Royal Albert Hall that sad and sorry night.

'We've 'ad a groit toime,' she beamed desperately through those clenched white teeth as the evening drooled to a protracted fade-out. 'Oi 'ope you 'ave.' By then it was woefully apparent that the right phrase at the right time is not exactly Miss Fox's forte – as anyone might have known who had seen her on *Wogan* blithely philosophising that, 'In this business you get your share of knockers.'

And, to be fair, why should she ever have been thought to possess the cool of an Angela Rippon, the wit of a Victoria Wood or the elegance of a Jerry Hall?

Yet the warning signs were already clear that she was heading for a rift in her love-affair with her tabloid public. Her progress through America in pursuit of her more successful recording career must have given the organisers of the shambolic Brits 89 event some pause for thought before launching her as our latest TV hostess. Over there she was booed when she compèred one show. And she failed to endear herself to the working masses when she flounced out of a TV interview because the interviewer's questions failed to measure up to her own high standards of interrogation. What she would have given for a few smart questions – or even answers – at the Royal Albert Hall!

Samantha's sole mistake is in misjudging her limitations. It is not a crime. It is at worst a folly. And Miss Fox seems to me to be a lady with a native instinct for survival in a world where values are at best hazy. She has been taught to mistake gloss for glamour, notoriety for enduring fame, the fast buck for lasting good fortune.

The fault, surely, is as much ours as hers. She is photographed and fêted wherever she goes. She need only turn up at the opening of an envelope to get her name in the gossip columns. So why shouldn't she believe, like so many of her adoring fans, that expertise comes easy? That anyone can be a star if only enough people will believe it?

My bet is that, being the shrewd cookie she undoubtedly is, Miss Fox is today a wiser lady. And who knows, tomorrow, she might even sit down and learn to read an autocue instead of spending her time rushing off for fittings of a £2,500 sequinned suit that would have looked just as good on Charlie Drake. To stay at the top, you first of all have to get your priorities right.

Peter Ustinov in Person

Theatre Royal, Haymarket
***Daily Mail*, 22nd March 1990**

A sting in the tales of Peter the Great

Peter Ustinov's facility to distil life's irksome vagaries into a polished anecdote and drop it with consummate skill into the lap of his willing audience is an achievement he accomplishes with flawless precision. So flawless it might, at times, seem to devalue his own priceless coin. For behind the apparently bottomless treasury from which he dispenses his mixed bag of family history, professional actors' stories and wry philosophers' tales, is the living example of art concealing art.

We appear to be in the presence of some amiable, mildly eccentric, meandering uncle with family connections of global proportions. His mother met Queen Mary (Queen Mary did not say a word). He himself went to school with the son of Von Ribbentrop. His war was spent either at the mercy of a toothless sergeant who bit off his own tongue the minute his false teeth were delivered, or basking in the glory of being David Niven's batman.

Guinness, Gielgud, Richardson, Olivier and Laughton: he acted with them all and conjures up affectionate, if wicked, memories with one drop of his jowls or one rise of the vowels. Yet whether recounting tales of dining with the Reagans, or filming with Elizabeth Taylor, he deflects any hint of shameless namedropping with the best raconteur's favourite weapon: self-deprecation. He is forever the butt of his own success.

Yet even this is to diminish his worth as an entertainer of style and clout. For what could so easily pass for dinner party chatter of an elevated kind is a compulsively subversive mind at work. It is this which marks the true comic talent from all lesser jokesters. Ustinov, while seeming to inhabit a world of comfortable, intellectual privilege is, in fact, the Lord of Misrule. Puck disguised as Cardinal Wolsey.

He teaches us to mistrust our betters and learn from those less blessed. Even his most gentle satire carries the sting of humanising observation in its tail. With the world in its present melting pot, I would readily nominate Ustinov as the next Pope, were the notion not guaranteed to set him off on a whole new trail of irreverence.

Wayne Sleep
Daily Mail, 30th April 1990

Walking tall with Wayne

On most things, Wayne Sleep and I see eye-to-eye. Mother Nature herself saw to that. At a height of roughly 5ft 2in apiece, there is not much else we can do. Human nature on the other hand, is a different affair. And, truth to tell, there have been times when our eyeball-to-eyeball view of each other has been... well, frankly less than the sum of our tiny wholes. Indeed, a couple of years back, in a decidedly jaundiced interview to a newspaper whose market is even more down than our mutual eye level, Wayne complained bitterly: 'A minute theatre critic had refused to tip a taxi driver just because the poor man had confused our small but perfectly-formed frames.' Oh dear. Yes. It was I. Shame and innate honesty compel me to confess. But 'poor man' nothing. The dolt doggedly refused to accept my insistent assurances that I was not the little dancer he'd seen playing the Genie of the Ring with Danny La Rue in the Palladium pantomime.

It happens all the time. Please do not misunderstand: proud as anyone would be to be Wayne Sleep, it's just that I'm quite happy to be me. If occasionally being mistaken for Wayne Sleep is a hassle, what must it be like actually *being* Wayne Sleep?

'I was beginning to feel under pressure when I gave that interview,' he admits, though his wicked chuckle is not exactly contrite. Why should it be? Contrition is not what gave him the grit to fight his way to the top of the heap at Covent Garden, only to see the plum male roles go more often than not to dancers who lacked his skills, yet towered in height. Nor did self-doubt impede his great leap into the unknown when he founded his own commercial company which gave him the roles the Royal Ballet refused to create. In doing so, of course, he brought dance (and himself) to the notice of the masses.

Recently he went back to Covent Garden, but on his own terms and in a role of his own choosing, one which he'd been allowed to dance only three times before he fled the nest and starred in *Cats*. 'Luckily we played to full houses with *La Fille Mal Gardée*. I now feel that I've really danced it,' he says, another old score successfully checked off. And tonight he is back on the West End stage to put his own brand of fizz into Andrew Lloyd Webber's *Song and Dance* show at the Shaftesbury, a revival of his own second big solo commercial hit.

Of course, a high profile, especially on such a distinctly diminutive torso, can be a mixed blessing. From being fortune's darling he suddenly found the tabloid Press had turned against him.

His highly publicised dance partnership with Princess Diana had made him ripe for their plucking. 'It changed my life from the point of view of the Press. I think by discrediting me they thought, indirectly, they could discredit her,' he says now, still astonished at the subterfuges they used.

It certainly was a bleak time, especially for one so used to basking in easy camaraderie; he is blessed with a personality guaranteed to turn even the most mundane meeting into a party. A natural clown and effortless scene-stealer, sudden unpopularity hit him hard.

However, he is not built like a rubber bullet for nothing. Onward and upward is his instinctive reaction to any adversity. The money he accrued from his gruelling tours of *Dash* and its subsequent spin-offs he has poured into a private studio directly opposite the hide-away mews flat he would call home if he had managed to spend more than 30 days there in the past year...

At 42, he shows no signs of slowing up. A severe leg injury (sustained, ironically, not in the dance, but sitting on the floor and being tripped over by a large impresario) is mended.

For once, size is on his side; he still looks like a pixie and is determined to dance Puck in *The Dream* at the Garden.

No, not for a moment does he regret his long break with the Royal Ballet, nor the switchback ride he has experienced as a result ever since.

'Everything happened because I'd arrived in the commercial theatre as opposed to the ballet, where you can be a star for 30 years and no one would know you if you walked down the street. The popularity and notoriety is not important to me. The success is. Yes, it is nice not having to explain across a dinner table what you do to someone who may be half as talented as you, but is still a household name, and that you are in your own right a professional artist of some credibility.'

'When I was still dancing with the Royal Ballet, one critic even said I was too small to dance *Petrouchka*. A puppet! Nijinsky created *Petrouchka* and he was exactly our size. Did you know that?'

I didn't. But I'll walk taller whenever I think of it. How many taxi drivers would have recognised Nijinsky? I wonder.

WAYNE SLEEP

I used to go into Joe Allen's quite a lot in the old days, but I was always taught to keep away from critics because I was brought up by the Royal Ballet, and they never mix with the critics, unlike the English National Ballet, who entertain them in the intervals, and rely on them a lot, it seems. We were taught never to mix at that level – but I did a bit because the critic on the *Daily Telegraph* married Lesley Collier, who was one of my partners. It was generally discouraged. But once I relaxed, and became established in the West End I got to know Jack, and started to read his column.

We looked so alike – I was once at a first night, standing by the bar, and suddenly a woman came up and said 'Thank God for you.' I was very flattered, and began to think 'Well, yes, thank God for me'. 'You're just absolutely marvellous,' she continued.' 'Thank you' I replied, thinking that she was talking about my dancing. Finally it transpired that she was actually thanking me for being more generous than some of the other reviewers, and she was the producer of the show! That's when I realised that she thought I was Jack Tinker. I was so embarrassed that I just thanked her again and walked away.

He was also often mistaken for me. There is that incident with the taxi – apparently he once had this long taxi journey. For the whole journey the driver, who thought that he was me, kept going on and on to him about my dancing. By this time Jack had made quite a reputation for himself, his picture was under his column as well, and he had started doing television appearances, so he was known in his own right, as a name but also visually. He was rather put out by this driver, particularly since the journey was so long and he just would not let up. He got so fed up, that when they reached his destination he refused an autograph and did not leave a tip to make me look mean!

He took me to see the Adrian Noble production of *The Comedy of Errors* at the Barbican. We were sitting there in the stalls, watching this play about identical twins, and whispering to each other that we should be up there doing this. At the end of the play, the two look-alike servants make a great show of politely asking each other to go first. So as the audience filed out, Jack and I began to noisily imitate this, a routine that went on long into the night.

We had appeared in a couple of charity shows together, and always planned at some stage to perform the song *Sisters* together, in drag I suppose. Sadly, we never got around to it. He would have loved to have been a performer. He just loved it, you could never get him off once he was out there, and he never seemed nervous. Whereas the rest of us who perform for a living are always aware of what can go wrong, and worried about being judged, he was amongst everyone he knew, in a world which he loved, and full of beans.

Jack turned a lot of people on to the theatre. He was certainly a populist writer. In fact, he crossed over the traditional fence and became personally friendly with many artists – something that, because of my Royal Ballet background, I don't really approve of.

Not many critics would get away with that, but he earned the trust of a great many performers. People stopped seeing him as simply a critic. He went beyond that role – his page became something of a personality page, a feeling strengthened by his general column. How he wrote became as or more important than what he wrote. In a way it's the same thing that happened to me – I crossed over from ballet to theatre, and I was attacked for selling out. That's very typical of the attitudes in this country – you are pigeon-holed, and disapproved of. In the same way, perhaps Jack the serious critic suffered in the way he was viewed. But he built a bridge and was able to cross it.

Glenn Close
Daily Mail, 23rd October 1990

The magic that makes a true star

Lux has clearly given up the quest. The soap company that paid suitably astronomical fortunes to use stars such as Marilyn Monroe, Elizabeth Taylor and more recently Michelle Pfeiffer in their adverts has instead opted to sign up a pretty coffee shop owner who has never been in the limelight before.

And while they might be very nervous about their decision – not to mention the £1 million annual sales dependent on young Claire Wogan's selling capacity – I think the executives at Lux have done precisely the right thing... for finding a star these days is no easy matter.

True, every once in a while some bright and shining personality appears in the firmament of headline entertainers. But how do they fit in with our concept of a star?

Last week Mr David Puttnam, seemingly still the sole white hope of the flagging British film industry, offered up his personal candidate to the hall of the immortals.

It was, wait for it... Ms Glenn Close. 'The best screen actress of her generation,' eulogises Puttnam.

Now some might say: 'Well he would, wouldn't he?' For Ms Close is the star of his latest film, *Meeting Venus*, and we all know what producers will say in order to sell their newest product. Ms Close, for her part, plays the accolade very cool indeed.

'I sometimes laugh at myself and say: "What? Is this the stuff movie stars are made of?" I feel very ordinary at times,' she demurs. And how wise she is to do so. For however great an actress Ms Close might be, and few would quarrel that she is up there among the best, a 'star' is a different thing entirely.

Star quality is no respecter of talent, of hard work, virtue or ambition. Each of us lesser mortals recognises it the instant we are in its presence, yet never has it been successfully defined.

It touched the likes of Garbo, Monroe and Dietrich and lent them mystery and mythology. It radiated from Davis and Crawford.

Bogart, Cagney, Brando and Dean all shone with its elusive light. But this was the only uncommon denominator they shared. No two stars are the same.

Bette Davis herself came near to defining it when she declared: 'A star is someone who, when their name goes up above a marquee, a queue forms below it.'

That's near but not close. Not Mr Puttnam's Close anyway. For we seem to have lost the knack of breeding that genuine, dazzling star object whose brilliance blinds you to their defects, turns limitations into distinctive traits. Even the term 'star' today is a devalued term hung on any passing fad from Jason Donovan to the deluded Chris Quinten.

Each generation has needed its stars to steer its dreams by. The Keans, the Macreadys and the Irvings of the theatre's old barnstorming past gave way to the glossy silver-screen idolatry of Hollywood's studio system. Yet even here, in spite of the hype and the hypocrisy, the real thing shone forth.

For a rare few, like Garbo and Dietrich, it lasted a lifetime. For others, like Vivien Leigh, it blazed forth through only two or three incandescent individual films. Poor, star-crossed Marilyn clearly felt it was slipping from her grasp in those last muddled months of her short life. And – who can tell – maybe, like Garland, she was about to outlive her own magic. For star quality's shelf-life is as indeterminate as its very nature.

Can David Puttnam seriously be comparing the worthy Ms Close to the intemperate Monroe?

Surely not. She is simply a fine jobbing actress, and this is the way her profession is going.

Time was when Gloria Swanson was able to say without fear of contradiction: 'I am still a big star. It's the movies that have got smaller.' Now it's the stars who have dwindled.

The Elizabeth Taylors and Barbra Streisands hang on in there like a stricken breed of dinosaurs awaiting extinction.

The film's the thing, not the name above the title. Do avid queues form for the next Michelle Pfeiffer or Debra Winger movie?

Likewise the pop industry – that prime devaluer of star status – has become the repository for all manner of disposable freaks.

Yet they, too, are paraded across the pages of our newspapers with the megastar status of the giants like Presley, the Beatles, or Jagger among the golden age of rock, and Prince or Jackson from the newer claimants to their crowns.

Just to see Olivier on any stage would make you forget every other actor you had ever seen in the same role. Just to see Dietrich in concert, even at the end of her long career, taking her teasingly prolonged curtain calls, was to rob one of all rational response.

If star quality could be distilled and bottled there would be a run on the bank. Just to know such luminary creatures are actually of the same species, walking the same planet as ourselves, lifts the human spirit.

And such a person, I suspect Lux knows better than most of us, is to be found few times in a lifetime. I doubt even Ms Close would claim as much for herself.

ANDREW LLOYD WEBBER

Some people just have a magnetic quality which draws you in. It is also a question of finding the right role. Hal Prince said to Elaine Paige very early on that if you find one star role that is perfect for you, you are very lucky. Mary Martin found three. The important thing is to stay with them.

Glenn Close, for instance, is desperate to star in a properly made film for video of her performance in *Sunset Boulevard*. Certainly she was extraordinary in the role, despite not being the world's greatest singer. That is an example of a star – she was able to take the part and add a dimension that, I have to say, was breathtaking. Yul Brynner stole *The King and I* and stayed with that role until doomsday.

It is not, however, a good idea to set out to write a star vehicle. Once you try to do that, you are done for. The only time that I have come close to that is when I wrote Christine in *The Phantom of the Opera* for Sarah Brightman. In that instance, she and Michael Crawford brought something special to the lead roles that I have never seen equalled. I have seen it nearly as good, but there was real star quality.

MICHAEL CRAWFORD

It is true that certain stars need to find their one role and hang on to it. Cary Grant could not have played the Phantom of the Opera. He and many great film stars have stuck to their own style and achieved marvellous things within it. Not for the world should one want to change that.

There are others, like Alistair Sim, Alec Guinness, who made their careers from being extremely versatile. Jack gave one the freedom to do that, as I did. He appreciated what individual artists try to do over a period as well as in the moment. So he embraced all the facets of stardom.

I never think about trying to achieve fame. As a performer you must simply follow your instincts. You cannot try and design a career, or any part of your life, against your natural inclinations. As long as you follow your own path, you will have a heck of a time. It will not always be easy, but those are the clues to follow to choose which parts you should play.

Pavarotti: the 30th Anniversary Concert

Hyde Park, London
Daily Mail, **31st July 1991**

Serenaded and charmed by the big man of the people

Like some giant panda, a rare and endangered species, Pavarotti's impressive bulk suddenly hove into view from the recesses of a vast and vulgar fake pink temple.

He paused to survey the sodden masses spread out before him across Hyde Park. The masses, alas, were huddled beneath a humpy carpet of streaming umbrellas as the rain pelted down in steady grey rods. If he could not see us, so we could not see him.

Perhaps, under the circumstances, *0 Paradiso!* was audaciously inappropriate so early in the programme, rhapsodising as it does on the wonders of an African queen's tropical paradise.

But no. This is Pavarotti. Il Grandissimo. The greatest crowd-pleaser since Caruso; the only opera singer in the world who could fill Hyde Park on such a cold and wet summer's night and leave us stomping, yelling and chanting for more.

Of course, he had left *Nessun Dorma* – better known, thanks to him, as the World Cup theme song – until his final encore. *Nessun Dorma* indeed: not when Maestro Pavarotti is on the stage. Not only did they not wish to sleep, they did not wish to leave.

Even before his first notes had filled the park's open acres, silencing the birds, drowning out the overflying jumbo jets, his audience – or most of them – had surrendered. Down came the umbrellas as if in a slow

233

court curtsey, daring the elements to do their worst and willing him to give us his best.

Both duly obliged.

Although, perversely, the rain ceased when he came to the tear-jerking Scene One finale from *Pagliacci*. It was, however, no contest as to who won. Only a few faint hearts fled from the impossibly-priced enclosures where Charles and Diana sat.

And then only when it became clear that the aficionados brooked no sheltering brolly blocking their view of Il Grandissimo. 'Get that thing down, you rich bitch! Never mind your perm, you're lucky to have a seat!' some ungallant groundling called to an immaculately-coiffed lady resolutely refusing to lower her shade.

Not even Pavarotti's music soothes every savage breast, it seems. There are, of course, those purists who claim that Domingo's voice is finer, more subtle in its phrasing, less showy in its tone.

They were not to be heard even whispering such heresies here. This is the Big Man who understands and commands the Big Occasion. He is an unrepentant populist. His presence embraces his audience, his heroic voice enfolds us in its power.

People who have never been to an opera house respond as instinctively to his richly romantic rendering of *Recondita Armonia* from *Tosca* as they do to the inevitable and over-familiar *O Sole Mio*.

The man, quite simply, is a star and stars write their own rules. Who but he would have dared to introduce his encore from *Manon* by translating the title, in his heavily-accented English, 'I Have Never Seen A Woman Like That'? ... and then, with a large and wicked wink, dedicating it to 'Lady Diana'?

Even if he had not quite got his tongue round the complexities of royal titles, he certainly has his finger on the pulse of the man and the woman in the street.

Sodden or not, they adored him.

Jimmy Tarbuck

Daily Mail, 7th November 1992

A whole generation has missed the joy of his patter

Two burning resolutions buoyed me along as I reluctantly stepped ashore at Southampton from the majestic QE2. The first is to return to this cosseted cocoon of well-being as soon as my diary and pocket permit. But then it always is. I met a woman who has made no fewer than 110 voyages aboard the last and the largest of the great liners still afloat. And she's already planning the 111th.

But on to the second and more important resolve. This is to slap an instant injunction on one Mr James Tarbuck, late of Liverpool, the London Palladium and the vanished variety halls of Great Britain.

Mr Tarbuck, I declare, is a national treasure. And as such he has his duties. One being that he is compelled to appear at least twice a year on any stage in the country for extended seasons before live audiences. One-night concerts and TV quiz shows do not count. If necessary, a royal edict should be sent out to this effect forthwith. Actually, one has been. Tarby will star in this year's *Royal Variety Show*. But that is not the same. The six-minute spot on prime-time TV will not give you the unforgettable experience of witnessing this master of the wisecracking vaudeville tradition in person.

To know him, you have to be there in the heaving, aching flesh. Like sex, it is not the same second-hand.

Why do I suddenly rhapsodise about this persistently roguish vagabond who, until last week, I had not seen live on stage for the past decade? Because Tarby was part of our non-stop shipboard entertainment. And among the thousand or so passengers who crowded into the ship's Grand Lounge for his two shows, I was forcibly reminded, as were we all, of what we have been missing.

Some good souls even missed their five-course dinner so as not to lose their favoured seats.

Like Keith Barron and family, fellow passengers and Tarby devotees like myself, I had to stand on tiptoe at the back for a full hour so as not to miss a second of his street-wise mischief.

It was a small sacrifice. For like the great and good Doddy or that Poet Laureate of misanthropy, Les Dawson, he is one of a disappearing breed who can turn 2,000 complete strangers into an instant conspiracy of camaraderie at the raising of an eyebrow.

Forget Bèn Elton. Don't even think on Tony Slattery's half-baked efforts to evoke this priceless effect in the otherwise flawless piece of West End escapism, *Radio Times*.

Tarby is the genuine article.

Had I been casting *Radio Times*, by the by, it is to Tarby I would first have turned. But would Tarby have bitten on the bait of a long-term West End hit?

I fear not. For while some men find God, others get golf. And both are all-consuming passions. Life, travails and ambition become secondary.

It was, therefore, no coincidence that Tarby completed his little night jobs before our ship reached Lisbon. For here the serious business of the trip awaited. A golf tournament. What else?

There he was after breakfast, resplendent in the sort of pastel-shaded gear no grown man would be see dead wearing anywhere but on a golf course.

Except, perhaps, in the lager bars of Torremolinos.

I told him of my plan to compel him to return full-time to live theatre. 'I'm doing Panto in Bromley at Christmas!' he protested. And so he is. But how long is it since he did his last panto season anywhere? Fifteen years. A whole generation has grown up not knowing the joy of this splendid patter-man. And that is a crime.

The Magic Man: Paul Daniels
Prince of Wales Theatre
Daily Mail, 11th February 1994

Hail the conjuring hero! I'm already happily under his spell

As ever, I am lost in amazement, true amazement, at the sheer breadth of Paul Daniels' talent. In the ordinary way, illusionists leave me, if not cold, then no more than lukewarm. Clever, yes. But we all know it's a trick. Finally, it's a big 'so what?'

But Daniels is different. He is the master of something I find infinitely more dangerous than a disappearing biker and his Harley Davidson (which he does), a thousand times more mysterious than discovering the missing part of a torn £10 note within a walnut shell concealed within an egg, hidden in a lemon, all of which have been conjured together before our very eyes – a trick made even more memorable by the owner of the missing tenner being a bona fide police inspector hoping to enjoy an off-duty treat with his daughter and her friends.

No. Wondrous and mind-blowing as any of this may be, my unbounded admiration for Mr Daniels lies in his ability to mesmerise his audience on a different level entirely. He is that rarest of things, a true entertainer. A pied piper who can persuade 2,000 people that reality has stood still and life has become one long and merry party. In short, he is that most endangered of species, the great stand-up comic.

His opening song and dance routine says it all, when he appears out of nowhere sitting on a previously empty chair grinning like some nonchalant little gremlin of infinite mischief. 'It's about magic,' he trills with his chorus line of busty, lusty girls. 'It's about wonder.' Well, I can't think off-hand of any simpler definition of what theatre at its best should be. Can you? Wonder and magic. Mr Daniels supplied them by the bucketful.

He gives us the magic of a comedian who can enfold an entire audience in his own brand of humour and wrap it around us like a magician's cloak. He supplies the wonder of an entertainer who can take a row of Malaysian medical students, a West End copper, a gauche little Essex girl on her ninth birthday and a compulsive cackler in the circle – and weld them all together into an enchanted circle, making them, and us, feel as privileged and special as if they were members of the cast....

There is about this master of the song, dance and chat a generosity which is impossible to resist. I will go and see him as often as I have free nights. He is a tonic you feel instantly better for having taken – even when he taken you in.

PAUL DANIELS

Jack and I were laughing friends. I opened at The Prince of Wales Theatre some years ago, and one of the critics who attended was this fellow called Jack Tinker. The thing that impressed me about his write-up of the show was his awareness of show business, in which I am something of an oddity. I do not fit into any defined scene, and he seemed to have a rare understanding of the comedic aspects of my performances.

Times go by, and as I appeared in other places, this Jack Tinker character kept giving me good reviews. Then I took a cruise on the QE2, and there I found Jack giving a lecture – stories of shows he had seen and actors he had known, and so forth. I thought, 'So this is Jack Tinker, this tiny leprechaun of a man.'

By his own admission his talk was far from smooth. He was quite good, the stories were good, but he was relying a great deal on technology, sound-bites and vision-bites. He had a screen which failed to work and he was not prepared for that. Unsure what to do while the video was being fixed, he hesitantly asked if anybody had any questions, which is a terrible moment for a performer, it always creates an appalling hiatus. So, to help him out, I shot my hand up, with a question. 'Good God,' he said, 'it's Paul Daniels.' 'I've got to be somewhere,' I replied.

After I asked him a couple of questions, the show started to roll. Afterwards we had a drink. He thanked me, and I asked whether he minded if I gave him a few pointers. The ingredients were there, but in the wrong order. He was eager to learn, and over the next couple of days we rebuilt the show completely. I got rid of the video and the sound-bites, and told him, 'You are the show. It's always the performer, whether it is opera, ballet or theatre, the performer must be the focus. In your case, you have got great stories, but you are a naturally good raconteur and people like you.'

There of course is the biggest secret of Jack Tinker – people liked him.

He already appreciated the power of theatre, the way an audience can be controlled. I think he felt it all the more because he was physically small, which gave him a developed sense of vulnerability in some areas. I taught him about different sizes of arenas, and how to alter your body language for the size of the audience, where to look, how to harness and direct the performer's influence. Most important, I showed Jack how you can turn a huge theatre into a living-room. All of this I was able to pass on to his show, and he picked everything up instantly.

Jack took my advice, the show was a success and he took it to the Edinburgh Festival and elsewhere. He always gave me credit for my part in it. Whether true or not, he once told me that had we not got the show right then, he probably never would have taken it on again. After that, we formed the Daniels-Tinker Mutual Admiration Society. It was a great friendship.

He always went to the theatre believing he was going to enjoy himself. I once told him that he was the nearest thing to my ideal – an 'enjoy'. The word critic, by its very title, suggests that its incumbent has to criticise. People buy tickets to the theatre to have a good night out. I want publishers to employ and enjoy. That was Jack, and he was a better critic for it.

The truth is that nobody likes their idols bashed for the sake of it. Yes, you might be swayed to like the subject of a vindictive article less, but you will also dislike the journalist who inflicted the criticism. Jack appreciated that, he cared about journalism as much as he did about the theatre. He knew that to wilfully destroy our own business is a self-defeating task.

Michael Barrymore

Opera House, Blackpool
Daily Mail, 9th June 1994

Barrymore's back, and he's awight!

Michael Barrymore bounced back from the ropes last night like a prize-fighter reclaiming his title. Even before he had time to speak his famous catchphrase – 'I'm awight' – the capacity audience was on its feet welcoming him back with an ovation which momentarily brought tears to his eyes.

If there was any doubt before, this dispelled it. The man is the most dearly-loved performer currently headlining in Britain today. His problems are our problems. His joys ours, too.

There could not have been a soul in the house who did not know where he had been these past few weeks. The clamorous public revelation of his fight against a chronic drink problem had stunned fan and friend alike. So when finally he was able to assure us that he was indeed 'awight,' it simply brought the house down once again. For that is exactly what everyone willed him to be. 'Thank you for making this a night to remember,' he told us, adding wryly, 'There has been a lot I've forgot.'

So there we had it. He was going to be upfront and open as ever. When you've attained the status of a National Treasure, as he undoubtedly has, you can't crack up even in private. You have to share it with this vast extended family. You have to stand up there and face it out, turn it into a huge joke and then laugh it out of sight. Which, of course, being the man he is, is exactly what he did.

When a bewildered woman with hair like Blackpool candy floss wandered into view complaining: 'I'm lost,' he simply shrugged and told her: 'Yes, love. I was too for five years.'

And then he proceeded to haul her up on the stage until her anxious husband rushed forward to claim her. Barrymore immediately went into the role of the lover caught in the act. It was hilarious.

For in reality, it was he who made it an evening to remember. He was firing on all cylinders with power to spare. The timing was razor-sharp. Not a thing did he miss.

Catching sight of the *Sun* newspaper's dreaded telly-basher Gary Bushell scribbling away in the audience, he immediately confiscated his notebook and ordered him out of the theatre in a wondrous elaboration on his usual routine of turning out supposed troublemakers. 'Last time I saw you, Gary, you were disguised as a tree,' he beamed amicably.

It was, of course, an all too heartfelt reference to the antics of the world's Press, which had besieged him in the Maryland retreat where he so famously checked in for a period of dedicated rehabilitation.

But, radiating health and well-being, he clearly bore no malice. After one more sideswipe at his erstwhile persecutors – chasing a reporter from the local press agency right round the auditorium – he was all smiles and forgiveness. Even Bushell was allowed to sneak back to his seat. Which was just as well. For anyone to have missed this dazzling display of a man at the top of his form would have been a crime.

This was a star indeed. I have seen him galvanise an audience before. At the *Royal Variety Show*. In the television studios. But this was truly special. He knew everyone in the house was willing him to excel. And he exceeded all our wildest wishes.

Inveigling an 88-year old Blackpool landlady called Doris up on to the stage for no better reason than he loved her smile, he proceeded to perch her on his knee and serenade her in a routine of humorous affection that is his hallmark.

With pensioners and children alike, he brings out the very best in them and in himself. They warm to him. They may never quite know what he's going to do or say next – that's the uniqueness of the man. But they trust him implicitly. And he in turn transforms them for just one moment into a star.

Handing Doris a bottle of champagne, he grinned: 'No dear. It's for you. I'm not going to touch it.' Then, shooting one of those knowing glances of despair into the ceiling, he added: 'Can you just hear them – get that bottle off him quick!... I'm going to have to live with that for the rest of my life.' From where I was sitting he certainly looked as if this would be no problem at all. 'I was apprehensive, of course, before tonight,' he confided to us. 'But at the end of the day, you just have to get up, dust yourself down and start again, whatever business you're in.' And they cheered him to the echo.

There was no mistaking the message. Taking his cue from one of the many showstopping song and dance routines with which he can outstep the best hoofers on any stage, he was most definitely, most triumphantly, most enduringly 'Back in Business.'

For a moment, there were tears once again in his eyes as the audience rose and refused to leave. And, I have to confess, there were tears in mine, too.

MICHAEL BARRYMORE

I remember a particular article of Jack's that truly gave me back the will to live. I was at a particularly low ebb in my life – at a rehab centre, and you can't get lower than that – when Cheryl brought me in a piece that Jack had done and it did her as much good as me – in this Jack had written about my recently finished Barrymore series that he was 'utterly bereft and quite certain that nothing fresh or unexpected will light up our screens again until this miraculous Pied Piper of national goodwill returns.'

This was the turning-point in my recovery. That article at that time in my life swung the balance. I can almost recite it word for word. I've still got it – I could never part with it:

Goodbye Jack and thanks a million.

CHERYL BARRYMORE

Michael and I had known Jack professionally for quite a few years. However, we did not know him socially for a long time. He was a great sender of cards, though, and we have loads of little messages from him around the house.

We were in Palm Beach when Michael first became ill. It was Jack that I phoned, in absolute desperation. He immediately arranged for someone to help. Michael had to enter a rehabilitation centre, and I was left in Palm Beach. I had promised Michael that I would visit him, but the centre would not allow me to – it was one of their rules. Every week when the family visiting-day came round, I would feel plagued by guilt.

Jack took my mind off it, speaking to me for the whole day, every day. After a month, I was allowed my first phone-call to Michael. The occasion coincided with Jack's piece entitled *A Peerless Star*. I read it to Michael over the phone. He was so overcome, he cried his eyes out. To this day he keeps a copy of that article in his wallet.

There were not many times when Jack was upstaged. One night, when Michael was working, Jack and I arranged to go out to the theatre to see *Martin Guerre*, and then Jack had booked a table for three at The Ivy.

Michael had promised to try and meet us. We came out of the theatre and looked around to see if he had been able to make it, but he was not there. As we began to make our way to the restaurant, we and about a thousand other people heard a song blaring out at full volume from a car radio and Michael's voice. There was Michael, standing up in a convertible, serenading me for all he was worth with the song *I don't Know Why I Love You But I Do*. For once, even Jack was agog, but enchanted. Then Michael bundled us both into the car, and we sped off.

Julie Goodyear

Daily Mail, 17th September 1994

Bounteous Bet is streets ahead of the froth

Naughty is an altogether laughable description of a world where a female assistant building society branch manager can be kidnapped in her home, terrorised and finally done to death by ruthless thugs. And all for the comparatively meagre sum of £15,000.

However, in a week when once more our tiny patch of universe seems to have turned in upon itself, two small candles were lit for those of us who still cling against all the evidence to the illusion that God is in his heaven and all is right with the world.

As usual, it was in that fictional shelter of humanity, *Coronation Street*, where I found my spiritual succour. For lo! the Bambi of all barmaids, Raquel, was back on our screens once more, rescued from the outer darkness of Croydon by bounteous Bet, the all-seeing Delphic oracle of the Rovers Return.

And behold! Bet's *deus ex machina* descent on the lost town of Croydon in search of the emotionally dysfunctional barmaid and Raquel's tremulous return, was the stuff that dreams are made of. The writing, and above all the acting, was of an exceptional order, even for this bright burning beacon of excellence.

Yet behind these make-believe scenes performed with such style and subtlety by that veteran queen of the Rovers, Miss Julie Goodyear, and the infinitely appealing comparative newcomer, Miss Sarah Lancashire, there was an equally dramatic subplot being played out. For even as she filmed these taxing, dramatic and highly sensitive episodes, Julie Goodyear was under an insidious kind of siege.

The story was out that she was about to turn her back on the *Street* after almost a quarter of a century as one of its central players. Fuelled by the fact that she had spread her wings and recorded a chat show for her bosses at Granada, it was assumed in endless column inches of newsprint that the star was cutting up rough, refusing to toe the studio line and sign her £150,000-a-year contract and demanding more time off to do her own thing.

'Don't do it, Julie,' cried the fans in floods of letters to the Manchester headquarters. The newspapers were more censorious. A priggish note of 'Who does she think she is?' crept into their tone. 'The *Street* is bigger than its stars,' the pundits warned with brutal frankness.

And of course it is, in the same way that none of us is indispensable in the greater scheme of things. However, in life as on *Animal Farm*, some animals are more equal than others and some leave a greater emptiness when they are gone.

Yet all this was entirely academic. None of it happened to be true. Miss Goodyear duly, and I am told amicably, signed her contract. For its part, Granada took the unprecedented step of issuing a joint Press statement with the actress to quash the rumours once and for all. It categorically denied that she had declined to put pen to legal parchment until the studio met her demands.

For the record, the statement spelt out the facts: 'Ms Goodyear was not demanding more money. She was not demanding the right to film less episodes for the same amount of money. She was not demanding the right to work on a feature film or talk show. 'Any discussions between Ms Goodyear and Granada Television were nothing more than routine contractual negotiations.' Now you couldn't be less equivocal than that, could you?

However, on the very day this detailed statement was issued, certain down-market tabloids were still perpetuating the media myth that, though peace had broken out on the *Street* set, the turbulent star had haughtily got her way.

Sadly, it is part of that tired old British disease of building an icon up only to tear it down. But surely this diminishes the detractors more than the talisman they seek to topple.

Over the past decade we have seen our monarchy mangled, our police force persecuted, our judiciary ridiculed and our parliamentarians held up to contempt.

On the other hand, no fair-minded person could pretend that in the case of these once sacred cows, a great deal of the derision heaped upon them does not come uninvited. They have contributed fulsomely to the prevailing national mood of disillusion by their own follies, foibles and general crassness.

Yet what does Julie Goodyear do to deserve this kind of systematic demolition treatment?

She is a star of consummate charisma. An actress whose talent for conveying tough love, cast-iron common sense and a hidden tenderness which overrides all the natural instincts for self-survival has made Bet Gilroy one of the abiding joys of the best-loved serial in the English-speaking world. Three times a week (not counting repeats) she lights up our lives delivering some of the finest written lines on television. She does so with a skill which can turn comedy into tragedy and back again at the dip of those palely painted eyelids.

Such life forces do not come our way like swallows. They come singly and should be prized as an endangered species.

Julie Goodyear, like the character she plays, may not be bigger than the *Street* but she's bigger by far than all the mean-minded tosh the media slings her way.

JULIE GOODYEAR

Jack was a free spirit. He was magical, ethereal, a small child in a grown-up world. Very wise, witty, with a penchant for getting his own way, and letting you think it was your idea. A very naughty little boy sometimes, but never cruel.

The twinkle in his eyes was wonderful. His movements, his brain, were like quicksilver. He was dapper in his dress and always had shiny shoes, and small, beautiful hands.

Jack was a little tinker – a Lancashire expression for one full of mischief. I used to tell him he was small but perfectly formed. He loved that. In reality he was a giant of a man with a wicked sense of humour, a total perfectionist in every way. He never missed a trick.

Jack gave one unconditional love, which is very rare, normally only given by a mother. He believed in me and my work, and truly felt that I could do anything – so I often did, just to prove him right. An interview with Jack never felt like work because it was such fun. He always got it right.

We often had late night chats about anything and everything and laughed like a couple of kids at the hypocrisy of the show business world. There was in Jack a wonderful blend of masculinity and femininity I could identify with. He loved strong, glamorous women who could laugh at themselves: he loved me, and I loved him.

Robert Stephens
Daily Mail, 14th November 1995

Robert was one of nature's roisterers with a tangled life and a real genius for acting

'Dull people do not make good actors,' Sir Robert Stephens was fond of saying. It was a charge which could never be levelled at him. There was a generous recklessness, an over-abundance of energy and enthusiasm about Robert which marked him out as one of the most compelling actors of his age as well as one of the most companionable of men. Those fortunate enough to know him – and his friendships ranged literally from princes to paupers – treasured the time spent in his company just as audiences of complete strangers warmed instinctively to his presence on stage, film or television screen.

It also ensured a tangled love life, which he recorded with typically robust frankness and bravado in his aptly-titled autobiography, *Knight Errant*.

For he generated a sense of excitement spiced with danger which proved irresistible both as an actor and as a human being. It was a propensity which certainly did not make for a tranquil life and in all probability helped hasten his death on Sunday night in the Royal Free Hospital, Hampstead, at the early age of 64.

Prince Charles, one of his most ardent admirers and friends, had called in last week to make his farewells. Complications had set in after the successful but highly complicated liver and kidney double transplant Robert underwent there last year, before his knighthood was announced, yet he had neither the temperament nor temper to be an invalid...

On stage he could command a magisterial stillness. Larger than life by inclination he could, nevertheless, illuminate the small humanities in every character he played. Only three years ago he made a triumphant return to the classical stage with the Royal Shakespeare Company as an unforgettable Falstaff in *Henry IV Parts I* and *II*.

Avoiding all the obvious vulgarities of the role, which trick so many actors into playing the fat knight as knockabout farce, he showed us a magnificent wreck of a man in whom you could still see the brilliance of his early youthful promise. This was the first Falstaff ever to remind you that he had once indeed been a privileged page to a previous king.

In an ironic way it seemed a poignant commentary on his own professional life...

Elaine Paige

Minskoff Theatre, Broadway
***Daily Mail*, 13th September 1996**

Elaine, Queen of the Musical

Even before the reviews were out, Elaine Paige's Broadway début had caused queues around the block at the Minskoff Theatre this week. And even before she had sung a note, a sell-out audience gave her first preview entrance such a prolonged ovation that it seemed she would never be able to start the show.

As Norma Desmond, the faded star from the silent movies in Andrew Lloyd Webber's blockbusting *Sunset Boulevard*, Paige has finally made it to what was once the Mecca of every musical star. And Broadway seems all set to take her to its warm, but unpredictable heart.

It has been a long haul since I was first aware of her vibrant stage personality playing Michael Crawford's bit of rough in the Waterhouse-Hall-Black hit musical *Billy*, back in the early Seventies. Yet even then there was an extra fizz about her presence. It was, of course, Crawford's musical début at Drury Lane and few were allowed to twinkle too brightly in his presence.

Still, you could not help noticing the minute bundle of comic energy whose voice, even then, had a crystal-shattering intensity. To be honest, I cannot claim any such clear remembrance of her even more startling appearance in *Hair*. But then individual talent does notoriously tend to get mislaid on a stage full of naked flesh.

Since then, of course, she has carved out a career playing strong and gutsy ladies, not the sort you would find waiting at home for hubby with the pipe and slippers at the ready. I can still recall the thrill of her slow, gliding balcony appearance as Evita, the role which raised her from the ranks of promising second-leaguers and set her on the first step to Broadway's acclaim.

It was at that moment, radiant and commanding in her dazzling white Dior crinoline gown as she launched into the evening's show-stopping ballad, *Don't Cry for Me Argentina*, that every instinct told you all the potential of a major star had just arrived. And I wrote so.

However, in every career, as I never tire of warning, three ingredients are essential for staying power. They are – and in this order – luck, temperament and talent.

Elaine had already proved she had the latter. You do not get featured parts opposite Michael Crawford without it. The luck had come, at last, when she finally wrested the choice Rice-Lloyd Webber vehicle from her nearest rival, Verity-Ann Meldrum, who until the final furlong had been front-runner for the role.

The question was: would her temperament hold out for that perilous event in the build-up of any leading lady, the choice of a second starring showcase? The wait for that crucial make-or-break chance would have tested the nerve of lesser mortals, for zonking great roles for females in stage musicals do not fall off trees these days.

Yet again, luck was on her side. Dame Judi Dench's misfortune, having to drop out of the role of Grizabella in Lloyd Webber's mould-breaking show *Cats*, was Elaine's great gift. One song only as the bedraggled cat-lady of the night; but what a song it was. And, that extraordinary first night way back at the start of its record-breaking run, she sang it as if her life depended upon it. *Memory* was the song she needed to imprint her voice on the public consciousness. And like the seasoned trouper she already was, she saw her moment and seized it.

Piaf, Pam Gems's harrowingly frank musical portrait of France's greatest *chanteuse* and her next major stage metamorphosis, was the kind of artistic triumph every actress craves.

Utterly transformed into the tiny, physically awkward Little Sparrow of legend, she gave new voice to some of Piaf's greatest numbers without ever attempting crude impersonation, but making them her own.

Frankly, until Paige sang these songs, I could not bear to hear them trusted to anyone else. But her CD of the show is now among my most often played. Just like Piaf, she makes these simple street songs impeccable, powerful and personal.

ELAINE PAIGE

Jack and I had two things in common, a love of theatre and our height – we could talk to each other without getting neckache! He was so terribly knowledgeable about the theatre, you couldn't help but be caught up in his enthusiasm for the profession. If Jack rated a performance, I would rush to see it because I knew he was a fair and critical judge. He knew the vulnerability of being a performer, because he also trod the boards himself from time to time and maybe this is the reason he was so very generous at times in his appraisal, though he could also be quite blunt.

I remember one occasion in particular, a party at an art gallery where there were many studious and knowledgeable opinions being given about the art on display and Jack and I enjoyed a very funny five minutes sharing our anarchical views. He could be quite 'off the wall' and wacky and it was moments like these that I remember so well.

9

THE CRITIC: FRIEND OR FOE?

They won't turn me into a tame poodle!
Daily Mail, 28th August 1978

For the best part of the past decade, London's West End first nights have raised their curtains promptly at seven in the evening – give or take the odd 20 minutes to get the celebrities seated, the celebrity-spotters over their excitement and the cast over their last second panic.

Soon all this may change. The powerful Society of West End Theatre Managements – SWETM to their friends – are fed up with this arrangement. So, they claim, are the first nighters themselves. So, they add, are the casts.

So what is keeping the 7pm opening anyway? In two words: Overnight Reviews. The early opening helps the reviewers with their deadlines. Without it they would invariably miss the last act of every musical in town in order to get their copy into print.

But now the managers want their cake and eat it. They are proposing to start their shows at eight o'clock, or even eight-thirty and put a strict embargo on all critics' notices for 24 hours.

Now the folly of this proposal is plain to all who know that the only value of news is that it is new...

Is that what we really said..?
Daily Mail, 10th April 1979

The notices outside the theatre are ecstatic. 'Dazzling entertainment.' 'I shook with laughter.' 'The audience was convulsed.' That sort of hard sell still brings in the customers. You pay your money – anything from £14 per pair of stalls downwards. You take your seats and the entertainment which greets you makes you wonder if the blokes who previewed those immoderate phrases plastered outside on the hoardings were out on a day trip from St Dunstan's or members of the St Bride's Hard of Hearing Club, or both.

'Did we see the same show?' is the constant wail of readers who finally get round to seeing a hit show long into its run. Their wrath invariably falls on me and my kind when they are disappointed.

Of course in the theatre, more than anywhere else, one man's meat is another man's poison. But, personal preferences aside did we really see the same show? Is *Evita* really as good as those first night reviews? Does the entertainment on offer in many of our leading long-run theatres still match up to those rave reviews that helped turn them into money-spinners?

All too often the answer is: no. The original stars leave – often at the end of a short six month contract. The director, having notched up a hit and secured his percentage for the run, goes on to plough his energy into pastures new, more often than not leaving the succeeding casts to fend for themselves. With actors' egos allowed to run riot, it invariably becomes the survival of the strongest. Even original performances change beyond all recognition (and only sometimes for the better) when left to their own devices like this.

As one who has to carry the can for those cryptic unfulfilled promises, I decided to carry out a spot check on a half dozen of London's most popular long-stay shows. And frankly I'm amazed the public have not had the entire Critic's Circle summoned under the Trades Description Act long before now.

Of course we could plead Not Guilty and shop the management for gross misrepresentation. But has any one of the original reviewers been back to see *No Sex Please – We're British* since their glowing tributes helped turn it into the World's Longest Running Comedy?

I popped into a matinée – egged on by the words attributed to Sir Harold Hobson, doyen of our trade. I popped right out again at the interval. The general standard of performance on the stage of The Strand would have shamed a bankrupt end of pier show (a quote I freely bequeath the management of the pretty theatre).

We forget – but that matinée served as a sharp reminder – that this was the play in which Michael Crawford virtually created his Frank Spencer character eight years ago during a lull in his otherwise meteoric career. The twitching twit who holds together a virtually untenable play in his hands, became a magic, electrifying comic creation. Derek Fowlds, seven fat years on, struggles manfully with the bits of comic business Crawford left behind for his successors.

But would Sir Harold or any of the rest of us 'shake in our seats with laughter' at the show today, let alone encourage an unsuspecting public to witness the silly story line in all its shoddy implausibility by performances which are at best routine and in the case of the heroine, fit only for a straightjacket? (I charitably assumed her to be a martyr to St Vitus Dance.)

Peter Saunders, one of London's wilier impresarios, attempts to keep his all-time, record-breaking blockbuster (words not for quoting, please, Mr Saunders), *The Mousetrap*, free from the whiff of staleness by altering his entire cast every year. Sometimes it works, sometimes it doesn't. Personally I think this year's company no better and no worse than last year's. Neither one is going to have the RSC beating their dressing-room doors down.

But having guessed who did it shortly after the interval on first viewing, I'm not the best judge of what keeps the St Martin's Theatre stretched to capacity even on a wet and cold Monday night. And I've certainly never urged even Aunt Edna to include it in an itinerary of historic sights to see in London.

Oh Calcutta! was a *succès de scandale* when it opened nine years ago. Nudity was novel. Now Kenneth Tynan's hymn to sexual liberation seems merely nothing but novel. Most of the show's original intellectual pretensions have long disappeared in the bid to appease the tastes of its nightly audience of tired businessmen, late developing suburban swingers and non-English speaking Japanese tourists. A two-second glimpse of Diana Rigg's naked understudy in *Night and Day* – this season's solid hit play – is a hundred times more erotic nowadays.

Strangely enough, long-running musicals fare much better in keeping up original standards. *Annie* is still an enchantment. *A Chorus Line* never flagged through its two-year marathon at Drury Lane. I dropped into a Saturday matinée of *Evita* now that David Essex has been replaced by Gary Bond and found the show just as dynamic as on that electrifying first night.

After seven years packing 'em in at the Palace Theatre, *Jesus Christ Superstar* has actually improved. I was greatly underwhelmed on the opening night, but now find Jesus being given a blazing performance by Robert Farrant.

It is, perhaps, significant of the continued high standards of these two shows that on the nights I paid my random visits *Evita's* award-winning director, Hal Prince, was conscientiously checking out the first, and multimillionaire producer, Robert Stigwood, was out front appraising his property, the second. Significant... because it happens all too rarely.

How to tell the heartless truth, and still keep your best friend happy..!

Daily Mail, 21st January 1980

It's a dilemma anyone with a friend in a show has had to face. From the local amateur panto in the village hall to the star dressing room at Drury Lane, the after-show confrontation is landmined with moments that can explode the closest friendship sky-high.

The performer is hungry for praise. The backstage visitor, appalled by what he has just witnessed. What can you say? How can you possibly utter the unpalatable truth to someone waiting only to hear the inevitable: 'Darling, you were WONDERFUL'? And to lie to a dear one will be spotted immediately and forgiven even less readily than awful honesty.

In my experience, though, it is a situation not confined to the rarefied atmosphere of Thespians. For instance the man who goes home to find his wife has had her crowning glory ('Sweetheart, I love you with your hair loose and flowing.' How many times has he told her that?) cropped to the texture of the tufted front door mat knows the feeling well enough. And the best friend who has decorated the living-room a defiant yellow and purple opens up the same sensitive war zone. Never insult a person's choice of wallpaper even if you feel perfectly free to criticise his mother, offspring or bedfellow. It's a sure end to even the most beautiful friendship.

And last night John Osborne gave vent to a lifetime of being on the receiving end of honest opinion delivered at inopportune times. His play for ITV, *You're Not Watching Me, Mummy* dealt eloquently with the boredom behind the bright lights. In it Anna Massey was seen slumped in her dressing room after the curtain had fallen waiting for the onslaught of backstage ritual.

'Why do they come?' she demanded petulantly. 'Just sitting there as if they expected something to really happen in here after you've knocked your backside or for two and a half hours. Staring. Saying nothing. Waiting. Helpless. The world seems full of them. We slosh our blood all over the stage and what do they do? Sit and wait for a drink.'

Poor lady. But there is a brand of backstage veteran who can cover all emergencies without having to beat a quick retreat. Miriam Karlin is among the prime exponents of the art of dressing-room ambiguity. And though I avoid dressing-rooms – a critic is as welcome in one after a show as Mr Banquo at the Macbeths for dinner! – there are times when paths cross uncomfortably; when silence can only be interpreted as a dumb reproach; when we all need Miss Karlin's technique...

High on the list of get-out ambiguities is my own personal favourite, shamelessly stolen from Miss Karlin's artful armoury. 'I didn't be-LIEVE it, my dear!'

Now, besides being strictly nothing but the truth, this retort has the added lustre of feeding the recipient's vanity. It can be used as well for disastrous interior decor as for a dog of a show. Uttered with the right inflection it can even persuade a suburban housewife that her attempt at punk spiky hair is nothing but the sensation she hoped it to be when she let her hairdresser talk her into it.

But there are others, all of which work on roughly the same blend of high-octane delivery on the part of the giver, and easily ignited ego on the part of the receiver.

'What about YOU!' needs only the merest touch of innocence and awe to convince the listener that he or she has achieved something very special. And after all, special is just another word for downright odd. The trick is to rush on to the next topic before being asked to elucidate. In absolutely all such situations, gush is essential.

'You've done it again!' cried at full throttle and with a warm embrace to hide the embarrassment, can warm the cockles of a wife who has just had her hair dyed bright green, a friend who has mis-mixed-and-matched her old wallpaper to the new fitted carpets, or a faded star who has given several performances too many. The art of the hidden barb knows no barriers and no shame.

'My dear, if I hadn't seen it, I wouldn't have BELIEVED it!' is the whole truth, and nothing but the truth. But prefixed by a term of endearment – often quite genuine – it allays any suspicions of malice aforethought. We all believe the best about ourselves, after all.

Not even the world of heavy rock is free from the desperate need for reassurance. Look only at the scene Bette Midler plays in her film debut, *The Rose*. 'What did you think?' asks Midler with uncharacteristic lack of self-confidence. 'You were insane,' her visitor assures her – pop jargon for 'Only you could do it, darling'. And leaving them to pick the bones out of it as best they may.

NED SHERRIN

A friend of mine sat next to Jack during the opening night of a show I did called *The Sloane Ranger*. According to him, Jack was screaming with laughter all the way through. Yet when he opened his *Mail* the next morning he read an appalling notice about it, and could not reconcile the two things. Jack had this ability to watch something and laugh at it, and then later decide that it was worthless and say so without fear or favour.

He somehow managed to magically walk that impossible tightrope, a critic who mingled with performers. It is a difficult balancing act, although a number of people have done it over the years, Bernard Shaw for example. Jack brought it off. He was so engaging. I suppose the fact that he was tiny and funny counted in his favour – he almost became a theatrical mascot.

Secrets of my 1001 first nights

Daily Mail, 23rd February 1983

Suddenly I feel like Pavlov's dog. For the past 21 years I have been barking my head off in the line of duty and experience has taught me to expect no more than the odd curse or even kick for my response. Now, astonishingly, there comes a pat on the head and I find myself so stunned I doubt if I know how to wag a tail appropriately.

The critic's task of influencing people before he goes to bed almost guarantees he will wake up next morning with fewer friend somehow or other. I can appreciate only too keenly that the likes of Ms Elizabeth Taylor must feel that any prize handed out to a gentleman of my strange calling has been snatched from the tomb of her reputation. Why only this week the ghost of some unkind words I wrote about her – 'A dumpy little lady stomping her way through a great deal of kind lighting' – returned to haunt us both in a BBC news bulletin.

But now it can be told. Miss Taylor had her revenge even before those words had reached the printed page.

They had been scribbled down in the back of a taxi as I sped home to telephone my review with barely fifteen minutes to spare to my deadline.

Only when I reached my front door did I realise that my keys had vanished along with the cab. I hammered on the door of a neighbour. For when it comes to meeting deadlines, I have been known to manhandle old ladies out of kiosks in the middle of long-distance calls. So I spared no social chit-chat as I barged into this poor man's home and commandeered his telephone without giving him so much as a polite glance. Not until I had dictated my last full stop did I notice the naked blonde cowering in astonishment in one corner of the sofa.

'You didn't enjoy the play very much, then?' stammered the stunning stranger. My admiration for the way the British cope with unexpected guests has never been higher.

Of course this rough-and-tumble method of composing and delivering overnight reviews is fraught with more obvious hidden hazards. Tommy Steele was once saved from an entirely uncalled-for slur on his stainless reputation by the merest of good fortune – for both of us.

I had elected to begin an ecstatic paean to his maturing talent with the deathless words: 'Tommy Steele has thrown away the worn-out Lurex of his rock 'n' roll past...' Only the innate curiosity of a vigilant sub-editor prompted him to ring back and enquire why Mr Steele's method in disposing of his used family planning aids should be of the slightest relevance.

There is many a slip, as you see, twixt the telephone cup and the critic's lips. Speaking of lips brings me to the penalties of speaking one's mind in public about friends and artists one holds dear in private.

From the very outset of her career I heaped worship at the feet of Maggie Smith; she was and is, I believe, the finest artist of her day, on her day. So it was, I thought, as a long-standing admirer that I put pen to paper and warned her against falling prey to her own distinctive style of comic acting. Miss Smith let it be known through mutual friends that I had better not go within a mile of her... and for seven years I heeded her advice.

But we met up again in Canada and the reunion went rather too well. Next morning I woke up with severe bruising from head to toe and absolutely no recollection of the cause. I could only assume Miss Smith had had a change of heart and given me the treatment playwright David Hare dished out to my colleague Michael Billington in the foyer of the Royal Court, belabouring mightily about the head with hambone fists. Mercifully the phone rang and brought the distinctive nasal twang of Miss Smith at her most urgently confidential assuring me: 'Listen! I can tell you that you fell down two flights of stairs last night if you can tell me whose house we were in.'

During my 21 years Coming-of-Age as a critic, I have worked my way from nowhere to the exalted rank of Number Three on Mr Osborne's personal Death List. And I have the rude seaside card informing me of the award to prove it.

For myself I hold no grudges. Nothing gives me so much pleasure as sitting in front of a production that shines out with excellence, be it a Jacobean tragedy or a boulevard romp. I will bless Mr Osborne's name for *Inadmissible Evidence* and *The Entertainer* with my dying breath – even if he is the one to extract it.

DAVID NATHAN

Jack and I knew each other for twenty years or so. The relationships of theatre critics is usually odd. You see each other four nights a week, but after the show you quickly go your separate ways, particularly if you are an overnight reviewer like Jack and as I used to be. During the show there are only a few minutes before curtain-up and then the interval, when you may or may not get to chat. So unless definite arrangements are made, you cannot talk very much.

There was, however, a fairly regular tradition going back over a long period of between ten and fifteen years, whereby a few of us would always have a table reserved in The Dirty Duck after plays in Stratford-upon-Avon. There would be Jack, myself, Bill Hagerty, frequently Michael Coveney and occasionally Irving Wardle. Pam Harris, the manageress, also joined us. She was a great favourite with Jack. Speaking about the play we had just seen was frowned upon, because Jack would have already written his piece, and the rest of us still had to do so...

They'd love me on the critical list!

***Daily Mail*, 19th August 1989**

We have been bashed, we have been panned, we have been abused by the best. Critics, by and large, do not get a good Press. This week has not polished the image of the breed.

In the full glare of Edinburgh's annual media circus, Mr Steven Berkoff, actor, author and director extraordinaire, publicly moderated his offer to murder the *Guardian*'s Nicholas de Jongh only slightly. Critics, he conceded, were after all necessary to our daily functions, 'like toilet rolls.' He then added sadism and the qualities of a faded tart to the list of essential job qualifications. Fairly routine stuff for Mr Berkoff. Yet no sooner were his words uttered, than on television too the usually affable Stephen Fry began mordantly wondering how on earth any critic slept at night.

Unhappily, less emotionally stable artists do not confine themselves to harmless musings on the sleep patterns of the men they look upon as their natural enemies. They suit action to the insult. Even the late Olympian Lord Olivier was, in his more intemperate youth, driven to strike James Agate, doyen critic to two generations of theatregoers. Agate's offence? Returning late to his seat for the second act of the actor's performance.

It was ever thus. Where the artist's fragile ego is brought into conflict with the critic's right to express honestly-held opinions, sparks are bound to fly. I do not wish to come closer to David Storey's line in literary counter-attack than feeling the hambone mitt of this rugby-playing writer whistle past my ear to belabour the head of de Jongh's *Guardian* colleague Michael Billington. 'Silly man, silly man,' intoned Storey with each slap. Clearly for once his dialogue could not match his action.

Such hazards seem par for the course in this job. Tim Rice, a man of legendary calm conviviality and cheer – and a cricket player, too! – once informed me through uncharacteristically clenched teeth that had I been at my usual table the night previously he would have undoubtedly entertained the theatrical throng of diners there and punched me. Blondel, the show in question (my question) is now never mentioned between us.

Others are not so quick to forgive. De Jongh was again the recipient of a long-held grudge, this time a pint of ginger beer was flung full in his face by an outraged lesbian in defence of a gay play he could hardly remember reviewing. Clive Barnes, once known as the Butcher of Broadway, but in reality a gregarious, civilised Englishman abroad, suffered from a similar waste of drink when the contents of a wine glass were emptied in his direction by an angry primadonna of the ballet.

Yet none of these impassioned dousings can match the dramatic impact Miss Sylvia Miles achieved by emptying her lunch over the head of New York's most poison-penned operator, John Simon, in Broadway's celebrity honeypot, Joe Allen. Miss Miles, famed for her Oscar-nominated role as the predatory harlot in *Midnight Cowboy*, is a lady of outgoing instincts.

Meeting her not long afterwards in New York, I joked defensively: 'John Simon tells me you serve a mean spaghetti, Sylvia.' Miss Miles, a jealous guardian of the minutiae of her own legend and a dear friend, was indignant in her denials. 'Who told you that falsehood? I did no such thing!' she fumed. 'It was not spaghetti! It was chilli con carne!' In my book, hot food is hot food when it hits you in the face. It does not require a menu.

And yet perhaps not so. Eileen Atkins insists that she once pushed a pudding in mine during a discussion of Maggie Smith's suitability to play Virginia Woolf. I honestly have no recollection of the incident.

Memory obviously is selective on these issues. Like David Storey, John Osborne's fabled way with words also seems to desert him in extremis. I have a collection of cheerfully vulgar seaside postcards informing me of my progress up his own private hit list, happily the nearest thing to a death threat to have come my way.

At last count I had risen to third ranking, pipped to the post by the scholarly Benedict Nightingale, and, of course the ever-inciting de Jongh. However, my upwardly mobile rise in the hatred stakes has been impeded by an apparent lapse of Osborne's notoriously elephantine memory for grievance, signalled by the arrival of a long, charming and absorbing letter on the subject of Tennessee Williams' death. It bore the familiar autograph yet began, surprisingly: 'As you know I never write to critics...'

And here lies the nub of why critic and artist finds it so difficult to cohabit peaceably. Praise, the drug and driving force of the creative process, is a fickle and ephemeral thing. Nor is it helped by the language at its disposal. The British as a nation are not of generous, open-hearted stock. While the language we have created for abuse, put-down and censure is endlessly rich in wit, variety and invention, the words we reserve for our approval have a tawdry, overworked ring.

Rave reviews, while momentarily gratifying to artists and managements, are doomed only to be immortalised at best by being plastered up on theatre hoardings in tired clichés: 'Stunning', 'Tremendous', 'Superb'. Words rendered all but valueless through the necessity of repetition.

Yet every insult comes scorching hot from the press to burn itself into the memory and pass like new-minted currency around dinner tables from Hampstead to Hemel Hempstead. While I bet not one of you can conjure up one memorable phrase of praise from the long career of Katharine Hepburn, most are able to quote instantly Dorothy Parker's 50-year-old epithet to her talent: 'Katharine Hepburn ran the gamut of emotions from A to B.'

I once had cause to put this curious state of affairs to the test. Sir Peter Hall had publicly accused me of blatant prejudice, of not liking anything I had ever seen at the National Theatre. I was amazed. I sent him copies of my past 12 reviews. Three raves, three stinkers and the rest mildly in between. 'I still think you're prejudiced,' he replied. No doubt he did. Only the brickbats had struck home. The bouquets had already withered and died.

As the present chairman of the drama section of the Critic's Circle, I look round at my fellow members and find only one single factor common to us all. Not sadism, there are those of us whose children and loved ones would happily take up arms in our defence against such slanders. Not insomnia or the conscience of the Macbeths. As for the instincts of faded old tarts, let he who is without sin throw the first stone.

No. What binds this motley band of men and women, few of whose paths would voluntarily cross anywhere near neighbouring seats in the stalls, is a passionate love for and abiding interest in the theatre. That and the journalist's natural impulse to communicate his opinions to his readers in the most telling phrase to hand.

A good evening's work for me is a play which makes me laugh or cry, or know myself or my fellow man more keenly, the joys of which I can share with my readers. A bad night is when I can find nothing good worth saying. 'I liked the frocks,' for me is no valid reason to urge my readers into theatres at considerable expense to themselves, and not worth the printing.

At best our views are the opening salvo in an on-going debate which is settled only at the box-office. The public has the last crack of the whip. Meanwhile it is our lot to be maligned and misunderstood. I have every sympathy with a Scottish actor from the Royal Shakespeare Company who, spotting me standing patiently at a bus stop, raised his fist. The review of his performance flashed across my eyes even as I watched it clench.

'He has obviously studied at the Chris Quinten school of acting,' it ran. 'He can walk, he can talk and he can smile. But apparently not all of them at the same time.' He struggled to find words to match his feelings. 'Jack Tinker,' he spluttered, 'You're a... you're a... you're a...' The bus queue craned forward to hear his review of my own shortcomings, '...You're a twerp,' he ended lamely.

As an example of the critic's art it was not in the Tynan class; but as an example of an artist's justifiably wounded pride I found it genuinely moving and eloquent. Yet it gave me no sleepless nights. Nor have I revised my opinion of his performance.

STEVEN BERKOFF

I never really said that critics are toilet rolls – I would never say that anyway. It all started when I was taking part in a chat with Nick de Jongh in an Edinburgh talkfest. Nick suggested that we pretend to insult each other. It was those fake insults that got circulated. I might only apply them to one or two critics.

The idea of faded tarts emerged because a prostitute who sells her services frequently no longer has a feeling for the work. So I felt that a critic having to subject himself to so many performances, even with the best will in the world must lose some of his sensory perception and sensitivity. Never Jack, though.

There were similarities between Jack's work and mine – we were, indeed, kindred spirits. He had an extremely witty turn of phrase and could be very acerbic and sharp, sometimes snarling and catty. He was a very perspicacious man. Jack liked my work because he felt it was both radical and at the same time very professionally toned – what Ken Tynan might call high-definition theatre. That is what I have always aspired to. The criterion for Jack was skill, style and daring and that is what he saw in me.

Jack supported me and championed me in spite of and against the popular conventional taste. Against certain retroactive critics. When I won the *Evening Standard Award* for *Kvetch*, it was largely his influence – he led other critics to appreciate that play. He was the only one to give me genuine respect on the highest level of performance. Jack made me proud of what I was doing. I could cut his reviews out, I could paste them in my book, display them to enable me to promote my work abroad. It was not just a question of being made to feel good, I am beyond simple flattery because I can also take a bad review. There was something extremely positive about the way he stood up for me, it was like a cause. I felt that here was a man whose compass was very wide. He had a sharp nose that could sniff out what was phoney, spurious, facile. Therefore, if you had a good review from him you could trust it.

England is wonderful in that it has something like six daily newspaper critics. Whereas, a dump like New York only has one with all the influence and it makes no difference whether he is a good critic or not. It is very good that the English critics have a lot of power, because if a show is worthy, they can support it. It is a tightrope, but I like the way that we take our critics very seriously. We look at them, we study them, we get angry with them. It shows the high culture that we try to sustain in this country.

A critic is like a Geiger counter, he must test the values of our art. Even though I have been whipped by a few of them, I have been blessed by more.

NICHOLAS DE JONGH

I once wrote a review in the *Guardian* of some Restoration comedy. It consisted of a conversation between two theatre critics in a chocolate-house, talking about the play that they had just seen. There was Mr Smeer who could see no good in anything at all. Then Mr Gush arrives, delighted by the frocks, the sets and the sheer atmosphere of the production. I told Jack that I was Mr Smeer and he was obviously Mr Gush. He was delighted by this designation and we kept it up for years.

Jack loved emphasising our differences and how we never agreed on anything at all. That was not strictly accurate, we agreed on quite a few things. However, as with all satire, there was an element of truth in it. It is, however, quite wrong to see Jack as just a fan. He was very clear-sighted, eloquent and precise about what he admired in the theatre.

Jack was, intermittently, a controversial critic. He could be exceedingly outspoken and efficiently scathing. When Tommy Steele did *Singing in the Rain*, Jack reviewed his teeth. It was very cruel and very accurate.

Jack wrote that I was more prone to threats of violence from aggrieved performers than he was. I only received one death threat, though, from Steven Berkoff. Jack was a graceful apologiser. His size also helped – in some senses it was the making of him. Certainly in the business of disarming people. He had this diminutive, eternal youthfulness.

Time to say sorry to Liz and Shirley

Daily Mail, 6th August 1994

There are many salutary lessons to be learned as a critic from putting oneself on display, in captivity as it were, and allowing the public to come along and poke with sticks. This, basically, is what I do in the little show for which I am even now gathering up the nerve to take to the tumult of the Edinburgh Fringe.

Being a quiet week for first nights in London, I gave it an exploratory, low-key whirl this week at that brave outpost of theatrical enterprise in East Croydon, the little Warehouse Theatre. And there, despite the steaming heat and all the worst rigours of the train strike (yes, I still refuse to lose patience with those put-upon signal-persons in spite of all the Government propaganda) there was, amazingly, an audience.

Which was just as well as the show is optimistically titled *An Audience and a Critic*. Taking second billing to total strangers is bad enough, but to be left on one's own in such circumstances would have been a double humiliation. Anyway, I need not have worried. The audiences on both the nights I was there were on fantastic form – and not even a couple of thieves breaking into my dressing-room and legging it with my mobile phone as I gave my all on stage could dull my gratitude for the experience.

For the trick is that while I am seeming to explain and defend the curious role of the critic and spinning it along on a whirligig of anecdotes, I, too, am learning on my feet.

'Have you ever written anything you have subsequently regretted, and do you wake up at night worrying about it?' asked one sharp-witted inquisitor. Well, until that moment I had chosen not to think about chastising Elizabeth Taylor for not even being able to make an impressive entrance during her disastrous London dalliance with high drama in *The Little Foxes* all those years ago.

It was a terrible performance and surely the least you can expect of a star is that she knows how to walk on to a stage and make her presence felt. But in voicing my profound disappointment on seeing this luminous screen beauty reduced to the level of a jobbing actress in weekly rep, I broke one of the cardinal rules I set myself when I began reviewing theatre.

Never, ever, attack an artist for their physical deficiencies. It is cheap, it is cruel and, above all, people in glass houses are very ill-advised to enter stone-throwing contests.

However, such was my irritation at Miss Taylor's theatrical ineptitude that I threw taste and tact out of the window and described the poor, unhappy and, as it turned out, unwell woman as 'resembling an upturned cottage loaf' – then went on to accuse her of 'waddling into sight looking as if she was wearing her bustle back to front.'

The tackiness of the jibe did not strike me until I heard it read out next morning on Radio 4's *Today* programme. And I cannot describe the confessional relief it was to stand up there in downtown Croydon and purge the guilt.

That apart, however, I found I could honestly lay my hand upon my heart and say that no other review among the many thousand I have penned has ever disturbed my sleep. I learned very early in my career that in criticism, as in love, there is no joy in faking it and if you do so, eventually you will be found out.

Tell the truth and shame the Devil, my dear granny used to tell me. And it is surprising the moral strength an honestly-held opinion can give you, even when it provokes someone as decent and good-humoured as Tim Rice to wave a clenched fist under your nose as you're eating dinner in a crowded restaurant.

This said, however, there is one more review for which I am happy to have a platform to redress the score. The year I parted company with the legions of Liz Taylor fans, I also brought down the wrath of every Shirley Bassey freak in the land due to some rather terse remarks I made on the subject of a concert at the Royal Albert Hall.

To my eyes and ears the lady had become a grotesque parody of her own stage creation. The words were indistinct, the sentiments rang hollow and false. Indeed, most drag queens were doing better impersonations of her hits than she was managing on that night.

This was almost 15 years ago now, but Bassey aficionados still berate me for it. So I watched with growing fascination and admiration the revealing, aptly titled, documentary, *I Am What I Am*, which BBC1 devoted to the lady and her life last weekend. And I stayed glued to the screen for the full-scale concert they had recorded in Cardiff which they screened straight afterwards.

For this was, clearly, a formidable artist at the very peak of her form. Yet the miraculous transformation had been won at a terrible cost. The unimaginable trauma she suffered after the suicide of her youngest daughter had temporarily robbed her of her voice. On stage and in mid-concert, too. A devastating blow to any singer.

Reluctantly, Miss Bassey was persuaded to put herself in the hands of a voice coach to find a cure. And though it was evident (more from what was left unsaid than anything else) that this mercurial star has not been the easiest of pupils, it was also abundantly clear from the consummately controlled performance she gave before that vast, adoring throng in her native city, that the lessons had been well-learned.

Not once did the mouth slide round to the side of her face as if desperate to nibble her own ear. It remained where God intended and as a result the words rang out clear and true while the depth-charged emotions packed the punch of a true champ.

This was a world-class performance. Mature and vibrant. And I am more than happy to say so. For I can hardly believe it was the same woman who tortured those hit songs so many years before.

The shows that fail to produce

Daily Mail, 28th June 1996

Two more West End shows announce their premature closure. Both were award-winning musicals. But the long awaited *Mack and Mabel*, and Stephen Sondheim's *Company*, have given up the unequal struggle. The notices are up. Following so steamingly hot upon the heels of Felicity Kendal's singular failure to draw the town in *Mind Millie for Me* and the collapse of Zoë Wanamaker's short-lived impersonation of a dog in *Sylvia*, the professional mourners are starting up their much practised wailings at the death of the West End.

As with any sudden death, culprits must be found. And the fingers have pointed, inevitably, at such diverse villains as the IRA, the critics, the weather and the fickle public themselves.

I emphatically deny any culpability in the blood-letting. Critics rarely, if ever, kill plays. Shoddy productions, ill-advised scripts and indifferent audiences are what empty theatres. And it is the producer himself who delivers the final death blow. He or she alone decides when the final curtain falls.

Dancing on graves is never excusable. But I have to say that the only production among the latest quartet of casualties which I genuinely feel the West End is the poorer for losing is *Company*. Frankly I have no explanation for its all too sudden departure and lament it bitterly.

The reviews were justifiably ecstatic. The exceptional cast, led by the award-winning Adrian Lester and Sheila Gish, could not have been bettered. And Sondheim, notorious for his reluctance to pander to popular taste, has never been more accessible save, perhaps, for his earliest crowd-pleaser *A Funny Thing Happened on the Way to the Forum*.

Assuredly, had it been possible to keep the show running at the small and intimate Donmar Warehouse, for which it was originally conceived, it would have run for as long as they wished to play it. But transferred and exposed to the financial stringencies of the West End, maybe there simply were not sufficient aficionados out there.

And so it joins that list of inexplicable yet honourable failures such as the National's impeccable revival of *Carousel* and the haunting *City of Angels*, which possessed class, imagination and talent plus critical acclaim – but, alas, not audiences in sufficient numbers.

As for the rest, well without wishing to say I told you so, the producers themselves cannot say they went unwarned. The losses of *Mind Millie for Me* have been estimated at £500,000. No laughing matter. Unfortunately, neither was Millie, a fatal flaw in a farce.

Yet there it was in the obituaries: 'Poor reviews followed by poor audiences were blamed.' What about the poor jokes? Or in the case of *Mack and Mabel*, the poor sets and costumes? What looked suspiciously like Marks & Spencer knickers with sequins sewn up the sides for the chorus girls' big number might be considered an enterprising economy in an amateur production. To an audience paying West End prices and expecting West End standards, it is simply shoddy.

Nor was Caroline O'Connor's lively Mabel well served, having to sing Jerry Herman's big love song perched on the top of a flat kite-shaped piece of cardboard which turned out to be the prow of an ocean liner. One can only wonder how these glaring miscalculations were allowed to be exposed to the sophistication of a first night audience. Did not Sir Peter Hall, usually such a discerning director of other people's work, not notice his adaptation of *Mind Millie for Me*, Feydeau's fragile frolic, was a charmless chortle-free yawn? Did not Miss Kendal once complain that her character was a self-absorbed bitch for whom it was impossible to raise a flicker of sympathy, much less a smile?

These are imponderables about which, the more theatre I see, the less I comprehend. I suppose it is essential for any artist appearing in front of the public to believe wholeheartedly in the piece on view, simply to get him or herself on the stage each night.

CHARLES SPENCER

Jack was the critic with the highest public profile, and the only one who filed his report regularly on the night. He was always there, on page three, making the theatre seem very amusing and glamorous. I don't think that writing your reviews on the same night necessarily produces one's best writing – Jack's work came out every night in a great gush of emotion. It caught the excitement of the occasion, but was weaker on analysis. However, considering the time he had, his was an amazing achievement. Despite his air of frivolity, he took the job immensely seriously. He loved new writing, and this famous critic often went to the most obscure places to seek out good new plays.

He did not get sucked into trends. It is a sign that he was a discriminating critic that, whilst he hated Sarah Kane's *Blasted* at the Royal Court (though I believe he was less than happy with that knee-jerk 'disgusting feast of filth' headline), he loved Mark Ravenhill's *Shopping and Fucking*. That piece is equally strong, but is much better written. Interestingly, he trod a very delicate line at the *Mail*, he did not particularly adhere to the rather fanatical espousal of family values at the newspaper. He was gay, and made no bones about it, he was a Labour supporter, yet he achieved this remarkable balancing act of writing very much for a *Mail* audience, without any strain. So he could not be called a radical critic, but he was no conservative either. He was on the lookout for quality, in whatever shape it might come.

Private Eye dubbed him Jack Twinky, and that was the image everyone knew, him turning up in an immaculate costume at a major musical. He went through a period of wearing a little sailor-suit. There was a production of Alan Ayckbourn's *Way Upstream* which was undergoing horrendous technical difficulties with leaking water. Jack arrived at the press night wearing a yellow sou'wester and mac, and yellow boots, prepared for a flood.

It would have been very easy for Jack to become the sort of critic who likes everything and does not want to give offence. He remained very discriminating. He was, though, rather star-struck. My view is that critics should have as little to do with anyone in the business as possible, and just occasionally I felt that Jack was too close to the people he was reviewing. There is then a danger of personal involvement, but in his case it did not affect his work. He might perhaps have approached certain people with a more charitable spirit, but if they were awful he would say so. Jack was a fan, and that is a valid side of theatre criticism.

It is unlikely that Jack's work will survive in the same way as, say, Kenneth Tynan's. It is not as beautifully written as Tynan's, largely because of the speed under which he was writing. His real achievement was to keep theatre in the forefront of a tabloid newspaper. No mean feat, when you consider that *The Express* virtually abandoned its theatre criticism and the *Mirror* and the *Sun* do not cover it at all.

He was the great overnight critic. Absolutely right on the night. He championed shows, many of which might not otherwise have survived. I cannot see people reading him a hundred years from now, but there are very few critics of whom that would be true.

Apart from Tynan, there is only Hazlitt and Coleridge, perhaps Harold Hobson. Jack was not a supreme stylist, or one of those critics in whose reviews one could picture the show, though he did come up with some terrific lines. He was the instant judgement man on the night, and I do not think that Jack considered himself to be writing for posterity. His work was highly entertaining, with a sense of freshness and fun. It enthused people, it created that aura of excitement which theatre desperately needs.

As far as the West End goes, particularly with musicals, Jack's view was crucial. Cameron Mackintosh says that the reviews that count for him are the *Mail*, the *Standard*, the *Daily Telegraph* and the *Sunday Times*. It pains me to say so, but of those four newspapers, when Jack was on the *Mail* that was the paper which absolutely mattered the most.

He saw theatre in everything – life was a big theatre, and he was the jester at its centre. But, like all jesters, he could easily be hurt. You cannot be a good critic if you do not have a thick skin.

PETER HALL

When I ran the Arts Theatre in London's Great Newport Street I was Director of Productions, director of everything, and had to get to know all the critics. There was, is, a slight convention that there is a fence between those who do and those who criticise. It is peculiarly English that cordiality tends to reign, when most of them want to kill each other. It is not very pleasant to be lambasted in the press – if any of us ever criticise the critics, the results are usually stormy in the extreme. However, Jack straddled the doers and the criticisers in a rather interesting way. He cared about show business and was of show business, but was never sentimental or less than hard-hitting. If he did not like something, by Christ he said so. When the poacher turns gamekeeper or vice versa it can often be said that he ceases to operate well in either capacity. That did not apply to Jack. He was a bit of a performer, in life and in the business.

He was also a very popular critic in the sense that he persuaded an entirely middle-class audience, disinterested in the theatre (which I generally take the *Daily Mail* readership to be) that theatre was important, still an event. Jack did a great job reporting the visceral excitement and universality of a minority art to a very large public, most of whom would not see the show he was writing about.

MICHAEL COVENEY

Overnight reviewing is rapidly, and regrettably, becoming a thing of the past owing to a combination of factors: earlier deadlines dictated by the new technology; the reluctance of editors to carry the cost of changing a page where it is thought to be not strictly necessary; and the refusal of arts editors and critics themselves to treat first nights as news.

They do treat them as news, of course, the moment they are confronted with an Andrew Lloyd Webber musical or a Tom Stoppard comedy. It was a great boost to the theatre – in terms of prestige and box office realities – when all first nights, from Shaftesbury Avenue and the National to the Bush, were reviewed as a matter of course in the next morning's London editions. But now those notices trickle through over several days, and are invariably downpaged, without illustration, beneath the rising tide of routine interviews and puffing previews. As a result, the amount of theatre work actually reviewed has diminished; in this way, the print media have, in my view, reneged on their responsibilities and thrown away a large part of their influence.

You are more likely to read in a daily broadsheet a full-length feature about backstage conditions in the Barbican, or an ego-massaging interview with a leading lady, than you are any piercing jeremiad about the Royal Shakespeare Company's lack of new writing policy, let alone a full-length, fully illustrated descriptive account of last night's opening. The work itself is disappearing in a welter of PR-led ballyhoo, and the prime cause is the abrogation of the daily newspaper critic's responsibility to deliver last night's news.

In the national daily Press, Jack Tinker of the *Daily Mail* alone maintains the old standard, which is why he is the most influential critic in what used to be known as Fleet Street.

Extract from *The Aisle Is Full of Noises* by Michael Coveney, published by Nick Hern Books.

.

EPILOGUE

'Loved the show, loathed the finale.'

The nest I was desperate to fly still exerts a spell

Daily Mail, 30th October 1993

To me the most visible change to the road where I grew up has been wrought upon the house in which we lived. It seems churlish to resent it, but I do. A whole row of flat-topped two-up, two-down cottages with their outside lavs further down the hill have vanished, and the big house opposite has been outlandishly gentrified, but I pass this by without a pang stirring.

Truth to tell, though I lived here all the formative years of my boyhood and adolescence I never return with any overwhelming feelings of nostalgia. It is simply a ribbon of urban Victorian and Edwardian straggle which joins Oldham and Rochdale in what I still call Lancashire.

Of course, this lack of proper respect for one's own past fills me with guilt and I do dig deep for fond memories.

But these are always of the people, never the place. You can still drive through Royton without knowing you've left either of those once-proud mill towns, Oldham and Rochdale. And most people do.

Indeed, its only conceivable purpose was to provide the shortest possible thoroughfare between the two.

In those pre-postcode days you always had to add 'Near Oldham' when you addressed letters to us, the inference being that even the postman didn't know Royton was there. To confuse him further, the road itself was called Rochdale.

Our house was, and still is, at the end of a solid red-bricked terrace just before you reach the brow of the steep hill which gives the district its name: Summit.

Next door lived my aunt and uncle, a headmaster, with my cousin who always acted as an older brother. Down the sharp incline next to them was the town clerk and joined to him came the manager of the vast electricity station which was our answer to Battersea's.

At the bottom end of the terrace, on the corner of the road which led to a large wild national park, dwelt the headmaster of the local grammar school. And along the red-bricked side of his house ran the tree-lined street which led down to ornate park gates; it was dappled with more modern, detached homes built by minor mill-owners, bank managers and a bookie who sent whispers across the counter of the little shop by going bankrupt.

So there might have been some social aspiration in the name Summit as well as mere topographical mundanity

If there was, I never felt it. Not even then. My mother still speaks of the painful embarrassment I brought upon her as a child of only four when an old lady remarked kindly upon my, even then, distinctly affected and un-Lancastrian vowels.

'Ee, luv. I can tell y'don't come from these parts,' she cooed. To which I replied with excruciating frankness and lack of tact which have always been my downfall: 'Unfortunately I do.'

As soon as I said it I knew how hurtful it was and have been sorry ever since. So if I felt never to be quite part of this unyielding landscape, I have only myself to blame.

No doubt that strange sensation of living my entire childhood on the edge of nowhere in particular – not quite Oldham, nor yet Rochdale and certainly not Manchester – left its lasting legacy.

Ever since I left home to make my way in the world at the age of 18 I have felt compelled to live smack in the centre of places with distinct and vital personalities of their own.

First to Brighton, where I still keep a toehold, then on to London, where I roost above a theatre with Soho and Covent Garden on either side.

My own children, now grown up with homes and families of their own, have never even seen the house on Rochdale Road, Royton, Near Oldham, Lancs, where I lived for so long. They can't remember visiting that little anonymous town where I was born.

Yet, and this is the most peculiar thing, whenever I dream vividly of being at home and with present friends, family or foes, it is always in that old house we are gathered.

It was a long, deep place with rooms far larger and airier than seemed possible from its prosaic outside. No home I have ever owned since has had so much space, yet I think my father paid something like £650 as a sitting tenant for it after the war.

I recall all its details vividly, still actively regretting the marbled fireplaces my mother sacrificed in a burst of face-lifting modernity, still admiring the ornate plasterwork on the ceilings, still protective of the little back room which was entirely my own, though I shared a bedroom with my younger brother.

That room was where I dreamed and schemed a future which seemed quite improbable then, yet has turned out as so astonishingly like the blueprint that I might have been clairvoyant.

So, quite unreasonably, almost 40 years on I feel proprietorial outrage at the changes newcomers have made since my parents left, only shortly after I flew the nest.

The Edwardian bay has been replaced by one of those violently curved modern versions of Regency bow fronts. One of my childhood joys was gazing up at the exquisitely hand-painted pictures of birds which adorned each stained glass pane – perhaps even then I was contemplating flight.

Without any compunction I peer through this architectural affront to the modest Edwardian aspirations of the rest of the row and am astonished to discover that the two 'best' rooms I had once thought as big as any human being could reasonably desire have been knocked into one, which must give it the proportions of an elongated ballroom if the scale of my memory is accurate.

But very likely it is not. Time is a great shrinker. Tandlehill Road itself has dwindled.

That fine actress Barbara Knox, queen of *Coronation Street*'s Kabin, who once lived nearby and with whom I was recently reminiscing, summed up how the years rub away the gloss on past glories. 'To think, we once used to imagine Tandlehill Road was the end of the rainbow,' she sighed.

The substantial houses now look somehow diminished, the park beyond no longer a magical wilderness waiting to be explored. Yet something is bigger, grander, more breathtaking than ever I remember. The view, as the taxi takes me over the brow of the hill, stretches out far down across a vast valley and on to Manchester itself.

'Why on earth had I not remembered that?' I wondered aloud.

'Because you never saw it,' replied the driver with that strict Northern economy with words. 'There's no mills, so there's no smoke.'

And suddenly, in spite of the unfamiliar clarity of the air and splendid views across the rolling scenery – far greener than I ever recall – I feel intensely sad.

Those mills, though I hated the grime they spilled forth and felt intimidated by the brash loud voices honed from generations of shouting above their tumult, they were the heart of Lancashire.

They gave it its confident swagger. They were the basis of the vainglorious, inverted snobbery which believed implicitly: 'What Manchester thinks today, London will do tomorrow.'

The cast-iron confidence they produced inspired both stammering awe and secret contempt in me then.

But now no one is making cotton today. The Elk, the Robin and all those unlovely factories with their improbable names and towering stacks, are now just the husks of industrial dinosaurs. King Cotton is long dead.

Once I thought I would have danced on his grave, I felt such an outsider there. Now I could weep to see the stuffing knocked out of such proud people.

Jack Tinker on his daughter's death

Reprinted in the *Daily Mail* as a tribute to Jack

There was nothing at all ordinary about the day. It was not just like any other. If it had been, I still tell myself, perhaps I might have listened to some inner voice warning me that something was wrong, whispering that my youngest and most fiercely independent daughter had died at the age of 24. Against all reason, that is the guilt which never seems to go: that she died without me having the slightest premonition.

The very fact that there was no theatre to review that evening made the routine entirely different from the usual. To this day, more than three years later, every detail of it stands out so clearly in my memory – as if the sudden shock and subsequent grief have etched it there in bold relief for ever. As a result, I have never again been able to stay in London overnight on the first of August.

At around midday, which was the time she died, I was hosting a 60th birthday lunch for my good friend Lionel Bart in my favourite restaurant. It could not have been more jolly.

After an afternoon in the office, going through a stack of mail, catching up on all the forward planning for the coming weeks, I went blithely off to Barnes for the eagerly anticipated highlight of the week – meeting my brand new goddaughter, Kate, for the very first time.

So you see I had every reason to be thinking about my own children, grown up and out in the world as they all three were. And I was. There is nothing like a new baby for bringing the memories of your own brood's infancy flooding back.

This was the warm, happy, mellow mood in which I arrived home. It was past midnight and even when I was told to sit down because something terrible had happened, nothing as terrible as that occurred to me.

Her mother says that as soon as she saw a policewoman waiting on the doorstep, she knew that something had happened to Charlotte.

But I had to be told several times before it sank in.

After that, nothing is entirely clear again until the inquest, some three weeks later. The funeral, perhaps. But mostly I threw myself into work – the Edinburgh Festival was upon us – and battened down the emotional hatches until we could know the real facts.

We had all suspected what might have happened. From childhood, she had been subject to petit mal and asthma but she always hated to be over-protected, so we tried not to fuss. A sudden attack of either of these could have been responsible for her drowning in her bath. She was found by one of the youngsters who shared the house she had just moved into. But, of course, it was not until the inquest that we could be entirely certain. For some reason, by my own choice I went alone. And, sure enough, it was the epilepsy which had caused her to drown.

In the end, it was the coroner's kindness, his genuinely touching words about a useful young life cut short, which caused me to break down for the very first time since it happened. I had been prepared for everything except simple humanity, and I had to be helped from the court.

Ever since then, of course, I cannot read about any child or young person dying without my heart aching for the parents. There is, I am sure, a bond between people who have lost a child (and when do your own offspring ever stop being your children?). Because nothing ever prepares you for this loss. Not nature, not literature, not popular song, not social convention. There simply is no frame of natural reference.

With partners, lovers, parents – somewhere in the dark recesses of your mind there always lurks the possibility of a permanent parting. Yet what in our folklore gives us a glimpse of that unthinkable time when the child you would lay down your own life to protect is no longer there?

You are simply left floundering with all the unanswerable questions and well-meaning people telling you time is a great healer.

Time, in fact, is no such thing. It is a great accommodator; it simply makes the grief bearable. How easily I could have accommodated my own grief if my daughter had died other than as she did, I cannot say. I marvel at those heroic fathers whose children were butchered to death by IRA bombers, yet have found it in their hearts to campaign for peace with the killers.

My daughter was not the victim of terrorist violence, of mindless joyriders, of a callous sexual attack. Whether or not I would have found their heroic human spirit, I cannot say. I can only hope I would.

In the immediate aftermath of the event, the overwhelming kindness of friends and strangers, often from where you least expected – even the local paper was solicitous – helped to deaden the worst of the pain. Somehow you are carried through to each tomorrow with a renewed faith in the innate goodness of your fellow creatures, or at least I was.

Many urged me to go into grief therapy. But it seemed to me an affront for some total stranger to tell you how to mourn your own child. It was, however, an act of supreme wisdom as well as generosity which helped me conquer the worst and cope with the rest.

Among the literally hundreds of letters was an envelope from one of my most valued friends, the astrologer Patric Walker. Instead of the usual condolences, inside there was a return first-class air ticket to the Greek island where he lives, and the message 'Come when you need to' written on it.

Eventually I went, and was given that healing peace and seclusion impossible among a family in which each member is having to come to terms with his or her own personal sorrow.

It was only as I was preparing to leave that we even discussed Charlotte's death. And it was then that he gave me the advice I have carried like a talisman ever since and which I always pass on to parents who have suffered any similar circumstances, though each loss is unique and private.

'Don't look on it as a life interrupted,' said Patric. 'Try to think of it as a life completed and then you can take it with you for the rest of your life.'

And suddenly it seemed to make the first real sense since I had come home on that awful night. Of course, every parent must sooner or later realise that their children are only on loan and learn to let go. But I looked back and remembered how, even as a baby, what a hurry she had been in to overtake her elder sisters. How she had thrown herself into life and always seemed so heedless of what might lie beyond. I even blessed the fact that she had done all those mad adolescent things I had expressly advised against.

We had had lunch together only two days before it happened. She had come breezing into the restaurant triumphant, after a harum-scarum university career, in having secured the highly responsible social services job she had set her heart on. We celebrated her good fortune and her new flat. And but for Patric's advice by now I would, I know, be corroded inside by all the 'If onlys' and 'By nows'.

As it is, for most of the time, I have learned to accept hers as a life complete. Looked at like that, I can have no happier last memory. Sometimes, of course, the trick simply doesn't work.

INDEX

42nd Street, 8-9, 16-17, 135
84 Charing Cross Road, 140
900 Oneonta, 186, 187
Absence of War, An, 108-110
Adams, Ian, 192-193
Adams, Jonathan, 24
Adams, Polly, 95
Adler, Marion, 51
Aeschylus, 78
Agate, James, 254
Aitken, Maria, 162
Albee, Edward, 114
Alda, Alan, 146
Alderton, John, 116
Aldridge, Michael, 81
Alexander, Bill, 58, 62
Ali, Muhammad, 207-209
All My Sons, 77-78, 101
Almeida Theatre, 187
Amadeus, 138, 162
American Buffalo, 89
Amy's View, 200
An Audience and a Critic, 258
Anderson, Kevin, 35
Anderson, Miles, 41
Andersson, Benny, 51
Annie, 249
Antony and Cleopatra, 61
Arcadia, 107-108, 187
Archaos, 125
Armstrong, Alun, 34
Arts Council, 153
Ashfield, Kate, 120
Ashton, Joe, 164
Aspects of Love, 24-26, 31, 37, 169
Atkins, Eileen, 119, 254
Attenborough, Michael, 176
Augustus, Hope, 30
Awakening, 82
Ayckbourn, Alan, 8, 74, 90, 94, 95-96, 149, 155, 160, 163, 173, 175, 176
Bacall, Lauren, 92-93, 133-134
Bailey, Robin, 14
Baird, David, 186
Baker, Lucy, 80
Bakewell, Joan, 124
Baldwin, Alec, 146
Ball, Michael, 25, 26, 43, 47
Ballard, Kay, 137
Barnes, Clive, 134, 254
Barnum, 9-10
Barrowman, John, 51, 52
Barrymore, Cheryl, 240-241
Barrymore, Michael, 238-240
Bart, Lionel, 40, 41-42
Barton, John, 55

Bassey, Shirley, 214, 259
Batt, Mike, 27, 28
Beaumont, Binkie, 8
Beck, Michael, 93
Beggar's Opera, The, 21
Bell, Elizabeth, 95
Benchley, Robert, 94
Benjamin, Louis, 153
Bennett, Alan, 104, 159, 179
Bennett, Michael, 133
Bent, 164
Berkeley, Busby, 17
Berkoff, Stephen, 123, 124-125, 253, 256-257
Berman, Ed, 76
Bernstein, Leonard, 15-16
Best of Friends, The, 97-98
Beyond the Fringe, 186
Billington, Michael, 30, 45, 254
Billy, 192, 245
Billy Liar, 192
Biograph Girl, 163
Bjornson, Maria, 19, 25
Black, Don, 24, 25, 34, 35, 37, 38, 50-52
Blair, Isla, 102
Blake, Peter, 2
Blakeley, Colin, 78, 163
Blasted, 120, 188-189
Bleasedale, Alan, 164
Blessed, Brian, 7, 57
Blood Brothers, 16, 28-29
Blythe, Peter, 118
Bock, Jerry, 39
Bogdanov, Michael, 77
Bohmler, Craig, 51
Bolt, Robert, 70, 223
Bond, Christopher, 5, 33
Bond, Edward, 105
Bond, Gary, 1, 37, 158
Borge, Victor, 207
Boublil, Alain, 18, 26, 30, 42, 49
Boulter, Russell, 29
Bowman, Simon, 27
Boyfriend, The, 22
Bradley, David, 67
Bragg, Melvyn, 135, 139, 140
Bramble, Mark, 16
Branagh, Kenneth, 59, 64, 68, 100, 101, 174, 177-178, 194, 195-196, 197
Braun, Professor Edward (Inquiry into directors training), 196-198
Brecht, Bertolt, 90, 91
Brenton, Howard, 155, 156, 159
Briggs, Raymond, 84
Brightman, Sarah, 19, 20, 142
Brighton Evening Argus, 154
Broadway, 133-151
Bron, Eleanor 128
Brooks, Joe, 23

Brown, Georgina, 17
Bryan, Dora, 8, 173
Bryant, Michael, 110
Brynner, Yul, 4, 232
Buckley, Betty, 38
Burke, Vincent, 157
Burrows, Abe, 11
Burton, Richard, 85-86
Bush Theatre, 187
Busybody, 72
Byatt, Jonathan, 80
Cabaret, 16
Cadell, Simon, 95
Cahoot's Macbeth, 75-76
Caird, John, 18
Calder, David, 101
Callow, Simon, 197
Camelot, 13-14
Captain Brassbound's Conversion, 81-82
Carousel, 9, 32-33
Carr, Jane, 139, 221
Carrie, 22-23, 142, 175
Carroll, Lewis, 28
Carteret, Anna, 77
Cartwright, Jim, 179
Casey, Warren, 36
Cassidy, Joseph, 137
Cat on a Hot Tin Roof, 176, 218
Caton, Juliette, 50
Cats, 6, 8, 9, 24, 31, 39, 141, 154, 165, 228, 245
Cazenove, Christopher, 75
Cerveris, Michael, 150
Champion, Gower, 17
Channing, Carol, 167
Chappell, Jacquey, 21
Chekhov, 143
Chess, 51, 142, 167
Chicago, 16, 166
Choi, Hye-Younce, 4
Chorus Line, A, 6, 16, 192, 249
Churchill, Caryl, 113
Cinema: see Film
City of Angels, 36
Clause 28, 175
Clayton, Stanley, 71
Clift, Montgomery, 35
Close, Glenn, 11, 146, 230-231, 232
Cloud Nine, 113
Codron, Michael, 152-153, 187
Cohen, Lawrence D, 22
Collier, Lesley, 229
Collins, Joan, 65
Collins, Pauline, 99
Comedians, 200
Company, 45-46, 260
Congreve, William, 220
Connolly, Billy, 65
Conti, Tom, 6, 192

Cooke, Barbara, 23
Coronation Street, 241-243
Courtenay, Margaret, 17
Courtenay, Tom, 138, 162
Coveney, Michael, 45, 253, 263-264
Covington, Julie, 20-21
Coward, Noël, 42, 85, 162, 174
Cranham, Kenneth, 106
Craven, Gemma, 6
Crawford, Michael, 9, 10-11, 19-20, 165, 166, 167, 192, 233, 245, 248
Crazy for You, 8, 144-145
Critic, The, 93- 94
Critics, 247-264
Crowley, Bob, 32, 64, 69
Crucible, The, 76
Crumb, Ann, 25, 26
Cryptogram, The, 186
Cutler, Horace, 162
Daldry, Stephen, 106, 114, 120-121
Dale, Janet, 105
Dale, Jim, 11
Dalton, Timothy, 61
Dancin', 136
Daniels, Jeffrey, 15
Daniels, Paul, 236-238
Daniels, Ron, 74
Davies, Andrew, 160
Davies, Howard, 91
Davies, Russell, 186
Davis Jr, Sammy, 204
Davison, Peter J, 111
Dead Funny, 186
Dean, Felicity, 119
Death and the Maiden, 146
Dee, Janie, 32
Defferary, Jacqueline, 113
de Jongh, Nicholas, 42, 123, 129-130, 178-179, 253, 254, 255, 257-258
de la Tour, Frances, 115, 162, 173
de Marco, Richard, 126
Dench, Judi, 83, 90, 91, 101, 105, 162, 173, 174, 193, 200-201
Denison, Michael, 82
de Paul, Lynsey, 65
Desdemona – If Only You Had Spoken, 128
Destiny, 73-74, 155
Dexter, John, 73
Dexter, Sally, 40
Dido and Aeneas, 127
Dietrich, Marlene, 31, 202-203
Dillon, George, 132
Directors (Braun Inquiry), 196-198
Dodd, Ken, 31
Dogg's Hamlet, 75-76
Donnellan, Declan, 33, 34, 49, 128
Dorfman, Ariel, 146
Downie, Penny, 61, 64

Dream Girls, 133, 134
Dresser, The, 138, 162
Drewe, Anthony, 51
Drury, Alan, 77
Dubin, Al, 16
Dudley, William, 167, 168
Duet for One, 162
DuFeu, Helen, 166
Dunlop, Frank, 1, 124, 126
Eddington, Paul, 81, 107
Edgar, David, 73, 155, 156
Edinburgh International Festival, 122-132
Editing Process, The, 113-114
Educating Rita, 160-161, 162
Edwards, Gale, 37
EFX, 167
Elephant Man, The, 162
Eliot, T S, 6-7
Elliot, Alistair, 111
Elliott, Denholm, 197
Emmanuel, Alphonsia, 110
English, David, xi, 147
Enjoy, 159, 163
Enter the Guardsman, 51
Entertainer, The, 156
Equity dispute, 156-158
Essex, David, 3, 167
Euripides, 110
Evans, Edith, 70, 223
Evans, Kathryn, 21, 37
Everett, Kenny, 28
Evita, 2-3, 20-22, 31, 147, 152, 249
Eyre, Richard, 11, 12-13, 110, 119, 170, 171,
  191, 196, 198, 200
Family Voices, 83
Farleigh, Lynn, 76
Farrah, Paul, 166
Farrant, Robert, 249
Feiffer, Jules, 138
Fiddler on the Roof, 39-40
Fielding, Emma, 108
Fiennes, Ralph, 64
Film (comparison with live theatre), 198-201
Finney, Albert, 173
Fitzgerald, Michael, 104
Five Guys Named Mo, 145
Flynn, Daniel, 105
Forbes, Brian, 57
Ford-Davies, Oliver, 109
Forsyth, Bruce, 206-207
Fosse, Bob, 136
Fouere, Olwen, 125
Fowlds, Derek, 248
Fox, Samantha, 225-226
Frayn, Michael, 80, 140
Friedman, Maria, 46, 47-49, 99
Fringe, Edinburgh, 123-132
Fry, Stephen, 253

Fuente Ovejuna, 128
Fugard, Athol, 103
Fugard, Lisa, 103
Fullerton, Fiona, 14
Galileo, 173
Galton, Ray, 1
Gambon, Michael, 95, 96, 162, 172
Garland, Patrick, 221
Garnett, David, 24, 25, 37
Gay, John, 21
Gelbart, Larry, 154
Gems, Pam, 245
Gentle Jack, 70, 223
George, Tricia, 166
Gere, Richard, 36
Gero, Frank, 187
Gero, Woji, 187
Ghetto, 98-99
Gibson, Debbie, 36
Gielgud, John, 97-98, 107, 173, 174, 177, 183-
  185, 193
Gillam, Melville, 8, 153
Gillett, Debra, 116
Gimme Shelter, 156
Gish, Sheila, 46, 88, 260
Glass Menagerie, The, 218
Glen, Iain, 50
Godfrey, Derek, 56
Goldwyn, Sam, 213
Goodyear, Julie, 241-243
Gordon, Hannah, 100
Gore, Michael, 22
Grade, Leslie, 210-211
Grade, Lew, 209-211
Grainger, Gawn, 117
Grant, Deborah, 10
Granville Barker, Harley, 127
Grease, 36
Greenwood, Paul, 60
Griffin, Hayden, 78
Griffiths, Trevor, 72, 200
Grown Ups, 138
Guys and Dolls, 9, 11-12, 145, 150
Hagon, Garrick, 78
Hagerty, Bill, 253
Hair, 9
Hall, Peter, 62, 65, 78-79, 154, 170, 171-174,
  175, 178, 196, 200, 255, 263
Hall, Willis, 51, 79, 80
Hamlet, 55-56, 68-69
Hamlisch, Marvin, 5
Hammerstein II, Oscar, 3, 32
Hampstead Theatre, 187
Hampton, Christopher, 34, 35, 38
Hancock, Sheila, 5, 94
Hancock's Half Hour, 222
Handl, Irene, 72
Hands, Terry, 23, 60, 174, 176

Hanson, Alexander, 37
Hardy, Edward, 49
Hare, David, 108-110, 156, 200
Harnick, Sheldon, 39
Harris, Pam, 253
Harris, Richard, 13-14, 102
Harris, Rosemary, 78, 83, 97, 98
Harrison, Rex, 84
Hart, Charles, 19, 24, 25, 37
Harty, Russell, 122
Harwood, Ronald, 116-117
Hateley, Linzi, 23
Having a Ball, 164
Hawthorne, Nigel, 104
Hayden, Michael, 32
Haygarth, Tony, 118
Heartbreak House, 83-84
Heggie, Iain, 124
Hello Dolly, 167
Hellman, Lillian, 212-213
Henceforward, 175
Henry IV (Pirandello's), 102
Henry IV part 2, 67-68
Henry V, 59-60, 64
Henry VI parts I, II & III, 64
Henshall, Ruthie, 43
Henson, Nicky, 81
Hepburn, Katharine, 135, 138, 255
Herzberg, Paul, 88
Higgins, Clare, 110
Hille, Anastasia, 115
Hobson, Harold, 70, 248, 262
Hodge, Douglas, 112
Hoffman, Dustin, 65
Hogg, Ian, 102
Holden, William, 35
Hollander, Tom, 114
Holliday, Jennifer, 134
Holm, Ian, 112
Hope, Bob, 205-206
Hopkins, Bernard, 54, 55
Horrocks, Jane, 179
Hothouse, The, 117-118
Howard, Alan, 114
Howard, Ronald, 71
Howard and Wyndham, 152-153
Hughes, Dusty, 23
Hugo, Victor, 18, 43
Hull Truck Company, 125
Humphries, Barry, 211-212
Hunter, Kathryn, 113
Hunting of the Snark, The, 27-28
Hutchings, Geoffrey, 221
Hyde, Jonathan, 94
Hypochondriac, The, 77
Hytner, Nicholas, 26, 32, 33, 99, 104
I, 140
Ibsen, 118

Iden, Rosalind, 195
Innocent, Harold, 102
Inspector Calls, An, 106, 186
Intimate Exchanges, 90
Into the Woods, 33, 142
Irons, Jeremy, 60
Izzard, Eddie, 186
Jackson, Glenda, 160, 173, 196
Jackson, Michael, 223-224
Jacobi, Derek, 64-65, 174
Jacobs, Abe, 165
Jacobs, Jim, 36
Jake's Women, 146
James, Geraldine, 66
James, Hannah, 46
Jarreau, Al, 51
Jaymson, Drew, 36
Jayston, Michael, 221
Jefford, Barbara, 54, 55
Jesus Christ Superstar, 31, 249
Jo, Haruiko, 63
John Gabriel Borkman, 118-119
John, Paul, George, Ringo and Bert, 149
Johnson, Terry, 186
Joking Apart, 74-75
Jones, David, 92
Jones, Freddie, 162
Jones, Ken, 84
Jones, Paul, 12
Jones, Peter, 118
Jordan, Louis, 145
Joseph and the Amazing Technicolour Dreamcoat, 1-2, 180
Just a Minute, 222
Kane, Sarah, 120, 188
Kani, John, 103
Karlin, 250
Kartell, Theresa, 30
Kaye, Hereward, 29
Keeffe, Barry, 155, 156
Keeler, Ruby, 17
Keith, Penelope, 81
Kempinski, Tom, 162
Kempson, Rachel, 195
Kendal, Felicity, 87, 107, 261, 262
Kennedy, Cheryl, 192, 193
Kennedy, James, 120
Kent, Jonathan, 111
Kenwright, Bill, 45, 46, 148, 187
Kestelman, Sarah, 221
Kind of Alaska, A, 82
King, Denis, 79
King, Stephen, 22
King and I, The, 3-4, 232
King Lear, 182
Kinnear, Roy, 94
Koltai, Ralph, 23, 24
Kretzmer, Herbert, 18, 42, 44-45

Kuhn, Judy, 23-24,
Kvetch, 257
Lan, David, 98
Land, David, 22
Lang, Fritz, 23
Lange, Jessica, 146
Langford, Bonnie, 7, 51
Lapine, James, 46
Lapotaire, Jane, 69, 138, 161
Laurenson, James, 17
Laurents, Arthur, 15
Lawrence, Stephanie, 15, 21, 28, 29, 148
Lawson, Leigh, 65, 66
Leach, Clare, 17
Lechner, Geno, 117
Lee-Potter, Linda, 221
Leigh, Paul, 51
Leigh-Hunt, Barbara, 56, 106
Lepage, Robert, 130
Lerner, Alan Jay, 13
Les Miserables, 8, 18-19, 26, 27, 31, 42-43, 44, 50,
    141, 143
Lesser, Anton, 64
Lester, Adrian, 46
Leveaux, David, 112
Life in the Theatre, A, 197
Little Foxes, The, 212-213, 258, 259
Littlewood, Joan, 5
Lloyd, Phyllida, 116
Lloyd Webber, Andrew, 1- 2, 6-7, 14-15, 19-20,
    22, 24-26, 31, 32, 34, 35, 37, 38-39, 50, 142,
    143, 147, 154, 168-169, 228, 232, 245
Loesser, Frank, 11
Loewe, Frederick, 13
Longden, Robert, 29, 30
Look Back in Anger, 100-101, 159
Lupone, Patti, 35
Lynch, Kenny, 10
Lynne, Gillian, 7
Macbeth, 56-57, 161, 180-181
MacKenzie-Robinson, Mhairi, 128
Mackintosh, Cameron, 8-9, 22, 27, 30-31, 41,
    42, 43, 50, 51, 143, 144, 145, 169, 188
MacLaine, Shirley, 210, 215-216
MacMillan, Kenneth, 32
MacNaughtan, Alan, 102
MacNeil, Ian, 106, 114
Madam Butterfly, 26
Madness of George III, 104-105, 179
Madonna, 142
Majority of One, A, 164
Maloney, Michael, 67
Maltby, Richard, 26
Mamet, David, 89, 186, 197
Man and Superman, 87-88
Martin, Millicent, 135
Martin Guerre, 49-50
Massey, Anna, 83, 112, 250

Massey, Daniel, 77, 117
McAnally, Ray, 97
McAnuff, Des, 150
McCallum, David, 28
McCarthy, Siobhan, 3, 21
McCartney, Paul, 65
McDade, Sandy, 113
McDiarmid, Ian, 74
McEwan, Geraldine, 174
McGann, Mark, 28
McGovern, Maureen, 137
McKellen, Ian, 66, 94, 138, 143, 175
McKenna, Virginia, 4
McKenzie, Julia, 12, 33, 50, 51
McLachlan, Craig, 36
McManus, Mark, 76
McMaster, Brian, 126, 127, 130
Meadmore, Robert, 14
Me and My Girl, 142
Medea, 110-111
Meegan, Paddy, 52
Melville, Herman, 29
Mendes, Sam, 41, 45, 51
Merchant of Venice, The, 53-54, 62, 65-66, 183
Merman, Ethel, 165
Merrick, David, 17
Metropolis, 23-24
Midler, Bette, 251
Midsummer Night's Dream, A, 54
Miles, Sarah, 171
Miles, Sylvia, 218, 254
Miller, Ann, 136
Miller, Arthur, 76, 77-78, 96, 101
Miller, Jonathan, 122
Mind Millie for Me, 260, 261
Minnelli, Liza, 219-220
Miss Saigon, 26-27
Moby Dick, 29-30
Moffat, John, 221
Molière, 77
Monopoly, Tony, 30
Moonlight, 112
Moore, Claire, 51
Morris, Mark, 127, 130
Morrison, Diana, 26
Moss Empires, 152-153
Mother Courage, 90-91
Mousetrap, The, 248
Murmuring Judges, 108-110
Musical of the Year, 50-52
My Fair Lady, 13, 153
Napier, John, 14, 167, 168
Natel, Jean-Marc, 18
Nathan, David, 253
Nathan, George Jean, 10
Neagle, Anna, 71
New writing, 158-160
Nicholas, Paul, 7

Nicholas Nickleby, 18, 138, 160, 161, 162, 163
Night and Day, 249
Night of the Iguana, 218
Nightingale, Benedict, 45, 132, 147-148, 255
Nighy, Bill, 107
Ninagawa, Yukio, 63
No Man's Land, 107
No Sex Please – We're British, 248
Noble, Adrian, 59, 63, 68, 176
Noises Off, 80-81, 140
Nottingham Playhouse, 200
Nunn, Trevor, 15, 18, 25, 35, 66, 108, 161, 168
Oakes, Meredith, 113-114
Ockrent, Mike, 145
Oh Calcutta! 249
Old Possum's Book of Practical Cats, 7
Old Times, 91-92
Oldham, 163-164, 267-269
Oliver! 40-41, 42
Olivier, Laurence, 73, 167, 171, 184-185, 197, 254
Olivier, Richard, 99
Oman, Julia Trevelyan, 97
Once a Catholic, 139
Once and Future King, The, 13
Once in a Lifetime, 161
One Mo' Time, 136
O'Neill, Con, 148
Oresteia, The, 78-79
Orton, Joe, 115-116
Osborne, John, 100, 156, 159, 194, 250, 255
Othello, 66-67, 181
Other Places, 82-83
O'Toole, Peter, 56-57, 87-88, 161, 173, 194
Pacino, Al, 89
Paddick, Hugh, 223
Pagett, Nicola, 92, 116
Paige, Elaine, 3, 7-8, 21, 167, 193, 244-246
Pal Joey, 192
Papp, Joseph, 136
Parker, Dorothy, 255
Party, The, 72-73
Pasco, Richard, 106, 109, 110
Passion, 46-47
Pavarotti, Luciano, 233
Payne, Sarah, 10
Peacock, Trevor, 12
Pearce, Joanne, 69
Peck, Bob, 101
Pennington, Michael, 56, 74, 117
Peron, Eva, 2, 20, 21
Person Unknown, 71
Pertwee, Jon, 80
Petherbridge, Edward, 94
Phantom of the Opera, The, 19-20, 24, 31, 34, 39, 141, 142, 143, 168, 169, 232
Phillips, Arlene, 15, 36
Phillips, Siân, 192

Piaf, 138, 161, 245
Pickup, Ronald, 73
Pinter, Harold, 82, 91, 93, 107, 112, 117, 118, 159
Pirates of Penzance, The, 136, 140
Pitchford, Dean, 22
Plantagenets, The, 63-64
Plenty, 156
Plouviez, Peter, 157
Plowright, Joan, 163, 221
Political correctness, 180-182
Polycarpou, Peter, 27
Popplewell, Jack, 72
Powell, Dick, 17
Preston, Duncan, 88
Previews, 152
Price, The, 101-102
Priestley, J B, 106
Prince, Hal, 2-3, 4-5, 19, 21, 34, 143, 193, 249
Private Lives, 85-86, 162
Pryce, Jonathan, 27, 41, 162, 200
Purves, Peter, 21
Puttnam, David, 231
Quilley, Denis, 5, 33, 34, 51, 73
Racing Demon, 108-110
Raise the Titanic, 210
Ravenhill, Mark, 119
Rawle, Matt, 50
Rawlings, Adrian, 96
Real Inspector Hound, The, 93-94, 152
Real Thing, The, 86-87, 140
Redgrave, Michael, 195
Redgrave, Vanessa, 61, 119
Redman, Joanne, 30
Reed, Mike, 11
Rees, Roger, 87, 138
Reid, Beryl, 173
Relatively Speaking, 8
Rent, 9, 144
Rice, Tim, 1-2, 20, 168, 254
Rich, Frank, 134, 142, 144-146, 147, 148, 150
Richard II, 64-65
Richard III, 57-58, 64, 182
Richard, Cliff, 167
Richardson, Ralph, 53, 55, 107, 194, 216-217
Riding, Joanna, 32
Rigg, Diana, 83, 110, 111, 178
Rise and Fall of Little Voice, The, 179
Robbins, Jerome, 15
Rodgers, Richard, 3, 32
Rogers, Paul, 138
Romans in Britain, The, 159, 162
Rooney, Mickey, 136
Roose-Evans, James, 97
Rose, 160
Round the Horn, 222, 223
Routledge, Patricia, 33, 60, 80, 84
Rowe, Clive, 33

Royal Court Theatre, *passim*
Royal National Theatre, 170-174, 179-180, 189-191, *passim*
Royal Shakespeare Company, 176-177, *passim*
Royle, Carol, 56
Rudman, Michael, 173
Runyon, Damon, 12
Russell, Willy, 28-29, 99, 148-149, 151, 160, 161
Ryan, Madge, 111
Ryding, Antony, 120
Sacks, Oliver, 82
Sager, Carol Bayer, 5
Salad Days, 22, 188
Salome, 124
Salonga, Lea, 27
Sarruf, Valerie, 54
Satton, Lon, 15
Savage, Lily, 129
Scales, Prunella, 114
Schaffer, Peter, 138
Schonberg, Claude-Michel, 18, 26, 42, 49
Scofield, Paul, 119, 162
Sea, The, 105
Searle, Adam, 40
Seiphemo, Rapulana, 103
Serious Money, 113
Shakespeare, William, 53-69
Shankley, Jeff, 15
Share My Lettuce, 188
Shaw, George Bernard, 81, 83, 87, 88
Sheen, Michael, 112
Shell, Ray, 15
Sher, Antony, 48, 58-59, 62
Sheridan, Richard Brinsley, 93-94
Sherrin, Ned, 251
Shirley Valentine, 99-100, 148
Shopping and Fucking, 119-120
Shrapnel, John, 69
Simkins, Michael, 46, 95, 96
Simon, Christopher, 117
Simon, Neil, 5-6, 146
Simpson, Alan, 1
Sinatra, Frank, 193, 204-205
Sinclair, Belinda, 12
Sisterly Feelings, 163
Skriker, The, 113
Sleep, Wayne, 7, 192, 227-230
Small Family Business, A, 94-95
Smith, Maggie, 48, 89, 114, 179, 188, 197, 220-221, 252
Soans, Robin, 120
Sobol, Joshua, 98
Society of West End Theatre Managers, 157, 161, 247
Sondheim, Stephen, 4-5, 15-16, 32, 33, 45, 46, 142, 143, 163
Song and Dance, 228
Sophisticated Ladies, 136

Speed the Plow, 142
Spink, Ian, 113
Springtime for Hitler, 28
Stafford-Clark, Max, 120
Starlight Express, 14-15, 24, 31-32, 142, 169
Steadman, Alison, 75
Steele, Tommy, 252, 258
Stein, Joseph, 39
Stein, Peter, 130
Steiner, George, 130
Stephens, Robert, 67, 243-44
Stevenson, Juliet, 146
Stewart, Michael, 16
Stigwood, Robert, 22, 249
Spencer, Charles, 261-263
Stiles, George, 51
Stilgoe, Richard, 14-15, 19
St John Stevas, Norman, 163
Stoppard, Tom, 75, 86, 93-94, 107-108, 140, 152
Storey, David, 254, 255
Stott, Ken, 105
Streetcar Named Desire, A, 88, 146, 217, 218
Stubbs, Imogen, 67, 186
Stubbs, Una, 80
Sugar Babies, 136
Sunset Boulevard, 34-35, 38, 39, 169, 232, 244
Suzman, Janet, 173
Swanson, Gloria, 232
Sweeney Todd, 4-5, 33-34, 163
Sweet Bird of Youth, 92-93
Swerling, Jo, 11
Swift, Jeremy, 116
Sylvester, Suzan, 96
Taking Sides, 116-117
Tanaka, Yuko, 63
Tarbuck, Jimmy, 234-236
Taylor, C P, 127
Taylor, Elizabeth, 85-86, 136, 212-213, 251-252, 258
Tempest, The, 62-63
Tennant, David, 116
Terry, Ellen, 81
Thaw, John, 110
Theatre Workshop, 5
They're Playing Our Song, 5-6, 163, 192
Thompson, Emma, 101
Thompson, Sophie, 46
Three Musketeers, The, 51
Three Sisters, The, 139
Three Tall Women, 114-115
Time, 167
Tingwell, Charles, 71
Tinker, Jack: *passim*
    Brighton *Evening Argus*, joins, xv
    Daily Mail, joins, xv
    Daily Sketch, joins, xv
    Daughter, Charlotte's death, 270
    Early career, xv

Jack Tinker Award, xv
    Stage shows by, xv, 258
    Tinkies and Stinkies, 174-176
Tobias, Earl, 30
Toksvig, Sandi, 131
Tomelty, Frances, 57
Tommy, 150
Toms, Carl, 55
Tony Awards, 141-143, 144, 145, 146
Top Girls, 113
Topol, 40
Townshend, Pete, 150
Toye, Wendy, 54, 55
Travolta, John, 36
Triplett, Sally Ann, 36
Triumph Productions, 153
Turner, John, 82
Twelfth Night, 125
Tynan, Kenneth, 42, 45, 249, 262
Uggams, Leslie, 205
Ullmann, Liv, 92
Ulvaes, Bjorn, 51
Ustinov, Peter, 50, 226-227
Valley Song, 103
Verdon, Gwen, 166
Victoria Station, 83
Vidale, Thea, 126, 127
Vieux Carré, 218
View from the Bridge, A, 96
Wall, Max, 31, 137
Walter, Harriet, 108
Walters, Julie, 173
Ward in Chancery, 137
Wardle, Irving, 45, 253
Warehouse Theatre Croydon, 258
Warren, Harry, 16
Warren, Marcia, 75
Waterhouse, Keith, 79, 80
Waters, Jan, 81
Way of the World, The, 220
Wayne, Carl, 29
Weapons of Happiness, 155
Webb, Marti, 21
Weir, Judith, 113
Wentworth, Scott, 51
West, Sam, 105
West Side Story, 15-16, 32
West Side Waltz, 138
What the Butler Saw, 115-116
Wheeler, Hugh, 4, 33
When the Wind Blows, 84-85
Whistle down the Wind, 154, 169
White, Michael, 137, 140
White, T H, 13
White, Willard, 67
Whitemore, Hugh, 97
Wickham, Saskia, 110
Wild Honey, 143

Wilder, Billy, 34, 38
Wilkinson, Colin, 18, 43
William, David, 54
Williams, Kenneth, 70, 186-188, 222-223
Williams, Tennessee, 88, 92, 93, 146, 149, 176, 217-218
Wilson, Richard, 116
Wilson, Robert, 130
Winter's Tale, The, 60-61
Witter, William C, 10
Wolfit, Donald, 195
Woman in Black, The, 186
Woman of the Year, 133, 134
Wood, John, 62
Woodvine, John, 99
Woodward, Sarah, 105
Woodward, Tim, 110
Worzel Gummidge, 79-80
York, Susannah, 127
Yuriko, 4